PLEASURE AND AMBITION

For

Gail
Gill
Joan & Peter
and
Polly

PLEASURE AND AMBITION

THE LIFE, LOVES AND WARS OF
AUGUSTUS THE STRONG
1670–1707

TONY SHARP

BLOOMSBURY ACADEMIC
LONDON • NEW YORK • OXFORD • NEW DELHI • SYDNEY

BLOOMSBURY ACADEMIC
Bloomsbury Publishing Plc
50 Bedford Square, London, WC1B 3DP, UK
1385 Broadway, New York, NY 10018, USA
29 Earlsfort Terrace, Dublin 2, Ireland

BLOOMSBURY, BLOOMSBURY ACADEMIC and the Diana logo
are trademarks of Bloomsbury Publishing Plc

First published in 2001 by I. B. Tauris
This paperback edition published in 2021 by Bloomsbury Academic

ISBN: HB: 978-1-8606-4619-5
PB: 978-1-3501-8024-6

Typeset in 10/12 Baskerville by The Midlands Book Typesetting Co, Loughborough

To find out more about our authors and books visit
www.bloomsbury.com and sign up for our newsletters.

Contents

Acknowledgements

The letters of English diplomats used in this work are three centuries old, while most of the German-language articles upon Augustus date from the nineteenth and early twentieth centuries. I would have been unable to write this biography, had it not been for the courteous efficiency of the staffs of the Public Records Office in Kew, the British Library in Central London, the British Lending Library in Boston Spa and Worthing Public Library. I express my deep indebtedness to them all for their help.

Mike Shaw and Gill Regan were kind enough to read an earlier draft of this book and offer many perceptive comments. Christine Napthine gave me invaluable assistance in readying the manuscript for publication.

At a much earlier stage, Professor Norman Davies and Dr Derek McKay, both of the University of London, generously gave of their time to discuss sources which I might pursue. The Royal Commission on Historical Manuscripts provided me with an excellent guide through the maze of George Stepney's papers.

Dr Lester Crook at I.B.Tauris never wavered in his support of this work, and I remain profoundly grateful for his kindness and encouragement.

Tony Sharp
Godalming

Le plaisir et l'ambition sont ses passions dominantes, cependant le plaisir est la plus dominant, bien souvent son ambition a été traversée par ses plaisirs, mais ses plaisirs ne l'ont jamais été par son ambition.

Jakob Heinrich von Flemming, 1722

SAXONY AND POLAND
c.1700

KARELIA

St Petersbur

INGRIA

Stockholm

Reval   Narva

ESTONIA

SWEDEN

Pernau   Dorpat

LIVONIA   RUSSIA

The
Øresund

DENMARK

Karlskrona

Copenhagen

BALTIC SEA

Wolmár
Wenden

COURLAND   Riga
Libau   Mitau   Kokenhusen
Joniškis   Bautzen
Polangen   Birsen

Düna

Gottorp

Schleswig

SAMOGITIA

HOLSTEIN
GOTTORP

Niemen   Kaunas

GRAND DUCHY

Hamburg   Wismar   Stralsund SWEDISH
Ratzeburg   POMERANIA
Lauenburg   POMERANIA

Königsberg

Vilnius

OF

Danzig   Heilberg
Elbing
Marienburg   PRUSSIA

Johannisburg

Minsk

Grodno   Nowogrodek

Tykocin

BRANDENBURG   Warta

Thorn

Elbe   Oder

Potsdam   Berlin

Magdeburg   Frankfurt   Kaźmierz

LITHUANIA

Quedlinburg   Wittenberg   Poznań

Gniezno   Pułtusk

Brest-Litowsk   Pinsk

Mansfeld   Oranienbaum   Pünitz

Warsaw   Praga

Torgau   Liebenwerda   Fraustadt

Łowicz   Błonie

Leipzig   Glogau   Rawicz   Kalisz

PODLESIA

Erfurt   Altranstädt   Meissen   Steinau   Łódź

Borna   Dresden   Bautzen   Breslau

Piotrków

Lublin

POLAND

Freiberg   Görlitz   Ohlau

Łuck

Teplitz   Königstein
Pillnitz   Bischofswerda

Karlsbad   Moritzburg   Tarnowskie   Kliszów

Pilsen   Piekary Śląskie   Sandomierz

Rawa   VOLHYNIA
Ruska

Prague   Katowice   Cracow   Vistula   San   Jaworów
Jarosław

Kie

Nuremberg

Elbe   SILESIA

BOHEMIA

Lwów

PODOLIA

Brno

Budweis   MORAVIA

Munich   Linz

Danube

Kaminiec-
Podolski

Vienna   Bratislava
Baden
Sopron

Tokaj

Buda   Pest

Tisza   Debrecen

Dniestr

State boundaries

Saxony

Swedish Empire

Internal boundary between
Polish Korona and Grand
Duchy of Lithuania

HUNGARY

Cluj

OTTOMAN

Szeged   Arad   Lipova

Zenta   Aranca   Bega   Deva

EMPIRE

Danube   Mureș

0   100   200   300 km

Futog   Novi Sad   Lugoj   Timiș
Petrovaradin   Temesvar

Belgrade

BLACK
SEA

Introduction

'Ambition and a lust for pleasure are his chief qualities, though the latter has supremacy. Often his ambition is curbed by his lust for pleasure, never the latter by his ambition.' So wrote Jakob Heinrich von Flemming, when producing his shrewd character sketch of 'Augustus the Strong', the master that he served so long and intimately. The entire portrait of his sovereign can be found in Appendix 2.[1]

'Augustus the Strong' (known as 'August der Starke' or 'Augusta Mocny' in the lands over which he ruled) lived from 1670 until 1733, but never enjoyed the appellation in his lifetime. From 1694 until his death he reigned as Elector Friedrich August I in Saxony. In the years 1697–1733 he was also King Augusta II of Poland, although technically he was dethroned in favour of a Swedish puppet between 1704 and 1709.

Until recently, I would have had to work somewhat harder to inform the general reader who Augustus was. Following the success of Janet Gleeson's elegant and interesting study of Augustus's role in the development of Dresden and Meissen china, however, I can at least assume some greater awareness of his existence.[2]

Although Augustus starred silently in the 1920s film *Der Galante König*, previous English readers would have only met him playing walk-on parts in works featuring 'Peter the Great', Charles XII of Sweden and 'Frederick the Great', or perhaps in histories of Poland. And in most of these Augustus has hardly been showered with critical acclaim. What has been written about him in our language has been largely a potage of inaccuracy, ignorance and fiction, seasoned with the tendentious and sometimes stirred with bias.

Augustus is rightly credited with being of Herculean strength and having many mistresses. He is falsely saddled with the paternity of over 300 bastards, whereas the true figure is between eight and ten. He is often portrayed as the most duplicitous ruler of his time. Not only is this something that cannot be measured without advancing effective standards to define the concept of integrity; but it is ludicrous to ignore the competition to be found in a Europe dominated by the mores of Louis XIV. Augustus is also written off as an exotic and profligate German princeling, who acted out of his league. The contemporary view that treated him as a major player in European affairs is unknown, ignored, or suppressed.

That he bled his realms to finance his ambitions is undeniable, as is the fact that he lavished a large part of his budget on mistresses, favourites and a gamut of personal pleasures. Yet it is generally overlooked that much of his expenditure also helped turn Dresden into a 'Florence on the Elbe', which rivalled Prague and Vienna in its baroque beauty until the Royal Air Force flattened it in February 1945. The current visitor to Dresden will admittedly see on the skyline more cranes than spires, but can also appreciate the Phoenix of Augustus's creation arising from the ashes.

Even if the Zwinger and other examples of baroque architecture do not engage him or her, it is a rare traveller who can avoid gawking at the fantastic collections of jewels and models in 'Das Grüne Gewölbe' ('the Green Vault'), or revelling in the display of paintings in 'die Gemäldegalerie Alte Meister'. Augustus was instrumental in building up both hoards, as well as various scientific collections. Then there is the little matter of his role in founding and funding the Meissen and Dresden porcelain industries.

Pracht kündet Macht ('Splendour denotes power') goes the saying. 'Splendour' in isolation does no such thing, however, as the Prussians demonstrated conclusively in their early commitment to power blasting out of the barrel of a musket. Augustus knew this too; by the end of his life the Elector-King had fashioned an impressive standing army. The problem was that Frederick William I of Prussia (r 1713–40) controlled a bigger and better one, having consciously forgone splendour in favour of firepower. His successor Frederick the Great (r 1740–86) used this formidable force to remove Saxony forever as a competitor in the affairs of Germany.

Unsurprisingly, the victor imposed not only his will, but also his version of history. It is no accident that we can trace the origins of the skewed portrayal of Augustus, as nothing but a feckless and shifty womanizer ruling over some Saxon Sodom, to court circles in Berlin. Wilhelmina, the Marchioness of Bayreuth, was Frederick the Great's older sister, while Baron Karl-Ludwig von Pöllnitz took time out from the life of an 'adventurer' to perform as master of ceremonies at the Prussian court.[3]

Wilhelmina's memoirs ostensibly portray the degeneracy of Dresden in 1728. Dealing with her account can be left to a study of Augustus's later years, save for the item about her tally of Augustan bastards being reminiscent of the number of days in a year. This is precisely the point. In German speech of the time, a house with 365 (or some such number of) windows was simply a dwelling with many windows. Similarly, Augustus had between eight and ten illegitimate children, which is a lot of bastards; while taking the figure literally is also a lot of nonsense.

Von Pöllnitz's study of Augustus's amours was published in French shortly after the Saxon's death and translated into English by 'a gentleman of Oxford' in 1734. As such, it is the only book-length work on Augustus in our language. Its 'scandalous' portrayal of his love life, complete with 'authentic' dialogue, titillated at the time, and it was last reprinted here in 1929. However, a generation raised upon the foibles of the House of Windsor would be yawning by the second page, and in truth it is a tedious read.

More important for the historian is its status as a source. The book is not entirely worthless, but it is strewn with so many blatant errors that it has little value, save in indicating the sequence of Augustus's major affairs. Even in this respect it is frequently faulty.

Needless to say, neither work provides any significant context to Augustus's life. The Great Northern War, which Augustus brought crashing down upon his own arrogant head, occupied him from 1700 until 1721. In von Pöllnitz's study, it rates a few lines as Augustus leaps between the sheets. Wilhelmina warbles incomprehensibly about Saxony's relations with Vienna. There is not a word about Augustus's lifetime dream of replacing the Habsburgs upon the Imperial throne with his own dynasty. More relevantly, this fact, as well as other objectives of Augustus's considerable ambitions, are equally absent from more serious accounts.

The point of the above paragraphs is not to present Augustus as white as driven snow. This would be impossible for a personality marred by so many flaws; and some of the stains are ineradicable. However, he should also be credited with many characteristics that must be deemed advantageous to a ruler of his time. The sketch by his long-time minister Flemming provides a useful resumé of his virtues and vices. Others will emerge from the text.

From one fault Augustus did not suffer at all, and that was pre-dictability. Phrases such as 'his active temper' and 'a prince who would not lie still' figure frequently in reports of his behaviour. He was constantly on the move from one project to another, driven by both his complex personality and his status. Foreign policy, military matters, financial reforms and domestic affairs all vied for his attention along with architecture, hunting, alchemy, extravaganzas, women and wine. Yet for too much of the time the achievement of his aims was circumscribed by his hedonism, as Flemming emphasized.

Too often the consequence was that schemes went off at half-cock, and, with resources misapplied, dreams foundered upon harsh reality. The unprovoked attack upon the Swedish Empire in 1700 was cretinous in conception and cavalier in conduct. Augustus blundered into a war that consumed a third of his life and the entire existence of many thousands of his subjects. Although it was not his intention, the outcome of his crass act was to draw Peter the Great's Russia westward. Such might have happened anyway, as those who love 'iffing' about with history's non-events will confirm; but Augustus's overweening ambitions ensured that it came to pass.

Augustus has a place in European history. He was never as great as his ambitions, yet he was never mediocre. His failures are on the epic scale; his limited achievements durable. Despite standing only in the second echelon of those imprinting their mark upon our continent, he was a first-rank dreamer and schemer. His life encapsulated a small-scale version of a constant folly: boundless ambitions underpinned by finite resources.

However, it was a full and multi-faceted life that could have been much shorter. Augustus overcame malaria, smallpox and dysentery, as well as a host of lesser ailments and wounds. For the last 15 years of his life he fought diabetes, while from 1727 an amputated toe hindered him further. Like his immediate forebears, he was also an alcoholic, who left the world a few weeks short of his sixty-third birthday following one final heroic binge.[4]

He conducted his life with charming selfishness, considerable personal courage, and an acute talent for self-publicity. In our day he would have been a tabloid editor's dream. In his own he was a nightmare to a settled domestic and European order. To the horror of his Lutheran subjects, he converted to Catholicism during his bid for the Polish throne. To the despair of the anti-French alliance, he began a war in the east of Europe.

He was in love with glory and, like many contemporaries, he had mulled over Machiavelli. Yet his character prevented him from ever consistently applying the requisite power to the realization of his grandiose objectives. As a ruler, Augustus proved to be only a strong, but ultimately unavailing, swimmer against the tides of history.

George Stepney was a British diplomat and poet who lived from 1663 until 1707. There is no doubting that at his death he had a greater grasp of the affairs of Germany than any of his countrymen. Nor can we contradict his own view that he knew Augustus and Saxony 'as well as any Englishman can know them'.[5] During his time abroad he headed three missions to Augustus, in 1694–95 and 1698, and visited Saxony upon two further occasions. In other years he reported extensively upon Augustus's activities from his posts elsewhere.

On his death in September 1707, Stepney left behind him a hoard of 'fairy treasure', to use his own phrase:[6] thousands of letters, of which a few hundred relate to Augustus and Saxony. Of these, precisely *one*, which was published long ago, has been utilized by German authors.

It is these neglected letters of George Stepney which provide the core of this book. Using these, along with some correspondence of Stepney's fellow diplomats, and supplementing these sources with German-language biographies and articles, I have sought to portray Augustus's life and environment in the years from 1670 to 1707.[7]

Although Stepney was dubbed a poet in his own era and for some time thereafter, nobody seriously rates him as such these days. He was, however, a talented writer, and his prose, as expressed through his letters, is cited throughout this book. For sources of his letters, and indeed for the whole question of references and notes, I refer the reader to p 263. I would also emphasize that this book can be profitably read without consulting the notes (n) or the appendices (A), or skipping to pages (p) and chapters (C) as indicated in the text. The notes largely provide supplementary information, which would have burdened the main text. Such will interest some readers, but not all.

Most German and French quotations have been consigned to the notes and left in their original form. And with Augustus, who wrote as he spoke, penning both German and French phonetically upon the basis of a strong Saxon accent, 'original' is the operative word. However, the spelling of Stepney and other English writers has been modernized throughout. I have removed capitals from English nouns, altered some punctuation, and dispensed with the non-existent 'ye' in favour of 'the'. Overall, the reader should find it no harder to understand Stepney and his fellows than the King James Bible.

For the sake of simplicity, I have used England and Britain, Prussia and Brandenburg, Austria and the Empire, Russia and Muscovy, Holland and the United Provinces as synonyms, while Brunswick, Lüneburg and Celle are all subsumed by Hanover. For personal names I have applied the most commonly accepted modern spelling and indicated where there is no agreement. For most place-names contested by more than one language, I have indicated both contemporary and current usage.

In the 1600s New Style (NS) dates were ten days ahead of Old Style (OS), and from 1700 the difference was eleven days. When this work commences, England, Saxony, Prussia, Sweden and Russia used OS and France, the Empire and Poland NS. The first 11 chapters are dated OS with double-dating (e.g. 10/20 May 1697, 10/21 May 1700) given where necessary. Thereafter I have used NS dates or double-dated.

References to distance are not always clear, however, a German mile was equal to four British miles. Money and its value is always a problem. The main Imperial currency was the Reichsthaler (RT) or simply the thaler or taler, otherwise known as the dollar or Rixdaler. A flood of florins, crowns and ducats, and many other currencies, also circulated. There were four dollars to the pound sterling. Ms Gleeson asserts that the values of the early 1700s can be converted into current values by muliplying by 65.[8] Therefore RT 4000 equals £65,000 in today's money (4000 divided by 4 and multiplied by 65). I would not argue with her formula, although, upon 'life is too short' principles, I have not tried to apply it; not even to assess Augustus's vast outlays in purchasing the Polish crown (C13).

In original sources I have used ( ) wherever brackets occur; any use of [ ] denotes my own interpolations. For example, a word followed by [?] indicates my guess at its true transcription, when the original in the letter was not clearly legible.

'A prince of great hopes'
Trials of a second son 1670–1694

Chapter 1

'Nothing other than a sword'
A portrait of Augustus 1670–91

'A GLORY-SEEKER'

In the early hours of Ascension Day, 12/22 May 1670, Anna Sophie, the 23-year-old Electoral Princess of Saxony, gave birth to her second son, Frederick Augustus. We know nothing of whether her delivery in the Electoral Palace in Dresden was difficult, or whether, given the fantastic strength of his manhood, Augustus was a 'big' baby. We do know from portraits that the boy came to resemble his mother physically, sharing her thick dark eyebrows and long curving nose.

A devout Lutheran, Anna Sophie was a daughter of King Frederick III of Denmark (r 1648–70). She was an educated woman, who knew German, Latin, French, Spanish and Italian, besides her native Danish. It seems reasonable to credit her for the intelligence with which both Augustus and her elder son John George (Johann Georg) were endowed. Although in later life Augustus would oppose his mother upon a whole range of issues, there seems little doubt that he loved and honoured her, and sought her approbation for his actions.

She received little, if any, of such emotions from her husband, the Electoral Prince (Kurprinz). He, another John George, was to be the third of four Electors bearing that name who ruled Saxony consecutively in the seventeenth century.[1] The future John George III was a short stout man, taciturn by nature and bellicose by temperament. Like Anna Sophie, he was born in 1647, and they were married in 1666; their union being no love-affair but an affair of state. Anna Sophie's relevance to the process was simply that she was a female member of the royal house of Denmark, with which the Wettin dynasty of Saxony cemented several marital alliances. Their other main source of spouses was the Hohenzollern family, who ruled in Brandenburg, ducal (East) Prussia and various small territories of the fragmented German lands which composed the Holy Roman Empire.

Like most princesses, Anna Sophie's function was to breed and not be heard. She had her children, religion and – within the bounds prescribed by her sex and status – her intellectual pursuits, upon which to focus. John George, meanwhile, devoted himself to his interests of drinking, hunting and warfare, and spent his spare time with a string of mistresses, one of whom bore him a son.[2]

In much of his behaviour he merely aped his father, the current Kurfürst or Elector of Saxony, John George II (1613–80), whose reign had commenced in 1656. Renowned as a hard drinker, John George II enjoyed sufficient moments of sobriety to indulge the cultured side to his nature, which saw the introduction of the theatre, opera and art collections into Dresden and the construction of new buildings and gardens in his capital.[3]

His son and successor John George III had little interest in such sissy sidelines, although the opera furnished him with one of his noted mistresses, the Italian singer Margherita Salicola. Instead, the 'Saxon Mars' would apply himself to introducing a standing army in the Electorate, and leading his troops into various battles as the loyal servant of the Habsburg Emperor, most notably in the famous relief of Vienna from the Turks in September 1683.

So, whatever may be the diverse effects of nature and nurture upon the development of a human personality, Augustus and his brother were exposed from the outset to contradictory influences. The formal piety of their early education, plus the devout maternal guidance, contrasted sharply with the licence of the court, epitomized by the lifestyles of their father and grandfather. To be a ruler suggested little in the way of personal responsibility, but much about selfishness and pleasure.

Both princes were initially brought up by ladies-in-waiting sent to Dresden by Queen Sophie Amalie of Denmark. But in November 1672 these toddlers acquired their own tutor, who was instructed to develop in them Christian virtues and princely manners through 'prayer, reading and writing, devout study of the catechism, jolly little sayings and short psalms'. As they grew older and their powers of comprehension increased, the boys were 'to diligently study the Holy Bible' and other pious (i.e. non-Catholic and non-Calvinist) books.[4] Every lesson was to begin and end in prayer, while secular studies commenced with reading and spelling. They were also taught to speak slowly and clearly and not to swallow their words.

Early in 1676 the two princes were given their personal household (*Hofstaat*) under the direction of their own steward (Hofmeister), the chamberlain (Kammerherr) Johann Ernst von Knoch (1641–1705). Besides Knoch and the pages, there were 15 members of the

Hofstaat, one of whom had the task of watching the princes closely day and night, to ensure that they were never spiritually 'endangered' by Papists, Calvinists, or other sects.

Despite having a specialist teacher (Fachlehrer) for writing, Augustus developed a crabbed hand, penning everything in lower case, including proper names and the first words of sentences; all of which places a premium upon the eyesight of the researcher. Even more of a problem results from his spelling. His literal obedience of the injunction *Schreibe wie du sprichst* produced both French and German written phonetically upon the basis of a broad Saxon accent.

Such defects arguably stemmed from a greater failing, for at this crucial age Augustus was completely uninterested in his studies. John George was the scholar; Augustus saw himself as 'a lively fellow', who loved hunting and simply having a good time. Most of all he wanted to be a soldier, who 'needed nothing other than a sword to ensure his progress in life'.

His father could have asked no more from his lad, and there seems little doubt that John George III favoured the younger boy and his inclinations. There is a story of the brothers accompanying him to Leipzig Fair. The bookish John George selected mathematical instruments and tomes from the stalls, while Augustus purchased a carbine. His delighted father bellowed that Augustus ought to become Elector.[5]

This was the nub of the problem. Augustus may have been first in his father's affections, but as far as the succession was concerned he was strictly second. His brother John George was in reasonable health and little older than himself. As the lineal heir John George was the focus of constitutional attention: he was expected to govern at some time and was prepared accordingly. If he had male children they, not his younger brother, would be his successors. Hence, if Augustus saw himself as virtually excluded from the succession, there was little reason why he should not follow his inclinations and be an ill-educated warrior; or, to use his own words, 'a glory-seeker' ('eine ehrliebente sehl'). In an era of almost continual warfare, such a bent at least provided an occupation.

However, until such time as he could make his own way, Augustus had to endure the proximity of his sibling; and the characteristics of the two dissimilar brothers clashed so deeply that their relationship was one of both deep-seated antagonism and mutual jealousy. Augustus gave his view of the conflict in 1690: recovering from smallpox, he penned a few pages of autobiographical 'sketches'. For one section he used the popular guise of a romantic novel to describe the relationship of two brothers, Kodrus (John George) and Pallantes (Augustus), ostensibly as it was in 1680, but in truth as it remained current a decade later, and indeed until his brother's convenient death in 1694.

He described John George, who was born on 18/28 October 1668, as delicate and sickly, weak-natured and weak-limbed, sombre, melancholy, reflective, scholarly and extremely hot-tempered. It is not a bad assessment, since most characteristics are also remarked upon by others and his violent tantrums nearly resulted in him murdering his wife (p 55). Such bouts of rage may have resulted from inflamed kidneys and gallstones, for as a child John George suffered from gripes, like his grandfather, and sediment was found in his urine.

Augustus is totally dissimilar. In his self-appraisal as Pallantes, he is strapping, strong-willed, gracious, generous, frivolous, even-tempered and proficient in military skills, and allows nothing to bother him. Yet he contradicts himself; for something *did* trouble him. As he phrased it, 'the younger brother begrudged the way nature had made Kodrus different from himself'.[6]

Different in what way: intellectually? Perhaps Augustus neglected his studies because his brother so outclassed him in this sphere. However, 'nature' had made him different from John George in another more profound sense. It had made Augustus a second son, literally an inferior of his brother, the heir apparent. Perhaps the real source of the conflict between them was Augustus's belief that he was more fitted to the succession than John George.

'MISERABLY INFECTED WITH THE PLAGUE'

In 1680 plague arrived in Dresden from Austria. John George II fled to Schloss Friedenstein in Freiberg. His son decamped first to Görlitz and then to Bautzen. Anna Sophie and her two boys bolted for Lichtenberg near Torgau. There the princes stayed until November, their father refusing the Elector's entreaties that they be sent to Freiberg because he knew that the plague had already reached that town. Indeed, it had reached John George II.

'The general opinion' in Berlin was that he 'will very soon die', wrote Sir Robert Southwell on 2 June 1680. The British diplomat had been accredited to the Saxon court in May, and his mission did not end until October. It seems, however, that he never set foot in the Electorate, which was so 'miserably infected with the plague, and suffers all manner of inconveniences accordingly'. Since the envoy wisely declined to endure such 'inconveniences' himself, he lingered in Berlin and reported from there. Nor is there the slightest indication of what his abortive mission to Dresden was designed to achieve.[7]

On 23 June Southwell reported that John George II was 'under a formal cure for the pox, and that his room is so nauseous that not above three or four come near him'. Apparently, the 66-year-old Elector caught the plague 'from a page that used to lie with him, because of his frequent distempers into drink'. On 20 August the failing John George was 'put into a bath, and had four harlequins dancing round him, and talked nothing but of music and fresh journeys and pleasures that he intended'. But two days later he was 'no longer able to resist the infection which gave him so much pain and shame', and when 'death came he was serious and made a quick end'.

Augustus's 33-year-old father was now Elector of Saxony. He had refused all paternal summonses to Freiberg, but instead had ranged about the Electorate 'from place to place on horseback', during which period he fell 'from a precipice, but he recovered after keeping his bed for some days'. When the plague receded, John George III brought his family back to Dresden.

'ALL PROPER PRINCELY VIRTUES'

In April 1681 both princes climbed into the saddle for the first time. Augustus would prove to be a horseman of the highest calibre, though probably outshone by his nemesis Charles XII. Eighteen months later the boys started hunting on horseback and became life-time addicts. They were also inveterate gamblers, abetted by their grandmother, the Dowager Electress Magdalena Sibylla, a princess of the same Brandenburg-Bayreuth family into which Augustus too would marry.

Academic education also progressed, as the princes took up dancing, fencing, civil and military engineering, drawing, mathematics, languages and 'exercises' – a word which in the original French encompasses military drill and training. Augustus showed some talent at drawing and painting as well as his beloved 'exercises', but the scholarly John George led the way in the more cerebral pursuits. He was proficient in French, Latin and Italian, and pursued his own interests in history, politics and genealogy. Nor was the elder brother inept in military studies, whatever Augustus might want us to believe.

From late 1684, now aged 16, the Kurprinz was taken increasingly into state affairs. The following April, perhaps because the educational requirements of the brothers were diverging, but possibly because of their constant enmity, Augustus was provided with his own Hofmeister, the military counsellor (Geheim Kriegsrat) Christian

7

August von Haxthausen (16??–1696). That same year, the first known portrait of Augustus was painted. Later in 1685 John George was entirely out of his life for a while, when he embarked upon his *Kavalierstour*: the 'Grand Tour' which provided a form of finishing school to many privileged Europeans in the seventeenth and eighteenth centuries.

On 7 November 1685, John George, barely 17, and travelling as the Graf (Count) von Barby, left Dresden, escorted by his Hofmeister von Knoch and a travelling entourage (Reisehofstaat) of servants and courtiers. The 15-year-old Augustus accompanied him as far as Leipzig. From there the Kurprinz headed via Strasbourg to Paris, where he remained from December until May 1686. Other German princelings were there too, basking in the radiant court of *le Roi Soleil*. Like them, John George studied French, Italian, dancing, riding and fortifications and spent his free hours gambling and at performances of French and Italian comedies. He was received at court and Liselotte, Louis XIV's formidable German sister-in-law, ran the rule over him too.

In June 1686 John George left Calais for Dover. In London he was received by Charles II's widow: they conversed in French. Otherwise it was one social round. On 3 July the Kurprinz sailed from Chatham, where the fleet was at anchor, and travelled via the Spanish Netherlands (Belgium), Holland, Bremen, Hamburg and Holstein to Gottorp to meet his Danish relations, including his uncle King Christian V (r 1670–99). He also met some German kin: brother Augustus was there with his mother and aunt, enjoying a first venture into foreign lands. In October John George continued his journey, now shorn of its Italian leg; travelling southward into the Palatinate and then east, he returned to Dresden on 24 November 1686.

One reason why Anna Sophie had taken Augustus to Holstein that summer was to get the 16-year-old prince away from his first known mistress. Marie Elisabeth von Brockdorff was a lady-in-waiting (Hofdame) from Holstein. She had arrived in Saxony in the retinue of Augustus's aunt, Wilhelmine Ernestine von der Pfalz, when that widowed Electress came to live with her sister Anna Sophie in 1685.

How old the Hofdame was at the time of this affair is not known, but she was worth a page in the 'sketches' Augustus composed in 1690. In this he noted that, as a 'hoftahme', Marie Elisabeth was 'nicht in stande zu heirahtten'.[8] This was a statement of the obvious: as a prince, Augustus could only marry a woman of 'equal blood'. Whether he wrote it to indicate that she was his first love, or that he would have married her if circumstances had been different, is mere speculation. In any case, it is hard to imagine that their relationship

8

would have survived his pending travels. For now the time had come for Augustus to undertake his own *Kavalierstour.*

On 30 March 1687, ten days after his mother's death, John George III ordained that 'his beloved younger son' Augustus was to travel to foreign lands in order to make himself yet more perfect 'in all proper princely virtues'.[9] The original tour was intended to last three years and Augustus's Reisehofstaat of 20, headed by his Hofmeister von Haxthausen, included a doctor and a chaplain. The young prince was furnished with passes, made out in Latin and German, for one Graf von Leisnig; the pseudonym permitting him to avoid some of the more wearisome charades of court protocol in other lands.

First Augustus set out for Freiberg, where his grandmother was buried on 4 May. Three days later he said farewell to his father, who now headed for the spas of Karlsbad (Karlovy Vary), while his younger son returned to Dresden in time to celebrate his seventeenth birthday on 12 May. The next day Augustus left Dresden to spend Whitsun with his mother and aunt in Lichtenberg. On 19 May 1687 the great journey began. Travelling via Erfurt, Frankfurt and Strasburg, on 14 June Augustus and his party reached Paris, where they would remain until 16 September.

The move to France had immediately resolved one worry for Haxthausen, who could report that Augustus did not miss German beer in the slightest. Hardly had he crossed the frontier when he commenced a lifelong love-affair with red wine (and champagne), finally favouring strong Hungarian vintages – a predilection he shared with Peter the Great and George Stepney, to name but two of the many fans of Tokaj (C10 n3).

This new-found love of wine, together with other features of the young prince's lifestyle in Paris, emerge from a monthly budget for Augustus's household, which Haxthausen prepared for the Elector's perusal. From an allowance of 2000 Reichsthaler (RT), two-fifths was swallowed up by Augustus's bibulous table. Clothes took nearly RT 400, rent 175, while trips to Versailles, the opera and the theatre consumed another 160. Servants, doctors' bills, a hired coach, the blacksmith and pocket-money used up all but RT 110. And this last was the less than princely sum which Augustus disbursed upon his lessons, with the bulk spent upon 'exercises'. In short, he continued to enjoy himself at the expense of his studies.

On 24 June Augustus was received under his pseudonym by Louis XIV at Versailles, and conducted himself in a 'wohl gouvernirt' fashion, according to Haxthausen's report. He also met Liselotte (1652–1722). Born Elisabeth Charlotte von der Pfalz and now Duchess of Orleans, in 1671 Liselotte had been drafted into her pitiable marriage with the Sun King's bisexual brother Philippe. Despite such ambivalence her husband was known in the Versailles hierarchy as Monsieur and the earthy Palatinate princess had to settle for Madame.

As sister-in-law to Augustus's widowed aunt, Liselotte doubtless knew something of that young man's doings in Dresden. Moreover, acting as one pivot of a network of incessant correspondence centred upon her own aunt Sophie, the Duchess and later Electress of Hanover (1630–1714), she was well-informed over a wide range of issues. Much of the news which passed between these remarkable ladies stood at a far higher level than the typical court gossip (Hofklatsch) which riddled most contemporary letters, including those of diplomats.[10]

In her voluminous correspondence Madame provides a number of observations upon Augustus's life. Her first treatment of the prince is a pen-portrait as she saw him that summer, which remains one of the few existing written sketches of Augustus. She wrote her first impressions to Sophie in July 1687 and expanded upon her initial letter in another which she sent almost a decade later.[11]

Liselotte did not find the youthful Saxon's face attractive, particularly his large mouth (although the nose apparently passed muster). However, he was a well-made young man with a fine bearing. He certainly seemed more vivacious than the melancholy John George, whom she had met the previous year. Since Augustus spoke little, she felt unable to pronounce upon what might lie behind the exterior. Already he was very strong; with two fingers he had heaved up a weighty pipe from the ground 'as though it was a pin', and held it out before him. Nobody could emulate his deed. When the ladies of the court had got to know of the young prince's strength and physique, they had pursued him in a frightful manner. Despite this, von Pöllnitz produces not a single Parisian liaison, real or invented.

Poor Augustus! Addled with wine, pursued by women, surrounded by the diversions of Paris, possibly suffering heatstroke during that broiling summer and paying but pittances for his teachers; was it any wonder that his studies suffered? Nor was von Haxthausen loth to enjoy himself; he was hardly the spur that his young charge needed. His reports to the Elector he simply fudged. Augustus was profiting from his riding lessons 'for which he showed a great inclination', while dancing and languages were progressing more slowly. Naturally, Haxthausen never failed to remind the prince to make every use of such golden opportunities.[12] Yet there is no indication that John George III expected much more; nor did he appear ruffled by Augustus's bland and uninformative letters home.

'THOROUGHLY SPOILT'

On 14 September 1687 Augustus took his leave of Louis and his court, and two days later his party left Paris for Spain. Augustus grew sick on the Garonne and by the beginning of October was very ill, probably with malaria. For nearly two months the party remained at Bayonne, while the prince, sleepless, delirious, off his food, first fought for his life and then made a slow recovery. 'Il n'est plus que l'ombre de l'Hercule qu'il présentait quasi autrefois', a relieved Haxthausen informed Dresden on 2 November, shortly after the fever had broken.[13]

On 15 December Augustus resumed his journey, and 15 days later the party arrived in Madrid. Augustus was deeply impressed by the Escorial; we can be less certain, however, about the fun side of his stay in the Spanish capital. That he, who had so recently resembled but 'a shadow of Hercules', had the strength to kill a bull with his bare hands, would seem to be but another of the legends surrounding Augustus the Strong. Although the Spanish dalliances may be true, our only source for them is von Pöllnitz.

On 22 January 1688 Augustus had an audience with King Carlos II, a sickly and sterile product of Habsburg interbreeding. His demise without an heir was anticipated throughout his reign and kept the courts of Europe busy with grandiose plans for disposing of the Spanish Empire. Ever burdened with problems, that day 'Carlos the Bewitched' had another: whether or not to wear his hat to receive Prince Augustus (alias the Count of Leisnig). Spanish etiquette finally decreed a bare-headed audience.

On 31 January Augustus and company headed west, reaching Lisbon on 15 February. One source implies that Augustus was there to compete for the hand of a Portuguese princess; if this was true, nothing came of it. Whether anything came of anything else is unknown, for even von Pöllnitz is unable to conjure up a single Portuguese beauty for the gallant Saxon to woo. King Peter, who received Augustus with his hat under his arm eight days after his arrival, presented our hero with a diamond-studded bauble worth RT 8000–10,000 on his departure. As his 'sketches' show, Augustus had wanted to stay longer in Portugal but Haxthausen refused to permit it. On 1 March, 'mit grossem Chagrin', Augustus resumed his travels.

Through Toledo, Aranjuez, Barcelona, Narbonne and Toulouse they journeyed, Augustus celebrating his eighteenth birthday on the road, until on 20 May 1688 they reached Paris again. Their second stay would last six months and was shadowed throughout by the gathering clouds of renewed war between France and the Empire.

11

This led to French occupation and devastation of the Palatinate that autumn, and in 1689 to the outbreak of the Nine Years War, also known as the War of the League of Augsburg.

Haxthausen, when not sending reports that amounted to thinly veiled espionage, continued his losing battle with Augustus's education. Progress in French and dancing still lagged, riding was so-so, only in fortification and siegecraft was he making progress; although such would be little in evidence outside the walls of Riga in 1700 (C16). The problem, throughout the six-month stay, remained the same; too many diversions and dalliances. Augustus was quite frank about it in his 'sketches'.[14]

Eventually, France grew too hot for a German prince who might be taken hostage in the event of all-out war. Any idea of visiting England, Holland and the major Rhineland towns in the new year went by the board. At the end of October Augustus again took leave of Louis and his court. He informed his father that the French King had received him 'gar honnet und mit gar fihller distinction'. And why should a monarch on the verge of a major war treat a potential enemy with so much courtesy and distinction? The simple answer is that Louis was looking for Saxon neutrality, to leave the Emperor's armies short of a few thousand troops (C3).

On 7 November 1688 Augustus's party left Paris for Italy. Journeying via Lyon, they traversed the Alps in severe winter weather and arrived in Turin three weeks later. Hardly had Augustus crossed the Savoy frontier when the order went out from Paris to arrest him; typically, John George III had plumped for the, Empire. On 5 December Augustus had an audience with the ruler of Savoy, Duke Victor Amadeus II, and despite the attempt to remain incognito was splendidly received. Hunts, balls and a fresh bevy of damsels soothed away any memory of near-arrest. Genoa came next, then Milan: Augustus managed a visit to the Ambrosian Library on New Year's Eve, but this and other cultural forays fail to remove the impression that Italy was mostly pleasure.

This was certainly the case with Venice. Travelling from Milan by way of Cremona, Brescia, Vicenza and Padua, the Saxons reached Mestre on 11 January 1689. From there they crossed to the lagooned city by gondola. On the next day Carnival began, and Augustus stayed to its end. Operas and masked balls, the theatre and love-affairs, together devoured his days.

In Venice he received an instruction not to visit Rome, and only to travel as far as Florence before beginning his return journey. In view of Augustus's later conversion (C13), the ban on visiting the Holy City is often interpreted as concern that the prince was already flirting with Catholicism. However, there is no hard evidence of this, and the probable reason was lack of time. John George wanted his lad in Vienna at Easter, before he set out on campaign against the French.

Nor had Augustus renounced glory. From Paris, Lyon and Venice, he implored his father not to forget him when he marched. The Elector had only to give the order, and his son would come to him booted and spurred, honoured to begin his military career under such leadership.[15] But there was no need for a premature return, and when Carnival ended, Augustus travelled via Ferrara and Bologna to Florence. Tuscany's Grand Duke Cosimo III had been well received in Dresden in 1668 and now reciprocated the hospitality. However, there were no balls nor operas, since Cosimo had given them up for Lent.

The main leg of the return journey took the party back to the Alps. After travelling through the Tyrol, Carinthia and Styria, they entered Hungary, celebrating Easter in Pressburg (Bratislava), then moved on to Vienna. The ultra-Catholic Emperor Leopold I (r 1658–1705) drew on his reserves of affability to greet the son of his loyal Protestant ally and even chatted to the party's Lutheran chaplain. Augustus enjoyed the honour of the Imperial table and a hunt in Laxenburg before travelling via Prague to meet his father and brother at the spa of Teplitz (Teplice) in northern Bohemia, where he arrived by post-coach on 14 April.

The Elector was taking the waters along with 'das Haugwitzische Frauenzimmer'. This menage was headed by the Austrian countess married to Saxony's Grand Marshal von Haugwitz. Also there was her niece, the 28-year-old Countess Susanne Margarethe von Zinzendorff, who was John George's current mistress. Augustus spent a week in their company before setting out on the last brief stretch of his journey.

Shortly before eight on the morning of Sunday 21 April 1689 our hero arrived back in Dresden. After changing his clothes he attended divine service (Gottesdienst), following which the senior court chaplain (Oberhofprediger) gave thanks for his safe return and the congregation sang 'Nun lob mein Seel den Herrn'.

And was Augustus's soul praising the Lord as he stood in the court chapel? Was he thanking God for his safe return? Indeed, was he pleased to be home after a sojourn of 23 months in foreign parts, or did everything seem somewhat parochial? Was he gawking around to see who was with whom these days? Was he running his eye over possible conquests and contrasting the maidens of Dresden to the Latins he had so recently known? Did the language sound strange? He may have skimped his studies, but he certainly spoke some French and Italian now. Was the Lutheran service somewhat alien? After all, he had been solely in Catholic countries for two years. Were the buildings, people, churches, even the scenery and weather, all rather incongruous? Was he just glad to see his mother again? Or was he solely elated by the imminence of his first campaign, with all its prospects of glory?

Who knows what he was thinking? It was probably along the lines above. For it seems far more realistic to conjecture the random thoughts of someone verging on 19, than to try and link his recent experiences to his later deeds. It is absurd to suggest, as some authorities do, that having seen Versailles, El Escorial and the marvels of the Italian cities, Augustus was already imbued with ideas for converting Dresden into its later status of 'the Northern Paris' or 'Venice (or Florence) on the Elbe'. It is equally fatuous to contend that his brief stay in Denmark in 1686 gave him notions about the need for absolutism in Saxony.

Such arguments are founded upon perfect hindsight, and in any case ignore one vital fact: there was no guarantee that Augustus, the second son, would ever become Elector and thereby have the chance to implement such policies. For this reason it is important to emphasize that in 1689, Augustus remained what he had been before his travels: a workaday glory-seeker, one who sought fame solely in battle. Ideas of wholesale glory, incorporating diplomacy, architecture, absolute rule, patronage and more, would only come to fruition later. And the prerequisite for their maturation would be that he was a ruler, supreme in his realm, and not just an inconsequential second son.

'Paris has thoroughly spoilt the prince', opined Liselotte.[16] Augustus, however, had been stirred not only by Paris, but by his entire spectrum of experiences. He would have needed a soul-transplant, had he remained untouched by the barrage of impressions which had regaled his senses. And whatever his many faults, Augustus was a sentient and a sensual being. But for the present he remained in a latent state; touched by much, but incapable of giving expression to any changes wrought in him. For that he would need power, and even more the power to use incredible amounts of money. Then the seeds planted in him by his *Kavalierstour*, and watered by the ongoing experiences of a life driven by ambition and pleasure, would have a chance to bloom.

'DOING ALL HE DESIRED'

In 1689 Augustus went off to war against the French. The Saxons were normally positioned on the Rhine, and he would see a lot of that river during the three campaigns of 1689–91. In his first year of war he took part in the siege of Mainz, winning praise for his cool-ness under fire. When Imperial forces stormed the fortress, he was grazed in the head by a bullet. In June he chipped a bone in his thumb, when a musket, which he had double-loaded in order to fire across the river Main, exploded in his hands. In his 'sketches' he recalled another occasion when he nearly broke his neck.

Beyond such events, there was little to report. The Nine Years War was not a spectacular conflict, particularly on the Rhine front. There was much in the way of manoeuvre and little in the way of engage-ment. It was certainly not a glorious war. Augustus was undoubtedly brave; he performed his duties; he learned about the realities of combat; and when the campaigning season was over he went home or visited Vienna, where he began a lifelong friendship with Joseph, the heir to the Empire.

In the winter of 1689–90 his father sent Augustus to Bohemia, with a view to his possible marriage to one of the daughters of the late Duke of Lauenburg, a duchy on the lower Elbe between Hamburg and Mecklenburg, which was contested between Saxony and Hanover. Nothing came of it. In late 1690 Augustus contracted small-pox, and during his recovery he penned his 'sketches' and read many historical novels.

Then it was back to the Rhine. However, in 1691 the Saxon contingent of 12,000 had a new fieldmarshal, Hans Adam von Schöning (1641–96). Born in Küstrin, Schöning had played an important role in Brandenburg's affairs during the reign of the 'Great Elector' (1640–88). He was a major-general in the Prussian army at 36 and governor of Berlin seven years later, and took part in the liberation of Budapest from the Turks in 1686. Absolutist and anti-Habsburg in his aims, Schöning sought to mould from the squabbling princelings of the Empire a German champion to contest the rule of Vienna.

The Great Elector's successor endeavoured to curb his influence. In August 1689, now commander of Brandenburg troops on the Rhine, the fiery fieldmarshal gave his enemies their chance. A clash of military plans led to Schöning's arrest, dismissal and exile to his estates. Now an avowed enemy of Berlin as well as Vienna, Schöning entered Saxon service in early 1691.

We can only surmise that the *Kaisertreu* John George III had taken on Schöning for his military skills and not his political predilections. His two sons were guests at Schöning's headquarters in mid-July. Although it was a relaxed and boozy occasion, with Augustus toasting the fieldmarshal while mounted on a mule, there were serious consequences to the meeting. Both princes came under his spell, and were to use Schöning as their chief adviser when they became

15

electors, while his imprisonment by the Emperor was to bedevil relations between Vienna and Dresden (C3).

For an era was coming to an end. On 1 September 1691 the secretary to the English envoy in Berlin sent a despatch to London. This appears to be the first of his many letters relating to Saxon affairs in general and the life of Augustus in particular.[17] George Stepney reported that John George III had been brought to Tübingen on 23 August, 'where he lay desperately sick and speechless'. Moreover, both of his sons were 'also indisposed', particularly Augustus, 'who is carried off to Nuremberg'.

Three weeks later Stepney recorded that John George had died about eight in the morning on 12 September, after 'being violently attacked by an apoplexy'. It was not a peaceful nor a dignified death for the 44-year-old Elector, any more than would be those of John George IV and Augustus. 'He had his understanding and was present to himself till the last minute'.

Possibly the dying ruler was aware that it was a anniversary. Eight years earlier he had charged down the Kahlenberg slopes outside Vienna with Jan Sobieski, the King of Poland, to put the besieging Turks to flight. Leopold had repaid this and other acts of fealty with scant gratitude, other than making the bluff huntsman his Reichs-jägermeister (Imperial Huntmaster). Well might Stepney remark that 'the Emperor has lost a prince who took pleasure in doing all he desired'.

When John George III went to the happy hunting-ground, his successor, not yet 23, was by his bed, while Augustus was reported to be returning from Nuremberg. Stepney had little to say about these two young men, save that Augustus had 'a spirit and ambition difficult to be governed', while the new Elector was 'inclinable to the hereditary vice of the family'.

John George IV, however, was more than 'inclinable'; he was addicted to a teenage nymphomaniac. She and Schöning would dominate the 31 miserable months of the young Elector's reign, and Stepney would observe much of what occurred from a grandstand seat.

Chapter 2

'This marriage will not end well'
John George IV, Eleonore and
'the Family' 1692

'A LEWD AND WHORISH EXISTENCE'

Ursula Margaretha von Neitschütz was born into the noble Upper
Lusatian family of Haugwitz around 1651.[1] Her older half-brother was
Friedrich Adolf von Haugwitz (1637–1705), who held the post of
Grand Marshal (Oberhofmarschall) of the Saxon court from 1680
until 1697. Ursula also had an unmarried sister who was a Roman
Catholic, a faith professed by only a minority in Lutheran Saxony,
the cradle of the Reformation.

Ursula married Rudolf von Neitschütz, another Lusatian noble. We
do not know when, nor how old her husband was. He first surfaces
as a major in the Saxon army in 1668. Having participated in several
campaigns against the French, he was with John George III at the
relief of Vienna in 1683. There is little reason to think that he was
other than a dutiful soldier and weak-willed man, who was no match
for the wiles of his pushy and depraved wife. After Rudolf's promotion to lieutenant-general in 1693, Ursula was referred to as 'die
Generalin'; but she was in command of events long before that.

Their marriage produced eight children, four of each sex. How
many of them Rudolf fathered is an open question. Only three of the
offspring are identified by name, and our concern is with the most
notorious: the oldest daughter, Magdalena Sibylle or 'Billa', later
Countess of Rochlitz. It was Billa who became the mistress and
nemesis of John George IV. She was also the young Elector's morganatic wife, probably the mother of his daughter and quite possibly
his half-sister. Billa was also a covert Catholic, who sought both to
become Electress of Saxony and to return John George and his realm
to Rome. This heady brew of sex, politics and religion bubbled away
throughout the brief reign of Augustus's elder brother.

Magdalena Sibylle was born on 8 February 1675[2]. The then

Kurprinz, later John George III, may have sired her. Her mother Ursula had many affairs when young, with John George identified as one of her lovers. Ursula, as a von Haugwitz, was presumably to be found in the ranks of the 'Frauenzimmer' and John George III may have drawn from this well more than once for his extra-marital liaisons. So it is quite possible that Billa was the fruit of a fling between Ursula and the Kurprinz, while Rudolf von Neitschütz was away with his regiment.[3]

However, the only real 'evidence' of such paternity is a lampoon (*Pasquille*) circulating in Dresden after the deaths of Billa and John George IV in April 1694; by which time Ursula was to be charged with witchcraft and murder (C7). In this, *die Generalin* is denounced as a woman who led 'a lewd and whorish existence throughout her life', who openly prostituted herself with John George III, illegitimately spawned the Countess of Rochlitz (Billa) from this liaison and thereafter procured Billa for her half-brother John George IV, binding him to incest through witchcraft.[4]

These grave charges can be read in two ways: either as part of the propaganda barrage surrounding the fall of the Neitschütz family and pandering to the hysteria of the time; or as a genuine statement of suppressed facts, which could only be published safely in the wake of this clan's collapse in power. The fact is, however, that we do not know whether John George IV and Billa indulged in an incestuous relationship; or if they did, whether they knew it was such.

We can speculate upon the intensity of their bond to suggest that they were aware of the truth. We can note too that Ursula addressed John George IV as 'Herr Sohn'. But this does not prove that the lovers knew of a blood relationship between themselves. However, the parents may have known. John George III would hardly have disapproved of his older son having a mistress as such; that he acted to keep both of his sons away from Billa, and even banished her and Ursula from court, may suggest a fear of incest. On the other hand, he might simply have disapproved of the ardour of his heir's feelings for a mere mistress. It is noteworthy that Stepney, who sniffed out plenty of dirt to titillate his masters in Whitehall, does not once mention the subject of incest in his correspondence.

While the question of incest remains open, the matter of the marriage of Billa and John George is more clear-cut (p 38). However, it could not even figure in the initial relationship, since Billa, although of noble birth, was not of 'equal blood' to John George; who, for the purposes of producing an heir, could not marry a woman of lesser rank than a princess. And such elevation for his mistress was impossible, before he was in a position to do something about it; until he became Elector. Moreover, such aspirations seem to have developed with the relationship, which in its early years was pretty rocky, given Billa's record. Even allowing for the imprecision of the evidence, we are compelled to conclude that she 'started young' and continued as she had set out.

In 1687, when Billa was only 12, none other than Christian August von Haxthausen fell for her, with the intention of marrying her when she was a little older. We know that Haxthausen died in 1696, but none of the sources give his date of birth; it is hard, however, to think of him as less than 30, when he was appointed as Augustus's Hofmeister in 1685. Now, two years later, the courtier charged with overseeing our hero's educational and spiritual development was seeking the hand of a child, whom by his own account he at some time bedded. For in June 1694 Stepney decorously reprised Haxthausen's claim that John George did not have Billa 'to himself, but he had the favour of being His Highness's taster'.[5]

There were certainly other 'tasters' throughout the relationship. Inevitably Augustus is identified as one, with the two brothers allegedly crossing swords for the nymphet's favour. When the Elector learned of their daggers-drawn behaviour, both princes were banned from any further contact with her. So while Augustus and Haxthausen travelled to France that May, John George was watched. Despite this he met clandestinely with Billa. When their meetings were discovered, she and her mother were banished from court and they left for their estates in Lusatia.

It is impossible to say whether Billa and John George kept in contact by letter; although it seems that Ursula, ever the manager, was ready to pen some of her wayward daughter's correspondence with her lovers. Only during the 1689 campaign did Billa and the young John George definitely meet again, when Ursula and her daughter turned up at her husband's camp in Schweinfurt. Such a 'coincidence' displeased John George III, and this episode cost Rudolf von Neitschütz his command. But later that year the affair resumed in Dresden. In consequence John George was sent away, this time on a tour to Rome, early in 1690. How it played thereafter is hazy. But the events which changed everything were the death of John George III in September 1691, and the accession of his namesake as Elector.

Once John George IV returned from the army in early October, he openly installed Billa as 'favourite'. She was given the same apartments and private galleries as his father's mistress Susanne von Zinzendorff. Ursula too went on the payroll with a pension of RT 2000, but was able to increase her takings by control of her daughter's 'court', to which all serious petitioners and office-seekers now addressed themselves. The new Elector was bewitched enough to provide an authorizing signature upon the necessary documents.

19

Nor was Billa's father forgotten. Rudolf was both reinstated into the Saxon army and promoted to lieutenant-general of cavalry. Her brother Christoph Adolf, an educated linguist of little moral character, advanced in his position as court chamberlain, while her brother-in-law, Wolf Dietrich von Beichling (1665–1725), prospered too. Married to Billa's younger sister Anna Katharina, who appears to have been only 13 or 14 at this time, Beichling now became an adviser (Geheimder Referendarius) to John George and an important 'fixer' for the Neitschütz family (p 53).

And what was Augustus doing while 'the Family' was raking in its spoils under the besotted eyes of the new Elector? The answer seems to be that he was rather passive. As heir presumptive, he was no longer just a second son but first in line, at least while his sibling remained without issue. However, he was now also a subject of his brother, to be disposed of as John George wished.

'The Elector's brother is to be no more called Prince but Duke Frederick', advised Stepney from Berlin on 24 November 1691. 'The Elector has assigned him a noble palace, where he is to live with his bride the Princess of Brandenburg-Bayreuth'. This is the first intimation of the marriage which would take place on 10 January 1693. Naturally, the betrothal placed no curbs upon the sexual appetite of the young Wettin. But other than that there was little: just a town house, a country estate and a pension of RT 50,000 – a sum which Billa grossed each time John George showered her with jewellery. Beyond that, Augustus was duke of nothing. The best that was offered in his father's will was the disputed Lauenburg, if it could be prised from Hanover's grasp. Otherwise, in 1692 it was back to war, still looking for some evanescent glory.

This may all have suited Augustus still, but possibly it did not. If he continued to believe that he was better suited to rule than John George, then the spectacle of 'die Neitschin' (as Augustus called Billa) and her grasping family ruling the roost could only have reinforced such a view. This was greed not glory, crass not class. Yet there was time enough for him to continue his old life while John George remained unmarried. However, this too was to change. Although it originally appeared that the Elector had settled for the status quo, very soon thereafter, possibly spurred on by Billa's bouts of infidelity, he opted for marriage, and with it all manner of new problems.

'THE BARGAIN IS MADE'

On 19 December 1691, Stepney reported that John George 'begins openly to shake off' his previous obedience towards his mother, because she had been 'too severe with him upon his amourettes with Fräulein Neitschütz'. Piqued by her interference, he had taken the opportunity 'to break his mind to her'. He was abandoning the plans, made 'more by his compliance than inclination', for him to marry her niece, a Danish princess. To convince her that 'these were not words only', he returned all gifts to the Danish court. Not only was this 'a great mortification' to his mother, but King Christian V was 'naturally warm in his resentment'.

Yet, however engaging he made this little story of a son taking the shears to apron-strings, it doesn't ring true. Within two months Stepney was outlining the negotiations for another marriage contract, this time linking Dresden and Berlin. He doesn't analyse the change or refer back to the abortive Danish match, probably because such switches were so commonplace. The fortunate Danish princess who had been jilted by John George was simply replaced by a tragic pawn of the Brandenburgs. There was going to be a marriage; the politics of heredity decreed this. The bride's identity depended simply upon the lottery of current alliance politics.

John George's bride-to-be was a widow nearly six years older than himself. Eleonore Erdmuthe Louisa von Sachsen-Eisenach was born on 13 April 1662. A sister of the current Duke of Sachsen-Eisenach, in her late teens she had married Markgraf Johann Friedrich von Brandenburg-Ansbach, to whom she bore a son and a daughter. After Johann's death in 1686 her children had been brought up in Berlin with the Brandenburg Kurprinz, the future Frederick William I. And it was his father, the Elector Frederick III (r 1688–1713), who promoted her re-marriage. In November 1691 Eleonore arrived in Berlin. In January 1692 a Saxon Geheimrat (privy counsellor) was sent there to conduct John George's courtship; that is to say he negotiated the financial and political terms of the marriage contract. Then the principal parties took over.

'At present', wrote Stepney from Berlin in February, 'we are taken up with the several divertissements, which are prepared to entertain the Elector of Saxony and his brother, who came on the 4th to Potsdam and the 5th had their public entry here'. For eight days the Saxons enjoyed 'serenades, fireworks, balls and continual feastings'. In return Augustus regaled the Prussians with some awesome feats of strength.

On 9 February Stepney reported that 'the match is looked upon as concluded, after the hard drinking last night'. The deal cost Frederick several of his best glasses, smashed to smithereens by a paralytic John George. The next day the two Electors signed a treaty. On 14 February John George left for Dresden for a meeting of his States (Parliament).

Some two months later, as the wedding day approached, Stepney penned portraits of those involved in this match made in hell. John George he described as 'of middle stature, round-shouldered, of a sullen look, which I believe does not belie his humour'. He was 'of a saturnine temper, seems to think, talks little, offers no jest himself, and is not pleased when others do it'. However bad his decisions, 'when he has once taken them, he is obstinate and hears no persuasion'.

The envoy added an observation of particular relevance to the young Elector of Saxony, given his known kidney problems. 'He would appear not to love drinking', said Stepney, 'nor has he the constitution which can bear that exercise'. The smallest 'debauch ruins his health, and as the custom of his country engages him in frequent ones, I look upon him as a man that will not be long-lived'. This he viewed as 'so much the better for his country and for his brother, who is a prince of great hopes'.

And what of his prospective bride? 'She is handsome, well-shaped but too lean', wrote Stepney of Eleonore. 'She is a princess of great virtue and piety', a Lutheran, 'and one who passes for a bigot in that persuasion'. Yet such zealotry had not doused the belief that she had been prepared to convert to Catholicism to marry the Elector of Bavaria. Perhaps she simply wanted another husband at any price, and she knew that the Elector of Saxony did not come without cost. 'She is of a mild nature, and prudent'; therefore she would tactfully 'comply with his humour that is quite contrary', and ''tis to be wished, if they have children, that her goodness may correct the breed'.

Of course, the abiding problem of the 'breed' was a proclivity to prefer other women to their wives. As soon as Stepney explored the third side of the eternal triangle his optimism beat a hasty retreat. He had never seen Billa, but had heard that she was 'young, gay and handsome'. Ostensibly she had been 'sent away' and promised in marriage to a Swedish count. But it was 'more than ever a wager', that when John George had 'tried t'other, his first flame is not so thoroughly extinguished, but it may catch again, which may render the match very unhappy'.

Having tendered his gloomy prognoses, Stepney turned to more congenial matters and wangled permission to attend the festivities in Torgau. He left Berlin with Frederick III and his entourage on 12 April. Eleonore travelled without her children, in order 'to be less a burden to the court of Saxony'. Wending their way via Potsdam and Wittenberg, the Brandenburg party reached Leipzig on 15 April.

There, on that same day as his intended arrived, John George visited Billa. Her fleeting exile had ended, if indeed it had ever occurred, while rumours of a Swedish husband had been but a ploy

22

'to quiet the spirit' of Eleonore. What transpired between the lovers at this tryst remains a mystery; but on 17 April 1692, with his brother and mother still in Dresden, preparing for a wedding scheduled for Torgau some days hence, John George married Eleonore.

'The despatch with which the marriage was clapped up at Leipzig', with 'little more ceremony than is used at ... Knightsbridge', affronted Stepney. Nor was he impressed that it was 'consummated with such an air of debauchery', when that same night and 'without ceremony', the Elector 'bedded his bride in her own apartments', before returning at 5.00 a.m. on 18 April to his quarters.

Why the rush? Stepney referred to the rumours of sorcery, which were to explode into hysteria two years later; with many already believing the 'stories of filters and incantations', by which Billa had ensnared her prince. Therefore an immediate marriage, which his advisers pressed for, would at least provide an opportunity of regularizing the succession before a bewitched Elector changed his mind. However, Stepney thought that the real reason for haste was John George's 'violent passion which he is not the master of, and a certain irregularity which is too observable in all his actions'. This may well be true; yet John George had little to lose. Sporadically servicing the succession would symbolize those rare occasions when he intended to quit Billa's bed for that of his wife.

Eleonore was introduced into Torgau on 20 April 'with an entry that was very magnificent'. Now the festivities could commence. The next day there was a ball; Augustus missed it, being laid up 'with an ague'. However, he arose on 22 April for a carousel, 'in which he could not forbear playing his part, which he did to admiration'.

First John George 'entered the lists at the head of eighteen knights all clothed alike in red, with gold trimming, broad shoulder-blades and green plumes'. Then came his brother leading an equal number garbed in blue, with silver trimmings and white plumes. 'They performed three times round by two and two', various exercises with spear, javelin, pistol and sword, 'at which they were very expert'.

On 25 April came the second part of the carousel. That evening there was a banquet just south of Torgau, after which John George and his bride floated down the Elbe 'in a sort of Venetian gondola'. For those still hungry supper followed, as a prelude to 'a very good fire work built on boats upon the water, with the names in cypher of both the Electors and Electresses'.

There were fireworks on land too; Billa 'was there and at the same table' as the newly-weds, 'where she received all the dalliances and discourses'. Stepney deprecated such behaviour as 'not civil at any time, but in the first week seems desperate and scandalous'. Similar

23

thoughts occurred to Saxony's ministers, who advised John George 'at least to counterfeit kindness' while the Brandenburg court was there, 'and not own so publicly where his true inclinations lay'. Eventually, with typical ill grace, the groom managed 'to direct his courtship aright', but 'so awkwardly that the constraint was too visible'.

Whatever her private feelings, Eleonore knew that 'the bargain is made' and was prudent enough 'to dissemble her grievance'. Stepney fancied that she seemed 'contented with the title' of Electress, adding snidely that this would be 'all she gets by the marriage'. For it was an unalterable fact that 'liberty has been established in the family by the example of two generations at least' of the Wettin dynasty. In any case, having a mistress was 'excusable if it goes no further'. While Stepney dared not insinuate that John George 'had two wives', he had noticed that Billa was referred to as the 'young Electress in opposition to the other'. In general, everything seemed to confirm 'the opinion that this marriage will not end well'.

Such too was doubtless the wish and expectation of the Neitschütz clan. Both *die Generalin* and her husband turned up at Torgau, along with their wanton daughter. One almost wonders whose marriage it was, for they seemed as happy as any in-laws. General Neitschütz was 'mightily pleased at his daughter's advancement', and 'the mother does not appear less satisfied'.

In fact the only person – besides Eleonore – who had a less than jolly time at Torgau was Augustus's mistress, the daughter of his late tutor von Klengel (p 86). Unlike the members of 'the Family', who were presented to the Electress, the young Klengel (also named Eleonore) did not have 'the happiness to be so well treated'. Not being of a noble family, which 'it seems is necessary in all callings, she was commanded to appear no more at court'. However, Stepney's expectation that this would oblige Augustus 'to marry her to some person' proved false, at least in the short term. He was still recounting their liaisons some three years later (C8).

For the moment there were fresh revels to depict. On 26 April a wolf, two lynxes, four bears and 19 wild boars 'were brought in chests into the court of the castle and baited there'. Two days later the guests were entertained by 'an Italian opera, where Bella Margarita [Margherita Salicola?] sung to admiration', and the 'night ended in masquerade'.

On the morning of 29 April the two Electors went hunting 'in a wood hard by', where 150 stags and some wild boars were 'surrounded with foils' and shot. The sportsmanlike envoy, a fan of fine distinctions, disapproved. 'This', he commented sniffily, 'the Germans call a royal hunt, though it be rather butchery than sport'. That afternoon Frederick III left Torgau. 'He could not dissemble his being very weary in Saxony', since their chief recreations were riding and hunting 'which he is not made for'. Stepney naturally accompanied his Elector to Berlin.

From there the Briton continued to keep tabs on happenings in Saxony, including the arrest of Schöning by the Austrians in June 1692. That August he noted John George's fall from a horse and Eleonore's miscarriage. The next month he pronounced them recovered. On 11 November Stepney reported that the Electoral Palace in Dresden had recently caught fire, 'but I do not hear the damage is considerable'.

This led him to pen a disparaging summmary of the first year of John George's reign. 'The world would have made no scruple of reflecting upon providence and divine punishment', if the Elector, in addition to seeing Schöning 'taken away by force', alienating his allies, nearly 'knocking out his brain' and causing 'his consort to miscarry',[6] had also had 'his palace burnt about his ears'.

It had certainly not been a good year for the young ruler, and it was only to get worse; there was nothing glorious about John George's brief tenure of the electoral cap. However, he and the Saxon army became objects of allied policy. This accounted for the presence in Dresden, first of Sir William Colt, England's envoy to Hanover, and latterly of Stepney himself.

Chapter 3

'To engage the Elector'
England and Saxony 1692–93

'THE ELECTOR OF SAXONY IS WARPED'

Following the death of John George III, Fieldmarshal Schöning left the Saxon army in winter quarters and arrived back in Dresden in October 1691; 'and 'tis thought he may have the greatest ascendant over the spirit of the new Elector'. Stepney's prognosis proved correct. Despite tales that Schöning had purchased John George's favour by procuring him a French pension when he was Kurprinz, it was the general's ambitions for Saxony and himself which most attracted the young ruler. He promoted Schöning to the posts of Geheimrat and Kriegsrat, and he came to dominate the Electorate's affairs.

In February 1692 the soldier-politician accompanied John George IV to Berlin. 'His natural insolence was greatly heightened by having this opportunity of showing his resentment and despising his enemies', scoffed Stepney. As for his apparent opposition to the marriage with Eleonore, this 'may be only in order for a better bribe'. Perhaps a better bride was Schöning's real objection, given his antipathy towards Berlin. However, he went along with the match.

His influence was more evident in John George's dealings with the Habsburgs. Schöning counselled that the days of unconditional Saxon subservience to Leopold should end. Future military aid should be contingent upon Vienna fulfilling its obligations towards Dresden.

These revolved around lack of Imperial support for the Electorate's position in the Lauenburg dispute and non-payment of outstanding subsidies of RT 500,000 occasioned by Saxon participation in the campaigns of 1689–91. To this was soon added a disagreement over winter quarters for the 6000 Saxon troops left on the Rhine; John George threatened to march them home if there was no satisfactory solution. The changed line did not go down well in Vienna. The new Saxon envoy there, the cradle-snatcher Haxthausen, reported in January 1692 that the Imperial Chancellor feared that Dresden was pursuing a generally hostile policy towards his court.

This concern was reinforced, when it became known that Saxony was listening to overtures from French agents, who had also approached Brandenburg and Ernst August, Duke of Hanover. Talk of a neutral bloc in north Germany was widespread at this time. 'We fear the Elector of Saxony is warped', wrote Stepney on 19 February, 'and has promised the French to be inactive, which is as bad as being neutral'. In his view, the Emperor 'has not been so careful as he ought in managing this Elector, supposing to find in him the same dispositions' as in John George III, 'who paid blind obedience to all that the court of Vienna could command'.

Faced with such a problem, there could be but one solution. Whitehall suggested awarding the Order of the Garter to John George. Stepney demurred, believing that the Saxon was 'engaged too far in a contrary interest, and the honour of the Garter will scarce be sufficient to reclaim him'. For the diligent French had been 'sowing tares which may choke the harvest of the next campaign'.

So for now John George remained unreclaimed and undecorated, while Vienna bought off Hanover by investing Ernst August with something more substantial than a ribbon. In return for realization of his dream, Hanover's elevation from duchy to the ninth electorate of the Empire, Ernst August signed a treaty in May 1692. This committed the first Elector of Hanover to supply a contingent of 6000 troops to an Imperial army taking the field against the Turks that summer. The usual sweetener – a subsidy from Vienna – also applied.

Since Brandenburg posed no problem, this left only the Saxons to be sorted out. Direct discussions between an Imperial envoy and Schöning finally commenced at Dresden in May. Both sides pitched their negotiating positions very high, almost as though inviting the other to abort the talks. Moreover, the Saxons hedged their participation in the 1692 campaign with so many conditions that it seemed that they intended not to march. The Austrians invited them to confirm this by deeds, and John George did so, ordering back from the Rhine all his troops save the 3000 that he was obliged to supply under the 'constitution' of the Empire. With the breakdown of negotiations, Schöning left Dresden to recuperate at the spas of Teplitz in northern Bohemia. His vacation would last over two years, mostly spent where baths were at a premium.

'HIS FALL IS NOT TO BE WONDERED AT'

Around 1 a.m. on 24 June 1692, Hans Adam von Schöning was 'surprised in his bed' in Teplitz by Imperial dragoons from the Prague garrison. Awoken by shouts, the general loosed off a couple of pistol shots through the window of his room, before soldiers battered down its door. Grappled to the floor, Schöning was bound and 'carried away in his shirt' by the troopers, who 'hurried him to Moravia' in case John George 'should attempt his rescue'.

'I am much surprised that so wise a man should venture himself at Teplitz in the Emperor's domain', Colt told Stepney on 30 June. In retrospect it does seem a strange, if not a reckless move by an avowed opponent of the Habsburgs, whom they had clearly targeted. For Haxthausen had stressed that Vienna attributed changes in Saxon policy not to John George, but to 'evil people' (*bösen Leuten*) in Dresden;[1] this was simply shorthand for Schöning.

Moreover, he *had* been in touch with French agents. There is no doubting this, nor that Louis XIV paid him an annual pension of 18,000 *livres*. From his prison, Schöning merely maintained that such contacts had not been prejudicial to the Emperor. Of course, an isolated and incarcerated man, with the axe hovering over his neck, could be expected to follow promptly the 'well, he would, wouldn't he?' dictum of Mandy Rice-Davies. However, the account that Schöning later gave to Stepney is not quite so innocent.

According to this version, Louis XIV had offered John George IV an annual subsidy of RT 400,000, 'if he forbear acting against him with more than the ordinary contingent, which he was obliged to furnish according to the matricule of the Empire'. Schöning did not reject the proposal, but went to Teplitz while it was under consideration. He admitted to Stepney that the idea of neutrality, with the Saxons heading a 'third party' balancing between France and the Empire, had attracted him. Moreover, such a scheme had the chance of coming to fruition under his aegis, 'because of the noise Schöning had made in the world', as Stepney spitefully phrased it.[2]

The envoy was equally malevolent on 1 July 1692, when he reported lengthily about the arrest to London. He was currently with the Brandenburg court at Cleves, and his views possibly reflected the 'spin' given by Schöning's enemies there. The general had 'been suspected to receive money from France' ever since his disgrace in summer 1689, and to 'revenge which ill-usage 'tis thought he has tried all means of doing mischief to the allies'. The chief product of his 'treacherous advice' was that John George had 'so shamefully kept his troops at home', giving the French the opportunity 'of drawing all their forces from the Rhine into Brabant', and thereby causing the loss of Namur in June.

Moreover, when Schöning went to Teplitz, he 'gave out he intended to use those waters' for six or seven weeks. Since he was commander of the Electorate's army, he thereby provided the French with 'a convincing proof' that Saxon troops 'had no design to disturb their projects by any diversion' in the near future. With such a record, Schöning had simply courted trouble by travelling to Teplitz, and therefore 'his fall is not to be wondered at'.

Stepney anticipated that Schöning was unlikely to be released soon, 'since I cannot guess at one prince who will appear to solicit his enlargement' – other than John George, of course, who 'will pretend a right of punishing him in his own territories, when it is proved he is guilty'. He thought that the Elector would 'lay hold of this pretext for continuing inactive'. However, in Stepney's view, Vienna was in the right, since Leopold had the jurisdiction to seize and prosecute suspected criminals in the hereditary Habsburg territories, as opposed to the Empire as a whole.

John George naturally saw things differently. He sent out a string of missives and envoys arguing the illegality of Leopold's act. He got nowhere with William III, who stood four-square behind the Emperor. This was hardly surprising: as Stadhouder of the United Provinces, and from 1688 as King of England too, William of Orange (1650–1702) had pursued throughout his adult life his dogged campaign of thwarting Louis XIV. Such a man had no time for anyone or anything that baulked his mission, and into this category fell Schöning and his policies. In fact, the Austrians even told Dresden that leading allied circles had demanded Schöning's arrest.

Whether or not this was true, the possibility existed that with Schöning out of the way there might be hope for the young Elector. Misguided, raw, prickly, he could be drawn back into the fold. William had got on well with the loyal John George III: in May 1688, while entertaining the 'Saxon Mars' in Holland, he had almost obtained Saxon forces to aid his landing in England. Even the necessary bribes for the ladies of the 'Frauenzimmer' were under consideration.[3] Such a policy could bear repeating; soon Billa and certain other Saxons would be in receipt of English pensions.

For now, John George IV huffed and puffed and made no progress. The Emperor held Schöning close prisoner in Brünn (Brno), and possession was nine-tenths of the law. Since John George could not free him, Schöning took matters into his own hands, with equal lack of success. In early September Stepney reported that Schöning 'had got an iron off the grate of his prison' while trying to escape; 'but his belly stopped him half-way, and he was found hanging ... betwixt heaven and hell' and lugged back in by his gaolers.

Perhaps John George was in purgatory too. Unable to do a thing about his general, he also had to contend with the pressures of 'the Family' and his obsession with Billa, who was pregnant. It was probably John George's child, since one Colonel Klemm, who had apparently fathered another on her, was on military duty at the time of this latest conception; but such 'evidence' demonstrates only that Klemm was not the father, not that John George was.

In December 1692 the Kriegsrat Count Julius Heinrich von Friesen was sent to Vienna. He had been in William of Orange's pay, and when he returned to Saxon service he retained close ties with his former master. Friesen was also linked to 'the Family' and had been, and possibly still was, one of Billa's lovers. His current mission was to endeavour to have the Emperor raise Billa to the rank of Imperial Countess (Reichsgräfin). Why Leopold should do this is not clear; conceivably Billa's conversion to Catholicism was already a factor. A straightforward trade-off, whereby she returned the Emperor's favour by working to bring John George back to the fold, is another possibility. Perhaps it was just one move in a series, designed to produce a deal between Vienna and Dresden.

It is hard to say how far John George was involved. Isolated, cut off from Imperial subsidies, besotted with Billa, he may have sought to mend his fences, using such influence as he could still apply. Although the Schöning question remained an obstacle, the Elector tried to call Vienna's bluff. Stepney reported John George's willingness for Schöning to be executed after fair trial, if the Austrians held 'real proofs against him', which he doubted.

He put added pressure upon the Emperor by reacting positively to an approach brought by a Danish envoy in November 1692 for resuscitation of a 'neutral bloc'. His advisers downgraded these negotiations to produce solely a defensive alliance. However, the possibility that the Elector might deplete Imperial forces again in the 1693 campaign caused both the Habsburg and English courts to take action. This was the beginning of direct British involvement in Saxon (and later Polish) affairs, which would last throughout the remainder of John George's reign and through most of Augustus's too.

'THE AFFAIRS OF GERMANY'

On 22 November 1692 Whitehall instructed Stepney to 'repair' to Vienna, and to remain there until he received orders to return to Berlin. After taking leave of the Brandenburg court, Stepney travelled by post-coach through Silesia and Moravia, reaching Vienna on 1 January 1693 (NS). En route he passed the castle of Spielberg, 'an eminence which commands the city Brünn in Moravia'. Behind its grim walls Schöning slumped in his cell, its door guarded by two sentinels clasping ready-drawn swords.[4]

On 25 November Sir William Dutton Colt (1646–93) was also sent upon a new mission by King William.[5] Quitting Hanover, Colt was to go to Dresden as envoy extraordinary, and deliver one Garter to 'our good brother the Elector of Saxony'. However, given 'the present state of the affairs of Germany' in relation to the war against France, William 'thought fit' to tender some 'further directions' to his ambassador.

Once the usual flummery of compliments was over, Colt was to address himself to specific points. First he was 'to engage the Elector' to join the Habsburg–Dutch alliance of 12 May 1689, into which England (on 20 December 1689) and 'many other princes are since entered for our common defence against the French King'. If John George would not join this 'Grand Alliance', then Colt was to propose that he enter into a specific pact with England and Holland. Should the Schöning affair cause problems, Colt was to give his masters 'speedy notice' thereof, so that requisite steps could be taken in Vienna.

Mindful of previous Saxon delays and shortfalls, Colt was to insist that Saxon troops be sent 'early in the spring to the Upper Rhine' and in 'sufficient force' either to parry the French there, or 'to divert them from bringing their whole strength into the Low Countries'. Colt was also 'to have a watchful eye' on French or Danish 'intrigues' to promote other Saxon proclivities, such as 'neutrality or to the forming or joining with a third party'. For 'the better effecting' of all his tasks, Colt was 'to keep a constant correspondence with such ministers as shall be residing in Vienna', which was where Stepney came in.

Colt and his wife arrived in Dresden on Monday 9 January 1693. Living 'upon our own purse', they took quarters in the old town. The house that they anticipated having was unavailable, because John George had given it to Augustus 'to live in with his new consort of Bayreuth, whither he went on Saturday last to be married to her'.

On 23 January Colt apprised Stepney that he had had two audiences with John George and that 'we have been most magnificently received'. This was as it should be, since grown men are not feted with Garters by other grown men every day of the week. This gripping ceremony took place on 26 January 'to the full content of the Elector and all his court', and Stepney received a meticulous account of how Colt had handled matters. As the contents of this screed are as riveting as watching paint dry, the reader is spared a summary.

On 17 February Christiane Eberhardine of Brandenberg-Bayreuth, fated since 10 January 1693 to be the consort of Augustus, made her entrance into Dresden. Colt bemoaned the consequent 'many marks of rejoicing, which will put some stop to our business'. His secretary, the German emigré Schweinfurt, was more enthusiastic, gushing to

Stepney on 20 February that since Eberhardine's arrival 'we do not want divertissements, for that every day produces something new'. Even a treaty was produced.

'MUCH IS DUE TO THE LADY'

On 25 January Stepney informed Colt of Dresden's conditions for an Imperial–Saxon treaty. First they required Leopold to release Schöning or to 'bring him to a fair trial'; second, Vienna was to abandon any support for the Albertine collateral lines (*Seitenlinie*) against the Wettins;[6] third, the Emperor was to decide the Sachsen-Lauenburg issue in John George's favour. Finally, he was to raise Billa to the rank of Imperial Countess, with 'that dignity to be continued to her posterity'.

Stepney accentuated Billa's importance, telling Colt that if he intended 'to do anything to purpose, you must make your court to that lady'. This, he teased, 'will be no difficult matter to you, after what you have been used to do to the Countess of Platen'. The last-named was the daunting mistress of Ernst August of Hanover.

Colt stood in no need of such advice, he had already traipsed up the back stairs. He reported to Blathwayt (p 43) that he had been conducted at night 'to the mistress and her mother' by the Hanoverian envoy. The German entreated Colt 'to give them the best words I could', praising 'the good offices they had done in keeping the Elector hitherto from acting against the allies'. Colt produced the requisite patter, and the two Neitschütz ladies 'gave me all the assurances possible that they would do their utmost'.

Such services did not come free: the Brandenburg and Hanoverian envoys both told Colt that 'there is nothing to be done but by the mistress, and they are soliciting to have her made a countess'. In the meantime Colt was made aware that 'money is the main point that will hasten our motions'. And so it came to pass.

Just prior to the signature of the Austro–Saxon treaty, Colt met with Billa, who now rejoiced in the title of Countess of Rochlitz. He supplied her with a gift of '6000 dollars in banco, which will amount to £1500 sterling'. The Dutch envoy was paying 4000 dollars, 'and so soon as I know what the others will contribute', he promised Blathwayt the particulars. All in all, Colt deemed it to be money well spent. For 'much is due to the lady', and without her assistance none of the envoys 'could do any great service at this conjuncture; the proofs I have are many'.

The provisions of the Austro–Saxon treaty of 20 February 1693, to which the English and Dutch were added as accessories in April, did not commit John George to enter the Grand Alliance. He simply made a specific agreement with Vienna, which remained valid until early 1694. Under its terms, Saxony was to send to the Rhine an army of 12,000 men, subsidized to the tune of RT 400,000, the English and Dutch governments picking up three-eighths of this tab. In addition, Vienna promised the Emperor's good offices in the Lauenburg matter and in John George's dispute with his cousins.

The agreement represented a climbdown by John George. He had gained a title for his mistress, some needed funds for his treasury and a Garter, and had also ended Saxony's isolation. Yet Schöning remained a prisoner; although some improvement in his conditions was promised, clearly the Elector had yielded ground on his freedom.

Colt never 'flattered the Elector with the hopes that Schöning would be released', therefore he always had a hard task in approaching the Saxon ruler direct. An added difficulty was the ambiguous personality of John George, which evoked mixed emotions in the diplomat. 'I never in my life saw so fickle a man', he wrote in mid-February, 'and all the intimacy I have gained with him hath been by the grossest flattery imaginable'. He also saw him, after he 'had drunk very hard', betraying 'many marks of anger, which had been fatal to one of his pages, if he had not nimbly escaped'.

Yet Colt also perceived 'a man of much better parts than I expected', who 'takes great notice of all things' and who was 'lost in his love' for Billa. Nor did Colt doubt his authority: 'the ministers can do little here, the Elector following only his own humour'.

'I am persuaded the Elector's intentions are good', Colt asserted at the end of March. 'I have presented him with a fine English horse' and 'I have gotten him some English dogs'. If a Garter and some homegrown pets were not enough, some more of the 'grossest flattery' was in order. Colt had continually assured John George 'of His Majesty's affection, and he daily expresses great desire to gain the King's good opinion'.

'THE MATTER IS STRANGE AND SURPRISING'

Augustus also sought King William's good opinion. At the end of February 1693, Colt reported that he 'desired me to assure His Majesty of his constant service'. The envoy observed that the heir presumptive 'had well drunk when he entertained me so freely with his thoughts'.

Made a lieutenant-general of cavalry for the coming campaign, Augustus had given Billa 'very hard words, for taking part with those who solicited' his brother to appoint General Chauvet as Saxon field-marshal. He made difficulties about serving under the newcomer, even to the extent of 'pressing the Elector' to appoint Rudolf von Neitschütz as commander. As Colt observed, Billa's father, 'though a very honest man to the cause', was completely 'incapable of such a charge, which his family are wise enough to know'.

Somewhat stranger than 'the Family' renouncing nepotism is the picture of Augustus trying to promote their fortunes. We can only guess at his real motives. Conceivably, the prospect of the experienced professional Chauvet actually winning some laurels at the head of Saxon forces was seen as a further blow to Schöning's position. If successful, the newcomer would be retained and would be able to fill the Saxon army with his placemen.

To those loyal to the fallen idol, this was anathema. In his letters Colt observed that 'the faction of Schöning is so powerful in the army' and that 'there was a great force for Schöning amongst the Saxon troops'. A kinsman of his was a lieutenant-general of foot and his son was a lieutenant-colonel of the guards. For all of these, the command of a 'seat-warming' duffer like Rudolf, with its inevitably mediocre results, would have ensured that, when free, the old plotter could return to his command in triumph.

In April 1693 there was another strange interlude involving Augustus: according to Colt, he asked leave of his brother 'to go to Hamburg and that his design was only gallantry'. Yet by 10 April his journey was giving John George 'great alarm and jealousy', and he despatched his Adjutant-General Carlowitz after Augustus 'to inform himself and to observe all his actions'. According to rumour, Schöning's son and 'another creature of that party' were with him in Hamburg; so too was the Danish ambassador, with whom Augustus had held frequent private conversations in Dresden. The fear was that he 'may be gained by these people'.

According to Haake, Augustus left for Hamburg secretly, but with his brother's consent, in order to stage a coup in Ratzeburg, the capital of the disputed Duchy of Lauenburg. If Saxony gained the duchy, it would fall to Augustus's inheritance under the terms of his father's will. Apparently, the plan was that he would head a Danish force provided by his uncle Christian V to capture the duchy, taking advantage of weakened Hanoverian defences there. In the event, certain correspondence was captured, the Hanoverians strengthened the garrison of the capital, and the whole project fell through.[7]

'I do confess the matter is strange and surprising', Colt admitted, 'for that we all thought ourselves sure of him in the party of the allies'. He presumed that 'a little time will give us more light in this matter'; instead, the Saxons generated a smokescreen.

Augustus's return was forecast for nearly one month. He was variously reported to be in Hamburg for sex, to watch a duel, and to see an alchemist make gold. John George even suggested that he might have gone on from there to Het Loo, to see King William. Although a coup was naturally not on the list of alternatives, Colt suspected that the inheritance of Sachsen-Lauenburg was somehow involved. John George's role in the matter was diversely described as complicit, 'not pleased', or ignorant of 'the bottom of the affair'.

Augustus left Hamburg on 25 April, met his brother at Torgau and on 5 May returned to Dresden. Colt thought that 'he seems very free and easy', while John George assured him that 'there was nothing to be feared' from Augustus's little trip, 'for that he did many things without thinking'. Yet by mid-May Colt was reporting 'a great coldness' between the brothers, perhaps because something like the full story was out. Certainly, Augustus was on the defensive, taking 'all occasions to justify himself', that he would never have undertaken 'so weak a thing as the world charged him withal, and that there could be no hopes of his keeping such a possession'. But the hubbub soon passed: the Saxons were needed at the front.

'PRESSING THE MARCH'

Now, the important thing for the British was to get the Saxons into the field. Colt would be with them, having been ordered by William to make the campaign. In May he quit Dresden for Hanover, where he spent a month catching up on business and preparing for rear-echelon duties.

In consequence, Stepney was left 'pressing the march' as best he could from Vienna, and John George was hardly in a hurry. Stepney predicted that the Saxon baggage and artillery would leave from Dresden on 10 May, with John George travelling to Frankfurt ten days after. He was late, waiting at Ochsenfurt 'till his troops come up' and not reaching Frankfurt until 14 June.

Stepney was pessimistic about future events. He feared that 'some scruple of honour and command among the generals may hinder their joining', whereby 'the charges His Majesty has been at to gain the Elector of Saxony may become ineffectual'. On 28 June he noted 'complaints' against the Saxons, who 'live licentiously, after all their promises to observe strict discipline' and only paid for two-thirds 'of what they call for'. Moreover, they 'still lag behind', as if 'they were loth to get out of these easy quarters'.

Blathwayt was less than impressed. In late May he had congratulated Colt and Stepney on their handling of the 'matter of the great alliance', which was now 'in the posture His Majesty desires'. One month later he was more concerned with posturing, as John George and Margrave Lewis of Baden (1655–1707) wrangled over the command. Blathwayt sternly informed Stepney of William's surprise at 'this dispute subsisting, after what you writ of accommodation'.

However, there was nothing that Stepney could do about this less than glorious campaign. He reported the 'unhappy rencontre' of the Saxons with the French 'at a pass called Zwingenberg' (east of Heidelberg) at the end of June, an action which Colt labelled as 'not of any great moment'. Here the survivors made their escape 'under the good conduct' of Augustus, who with a small force of cavalry and dragoons 'favoured their retreat'. It was the Saxons' only engagement that summer; thereafter they were ordered south to rejoin the main forces, reaching Heilbronn on 19 July. At the end of August the French broke off their Rhine campaign for another year.

'A MAN MAY HAVE TWO WIVES'

Not only Colt made the campaign with the Elector of Saxony in 1693. Whether or not her sovereign and lover had permitted it, the newly patented Countess of Rochlitz, 'very big with child', was there too, along with her manager-mother. On 25 June, during a rare interval from disputing the command with Billa and Lewis of Baden, John George became a father.

'On Sunday night', Colt briefed Stepney from Frankfurt two days later, 'the Countess of Rochlitz was delivered of a daughter a few hours after my arrival, and yesterday I have been Godfather'. He stood along with Augustus, the Saxon commander Fieldmarshal Chauvet, Ursula von Neitschütz and a Madame Arnheim. The baby was christened Wilhelmina Maria Friederika. The first two names, combined with Colt's presence, led to the erroneous story, assiduously promoted by 'the Family', that the envoy was representing King William and Queen Mary of England, who were the real godparents.[8] The name Friederika was a sop to the Danish royal family.

As to the child's status, she was heiress as of right to her mother, since the patent elevating Billa to countess applied also to her offspring, whether born in or out of wedlock. And she was also a legitimate daughter of John George, inasmuch as he considered himself married to Billa, as well as to Eleonore.

In March 1693, after the Elector had Billa made up to countess, Stepney told Whitehall that "'tis thought he will carry the humour so far as to marry her, though his Electress is still living'. The envoy predicted that he might soon 'assure your lordships a man may have two wives in Germany as well as in Turkey'. Despite the bantering tone, Stepney was reporting a rumour that was more than mere *Hofklatsch*, although he could not confirm its truth. Similarly, Colt wrote that Billa's parents 'would have the world believe there is more between the Elector and their daughter than can be made public'.

This was true: early in 1693 John George had signed and sealed a marriage contract between himself and Billa. The document actually bore the date 16 October 1691, thereby referring to a time *before* his marriage to Eleonore. That the contract was ostensibly back-dated was acknowledged by *die Generalin* during her later trial. The reason for this, as Ursula candidly stated (according to the official record), was to strengthen the position of her daughter, should the trivial matter of bigamy create any problems.[9]

The contract is tortuously worded and as convoluted as the predicament it sought to address; however, the main points are clear. In order to give Billa 'greater peace of mind' ('zu besserer Beruhigung ihres Gewissens'), John George had taken his vows before her parents. Although he recognized that such was not a formal union, he gave notice that he recognized as legitimate not only their marriage ('eine rechte Ehe'), but also their issue; although the latter were to have no rights of succession to the Electorate. However, since he was advised that neither the Bible nor the Lutheran religion forbade it, he felt free to take another wife of 'equal blood' ('und zwar von gleichem Geblüte mit mir'), and any issue from *this* marriage would be legitimate heirs to the Electorate ('die rechtmässigen Erben dieser Kur und Landen sein sollen').

In short, if Billa could now clamber to the higher rank of Imperial Princess (Reichsprinzessin), she could upgrade her morganatic marriage to an 'equal-blooded' version and become Electress, and her male children could succeed John George. She would be senior Electress, because this back-dated document gave her temporal precedence over Eleonore's wedding. Of course, if John George could meantime divorce the incumbent, matters would be much simplified.

That hapless woman had problems enough. Eleonore's hopes of producing an heir, and thereby cementing her position, were again shattered when she 'miscarried of a son' in February. When Colt left Dresden, he reported that she 'was under many and great afflictions'.

And what of the current heir to the Electorate? Augustus cannot have been any less aware than Stepney and Colt of the rumours of his brother's second 'marriage'; but we know nothing of his thoughts about this admittedly fluid situation. He was married himself now, to his pious cousin Eberhardine. She was merely inserted between his affairs and campaigns.

Although the Saxons did not march in 1692, Augustus obtained his brother's permission to participate in the campaign in the Netherlands that year, and in August he fought in the battle of Steenkerk. Otherwise he seems to have spent his days in camp piling up gambling debts, which would give a strange twist to his fate two years later (C9). In 1693 our hero would have his abortive outing in Hamburg, and some cut and thrust at Zwingenberg, but this was hardly glory. Perhaps it was all beginning to pall.

So what might he have thought, as he stood godfather to baby Wilhelmina? Nearby were assembled the brother he despised, his grasping mistress and her scheming mother. Was the fate of the Wettins, his own dynasty be it remembered, to be entrusted to this clique? What of Schöning and his grand designs? In 1705, in his 'memoirs', he recalled how Saxon courtiers had inwardly rejoiced at the arrest of this 'man of quality'.[10] While Colt might report in mid-August that John George had been 'extreme violent of late for the enlargement of Schöning', what was the guarantee that his brother would not abandon him again, in order to further the ambitions of his teenage mistress?

But did Augustus care that the undoubtedly fecund Billa might ease him from the succession? Did he intend to do anything about it? Or was he content to go on whoring and warring like his father? Even if we could divine his thoughts that summer, it would not alter the fact that Augustus soon had more to worry about than the succession; he was struck down by dysentery. Nor was he the only one.

On 25 August Schweinfurt reported that Colt was 'very sick of the bloody flux at Heilbronn', and that Augustus 'labours also under that distemper'. Five days later Colt died 'without making the least motion', and on 31 August he was buried in the town's Lutheran church.

Although on 30 August Schweinfurt had described Augustus as 'very sick' and 'also given over this morning', he did not die. On 8 September Schweinfurt announced that the Saxon 'begins now to mend' and would soon be in Frankfurt. And although Augustus had received a visit from his brother in Heilbronn, there was no question of John George dallying by the sick-bed.

On 8 September, John George was in Frankfurt 'with the Countess and his whole court'. Now he was heading for Leipzig. So too was George Stepney, who would also be a chronicler of deaths: those that would befall John George and his beloved Countess within a matter of months.

Chapter 4

'Carrying my cloak on both shoulders'
Stepney in Saxony 1693

'I HAVE STROLLED ABOUT LIKE A GYPSY'

George Stepney was born in Westminster in 1663, the son of minor gentry. His father died when he was three, and he and his two sisters were raised by their mother Mary. George's reference to 'my mother's care in my education' suggests that she provided her intelligent son with every advantage that she could afford.

Stepney attended Westminster School as a King's Scholar from 1676 to 1682. There he befriended two impecunious grandsons of the Duke of Manchester, Charles Montagu (1661–1715) and his younger brother James. Charles, later the Earl of Halifax, became a major political figure during William's reign and was Stepney's earliest patron and 'the best friend I have'. Another close schoolfellow was Matthew Prior (1664–1721), who, like Stepney, developed into a poet and diplomat.

In 1682 Stepney followed Montagu to Trinity College, Cambridge, graduating BA three years later and MA in 1689. In September 1687 George was elected a senior fellow of his college whilst he was abroad in Hamburg; appropriately it was a travelling fellowship.

At Cambridge Stepney acquired a considerable reputation as a writer of Latin verse. His papers contain various poems in that language (including an epitaph for Billa), as well as others in English, French and Italian. He also knew German and Dutch. On his missions in Poland and Hungary Stepney conversed and negotiated in Latin.

How Stepney entered upon his diplomatic career is obscure, and the sequence of his earliest postings is known in outline only. In July 1694 he wrote of 'having been abroad before the Revolution' of 1688, and that since then 'I have strolled about like a gypsy'.

He began as a member of Sir William Trumbull's mission to France, which ran from November 1685 to August 1686. However, we do not know if Stepney was in Paris for its entire duration. The first letter to specify his whereabouts is one from Montagu in November 1686, addressed to Stepney in Hamburg. There George spent some three years as secretary to Sir Peter Wyche, returning to England in May 1689.

Stepney's next post was in Berlin, where we first encountered him as secretary to James Johnston in late 1691. This position was set up for him by another patron, James Vernon (1646–1727). George writes of serving in Berlin for two years under Johnston, with a further year spent there on his own. This is broadly correct. Johnston was the delivery-man for the Garter awarded to Elector Frederick III of Brandenburg. Arriving in March 1690, he stayed on as envoy extraordinary, leaving Berlin (and an unpaid Stepney) in January 1692.

Stepney ranked his year alone in Berlin as his first mission. Next comes Stepney's service in Vienna, beginning in January 1693, and where he was still employed at the time of Colt's death. This was to be followed by eleven other missions, of which nine would take him into the German Empire.[1]

'SO THE KING BE SERVED'

'Wherever I am sent from Muscovy to the Mogul, is all alike to me, so the King be served, and I find my court': so wrote Stepney in July 1694. 'All corners of the earth are alike to me', he breezed upon another occasion. Granted the poetic licence, it seems to be a neat picture of a young, loyal career-diplomat and subject. It omits, however, his ambition, frustration and relative poverty.

It was not 'all alike' to Stepney. He was perfectly human; he desired status, influence and material well-being. He was good at his job and he wanted recognition of that ability. Moreover, remuneration varied with rank, or the 'character' designated in the credentials and instructions pertaining to an assignment; and those of noble birth were more likely to receive senior postings.

The quality of Stepney's reports, and his trenchant advice to senior envoys in his early years, all seem indicative of a man with top diplomatic status. Hence it is easy to forget that Stepney was merely 'Secretary of the King of Britain' at both Berlin and Vienna.

At the latter post he found himself transmogrified, early in 1693, into the King's 'Agent to the Emperor's Court and in other places in Germany', with a back-dated pay-rise. However, Stepney was not happy as an 'agent', which he deemed 'too vulgar an appellation'. Nor was he sure what the title signified; it was certainly a rare designation. Colt too was hazy about the nomenclature, although assuring Stepney that it was 'a title of distinction' and given 'as a beginning'.

And this was what it was all about: beginning at the bottom, but continually fighting one's corner for promotion, to receive a 'character'. Moreover, diplomatic service was often intended only as a way-station to some sinecure at home, possibly with a title, as a foundation upon which to build a career or to see out one's days. As one diplomat deftly phrased it: 'Foreign services may sometimes prove a good stirrup but never a good saddle'.[2]

The whole journey therefore required that one solicit and retain 'patrons': men who already had influence and were skilled at fighting to preserve their power within the fractious cockpits of English court and parliamentary politics. In his early years Stepney relied upon 'the triumvirate of my patrons', to wit Montagu, Vernon and, pre-eminently, William Blathwayt (1649?–1717).

When young, Blathwayt had served abroad. In 1683 he purchased the post of Secretary-at-War, which before the Revolution was but a clerkship. Retaining this position under William III, he held it until 1704. From 1696 to 1706 Blathwayt was also a commissioner for trade. Thanks to him, Stepney too became a commissioner in 1697, thereby pulling in an annual salary of £1000 as his 'sheet-anchor' during further diplomatic service. Blathwayt was also an MP during most of the years from 1685 to 1710.

His greatest influence, however, was exercised in his nominal role as Secretary-at-War. While a deputy took over such work as the King left to Whitehall, the multilingual Blathwayt accompanied William on his continental campaigns. There he effectively served as the King's executive secretary and as a third Secretary of State.

The two regular Secretaries of State jointly shared responsibility for home affairs. However, in foreign policy one covered the Northern Department (the Empire, Holland, Scandinavia, Poland and Russia) while the other headed the Southern Department (France, Iberia, Italy, Switzerland and the Ottoman Empire). The senior of the two normally supervized the South. In practice one of the posts might often be vacant, while the main work frequently fell upon deputies. This was the case with Vernon.

Vernon acted as secretary to the Duke of Shrewsbury (1660–1718) when the latter was Secretary of State in 1689–90, and retained the position under his successors. In contemporary terms he was a Permanent Under-Secretary. When Shrewsbury, a vacillating and reclusive hypochondriac, returned for a second stint in 1694–98, Vernon virtually ran his office. In December 1697 Vernon became a Secretary of State in his own right, holding the post until April 1702 and in this period often heading both North and South.[3]

'YOU BEGIN TO BE TAKEN NOTICE OF'

On 4 September 1693 Blathwayt contacted Stepney from William's headquarters at St Quentin in the Spanish Netherlands. He told him that Colt had been transacting a number of matters when he died. He was assigning winter quarters to the Saxon troops, endeavouring to bring John George into the Grand Alliance, agreeing the requisite subsidies, and trying to reconcile some dissenting German princes to Hanover's elevation to the status of ninth Electorate. By Colt's 'untimely death', these matters were 'left unsettled and are of too great importance to be neglected'.

For George Stepney, first came the good news: 'His Majesty therefore has pitched upon you for those performances'; not only because he was well satisfied with Stepney's 'diligence and abilities', but also because he knew that the young diplomat was acquainted with all these matters, through service at Vienna and his correspondence with Colt. The bad news was that his monarch 'does not give you the title of envoy extraordinary because you are to return to Vienna'.

Replying on 16 September, Stepney hid his chagrin. He was unable to 'sufficiently admire His Majesty's gracious favour' in employing him at Dresden. Playing to his strengths, he added with false modesty that 'as I am no stranger to the court of Saxony, I hope I may not be altogether useless there'.

Vernon sought to salve Stepney's disappointment. He should treat the Dresden mission as an opportunity to shine, for although George had 'been long abroad, it is not long that you have been in the King's business, I mean to act as a principal'. But from now on 'you begin to be taken notice of and to establish a reputation, which being confirmed, you may expect something substantial hereafter'. In short, much would depend upon how the young envoy handled his mission to Saxony.

Accordingly, on 20 September Stepney told Blathwayt that he intended to 'repair to Saxony' either that evening or the next morning. 'I hope to be at Dresden in four days running night and day', he added, and on the basis of information from Schweinfurt, he expected to 'find the Elector there'.[4]

'THROWN UP IN DRESDEN'

True to his word, Stepney left Vienna by 'running post' on 21 September. A gruelling journey lay ahead of him; but on 25 September, 'after having been a day and a night longer in the postwagon than Jonah was in the whale's belly', he could report that he was 'at last thrown up in Dresden'. However, he had just missed John George, who, having returned from Frankfurt three days before, had left that evening for his hunting-lodge at Moritzburg and was also intending to visit his mother and Augustus 'at their country-seats'.

Stepney therefore got down to business. He took a house in Dresden and made himself known to the Elector's chief ministers, 'who entertained me only with gentle discourse'. On 1 October he travelled to Leipzig, where he obtained most of Colt's papers from Schweinfurt.

The next day the Michaelmas Fair began; Stepney foresaw it as 'a dull one', telling an anonymous lady that he heard of 'no princes who design to be there except the Elector and his brother'. Doing his best as a star attraction, John George arrived from Torgau for the commencement, making 'a sort of entry' with Billa 'in an open chaise, though she affected modesty by muffling her hoods'.

On 4 October Stepney received his credentials, instructions and powers as commissary and deputy to the Saxon court. His instructions mandated Stepney to conclude a treaty and agree the requisite subsidies with the Elector, in order to ensure that the Saxons participated in the 1694 campaign against the French. The Briton sent copies of his credentials and powers to Grand Marshal Haugwitz, 'that he may enquire of the Elector when he shall be pleased to give me audience, which I believe will be done without ceremony to gain time'.

In fact Stepney's first audience with John George and his advisers took place on 5 October. He confessed that he could not 'much brag of the manner in which they treated me'. Despite this cool reception, Stepney still foresaw 'great hopes of our negotiation'. The Elector, he reported, was obliged to King William 'for these fresh assurances of his affection, and was ready to enter into stricter alliance with him for the *cause commune*'. However, the Saxons made it clear that they were awaiting the arrival of the Imperial envoy 'before any progress could be made [in] that affair'.

This was the nub of the matter in two respects. First, it was up to the Dutch and Habsburg envoys 'to make the first overtures', since they were the 'principals in this alliance, whereas His Majesty is only an accessory'. Secondly, John George (and later Augustus too) held back from sealing the conditions for Saxon participation in the 1694 campaign, so long as Schöning remained imprisoned by Vienna.

Already cast in a secondary diplomatic role by England's status in the treaty negotiations, Stepney wrestled also with his problems of personal standing. He rankled at his designation as commissary and deputy rather than envoy extraordinary, which led the Saxons to look upon him 'as an amphibious creature, whom they know not what to make of'. This lowly state also bred rumours at Dresden's 'foppish court' that he was not a gentleman. In consequence, and despite his claim that 'I set no extraordinary value upon nobility', Stepney laced his letters with accounts of his lineage. Moreover, his relative poverty in an 'extravagant country', where 'good eating and drinking is much in vogue', severely limited his opportunities to bribe and entertain.

Yet it was not lack of resources which affected the outcome of Stepney's mission in Dresden, but events. Ultimately there would be no lasting commitment of the Electorate's forces against the French; instead Saxon troops would find themselves in Hungary, fighting the other Habsburg foe, the Turks. Nor would their leader be John George; but his brother Augustus, supported by the freed Schöning.

Leading up to this would be the dramatic deaths of Billa and John George, followed by Augustus's ruthless purge of 'the Family'. Almost as a side issue, he would play a role in the original 'Königsmarck affair', which concerned the murder of the Count of that name, and led to the opening rites of another: the affair between Augustus and the Count's sister, Aurora von Königsmarck. To all of these events George Stepney bore vivid witness. As the young diplomat couched it, his time in Dresden furnished him 'with materials enough to form a novel (without adding any fiction)'.

'A WOMAN OF HER PROFESSION'

Stepney was hardly slow off the mark in recording the pecadilloes of the Saxon court. The day after his arrival in Dresden, he already knew of an adventure 'too notorious to be smothered', concerning Augustus. Poor Grand Marshal Haugwitz was 'under a cloud with the follies of his daughter', chaffed the envoy. This lady was married 'but fifteen weeks ago to a foolish Count of Zinzendorff, yet has been so quick, as to be fairly brought to bed within these three days'.

Although the cuckolded husband 'upon the first alarm talked of nothing less than death and divorce', later, 'at the Elector's persuasion', he 'abated part of his first fury', even to the extent of considering a reconciliation. 'The rather', added Stepney snidely, 'since 'tis believed this buttered bun has ducal blood in it'. Although to look at 'the little back-crooked piece, one would not have suspected such a commerce, betwixt her' and Augustus.[5]

Shortly after, he narrated to an unidentified lady a tale that he deemed 'fitter for chat in a winter night, than for letters which perhaps may be intercepted'. Stepney revealed to his correspondent that 'the Elector got hither three days before me, and has lain once with the Electress, and visited her three times'. This was 'extra-ordinary civil as things go here, for methinks I see the reign of good King Charles revived in Saxony', with Eleonore making 'much such a figure as quiet Queen Catherine'.

Stepney did not specify which of Charles II's many mistresses was mirrored by *die schöne Billa*, now Countess of Rochlitz. However, he was hardly ignorant of the roles played by her and *die Generalin* in the political life of the Electorate, and how Colt had put Billa on his country's payroll.

Part of Stepney's mission was to check that this source of influence remained well greased. 'You must needs find some means to wait immediately upon the Countess of Rochlitz', Blathwayt had told him, 'and to let her know you have the same orders' as Colt, 'and you must be very punctual in the performances'. In other words, Stepney was to continue her pension of 6000 dollars for 'as long as the Elector should continue firm to the allies'. Accordingly, on 4 October he told Vernon that he intended to 'make my court to the Countess' via Count Friesen, 'who is my good friend and her confidant'.

It did not prove quite so easy. Three days later Stepney recounted that Friesen had 'twice endeavoured to introduce me to the Coun-tess, but both times found the Elector with her, and (so he said) in ill humour'. However, on 20 October, two days after celebrating John George's twenty-fifth birthday, Stepney could tell Frans Stratford, his banker in Hamburg, that 'I made your compliment to the fair one and her mother', and 'my first entry there hath been very favour-able'.

Yet two months later, a certain misgiving crept into Stepney's cor-respondence. He reported the possibility of a renewed French bribe to Billa, even though she had apparently firmly rejected an offer of RT 100,000 from Versailles the previous year. But Stepney doubted that 'a woman of her profession', dedicated to making 'hay while the sun shines', could withstand 'so powerful a temptation'. However, he conceded that 'these stories may be industriously scattered by her friends', in order to make the allies 'more eager and generous in their pensions', through fear that 'she may be bought out of their hands'.

Yet, whatever the truth regarding a French bribe, there was another reason why Stepney was hedging his bets upon how far to back 'the Family', and this involved the Electress Eleonore. For John George's 'extraordinary civil' behaviour towards her in late Septem-ber was not the product of new-found decency or surfacing guilt, but was securely founded upon the politics of heredity. Apparently the Electress was pregnant.

'IF THE ISSUE BE SUCCESSFUL'

Eleonore was understandably annoyed with the English. Stepney described her as 'a little mortified' that Colt had stood as godfather to the bastard daughter of her husband and her rival. She was obviously one of those 'not of the secret', who 'believe and report to this day that this ceremony was done in the King's name'. Possibly Eleonore snubbed Stepney out of continuing pique. Alternatively, the grounds for denying him an early audience may have been those given by the diplomat: that she was 'indisposed with the burden she bears'.[6]

In mid-October Stepney confidently asserted that Eleonore was 'above eight months gone'. For those unable to detect any overt signs of pregnancy, there was the evidence of 'those who knew her in her state of breeding', that 'she carried her baby backwards to the last, without having any outward appearance of being near her time'. Anyway, Stepney at least was convinced about her condition, from which he drew the obvious political conclusion. If 'these lands may be blessed with a son', then possibly 'the tables may be changed, and the Electress get the better of the Countess'.

On 31 October he could report prayers in the churches for Eleonore, 'which is a mark that her being far gone with child is beyond dispute'. To Stepney, who had presumably now met with her again, 'she never appeared more gay and contented than she does at present'. Doubtless, she anticipated that 'the scene may change, if the issue be successful'. For this reason, the diplomat planned to be 'less public in my court of the Countess'. During the final period of the gynaecological guessing-game which 'will decide this matter', Stepney intended to balance between the two factions; 'carrying my cloak on both shoulders, I look upon to be the surest game'.

And as the game went on, others too grew surer. John George was one convert. Convinced by a wife who had 'the experience of being five times with child', and by doctors who 'gave under their hands and oaths' that she was pregnant, he sent 'for 4000 dollars of lace from Holland for baby clouts'.

Less inclined to such generosity were two others with vested interests in the birth. Although 'they are not very good friends among themselves', Augustus and Billa managed 'like Herod and Pilate' to combine 'in their ill wishes against' the Electress. Stepney further contended that Augustus, who would soon be travelling to his beloved Venice for Carnival, was getting 'out of the way on purpose'. Then he would not have 'to stand by and see an Electoral Prince come into the world'.

This may well be the reason why Augustus planned the trip,

doubtless in tandem with the sybaritic side of his nature. However, he must have departed for Venice at the end of 1693 with a smug look upon his face; safe in the knowledge that he remained next in line. For shortly before he and his brother went hunting on 18 December, Stepney learned that Eleonore was 'not with child, and that for these two months we have been praying to God Almighty to no purpose'. Reportedly, John George 'in his passion was near cudgelling the doctors, who were once of another opinion'.

So why was it, that when 'the mountain should bring forth, we have not seen so much as a mouse'? Obviously, the rockiness of Eleonore's marriage and status played a part in this phantom pregnancy, perhaps inducing a desperate act by a desperate woman; so too did the inexactitude of seventeenth-century medicine. However, the deflation appears to have been literal as well as metaphorical. 'It seems a little wind could not find passage', explained the envoy, 'and we have all this while mistook a fart for an heir to the Electorate'.

'The poor lady is inconsolable', wrote Stepney of Eleonore when her prospects blew away. 'She told me her misfortune till tears came', he recorded later. 'I pity her from my heart, and administered the best comforts I could in such cases'. Yet when Anna Sophie and her sister left for the country, the Briton suggested with cruel realism that 'our poor Electress' might accompany them 'and make a third at Ombre, for she is likely to be as little a consort as either of them'.

On the other side of the coin, it was clear that Eleonore's 'mistake makes well for the Countess, who now promises herself all the caresses', and for Augustus, 'who now looks upon himself as heir apparent'. This reminder of our hero's status proved to be chillingly prescient, since within a few months he was the new ruler of Saxony.

Chapter 5

'So many extraordinary changes'
Stepney in Saxony 1694

'CONCERNING HIS GENERAL'

Prior to his departure from Vienna, Stepney asked Blathwayt to inform him of their monarch's pleasure 'as to the confinement of Schöning, since I find the matter is now warm'. His patron replied that Schöning's 'release would be as unacceptable' to William and the Dutch as it was 'to the Emperor himself'. Stepney was 'therefore to hinder [it] privately, as much as lies in your power', without intimating in Dresden that either government 'concern themselves with Schöning'.[1]

These instructions probably suited Stepney. His missives already exhibited a hawkish view of Schöning's imprisonment, and suggest a genuine animus in his attitude towards the general. In some letters he even reduces the name to a Schweppes-like 'Sch——', presumably as a mark of disrespect. How much of this antagonism was purely personal is impossible to judge, although it certainly mellowed later.

Stepney's views were probably coloured by his service at Berlin and Vienna, and he was also aware that William too viewed Schöning as a French satrap. So, as a young diplomat endeavouring to make his mark, Stepney may well have prudently told Whitehall what he thought they most wanted to hear. To this end, he took every opportunity both to belittle moves by the general's family and supporters and to suggest that Schöning's residual influence at the Saxon court was on the wane.

However, Stepney was never able to square such biases with John George's continuing interest in Schöning's freedom; such as his threat to imprison three Saxon ministers posted to Vienna, if they did not 'act more conformably to the Elector's instructions concerning his general'. Stepney merely suggested 'that it is only the point of his own reputation, which makes him so much insist upon his liberty'. Indeed, on one occasion when John George heard a contrary opinion regarding Schöning's freedom, 'the impetuous humour of this prince' resulted in him 'laying his hand to his sword'.

Undoubtedly 'honour' played its part, but so too did Schöning's design for an absolutist Saxony to challenge the role of the cumbrous Empire in Germany's fragmented affairs. Both John George and Augustus had been strongly influenced by Schöning's vision, and his kidnap and imprisonment while in Saxon service was keenly felt by the brothers, both as a matter of honour and as a political issue.

Yet by February 1694 there was some movement in the Schöning affair. In January the general had been transferred from Moravia to Vienna, and although still confined and guarded he was allowed to receive relatives and friends. The issue of his liberty was decidedly on the front burner, while the temperature also rose in John George's torrid love life. Now the strains upon the young Elector began to show.

'LA DUPE DE L'AFFAIRE'

'We are here in the pleasures of a Carnival taken up with divertissements', reported Stepney on 9 February, 'and all business seems adjourned' until Adjutant-General Carlowitz should return from Vienna 'with the Emperor's final determination in the business of Schöning's liberty'.

Ten days later Augustus returned to Dresden from Venice. On his way back, noted Stepney, he 'took Vienna in his way, and was allowed to visit Sch—— for an hour'. Augustus recounted that the general 'preserves his beard till he shall be fully restored' to liberty and that although he had 'grown lean and pale', he 'still talks with the old heart'. Stepney identified our hero as 'ever a patron to Sch—— and his faction', and it was noticeable that 'since he has related to the Elector what he heard on this visit' John George was 'more eager than ever for having him again'.

In support of this point, Stepney described how on 21 February John George harangued the allied ambassadors with 'several abrupt discourses' on the subject. His general 'had been taken away by violence, and was kept close prisoner without being convicted of any crime'. For two years the Habsburgs had dangled the prospect of Schöning's release before him, 'of which he saw no effect'. No longer would he play '*la dupe de l'affaire*'. Instead he would recall his troops 'and leave the allies to look out for others'. On 23 February Saxon soldiers arrested the courier carrying the correspondence of the allied envoys and opened their letters. The next day, the Elector tried to kill his wife (p 55).

From this low point, the only way for John George was up. However, from here onwards the thread of negotiations becomes a tangled skein. Vienna now apparently offered to free Schöning so long as he did not re-enter Saxon service. There was talk that the Venetian Court was willing to enlist his services, but John George would 'give no ear' to this proposal, 'looking upon it as little better than banishment'. Moreover, in return for Schöning's release, John George was expected to support the Emperor's admission as a full member of the Electoral College in his capacity as hereditary King of Bohemia. All of this went into the negotiating pot, along with Saxon adhesion to the Grand Alliance and the terms of contingent subsidies.

John George was at Moritzburg when he received Carlowitz, his emissary to Vienna, on the night of 16 March. Early on 22 March, and again the next day he assembled his Privy Council in Dresden, to discuss the Imperial terms regarding the deployment and command of Saxon troops and the status of Schöning. Stepney was cautiously optimistic that 'we have the Elector fast for this year' and 'may hook him into the Grand Alliance'. However, given that there had been 'so many extraordinary changes' since he had been in Dresden, Stepney furnished 'no assurances'.

He was right to offer no guarantees. This complex tale still had some surprises in store, and while Stepney was able to detail certain events later, he remained in blissful ignorance of others. One of these was the purpose of the mission of Wolf von Beichling, Billa's brother-in-law, who was sent to Vienna on 26 March.

Stepney later contended that his function was to agree to the Emperor's proposition regarding Bohemia and the Electoral College. Another source asserts that Beichling's official reports dealt solely with the matter of Schöning's liberty. However, there are others who maintain that, in exchange for her promise to espouse the Catholic faith, Beichling also negotiated the question of raising Billa to the rank of Imperial Princess – such status being the essential prerequisite if she was to rise from mistress and morganatic wife to spouse and Electress.

'WHO GOVERNS ALL'

It is hard to assess from this distance, and with such fragmentary and often contradictory evidence, how near Billa came to this goal. Her power was not unbounded; John George clearly followed his own agenda in foreign policy and in the Schöning affair. 'The Family' might have some pull, when other factors also caused the Elector to waver; but there is too much evidence of his obsession with Schön-ing's liberty to believe that they could deflect him for long.

Nor is it clear how supportive John George was of Beichling's mission to make Billa into a princess, since he had aborted an earlier project. On 19 January Stepney reported the following concerning Billa:

> It has been discoursed as if Count Friesen, who from Vienna brought the patent of countess, should be sent back again for that of princess. But of a sudden the lady has likewise been mistaken in her reckoning, and after four months … proves no more with child than the Electress did, which makes her new dignity seem sus-pended for some time, at least till there is likelihood of issue.

In other words, if there was no heir in sight, there was no need for Billa to become a princess, let alone Electress. Conceivably, in this matter Beichling negotiated solely upon Billa's behalf.

However, on the domestic front, 'the Family' did rather well for themselves: rank for Rudolf, pensions and rake-offs for Ursula, 'allow-ances', bribes and gifts for Billa. Nor were her brothers forgotten; one married a Hanoverian countess and another obtained a regi-ment. But it was the chamberlain, Christoph Adolf, who did best; on 19 January Stepney related that the 'richest heiress of this country', Johanna Louisa von Miltitz, who had 'shown great reluctancy against a match which the Elector proposed betwixt her and the Countess's brother', had finally 'been brought to comply'.

Yet, whatever limits we propose to the power of the Neitschütz clan, there was no other faction that could influence John George, and Stepney was not the only diplomat to act consonantly. Hence, in his search for some lever to attain his monarch's objectives at Dresden, Stepney was obliged to dig deep into his slush fund.

On 6 February he revealed that he had disbursed '15,000 dollars of corruption', but realized that 'we shall not get clear for these bribes'. More was required to sweeten 'the Family', and through them John George, in favour of the treaty committing Saxon forces against the French. 'Besides 6000 to the daughter, the mother (who is the cun-niest witch I ever met with) has a great fancy to have 2000 or 3000 more for her share'. Yet Stepney considered such to be money well spent, since he saw Ursula as 'the woman of intrigue, who governs all'.

On 13 February Billa received Stepney. For one hour that evening they discussed certain matters which bore only tangentially on the Schöning affair, and his report is of interest solely as a glimpse into the young woman's methods. 'At night when she was in bed with His

Highness, she begun her complaint, as her *valet de chambre* told me, who came by her order at midnight' to brief Stepney. Perhaps all her influence derived from such initial pillow-talk.

There is another fleeting insight into the role of 'the Family' in Stepney's papers, and this suggests that *die Generalin* was frankly aware of the limits to her power. On the night of 18 February Billa threw a ball to celebrate her brother's marriage to Johanna von Miltitz. Stepney was a guest, and he talked to Ursula, who spoke candidly of the situation that would pertain if Schöning returned to centre-stage in Saxony. Although she expected John George would 'retain the personal kindness he has for her daughter', it 'would not lie in her power to be so useful' to the common cause, because Schöning was 'a man who will congress[?] all business to himself, and not suffer any other to intermeddle'.

Perhaps this prospect of Schöning's return was the key to Beichling's negotiations in Vienna that March. To ensure her future in this sleazy fairytale, Billa had to become a princess. Once she was of 'equal blood' with the Elector, she could rely upon her allures to ensnare him in marriage. In the meantime, she worked upon the open wound of John George's distaste for Eleonore and his evident desire to divorce her. The only question was whether the Elector truly wanted another spouse; if not, he would resist her elevation. In that case, Billa had to be able to offer the Emperor, through Beichling, something tangible on her *own* behalf; what better than the prospect of her converting to Catholicism and later bringing over John George as well?

The above is a purely speculative attempt to link the fragments of historical evidence into a coherent explanation. An additional factor is the possibility that John George was cognizant of Billa's plans and was prepared to become a Catholic for his own reasons. The suggested motive for such conversion was to qualify as a candidate in the election for the crown of Poland when that country's ailing King Jan Sobieski eventually died. If such was John George's plan, the irony is that it was his brother Augustus who executed it.[2]

'OUTRAGEOUS AND DANGEROUS'

On 24 February the Saxon court calendar (*Hofkalender*) chronicled an 'outrageous and dangerous confrontation' between the Elector and his wife, which stemmed from Eleonore's bitter protest about his gift to Billa of the valuable Pillnitz estate. The altercation grew so fiery that an incensed John George, ever readier to reach for a sword than an argument, 'had certainly stabbed her, if his brother, acquainted with the violence of his passion, and suspecting his design', had not disarmed him.

This Augustus did by 'tearing three blades one after another from his brother's hand' and in the process 'cutting all his fingers'. According to Stepney, writing much later, John George 'in a drunken fit ... wounded several persons, and would have stabbed his wife, had he not been disarmed by his brother'. For the record, we can note that this was neither the first occasion when Augustus had pacified his tempestuous sibling, nor the first time that John George had drawn his sword upon a defenceless woman. In another incident the Elector had threatened Billa with his blade.[3]

To show who was master in the Electorate, and indeed who was mistress and might yet become Electress, on 3 March John George 'obliged' Eleonore 'to receive a formal visit of the Countess'. The older woman obeyed. 'For a quiet life, the good lady was forced to salute her, but did it weeping.' Yet this, according to Stepney's further account, was but one stage in a continuing humiliation. 'I am told the Elector has twice bedded the Electress since their last broil.'

There is no date for the next event, which is mentioned only by Klotzsch; but if it occurred, then the time of Eleonore's deepest degradation would seem appropriate. Billa and a lady companion ate some pastry and both became sick. The other recovered quickly, but Billa remained ill and her body swelled. She thought – possibly hoped – that this was the start of another pregnancy, but the doctors disabused her. Therefore she decided that she had been poisoned and pointed the finger at Eleonore. John George took her accusations seriously and consulted the doctors again. Once more they demurred, suggesting that Billa's lifestyle might have something to do with it.

We might here note a small detail provided by Stepney on 2 February, shortly after Billa's four months of 'pregnancy' proved abortive. 'The Elector in a frolic took the medicines she did', remarked the envoy, 'and obliged several who were present to do the same'; yet one thing that seems clear about the melancholy and hot-tempered John George is that he was no great 'frolicker'. Perhaps he and Billa took drugs; possibly they were kinder to a constitution that could not handle booze. Perhaps he used them together. If any of these hypotheses are true, then both he and his mistress lived life in the fast lane; and by definition such a life can be left that much quicker too.

On 2 April Eleonore departed for her dowry-seat in Bretzen, which lay between Torgau and Wittenberg. Apparently her recent mortification had convinced her that, 'rather than be continually exposed to hard usage', she should live out her life in the country. 'But perhaps the crisis we are now in', suggested Stepney, 'may alter her circumstances'. The crisis that her rival was now in had certainly changed hers: Billa had contracted smallpox.

Chapter 6

'Je payeray la folie bien cher'
The deaths of Billa and John George
1694

'A DIVINE HAND HAS BEEN VERY VISIBLE'

Initially Billa's rash had come out 'very favourably' and in a manner
that gave hopes not only of 'her speedy recovery, but of her escaping
without being much marked'. All of which good news led to the bad,
which smacks greatly of disinformation. 'But it seems the mother',
wrote Stepney accusingly, 'for fear her fate should suffer, was for
trying tricks', and the remedies she applied 'have struck the distemper inwards, which has brought the fair lady into agonies'.

On the morning of 3 April 'she was taken speechless, and still
remains so'. The Elector 'scarce stirs from her bedside though he
never had the smallpox'. Her five doctors had consulted 'and shake
their heads'; they had used 'Spanish flies and syringes but all will not
help'. A minister attempted to give Billa the Sacrament, but they
could 'not get her mouth open, and I believe she may be dead
before I close up this letter'.

Stepney was not out by much, since Billa died around 7 a.m. on
the following day, 4 April. It was the Wednesday before Good Friday,
which is relevant only to one matter. On her behalf Beichling had
promised the Imperial court that Billa would publicly take Catholic
communion on the first day of Easter 1694.

Her death may have ruined Stepney's holiday plans. On Good
Friday he was busy with the quill, composing a long letter to Secretary of State Shrewsbury. However, in this missive of 6 April Stepney
paints a somewhat different picture of Billa's last hours, noticeably
omitting any mention of Ursula 'trying tricks'. Now he recorded that
Billa 'had taken cold, and perhaps drunk something that was refresh-
ing', which struck 'the distemper inwards and threw her into strong
convulsions' which lasted 24 hours, 'all which time she lay speechless
and was not in a condition of communicating'.

A very similar account is given by another contemporary witness, Augustus's wife Eberhardine, in a letter written to her mother and also dated 6 April. 'Last Wednesday, after lying sick from smallpox for nine days', the Countess of Rochlitz 'died quite unexpectedly, since she was completely out of danger'. However, 'while eating a meal she became speechless and unable to hear'. She lay in such fashion from 9 a.m. on 3 April until 7 the following morning 'without stirring, although her mouth was open, until she passed away'. Unsurprisingly, the pious Eberhardine saw in such fate 'a powerful example' of 'the wonder of God'.[1]

Stepney felt obliged to concur. He noted that the Lutheran clergy were 'very violent in their censures' and expressed 'great liberty in their reflections' upon Billa's death. In this he thought that 'they are not altogether to be blamed', since whoever knew 'this intrigue' from beginning to end 'must acknowledge a divine hand has been very visible'.

Not that such a nod to the Almighty prevented him from promising his reader a more carnal 'relation galante' about the whole affair, nor a last glimpse of Billa which, in deference to her demise, no longer portrayed her as a money-grabbing trollop. 'She was a beautiful brunette, not yet twenty years old, extremely good-natured, and one who did not concern herself with intrigues, which care she left to her mother'.[2]

The political future of die Generalin and the whole Neitschütz faction looked bleak. 'There is now a melancholy distracted family who will not find many to pity their misfortune', opined Stepney. One suspects that the only tears to spring from the eyes of Augustus were those of joy.

'SINGULAR LOVE AND ESTEEM'

Unlike Augustus, John George had never contracted smallpox and was not immune to the disease. Nevertheless, according to Stepney, he 'frequently visited the Countess and even eat with her during her sickness'. Moreover, following her death, he 'visited the corpse frequently after it was laid out, and once was bending to kiss it' before being pulled away.[3] 'Yet he could not be kept from pressing her hand' – and Stepney could not be kept from pressing the point that this was 'but a cold entertainment'.

On 6 April he and other diplomats went to court for a spicier variety, 'to observe how the Elector bore this disaster'. In Stepney's view he carried 'his loss better than I thought he would', and had 'grown more affable and tractable since his misfortune'. Perhaps it was the effect of shock. The envoys also found that 'he had changed his apartments (where she used to be frequently with him), for others more remote'.

There John George recounted that about 3 a.m on the day of her death, 'he was seized with a violent trembling at the heart', and his fingers 'contracted as if he had been in a convulsion'. This 'forced him to raise himself in his bed, just at the time' that he received the news that 'the pangs of death' had begun 'to seize the lady'. The Elector also spoke of 'the singular love and esteem' he had for Billa, emphasizing that 'had my passion proceeded for debauchery', he could find other women to 'make her loss less sensible to me; but my kindness hath been grounded upon better principles'.

All this led Stepney to observe that such feelings were far too fervent to be squandered upon a mere mistress, but rather tended to 'confirm the opinion the world has, that she was something more'. That this was indeed the case is clear from another letter sent by him on 6 April. Here he reported that John George had 'confessed to a good friend that she was his wife'.

Later, Stepney heard that the Elector had instructed Augustus 'to visit the mother, and to get out of her hands the contract of marriage'. He expected Ursula to surrender this, since it would be of little use now that Billa was dead. The envoy added that Augustus had also been tasked with the guardianship of baby Wilhelmina 'and to seal up what the Countess had left to be converted to her use'.

Stepney considered that Billa's death gave John George an opportunity for a fresh start. Now he was free 'from the public scandal of having had two wives, we shall soon see whither his inclinations will lead him next'. He had the choice to be 'reconciled and live well with the good Electress', or he might 'find some other person to divert him'.

As an alternative, he could of course 'give all his time to business, of which he is very capable, having a quick apprehension, a solid judgement and a very ready expression'. With typical disinterest, the envoys had told him that nothing would 'better divert his present melancholy, than making the campaign', for which he had all the necessary virtues: 'very warlike inclinations, an undaunted courage, a perfect knowledge of fortifications'. Moreover, he was 'an excellent horseman, and indefatigable in his exercises'.

Whether this litany of talents had formed part of the onslaught of diplomatic flattery is unclear. However, it is unlikely that their honeyed tongues had got round Stepney's peroration, which reads more like his personal prescription. The envoy considered that, if John George could 'apply himself, moderate his passion, and be governed', he might not only 'recover his reputation, which has much suffered by these two first years of his regency', but also 'prove a prince of fame, and make a very considerable figure in the world'.

Stepney's last words on this subject are interesting, in the light of a situation which would soon prevail, although he offered no hard evidence for such judgement, which seems awash with bias. He averred that John George's 'heart is very true to the Empire, and not at all inclined to France';[4] this he could not promise about Augustus, 'if he should come to the regency'.

'THE EFFECTS OF POISON'

For two days nobody at court followed John George's personal state of mourning for his late mistress. However, when Stepney and the allied ambassadors attended court on 7 April 'in our ordinary clothes', they found themselves to be 'the only persons in colours', and 'were looked upon as so many masques there'. The Briton viewed the now general deep mourning with distaste, as 'a sort of authorizing bigamy, to the prejudice of a virtuous Electress'.

Yet he also discerned new prospects for her, musing upon the advantages of 'a living wife, who perhaps may come again into play when the passion of grief' had eased 'and those of nature begin to operate'. But the main passions which now began to operate were suspicion and revenge.

On 10 April Stepney related that he had 'been to condole' Ursula. But he had also made it clear that she was now deemed a spent force, for which reason he hadn't promised her any of the money that he had previously paid to Billa. *Die Generalin*, however, was still in business: the business of retribution.

'The Countess has been exposed on a bed of state for four days', noted Stepney, 'but it seems her face is turned blue, and her breasts green, which the mother would make the Elector believe are the effects of poison'. As yet, John George was resisting this scenario, although keeping his options open. And although the body was exposed to public view, 'the Elector has not suffered the corpse to be opened, and no day is yet fixed for the burial'.[5]

Possibly Stepney was misinformed about the burial, or perhaps the decision to proceed represented an abrupt change of mind by John George. Whatever the case, Billa's funeral took place on the night of 12 April, with full mourning appearing somewhat incongruous in the gloaming. 'The burghers were in arms, and all in black upon the penalty of ten dollars to every one that appeared otherwise', recorded Stepney, while the Elector 'was in as deep mourning as it was possible to wear'. Augustus attended too in one of the 25 carriages that trundled behind Billa's cortège.

John George gave his mistress the treatment of a 'wife *de la main gauche*'. Countess Rochlitz was buried alongside three princes of the electoral house in a vault of Dresden's Sophienkirche, 'with almost as much solemnity as if the lady had been an Electress'. John George's device read, 'Ton sort est attaché au mien', and events would soon show that his fate was indeed bound up with hers.[6]

'Now she is underground', wrote Stepney optimistically, 'we shall observe if the Elector's passion be buried with her, or if he takes a fancy to any other person'. To help matters along, he overcame his desultory admiration for the virtuous Eleonore and – like any good diplomat – assumed the role of procurer. However, such attempts to stir the electoral fancy came to nought. 'The Elector is still mournful as a turtle that has lost his mate', and showed no bent for 'coupling afresh, though we have three young mistresses in our eyes for him'.

For the past was omnipresent. 'All the news I can tell you, relate only to the Countess', a frustrated Stepney informed Blathwayt. Ursula and John George were frequently together, and their 'discourses chiefly run upon the lady's being poisoned'; about which they had 'talked so often, that at last they really believe it, now it is too late to discover the truth'.

By now rumours of foul play, mingled with traditional Saxon superstition, were widespread. 'Grand Pescatore is quoted as an infallible author', who remarked in his almanac for April that 'a lady of quality may die of poison'. Stepney commented loftily that 'we have a thousand ridiculous stories of this nature'.

But the matter could not be shrugged off, because on this issue John George had now moved from neutral to committed. 'For the Elector says strict inquisition shall be made, and the death shall be revenged one way or another'; and there was a very strong hint about the prime suspect. 'The Elector pretends to have had a sort of dream or vision', in which Billa's 'death was revealed to him, and that of the Electress likewise'.

Whether or not John George was meandering into mystical mode, the implied threat was clear. When he had spoken to the ambassadors on 6 April, his 'vision' only extended to the death of his mistress. Now it encompassed the prospect of his wife's demise as well; although for the moment 'she is in good health'. On 12 April 'the Elector received a very obliging letter from her', but he responded 'as if he never intended to cohabit again with her'. Not surprisingly, Stepney now feared that Eleonore would gain 'but little advantage' from her rival's death. He viewed her as being already 'as much a dowager, as if the Elector were actually dead'.

Ironically these words were penned before Stepney was aware that John George had succumbed to smallpox. Until then he appeared to be more concerned with the Elector's mental health. 'He is really to be pitied, for never prince had so violent passions', wrote Stepney on 13 April, 'and any man who sees the agonies he suffers, cannot but be touched and suffer with him'. Around 16 April 'a black melancholy and distraction were visible in his looks and behaviour, which we imputed to his immoderate grief'. This was a retrospective view, but it mattered little. Stepney would never see John George alive again.

'AN HIDEOUS SPECTACLE'

On 20 April 1694 Stepney reported unsympathetically that the Elector 'has caught a distemper which he seemed to have coveted by so much assiduity'. The envoy does not mention a point made by one source, that John George, in seeking to lose himself in his memories, went for several walks in the dreadful April weather. Rather he attributes the cause of his illness to John George's state of mind, 'which made him uneasy both to himself and others', plus his earlier 'follies' in handling the Countess's corpse. However, in this despatch alone Stepney mentioned the following item. 'He has a fever, which is less to be wondered at', for on the same day that he was taken ill, 'he made a sort of debauch in strong Italian wines, to which he has never been used'.

Thereafter in Stepney's accounts about the progress of the illness, certain inconsistencies appear which might simply be attributable to sloppy reporting; but the main pattern of events would seem to emerge clearly. The first ambiguity concerns the date the illness began, which was apparently the same day that John George indulged himself in an alcoholic 'debauch'.

Originally, Stepney told Shrewsbury that on 18 April John George 'was seized with shiverings and pains in his back, which are the symptoms of the smallpox', and that since the night of 19 April 'little spots are broke out on him'. Later reports, based upon more information or disinformation, give a fuller but divergent picture.

Now it is on 16 April that 'he was taken with pains, on the 18th with shiverings'; On 19 April 'he received the Sacrament' and Augustus 'lay by him all night'. Either on this or some other occasion, the heir apparent ordered *die Generalin* to stay away from John George's bedchamber, on the grounds that 'she would be no agreeable object' to his brother's expected visitors, Eleonore and his mother Anna Sophie.

On 20 April (not, as before, on the night of the 19th) 'the spots of the smallpox appeared upon him' and 'came out very favourably'.

His mother visited John George on 21 April and his wife the next day. On 24 April Stepney ventured the opinion that 'they think he is out of danger'. Three days later he repeated this view, while noting that the 'smallpox are very thick upon the Elector', who would be left 'very much marked'.

That this bullish letter of 27 April was written upon the day that John George died, can be explained in two ways. Either Stepney was laggardly in obtaining information, or there was something like a 'news black-out' on the death. Stepney does not report the Elector's demise until 1 May. However, there is not necessarily anything suspicious about this, if we view the matter in terms of the pace of life in the seventeenth century and not in our own.

In any case, Stepney probably considered that he had covered this event, in terms of what John George's death might mean for future Saxon policy; however trivial his assessment might seem by the standards of today's 'in-depth analysis'. For although John George was 'a prince of a saturnine, obstinate temper', wrote Stepney on 20 April, 'I cannot promise the allies any advantage from a change'. For Augustus was 'as bad in the other extreme, of a mercurial volatile spirit'. He would 'content himself with his women, his wine, his exercises, and his frolics' and effectively 'leave the management of affairs' to Haxthausen, 'who took care of him in his travels'.

And on 1 May, Stepney took care of the Elector's last days in a detailed letter to Shrewsbury. From 20 April John George was allegedly 'very hearty', and talked 'of nothing but making the campaign' against France; precisely as recommended earlier by England's envoy. But on the night of 26 April 'he had a fever by being kept too warm, and was first perceived to be light-headed'.

The next morning John George 'came to himself and discoursed with much sense and devotion, promising to lead another life if he should happen to recover', while seeming indifferent whether he lived or died. At noon he 'eat heartily', but the fever returned at 2 p.m., and once more 'he grew light-headed, mistook his Electress for the physician' and 'continued raving mad' until he expired at five that same evening, 27 April.

Next came some gloss, which may or not be true but was undoubtedly of propaganda value for the coming struggle against 'the Family'. This information Stepney received from 'a person of distinction, who scarce ever stirred away' from the stricken Elector. It is impossible to say who this person was: all we know is that during John George's illness, Augustus and 'the chief officers of the court watch with him by turns'.

This anonymous source assured Stepney that after the third day of illness, John George 'never made the least mention' of his mistress or their daughter. Rather it was claimed that 'in one of his fits before his death', he tore from his arm 'a bracelet of her hair, worked into a cypher, and threw it away as it were with indignation'.

Moreover, during 'one of his lucid intervals', he was heard to say, 'Je payeray la folie bien cher'. As to which act of madness the Elector was paying so dearly for, the distinguished 'spin-doctor' offered two interpretations: first, 'the vicious commerce' he had with Billa; secondly, the 'unreasonable fondness' that he exhibited in visiting her sick-bed and handling her corpse.

Those who had seen the Elector's own carcass 'say it is an hideous spectacle, all crusted over like a tortoise'; for this reason it would not lie in state. However, John George's body had been opened, 'to convince the world there had been no foul play'; but 'no discoveries' had been made. All of which was very assuring, save that it was entirely hearsay.

Nor is it clear whether Stepney's version of the post-mortem report is simply a recital of what he was told, or his own poetic embellishment of the official verdict that there were no suspicious circumstances to the death. He writes that 'the noble parts' were 'all found in good condition'. This, avowed the envoy, 'confirms the opinion that the distemper lay chiefly in the blood and in the vital spirits', and that 'grief and strength of the imagination' contributed most to the Elector's death.

So Dr Stepney virtually suggests that 'a broken heart' aggravated by smallpox sped John George to his tomb. He was also told that the occasion of the Elector's death 'was very remarkable for being the eleventh day from the beginning of his sickness, the very same crisis that had been fatal to the Countess' (although Eberhardine's account specifies nine days).

In any case, to the sceptical eye, that which is 'very remarkable' is the speed with which obstacles were cleared from Augustus's path; but at the time, the issue was continuity. The next morning, 28 April, the new Elector was proclaimed and homaged by the guard and garrison of Dresden. So began, in the murkiest of circumstances, the unforgettable reign of His Electoral Highness Friedrich August I, which was to last almost 39 years.

66

'A restless ambitious spirit'
His Electoral Highness 1694–1696

Chapter 7

'To the ruin of that house'
Politics and poison 1694

'DESPATCHING PEOPLE WITHOUT NOISE'

Was Billa poisoned, or did she die of smallpox? The same question can be posed about John George IV. If they died of the latter, then we have to look no further than a major and undiscriminating killer disease of the time. Smallpox carried off William III's parents as well as his wife, plus a raft of Louis XIV's potential successors; and this is to name but a few of the most illustrious victims.

On the other hand, if the Saxon lovers were poisoned, then who murdered them? The degraded Eleonore, quitting Dresden for the country at the time of Billa's illness, is an obvious suspect in the case of her rival; but would she have murdered her husband as well? Indeed, would she have had the opportunity?

She certainly had the motive. Besides the constant humiliation he heaped upon her, John George's proposed 'strict inquiry' into the circumstances of the Countess's demise was a thinly-veiled threat against the woman he had already tried to murder. All this may have prompted Eleonore to eliminate her husband too, and arguably to find the 'strength' for the deed as well.

If Eleonore was not the poisoner, was Augustus? If so, did he act alone, or in league with a faction of the court that was interested in breaking the power of 'the Family'? If such a group existed and had a hand in Billa's death, then why commit regicide as well? It is possible that the pro-allied and pro-Imperialist cabal in Dresden was exasperated by the Elector's obsession with Schöning and his policies and by Saxony's consequent isolation. Yet putting Augustus in his brother's place would hardly produce an anti-Schöning outcome. More plausible grounds for liquidating the lovers were fears in Lutheran Saxony of both Billa and John George converting to Catholicism.

The above are all big 'ifs'. They have not been advanced as a prelude to erecting some unhistorical monuments to conjecture; rather, they are founded purely upon our lack of knowledge and represent the circumstantial evidence, which standing alone makes any 'conviction' unsafe. So, although we can provide Augustus with motive and opportunity and suggest the means, none of this proves that he removed either the Countess of Rochlitz or his brother. Nor can we be sure that they were murdered, by him or by anyone else.

We have already intimated that Augustus the glory-seeker saw himself as more fitted to rule Saxony than his brother. His elevation to heir presumptive in 1691 may have been sufficient for him at the time; but subsequent happenings possibly changed his outlook. When Augustus left for Venice in December 1693, he must have rated his future prospects poor indeed, unless he intervened in events and made things happen in his life. His brother was 25, only 18 months older than himself; he might reign for decades. If Augustus succeeded him, it would be at the fag-end of life, when he was too infirm or conservative to impose himself upon Europe.

Nor was there any guarantee that he would inherit. Eleonore's pregnancy had been a warning of his prospects if John George produced an heir. An even greater threat was that his brother would divorce Eleonore and formally wed the fecund Billa, once she had been promoted to princess. The very real prospect that this fertile young woman might produce a son would consign Augustus irrevocably to the sidelines of history: just one more German duke enjoying a small pension, a minor estate and some secondary command.

While John George lavished gifts and gold upon Billa, and *die Generalin* and her clan plundered the realm, Augustus was denied access to the financial resources of Saxony and was equally cut off from political influence. True, his brother shared the desire to redress Saxon honour by restoring Schöning to power; but in bouts of passion only, and not with the greater idea of promoting Saxony and humbling the ossified empire of the Habsburgs. And always there was Billa purring opposition in John George's ear.

To be a factor in European politics, Saxony needed a ruler dedicated to restoring the past greatness of the House of Wettin; a ruler with vision and ambition. Conversely, to promote these aims, Augustus needed a state and its resources. While John George could be petulant, he also remained petty; a minor German princeling who came at ten a penny. Augustus wanted more, and he could only attain his ends by having the power to do so. He had to be the Elector.

For this to happen required the elimination of his brother. As for Billa, he may have gone for broke by ending the power of 'the Family' as well, beginning with her murder. Nor should one doubt that Augustus was ruthless enough for such deeds: as we shall see, he kidnapped the Sobieski brothers in 1704, contemplated the murder of Charles XII when the Swedes occupied Saxony and had a 'contract' out on the usurper of his Polish throne, Stanisław Leszczyński.

As to the means, throughout this affair there was no mention of any other agency than the least detectable, namely poison. It could have gone easily into pies or pills for Billa and the Italian wines upon which John George 'debauched' prior to falling ill. If the latter showed any signs of recovery, then Augustus and other notables were at his bedside to top up the doses.

Poisoning was modish at this time, and not only south of the Alps. 'The fashion of poisoning people is becoming far too common', Liselotte inveighed to Sophie in December 1690. In her turn, the latter cynically christened poison 'la poudre de la succession'. The 'Great Elector's' second wife made several attempts to poison the Prussian crown prince, later Frederick III, to favour her own sons. Augustus's own aunt may also have fallen to the phial.[1]

Nor was Stepney naive on this subject. He often used the phrase 'princes have long arms'. In July 1694 he wrote in similar vein to James Cresset, the new English envoy in Hanover. 'I fear daggers and poison will be as familiar among you as they are in Italy. The princes have been often there, and they have learned the manner of the country, of despatching people without noise'.

And in February of that year, Augustus too had returned from this poisoner's paradise; the land of *aqua Tofana*, a secret potion, probably arsenical, named after its inventress, the Sicilian Teofania di Adamo. Not only was Augustus in Venice on this second trip, he journeyed further south to Rome, Naples and Sicily; perhaps he met men who could help. Maybe he interested parties in Venice who were fighting the Turks. 'I hear he promised the Republic to raise a regiment of foot for their service', noted Stepney, 'and upon his first returning hither the discourse of it was very hot'.

However, we know almost nothing of what Augustus did upon this second trip to Italy. There is the usual wodge of strong-man acts and gallantry by von Pöllnitz, who compresses the two trips our hero made to that country into one and includes an implausible audience with the Pope. Haake writes that Augustus returned with valuable books and the dedication to himself of the libretto of a contemporary opera, *L'Amore Figlio del Merito*. Perhaps there were also a few bottles of wine in his baggage, ready laced with *aqua Tofana*, as a gift to the Elector from his *fratello del merito*. Would the good doctors who opened up the bodies of Billa and John George have traced this concoction, before handing out their verdicts of no suspicious circumstances?

71

We shall never know. Perhaps the simplest answer is the best: that Dame Fortune simply beamed munificently upon Augustus. Billa and John George both died of smallpox, and Augustus was catapulted to the rank of Elector of Saxony a few days before his twenty-fourth birthday. Stepney never even hinted that Augustus was a fratricide or a poisoner;[2] nor did the court of Hanover later that year, when they must have longed to have had such an issue to counter Augustus's probings into the fate of Count Königsmarck (C9). Yet even for a guiltless Augustus the politics of poison remained a potent issue; and one to be turned against the person who had first placed it upon the agenda – Ursula von Neitschütz.

'PUSHING HIS RESENTMENT'

In 1705, in the sole fragment of genuine autobiography that he composed, Augustus touched upon his accession to the electorship. 'Everyone rejoiced at seeing me step into my brother's place', he recalled, 'since they were aware of my more gentle disposition'.[3]

In retrospect, it is hard to accept this self-evaluation unless it be deemed ironic. Whether the population in general rejoiced is impossible to establish. Certainly there was some joy in the offing for particular court factions, along with woe for the current top-dogs; but the 'gentle disposition' was little in evidence. More pertinent is Stepney's assessment, given in a long despatch of 1 May. The diplomat observed that 'now he begins to discover himself', Augustus had demonstrated by his first measures that he 'is of a violent temper, and is for pushing his resentment to the highest extremity against the proud [Neitschütz] house'.

Certainly the purge was rapid and ruthless and most probably pre-arranged. However, whether to distance himself from events, or because he viewed himself as being completely in control of them, Augustus did not even bother to remain in Dresden. Late on 28 April 1694, the newly proclaimed Elector left for Moritzburg 'to settle, more at his ease, the springs of government, and to resolve what changes he will make'.

'As yet', continued Stepney, 'I hear of no considerable ones, except in the Neitschütz family', who were likely 'to feel God's heavy hand in this revolution', since they had made 'an ill use of excessive power during their short reign, and too much slighted' Augustus. He now had it 'in his hand to do himself vengeance, and will do it to the ruin of that house and their adherents'.

Augustus certainly moved quickly. Within half an hour of his accession, the 'first act of his power was exerted' against *die Generalin.*

Guards were posted at the door of the Fürstenbergsche Haus, her dwelling in Dresden. Initially it was contended that this was a precautionary measure, 'to keep the mob from tearing the bawd to pieces'. Thereafter the real motive emerged, which was 'to stop the avenues of her house', and hinder her 'from conveying out of it several rich jewels belonging to the electoral family', which John George had given Billa. An additional reason was to prevent Ursula from spiriting away her grand-daughter.

There were also reports that *die Generalin* had been arrested and her domestic staff placed under guard. Moreover, Eleonore accu. ed her of being the 'cause of all the unhappy differences' between her and John George 'and pretends she should be treated as a person guilty of black practices'.

It would appear that the court's propaganda machine was already up to speed, creating an aura of witchcraft around the unfortunate Ursula. Although reluctant to transmit 'strange stories upon light reports', Stepney could not 'forbear relating one, which may have given grounds for what has been so confidently given out here of magic arts and enchantments'. This tale came from a woman called Naville, one of Billa's employees, who was a paid informer of Stepney's secretary, Plantamour (p 88).

According to this lady, upon John George's 'breast was found hanging a bag', which allegedly contained lizards' heads, snakes' skins, the livers and hearts of bats and 'other mixtures of this kind'. It is hard to judge how serious was Stepney's claim not to know 'if these be remedies used for the preserving and fortifying of the nerves'. However, he was rightly certain that 'those who seek occasions for ruining the Family, will not lose so good a one for making the world believe the force of charms and filters'.

It was also alleged that Billa's baby daughter was 'a supposed child, clapped into the place of the real one', which had died at Frankfurt 'soon after it came into the world'. Stepney observed that whether or not this was true, 'it may serve as a pretext for disinheriting the brat', not only of Billa's riches, but also of the County of Rochlitz and other lands, which John George had either 'dismembered from his domains or had purchased for her', and which Augustus wanted back.

Just 'as great ruins usually shake all the neighbourhood', the smaller fry of 'the Family' also felt the impact of 'this wonderful revolution'. Christoph Adolf, the court chamberlain, 'had his key taken from him', and 'now his house is fallen', and 'to aggravate his misfortune', he was also deserted by his wealthy wife. Another brother lost command of his regiment. Lieutenant-General Neitschütz, 'whose chief merit has been having an handsome daughter and an intriguing wife', was relieved of his post on 2 May, while Stepney's friend Count Friesen, 'a near relation of the Countess's and deeply entangled in her intrigues', also fell from favour.[4]

'I believe all other methods will be used to mortify the living', Stepney wrote with disdain, 'which are more to be excused, than the severity with which they pursue even the dead'. For on 30 April Billa's foetid body 'was taken up again' from the vault in St Sophia's and transported 'naked to another grave more suitable to her birth'. But it was not just a question of evicting an upstart from the family tomb: as is so often the case with Augustus's acts, money was involved, and in this instance possibly evidence too, since John George had placed several of his letters in Billa's coffin.

Once this was opened, it was 'rifled of jewels', and the long crimson velvet burial-gown was stripped from her body. The grave-robbers paid particular attention to retrieving a picture of John George 'set with diamonds which she wore on one arm, and a bracelet she had on the other of the Elector's hair'. Of the several rings yanked off Billa's fingers, one had been inscribed by John George with the words, 'Mon amour est tout pour vous'.[5] Doubtless some Augustan conquest would become its gullible recipient.

'SHE CONFESSES NOTHING'

Billa, however, was well out of it, while her mother's ordeal was just beginning – as was that of various oddballs from the occult world which flourished in Saxony, who had been rounded up to play their roles in Ursula's trial. 'The discourse we have had of late here seems so very fabulous, that I have been often in doubt if I durst relate them', Stepney told Vernon in May. 'Two old women (one a famous fortune-teller called Dromery) are laid up as close prisoners'. According to those 'wishing ill' to the Neitschütz family, they accused *die Generalin* of having poisoned John George III, 'because he obstructed the vicious commerce betwixt his son and her daughter'. They also claimed 'to have proofs of her having practised witchcraft' upon John George IV.

At 3 a.m. on 20 June 1694, Ursula was transported by coach from her home to Dresden's town hall. There she was 'strictly guarded', but Stepney could 'see her every morning' from his window. However, he viewed Ursula as 'a lost woman', for 'one way or another, they will find her guilty and take off her head'.

Yet if she was a lost woman, Ursula was a resolute female too, who 'after all this disgrace' still 'holds firm'. For, despite a rumour that 'she offered to hang herself (but was prevented)', Stepney was assured that 'she has presented a petition to the Elector, not imploring any favour but demanding justice'.

On 17 July Stepney reported that Ursula was still under guard in the town hall, 'but it is plain they are at a loss after what manner to proceed against her, because they are so tedious in doing it'. At the end of the month he again addressed her situation: she was still in confinement and had recently been 'dangerously ill'. Prior to that she had been 'questioned (but without torture) for the first time, upon the several heads that are to form her accusations'. However, 'she confesses nothing of what they lay to her charge'.

In September the envoy derided the Saxons, who treated him 'as little better than an atheist, for not entering into their credulity of witches'. As for Ursula's trial, this 'draws towards no end, and I believe they will make nothing of it'. He reckoned that the authorities in Dresden would go no further 'than prosecuting her for bawding her daughter (which by the old Saxon laws is punishable with death)'. However, since such was 'a practice so very familiar in Saxony and elsewhere', he thought that she would emerge 'with that infamy only which ought to attend so foul a crime'. She was still 'a close prisoner', and though frequently questioned 'confesses nothing that is material'.

Nor did she ever. Stepney's interest in the trial faded, and he appears to make no mention of Ursula's fate during his second mission to Dresden in 1695. This was despite the fact that it was then that the authorities literally threw the book at her, in a 36-page indictment. Augustus too seemed to have little concern for the proceedings. Matters dragged on until 1697, when Ursula was viciously subjected to thumbscrews and other tortures in the prison at Stolpen. Soon afterwards she was released. Of the remaining defendants, those who had not died under torture were flogged and banished. There were no death sentences.[6]

That Ursula was degenerate and grasping is clear. So is the fact that she rode to power on the back of her daughter's promiscuity; but in this she was hardly unique. For a while she turned Saxony into a family concern, but this fragile ascendancy rested solely upon Billa's hold over John George IV. Without him *die Generalin* was nothing, as is demonstrated by the ease with which Augustus smashed the hegemony of the Neitschütz clan.

Probably only such blatant facts prevented the authorities from adding to their preposterous charges by accusing Ursula of poisoning John George IV; since she was the last person in the world to gain from his death. As for the accusation that she murdered her former lover John George III, this was equally ludicrous; except to those who believed in her telekinetic talent for producing such an outcome by roasting waxen dolls. Such was the level of 'evidence' used in this farce of a trial.

Ursula dabbled in low-level 'magic', and there were few women in Saxony who did not. To call her a witch is absurd. Nor did Billa enjoy any supernatural powers. Her hold over John George IV was as commonplace as any exerted by woman over man; 'as if beauty, without filters, were not charm enough to make a prince of twenty-five love passionately as the Elector did', pronounced Stepney. Still, it had been an incredible tale; the envoy was right to tell a correspondent that if the full truth was made public, 'on la prendroit plutot pour un roman que pour une histoire veritable'.

Yet *die Generalin* knew the true story, and her three years of confinement, torture and injustice were not the stuff of fiction. Freed in 1697 after her ordeal, Ursula retreated to a family house in Gaussig. Her husband Rudolf died in 1703. Dubbed *die Zaubergräfin* ('the magic countess'), she lived on another ten years, an isolated old woman who always wore gloves to cover the stigmas left by torture; the marks of her fall, when another rose.

'HIS CHIEF QUALITIES'

Yet, however ruthless was the purge of the Neitschütz family early in Augustus's reign, once this 'wonderful revolution' had run its course, nothing very much appeared to happen. Augustus seemed to wait upon events rather than initiating them. There are perhaps three reasons for this, the first two deriving from Flemming's view that 'his chief qualities' were pleasure and ambition (A2).

First, having achieved the stature of Elector, Augustus simply took advantage of his new position to have a good time; perhaps 'a better time' more appositely describes his hedonistic behaviour. Second, until the return of Schöning there was nobody else to stimulate or channel his ambition. Von Haxthausen, whom Stepney identified in August 1694 as 'absolutely the favourite', and who acted as his chief adviser, hardly seemed to fit the bill of *éminence grise;* rather he appeared to be a greying prototype of Augustus himself. 'He is a polite man', Stepney averred, 'an exact courtier, very reserved, a bon vivant in all respects'. He impressed as someone who was 'pretty well at his ease, which he seems to love more than business', despite being 'very well-qualified, if he will be pleased to apply himself'.

Third, Augustus himself was ill-equipped for the tasks of government and statesmanship. He was still only 23. His education had been erratic and not that designed for a future ruler, but for that awkward customer the second son. He had shone only in war-related matters, and this was the sum intellectual experience that he brought to the office of Elector. Ever since he was 18, he recalled in his 'memoirs', his 'sole aim was to win glory as a warrior'. Having pursued no other profession, he hadn't 'the slightest knowledge of affairs of state'.

Irresponsibility, inconsistency and inexperience were obvious features of the first months of Augustus's rule. The first two were to remain ever-present in his career; products of his ambition, glory-seeking and hedonism. Inexperience was rapidly left behind with the speed and extent of his political learning curve. The next two chapters address first Augustus's personal affairs, and then his political operations, as evidenced by the first eight months of his reign.

Chapter 8

'So much to do'
Personal affairs 1694

'THE LAST OF HIS BRANCH'

On 30 April 1694 all members of the Saxon Privy Council were summoned to Moritzburg in order to renew their oaths. Beyond that they appeared to do little, spending the rest of the day 'drinking plentifully with their new master'. However, when Stepney and other envoys met him there on 4 May, the Elector was on the wagon.

'We were apprehensive he might have pressed us to hard drinking', as he always had in the past. But 'it seems now he has something else to do', the new ruler would 'leave off that ill custom, and manage a life on which so much depends'. Despite such sanctimonious twaddle, Augustus had hardly been cloistered with advisers, mulling the affairs of state: 'The Elector had been abroad all night, shooting at moorhens'.

Whether or not it was the consequence of this nocturnal carnage, the envoys found him 'in very good humour'. However, he had no wish to discuss alliance matters, fobbing them off onto his advisers. Stepney was sympathetic, judging that 'he is not yet sufficiently informed of the state of affairs (having affected ignorance in his brother's days)', and therefore he would not yet 'venture to talk of business freely'. Indeed, Augustus still appeared somewhat bemused by his change of fortune. When Stepney addressed him as His Electoral Highness, 'he told me he could not yet bring himself to believe that title belonged to him'.

Otherwise he seemed little changed. At his private table 'he still retains his old familiarity', and 'hates nothing more than that morose sullen temper and constraints' which made his brother 'more feared than esteemed'. To Stepney he spoke ritualistically with 'great affection as well as respect' about William III. All in all, the envoy anticipated few problems with this raw easygoing lightweight, concluding with the arrogant and erroneous judgement that 'we should have no difficulty of making him entirely ours'.

With regard to the deployment of Saxon troops against the French in 1694, Stepney was uncertain whether the new Elector would personally lead them into the field. This was not because Augustus 'wants courage or a desire to signalize himself', but because he would have 'so much to do in settling his government' and would be 'at a great expense in burying his brother'. Moreover, he 'ought to manage his health, being the last of his branch'.

From 28 April to 18 June, Augustus and Eberhardine remained largely ensconced at Moritzburg, although Augustus contrived a few escapes from the electoral hunting-lodge. He visited Dresden on 5 May to muster a regiment, and was back there a week later to celebrate his twenty-fourth birthday. On 15 May Stepney noted that Augustus was off to a small town, to be entertained 'for some days with the sport of heron-hunting'. This may have been a blind, with 'wild geese' substituting for 'herons', or if he went then it was for hours not days.

In any event, Stepney recorded Augustus travelling to Dresden on 16 May to meet with his Privy Council, and that Vienna's ambassador was attending a conference with the Saxons on 18 May. Possibly there had been a change in his plans, engendered by Austrian movement on the combined issues of the treaty and Schöning's freedom. These meetings saw the end of the log-jam, and the two states signed a treaty on 23 May (p 91).

Eight days later, Stepney wrote that Augustus had put his coach and servants into mourning. It was not in memory of his beloved brother; he had killed one of his chamberlains, Baron Nostitz. The accident happened on the night of 28 May at Moritzburg, when Augustus was 'at his sports'. The two men 'were shooting at marks with pistols, and unhappily the Elector's went off before he was aware', wounding Nostitz 'between the breast and the shoulder'. The 'poor fellow dropped immediately'. Falling to his knees, Augustus begged forgiveness. Nostitz asked only that his family be taken care of. The next morning he was brought to Dresden, where he died.

Stepney maintained that Augustus was 'much afflicted, and to heighten his grief, his mother has writ a very severe letter to him'. Such was unnecessary, since Augustus 'takes the accident so much to heart'. The event led the envoy to note similar incidents perpetrated by 'an unhappy family'. John George III had 'shot his favourite page dead at his feet by an accident of the same nature'; while John George IV 'had like to kill his Moor, and did really shoot his horse through his head'.

Some two months later, Augustus nearly put a bullet through his own brains. 'He'll never leave footling till he kills himself, as he did poor Nostitz', declared an exasperated Stepney on 24 July. 'He was playing the other day with a gun', which at first 'only flashed in the pan'. But later, while Augustus was 'handling it a little more familiarly, it went off in earnest, and a bullet pierced his hat'. He was 'the last of his line' and likely to remain so.

This was a theme that Stepney constantly emphasized; if Augustus died without an heir, the Electorate passed to the Duke of Sachsen-Weissenfels, who in Stepney's view 'makes now but a very ordinary figure in the world'. Yet he 'lives in hopes of the succession' and was 'much censured for not being discreet enough in hiding his impatience'. The envoy assessed this latest Augustan escapade as giving the Duke 'as fair-play for the Electorate, as if he was hired to make a vacancy'.

'EASY AND FAMILIAR'

On 14 June 1694 Stepney met again with Augustus at Moritzburg to present his new credentials. The envoy reported that the Elector 'received me very graciously, kept me at dinner with him', and that 'we were very merry over a bowl of punch'. There were no criticisms of 'that ill custom' upon this occasion.

Indeed, Stepney seemed to have fallen under the spell of the famous Augustan charm. He admitted being favourably impressed by 'a prince who loves to be easy and familiar' and was 'of a temper which I come very well to rights with'. Later he wrote glowingly that since becoming Elector, Augustus had 'always used me with marks of kindness'.

On 18 June Augustus and Eberhardine quit Moritzburg, coming 'to live in town till the burial' of John George. Following this, Stepney explained, 'the Elector goes a sort of progress' for about three weeks, 'receiving homage in the chief cities belonging to the Electorate'. After which, according to Count Reuss, who was to command the Saxon army on the Rhine, Augustus 'may have a fancy to run post to the army'. The envoy believed it possible, 'for His Highness loves such frolics'.

Augustus gave an audience to some Lusatian deputies in Dresden on 23 June, and that evening returned to Moritzburg 'for his devotions'. He was back in Dresden on the morning of 26 June to take condolences on behalf of the Duke of Holstein-Gottorp. The next day the Imperial representative had a like audience with Augustus.

On 28 June Count Friesen took his leave of Augustus 'and drank with him very plentifully'. Not only had the Count survived the fall of 'the Family', but he had been entrusted with the return of John George's Garter to William III and was leaving next day for Flanders.

Not surprisingly, Schöning's adherents were 'not well satisfied' to see the Elector 'so kind to him', and Schöning himself was unhappy that he was being sent to William, 'since he may be certain Count Friesen will do him no good offices there'. Friesen also took with him a gift of 'very good horses for His Majesty, knowing he had a mind to some from Poland'.

Friesen probably needed them all to help transport Stepney's own 'gift' to his masters. The envoy loaded up the Count with a copy of his hefty relation to Shrewsbury of 8 June concerning the treaty negotiations, along with a mound of supporting documents. If William and Blathwayt ever waded through these screeds, they must have rued the day that they sent Colt and the Garter to Dresden; while, once he had quit Saxony and rejoined William's service, Friesen became a constant headache to Stepney.

'THE TOMBS OF THE ELECTORS'

The funeral of John George commenced on 3 July. Burghers in arms lined the streets from the Electoral Palace to the Sophienkirche. At two that afternoon the procession began its march.

Following detachments of grenadiers, guards and artillery came 'the several schools singing psalms'. Behind them paced the Kammerherren and under-officers of the court, headed by its marshals and cup-bearers. A mass of rural gentry trudged by next, then members of the chief nobility 'bearing standards of the several counties and other territories belonging to the Electorate'. Each banner preceded 'an horse in mourning, hung with escutcheons', led by 'two persons of distinction in boots and cloaks, followed by a groom'.

Behind this throng filed Grand Marshal von Haugwitz 'carrying the electoral sword downwards'; the Saxon Chancellor bearing the seal on a black velvet cushion; and the Master of the Horse toting the electoral bonnet. Clattering in their wake was the Page of Honour, 'both horse and man in complete armour'.

Drawn by eight horses, with the coffin lying under a black and silver canopy, John George's cortège trundled behind. It was surrounded by gentry, chamberlains and pages, and guarded by trabants. Augustus followed on foot, the train of his cloak held by more chamberlains. Behind him plodded privy counsellors and members of other state and judicial bodies.

Having reached the church, John George's body was deposited for the night in an illuminated mausoleum draped with banners. Carpzov, the senior court chaplain, earned his pay by making 'a long harangue' in praise of John George. Largely neglecting his failings, he intoned a litany of his doings and honours, including his brief sojourn in England. Inevitably the award of the Garter found its place, although this shared billing with the Order of the Elephant, which had come by courtesy of his uncle King Christian V of Denmark.[1]

After all this, Augustus returned to his palace by coach. Perhaps he had an early night, since next morning he was back at the church to see his brother's body removed at nine o'clock. It was now to be hauled to Freiberg 'where are the tombs of the Electors of Saxony'.

As Augustus left Dresden, the cannons on the city walls fired thrice, and three more salvoes were let off by the guards and burghers. Only a small procession followed him, since most people involved in the ceremony had left early, 'to make the best of their way in a bad road' and to 'lie ready' outside Freiberg, with 'everyone in their right station for when the cortège should arrive'.

Quite likely they cursed the dead Elector, because it teemed down throughout these two days. 'I never saw thicker rain in my life', claimed Stepney. It was a little late for the heavens to wash away the sins of John George.

'THE SCENE CHANGES'

We are not told whether the weather was kinder on 5 July, when John George was finally lowered into the ground in the Fürstenkapelle at Freiberg. He was buried 'with the same solemnity as had been observed' in Dresden, 'with this difference only'. Once they left the church, the soldiers and officers turned their swords and arms upwards, 'and of a sudden the scene changes from mourning to homage'.

On 9 July it was the turn of the citizenry of Freiberg to render homage to Augustus. He remained seated before the assembly while the burghers and local miners repeated the oath; each 'holding up two fingers, which here they cut off for perjury, as they did ears in England'. The next morning Augustus travelled to Dresden, leaving almost at once for Königstein, 'a natural fortress he has four [German] miles from hence, on the Elbe, being a prodigious high rock'. He returned to Dresden on 11 July to receive homage from the gentry and citizens of that town. Two days later he set out for Wittenberg. On 24 and 25 July the burghers of Leipzig swore fealty to their new sovereign,[2] who then left again for Dresden.

On the morning of 30 July the Hanoverian ambassador had an 'audience without ceremony' with Augustus. Stepney managed a brief chat with him too. He imparted news of recent allied success against the French and complimented the Saxon on his gift of Polish horses to William, 'which he took well and told me he hoped His Majesty would find them "aussy bons que beaux"'.

Later that day Augustus left for Bautzen, the capital of Lusatia, for another oath of allegiance, before returning to Dresden on the night of 6 August. That seemed to be the end of such proceedings. Having been homaged throughout the land, Augustus was presumably ready for some undiluted pleasure.

'FATHER OF HIS PEOPLE'

Did Augustus initially try to live up to some of the responsibilities of his new status? Had he closeted himself with his wife in Moritzburg for over seven weeks in an attempt to behave like a mature and faithful consort? Was he dutifully trying to conceive an heir during this rare period of extended togetherness? Was the plan to appoint his father-in-law to command Saxon forces an attempt to please his wife?

We don't know the answer to any of these questions; we do know about certain outcomes. No heirs were conceived and Eberhardine's father did not get the job. Stepney noted that throughout the Margrave of Bayreuth's stay 'they kept him to hard drinking', then 'sent him home again without speaking one word of business'.

However, given his record, it seems unlikely that Augustus made any serious attempt at fidelity, as opposed to procreation. As Stepney observed at the end of May, consistency was not in the young Elector's nature, 'and he may be called in the literal sense a father of his people, as good King Charles was'. Augustus was 'an impartial distributor of his bounty', and 'while he's in the humour, the first woman that offers is sure of his caresses'. The envoy finished his assessment in French. 'Il n'est rien moins qu'orgueilleux, il boit avec tout le monde'.

This description of a man who was not too proud to drink with anyone seems to confirm the 'historical' portrait of Augustus as the sire of countless bastards. However, we must be careful not to accept literally the poet-diplomat's 'literal' judgement and confuse numerous affairs with numerous offspring. There is no doubting the promiscuity, but there are grounds for disputing the paternity.

In any case, even Stepney is ambiguous. In this same letter he remarks, 'I see little likelihood of the Elector having children; he has lived too fast'. Does he mean having 'heirs' or children in general? Is there an implication that Augustus at this time was seen as impotent? This would certainly seem to be the nub of a later comment by Liselotte (p 127). We can also note that besides the possible paternity of Sophie von Zinzendorff's child (p 46), Stepney's many missives mention no other scions of the 'father of his people'.

Stepney also suggested that the 22-year-old Electress Eberhardine might be the 'problem', for 'there appear no hopes of her having children'. The Briton dismissed her as 'a very devout lady', who was 'not much to be commended for beauty or wit'. And although von Pöllnitz would have it otherwise, as did Augustus in his courting days, she really was as plain as her portrait. This hardly mattered to Augustus, who fully understood marriage as a matter of state policy and beauty as a passing phenomenon.[3]

Augustus and the Electress 'live very well together, and he contrives all means he can find to divert her', Stepney told Blathwayt on 14 August. This judgement sits uneasily with what he wrote in July; that while Augustus was receiving homage throughout Saxony, 'his poor Electress has been left behind him in this progress, but his mistress [Eleonore von Klengel] and her mother (after the example of the Countess and hers) attend him everywhere'.

How Eberhardine felt about life with Augustus is hardly known. Her emotions were doubtless those of any forsaken wife; yet not before 1705 do we have any real evidence of her despair (p 221). Nor do we know if she accepted the idea that she might be infertile. Be that as it may, on 15 August, with Augustus promising to visit her 'within a fortnight', she was packed off 'to the wells of Teplitz, out of hopes that these waters may prepare her for child-bearing', while at the same time the Elector 'begins to drink here the waters of Egra'.

'A POOR WHORE'

While it was inevitable that with the wife away Augustus would play, this did not herald the remorseless rise of Eleonore von Klengel or any other female co-drinker. In Stepney's view, the death of Billa had ended the reign of the mistress in Saxony.

Certainly he did not think that Miss Klengel would make the grade. He assured Blathwayt that despite her beauty, she would always remain a 'poor inconsiderable w——', whom Augustus visited in private 'as if he was ashamed of his kindness to her'. He wrote similarly to Stratford, after the banker in Hamburg apparently suggested putting the lady on the English payroll.

Stepney demurred: 'As to your supposition that Kl—— may come in for a snack, I must tell you I see no likelihood of it'. She would always be 'a poor whore, because she has the misfortune not to be born a gentlewoman on the mother's side', and in Saxony 'quality is necessary even in scandalous professions'. So she 'must never expect to rule', and with 'the fatal example' of Billa 'fresh before her eyes, I do not believe she will venture to fly high'. While her mother was 'as intriguing' as Ursula, the daughter 'will never have any influence upon business' and therefore would 'deserve no sprinklings from us'.

Sophie Eleonore von Klengel (1674–1755) was 20 at the time that Stepney discounted her so summarily.[4] She was one of four daughters (there were also four sons) born to Wolf Kaspar von Klengel (1630?–1691) and his wife Marie (1645–1717). Both Augustus and John George IV were tutored in mathematics, artillery, architecture and fortifications by von Klengel. A noted soldier, he was also an imaginative architect and connoisseur influenced by long service abroad, particularly in Italy. Von Klengel impressed Augustus with his combination of military and civilian designs for the reconstruction of Dresden after the fire of 1685. Both brothers represented their father at Klengel's funeral in the Sophienkirche.

According to Gurlitt, John George III counted Eleonore, a lady-in-waiting to his wife, among his conquests. Presumably Augustus took over where his father left off, although when the affair began is unknown. Stepney first identifies a 'Fräulein Clingel' (later spelt 'Klengel') as a mistress of Augustus in April 1692.[5] He mentions her several times, before telling Blathwayt in May 1694 that 'she is a very beautiful black woman'. What we are to understand by 'black' isn't clear; von Pöllnitz describes her as 'beautiful brown'. Obviously her colour was not a factor in Stepney's assessment of her status. Whether it weighed with the court, in addition to her non-noble birth, is impossible to establish.

Her relationship with Augustus still had some distance to run. Only in 1695 did Augustus finally marry off Eleonore to the chamberlain Hans Adolph von Haugwitz, one of the Grand Marshal's relatives. There were three children to this marriage, and the couple lived on an estate rejoicing in the name 'Augustusberg'. Widowed, Eleonore remarried in 1714, her second husband being Baron Senffertitz. Now ennobled, Eleonore outlived him too, dying as a *grande dame* in Dresden at the age of 81.

'TO DIVERT HIS HIGHNESS'

On 10 August Stepney recorded that the young Saxon 'diverts himself in feastings and frolics' and it remained 'uncertain where he will pass the end of the summer'. He seemed to have his answer a few days later: 'Mr L'Electeur pendant la belle Saison se divertira a la Chasse', he informed the Dutch ambassador in Vienna.

But hunting wild animals could come later; for now there were other pursuits. 'The Elector revels and dances as merrily as if his brother had been dead four years and not four months only', Stepney observed captiously. On 24 August he was still more censorious. 'The Elector is continually in frolics and debauches', and 'certainly no prince (who ought to preserve respect in his subjects) was ever guilty of so public follies'.

Whoever else was involved in this partying, it was not Countess Maria Aurora von Königsmarck, who arrived at Dresden in early August. Almost eight years older than Augustus, with plenty of experience in handling herself at the courts of northern Europe, like certain other 'interesting' women Aurora was coy about her past. Some accounts give her date of birth as 1668, or even 1678, and her nationality as Swedish. Her most convincing biographer, states that she was born in Stade near Bremen on 28 April 1662.[6] Her father Count Konrad was German, although he served as a Swedish general, while her mother was half-Swedish. The family owned lands in both Sweden and Germany.

Aurora was an intelligent woman, a gifted linguist and a talented poet of her time. Her 'independence' is shown by the manner in which she later opted for the role of a seventeenth-century single mother. Despite such individualism, not to mention a name that would probably have earned her Hollywood stardom in a later era, she has yet to make it as a feminist icon, and we still await a sisterly biography in the English language.

She arrived in Dresden with the intention of getting Saxony's ruler 'to interest himself more warmly' in the fate of her younger brother Philipp Christoph. Cynically, Stepney supposed that 'the other side' of Aurora's visit would be to try and lay her hands on the 30,000 dollars Augustus owed Philipp in gambling debts (C9). For the moment, the Saxons had 'lodged her in the court'.

On 17 August Stepney informed Blathwayt that Augustus had treated Aurora 'with great distinction' and had 'supped with her twice', along with Haxthausen, at the latter's house. Later he noted that Haxthausen was 'very fond' of Aurora, 'contrives all means possible to entertain her', and either sought 'to pleasure the Elector thereby, or has her in the eye for himself'. It is not known whether this noble procurer was again thrust into his role of 'taster'. What does seem clear is that the 'court-wise' Aurora was not exactly swept into the electoral four-poster.

On 25 August Count Harrach, the new Austrian ambassador, arrived in Dresden; he had an audience with Augustus the following day. Possibly Vienna was picking horses for courses. Stepney certainly thought that these two would gel, with Harrach likely 'to hit the Elector's humour in hunting, tennis, and other exercises'.

On 28 August our hero was pronounced to be 'gone a hunting'. The next day he left to visit Eberhardine at Teplitz, 'to try what effects the waters may have had on preparing her body for a prince'. The Saxon stud arrived back in Dresden in early September, stayed two days and on 7 September was reportedly 'gone again a hunting'. A week later Stepney chronicled that the Elector 'comes this morning from hunting and goes again this evening'.

Whether from sated blood-lust, saddle-sores or fatigue, Augustus had his feet on the ground long enough to receive Stepney on Monday 17 September, just before the latter left Saxony for the first time. It was also the Elector's fasting-day, which he observed every week 'since the misfortune he had of shooting Baron Nostitz'; although to compensate for such austerity 'he usually makes a double meal of it in the evening'. That night Augustus was 'to sup with Count Harrach, who had Fräulein Königsmarck and several other ladies to divert His Highness'.

Stepney was no longer around to tell us how many meals Augustus got through that night. He had passed the chief quill to his friend and secretary Philippe Plantamour, ordering the Frenchman 'to write constantly' in his absence. He assured Blathwayt that he would be 'well-satisfied with his letters'.[7]

Unfortunately, Plantamour's extant despatches from Dresden only cover a few weeks in January–February 1695 (p 100). However, it is quite possible that the Frenchman had nothing much to write about before then, since Augustus was frequently out of Dresden from October 1694 until early January 1695, first at the Leipzig Fair and then with his in-laws in Bayreuth. Moreover, his 'frolics and debauches' were scaled down in late 1694, when he was afflicted with severe stomach pains.

Yet as the new year dawned, Augustus was ready to swing again, particularly as Carnival-time was approaching. By then too he was involved in certain consequences of the release and return of Schöning, which together with other affairs of state will now be considered.

Chapter 9

'Setting his government upon the hinges'
State affairs 1694

'WHEN ALL IS CONCLUDED'

When Augustus summoned his privy counsellors to Moritzburg to renew their oaths, Stepney described this as one step in the process of 'setting his government upon the hinges'. These particular hinges underwent little lubrication, since Augustus effectively confirmed his brother's government in office. It was a conservative act by an inexperienced sovereign. Given the state of treaty negotiations, it was a wise move. If Augustus wanted Schöning back with him, continuity was required in the first instance. More radical measures, with the general as motive force, could follow after his release.

It was with this unreconstructed administration that Stepney conducted his negotiations. Most of its members expected 'sprinklings' for doing their job, and it was normal for them to receive presents upon completion of the task as well, as indeed did Stepney. This did not prevent him from complaining to Stratford about Haugwitz and Haxthausen, 'who give but little help to our business, yet will have their pretensions to His Majesty's bounty, when all is concluded'. Since he had not 'been very well used' by the Saxons, he felt all 'the less reason to be prodigal'.

On 29 May he reminded Blathwayt that Colt's previous 'arrangement' had been to pay bribes of RT 2000 to each of Gerßdorff, Knoch and Bose, 3000 to Grand Chamberlain Pflug, and 6000 to Billa. According to his later accounting, Stepney 'sprinkled' somewhat differently. He paid 3000 to Gerßdorff and Haxthausen, 2000 each to Haugwitz, Bose and Knoch, and only 1000 to Pflug, who was not involved in his treaty negotiations. For a few dollars more he had also bought Billa's 'waiting-woman' and her daughter's nurse. The whole process involved some creative accounting, using such monies as he had not paid to Billa.

In this same long despatch to his patron, Stepney produced pen-portraits of three of the ministers with whom he was dealing. The envoy considered Haugwitz to be 'a very honest gentleman, true and hearty to the interest of the allies', but someone who 'easily takes fire when he perceives he is in any way neglected'.

Haxthausen, 'whose character you have had' (p 76), came in for some more analysis. Stepney probably did not know then that the putative seducer of 12-year-old Billa had now joined the side of the witchfinders and was claiming that Ursula had hexed him into baby-snatching.[1] However, the envoy still implied that Haxthausen had pimped for Augustus and, from 'a plentiful fortune', had helped fund his extravagances. He was a confidant of the young ruler 'because he has had part in his pleasure' and may have 'sometimes supplied his wants, for they say the Elector owes him 30,000 Rixdaler'.

August Ferdinand Pflug (1662–1712) was currently Grand Chamberlain (Oberkammerer), although Haxthausen would replace him on 1 July. A 'man of pleasures and of a ready wit', Pflug had served William when he was Stadhouder and participated in his landing in England in 1688. Stepney admired him as 'a man who has had only a page's education' yet was 'as cunning and complete a courtier as one could meet'.

His views of Gerßdorff, Knoch and Bose emerge from more fragmentary evidence. Nikol von Gerßdorff (1629–1702) had been director of the Privy Council (Geheimer Ratsdirektor) since 1686. Stepney described 'the good old gentleman' as 'a timid soul', with whom he got on well by expediently 'listening with attention to the old stories he usually tells of his negotiations'.

Knoch, the former Hofmeister of John George (p 4), had been President of the Consistory (Oberkonsistorium), a form of court, from 1687 to 1693. He left this post during Colt's embassy, 'because he very conscientiously refused to suspend the Elector's confessor', despite John George's command. The clergyman 'would not absolve' Billa 'or admit her to the Sacrament while the Elector lived openly with her in adultery'.

Christoph Dietrich Bose, 64 years old, was Saxony's General-kriegskommissar, something like a Quartermaster-General, and 'like all commissaries, the Devil of a fellow'. He too had 'disobliged' Billa, by refusing her 15,000 dollars 'out of the chest of war', when 'there was no money to be had' in the treasury.

These were the men who negotiated with Stepney. They also treated with the Austrians to obtain the release of Schöning, even though they shared a mutual detestation of the general, which he reciprocated. None save Haxthausen had much influence upon Augustus, while death and disagreement removed all but Pflug from his councils quite rapidly. Nor had Schöning long to serve his prince; but at least he would make an impact while he lived.

'THE BUSINESS HAD STUCK SO LONG'

Soon after Augustus donned the electoral cap, Stepney speculated whether he also 'inherits his brother's violent passions for having Schöning again'. While 'not so nearly engaged in point of honour' as was John George, Augustus 'always had a peculiar fondness' for Schöning, and was unlikely to 'absolutely abandon him'. Nor did he, and whether or not John George had been on the brink of gaining Schöning's release, it was Augustus who achieved it.

On 23 May 1694 Vienna and Dresden signed a treaty. In return for the old soldier's liberty and a subsidy of RT 400,000, Augustus agreed to send to the Rhine 12,000 Saxon troops, plus their supplies and artillery. In a separate article, the Emperor promised to back Saxon claims on Lauenburg and to oppose the pretensions of the *Seitenlinie*. For his part, Augustus undertook to support the re-admission of the King of Bohemia (the Emperor) into the Electoral College. Finally, on 6 June the Saxons joined the Grand Alliance.

The negotiations which led up to these two treaties were the subject of Stepney's massive missive to Shrewsbury of 8 June. A few points might usefully be distilled from its vapourings. First, Stepney saved his King over 20,000 dollars in subsidies and 'retrenched a dangerous clause'. Second, although Saxony's commitment to the Grand Alliance actually took place on 6 June, it was back-dated to 23 May in order to coincide with the Austro–Saxon agreement. Third, despite the Briton's belief that Augustus was 'riveted' into the Grand Alliance, it proved more a case of him being loosely-tacked (C10). Fourth, Stepney's attempt to expedite the matters of payment and ratification, in order to get the Saxons speedily into the field, foundered hilariously upon the fixed rock of protocol. It required another colossal '*relation*' to sort matters out.

However, all this toil brought no promotion. For when Stepney received fresh credentials upon Augustus's accession, they again designated him only as deputy and commissary. Stepney had little choice but to 'submit with due resignation' and simply pride himself on what he had achieved, despite 'the poor tools with which they have been pleased to set me up'. He had the honour of being 'perhaps the first man without a character' to have brought 'to perfection two treaties like ours'.

On 14 June the 'man without a character' presented his credentials to Augustus at Moritzburg, 'choosing rather to have a private audience without ceremony than do things by halves'. Afterwards he thanked the Elector 'for having at last finished what we have been so long labouring at'. Augustus replied that Stepney knew full well what had delayed matters, and it was no fault of his that 'the business had stuck so long'.

The envoy reported that two days before, the order had been given for Saxon troops 'yet loitering' in the Electorate to join others who had wintered in the lines. The entire army was then to meet Lewis of Baden, who in the absence of Augustus would be in overall command. Stepney hoped that the Saxons would arrive 'in time enough to be of use yet this year'. However, he was hardly sanguine: 'The worst is our artillery and proviant-carts are still here'. Stepney attached less blame to the Saxons 'for being so tardy' than to the Imperial court. Vienna 'might as well have granted the same conditions four or five months ago (as to Schöning's liberty) as those they have now given'. In such event all might have been 'in the order and readiness we could wish'.

The terms for Schöning's release were that he swore and signed a written undertaking known as a *Revers*, pledging that he would play no role in Saxony's affairs while the war against France lasted, without Imperial approval. Augustus adhered to these same conditions in article five of the Austro–Saxon treaty. Stepney was unimpressed, believing that the general would break his oath 'as soon as the first temptation offers'. Nor could the envoy reconcile the terms of Schöning's *Revers* 'with the favours the Elector has granted him', which included the return of his patent as Saxon fieldmarshal and the colonelcy of several regiments.

In any event, once Augustus's ratification of the treaty had reached Vienna, 'Mr Schöning will be permitted to begin his journey hither'. On 6 June 'his sword was sent to him' and later he even had an audience with Leopold. 'I suppose we shall have him here in a fortnight', Stepney surmised, convinced that once the general reached Dresden, 'we may expect nothing but intrigues and heart-burnings'.

For a few weeks there was no problem. Although given permission to leave the Imperial capital on 20 June, the former prisoner was in no state to do so. 'Mr Schöning's gout keeps him still in Vienna', Stepney merrily informed Blathwayt on 17 July. Ten days later, believing Schöning's arrival imminent, Stepney sought advice as to 'how I am to live with him'. Soon he was to find out.

'LETTING THE BEAR LOOSE'

Escorted by his henchmen and Saxon cavalry, Schöning arrived in Dresden on the night of 9 August 1694; an act which Stepney later likened to 'letting the bear loose which will never be quiet but in chains'. The general, 'much weakened by the gout', was carried in a chair to court 'and was alone with the Elector nearly an hour'. He was still laid up when Augustus visited him for two hours a few days later. 'I can yet make no just observations how far may reach his interest and credit', Stepney confessed to Blathwayt on 17 August, for he could obtain no information. All ministers were 'close'.

Four days later Stepney noted that the former prisoner had still not left his house. The Briton hoped that he might therefore 'leave him to himself without either caressing or neglecting him'. Schöning reportedly remained 'much tormented' by gout, but Stepney thought that he was keeping out of the limelight, to show Vienna 'how strict he keeps to his *Revers*, by not concerning himself in civil or military affairs'. By dint of such 'moderation' Leopold might become convinced of the soldier's sincerity and 'permit him to have command of the army next campaign, if the Elector thinks fit'.

On 24 August Stepney alleged that 'Mr Schöning begins to find himself warm' and, like a snake, 'will shortly move and sting'. The reason for this judgement was that he was seeing all the army despatches. But Stepney had to climb into the snakepit (or bearpit) sometime. He had been instructed by Blathwayt that 'the less you affect coldness towards him the better'. So, after Schöning sent a compliment to the Briton at the end of August, Stepney visited him on the morning of 3 September.

The old man gave his version of the events that had led to his arrest (p 29), emphasizing that he had acted in the best interests of John George IV and 'the public good'. However, the Saxon ministers, who were 'unwilling to allow any stranger a footing', had been 'pleased to see him sacrificed' by permitting 'sinister interpretations to be put on his best words and actions'. Stepney's verdict was equally ungenerous: 'in truth he has a tongue to deceive the Devil, if he were not well upon his guard'.

Schöning returned Stepney's visit on 6 September and 'offered to serve me with the small interests' he had with Augustus, whenever the Briton 'judged he might be useful'. The general added to this open-ended offer of goodwill by stating that it was he who had prevented Saxon troops withdrawing from the Rhine (ostensibly because of discontent over their supplies). He had acted so, both to deflect any 'ill impressions against' Augustus in foreign chanceries and to counter suspicions that it was Schöning's very presence in Saxony that had led to the incident in the first place.

Whether this was true seems doubtful. According to Schöning, the order for withdrawal had been issued without his knowledge. Then it was presented to the Elector 'unluckily as he was in his going a shooting'. Augustus signed the edict 'without informing himself of the contents, and so it was dispatched to the army'. A courier had to be sent in pursuit to get the orders changed.

It is hard to see who, other than Schöning, could have given an order that Augustus signed without reading. The possible exception was Haxthausen, who was clearly enjoying his 15 minutes of fame. 'As Grand Chamberlain he is nearest the Elector's person', Stepney explained, 'and exercises his office with such authority' that nobody had access to Augustus save 'by his permission'. But although Haxthausen's power was 'very great, if he is able to keep his ground', Stepney thought that he 'seems to grasp at too much' and made little effort 'to strengthen his party'. Moreover, Haxthausen had become 'insufferable proud, and takes airs'. As to his relationship with Schöning, the general had 'slighted him heretofore', and Stepney thought Haxthausen was 'of an humour to repay Schöning in the same coin'.

So it was conceivably Haxthausen who issued the withdrawal order, intending to embarrass Schöning. However, this is merely surmise. It is equally unclear who fanned Augustus's involvement in 'the Königsmarck affair'; always allowing for the real possibility that the young Elector required no stimulation.

'RAISING LAZARUS'

There is no point in reviewing 'the Königsmarck affair' in detail, either as a minor romantic tragedy or as a squalid love-affair. Many authors have raked over these particular coals, and although the researches of the late Professor Hatton may not have doused the fire of accounts stoked by partisanship, it is her sober portrait which provides the background to the involvement of Stepney and Augustus in these events.[2]

Briefly stated, on the night of 1 July 1694 Aurora von Königsmarck's younger brother Philipp Christoph was murdered by four courtiers in the service of Ernst Augustus of Hanover. Whether the Elector gave the orders, or his mistress Countess von Platen, is not germane. One person not involved was George Louis, the Electoral Prince, later King George I of Britain. Here Stepney confirms what other evidence shows. He told Blathwayt that George Louis was in Berlin, 'acting comedies and making merry with his sister', the Electress Sophie Charlotte of Brandenburg.

The motive for the murder was Philipp's affair with George Louis' wife, Sophia Dorothea, which began in 1690. Not that the Kurprinz was in any way a 'wronged' husband: he had taken many mistresses, including Aurora von Königsmarck; 'elle couche avec le prince', wrote Philipp.[3] However, unlike Augustus, history has essayed no inventory of the conquests of the Hanoverian.

Although unfaithful himself, George Louis would still expect fidelity from his wife, to ensure an electoral succession spawned by legitimate sperm. The priapic activities of Philipp, since 1689 a colonel in Hanover's army, could upset more than mere proprieties. Warnings to the lovers to end the affair were ignored by them both.

Perhaps the occasion, rather than the cause, of Philipp's demise stemmed from money matters. He lived opulently, maintained a grandiose household and was a compulsive gambler. Short of readies, upon Augustus's accession he went to Dresden to try to collect the RT 30,000 that the new Elector still owed him in gambling debts. Augustus, equally strapped for cash, offered him instead promotion and a Saxon regiment, which Königsmarck accepted.

This move led to fears that the now independent Count might seek to abscond with Sophia Dorothea, an act that would besmirch Hanover's newly won electoral dignity. It is unlikely that elopement was in Königmarck's mind, although he was last seen alive heading for his lover's apartments on 1 July. He never reached them, since he was murdered that night, and his stone-weighted body was dumped in the River Leine. George Louis and his wife divorced on 28 December 1694, by which time both Stepney and Augustus had lost interest in a matter into which the envoy stumbled quite by chance.

On 13 June, purely as gossip, Stepney told Cresset in Hanover that Königsmarck 'must be with you by this time'. He had been made a major-general in Saxony and was 'expected back shortly'. To Stratford he bantered that the Count's promotion in the Saxon army had not been for nothing. 'I suppose by that means the debt is paid', gibed the envoy about the thousands which Augustus had owed Philipp.

Some four weeks had passed before Stepney first touched upon the possibility of murder. 'We have whisperings', he told Blathwayt on 10 July, that one of Königsmarck's servants had arrived in Dresden, to inform Augustus that his master had been missing since 30 June, 'the day he designed to leave Hanover and come hither'. Stepney surmised that the 29-year-old Count was probably dead.

A week later Stepney reported that Königsmarck 'is not yet to be found'. He had heard that Augustus, 'upon the alarm of his being missing', had sent his Swedish-born adjutant Johann Bannier to Hanover, in order 'to prevent the blow if it was not already given'. Otherwise the matter remained 'all mystery'.

On 24 July Stepney asked Cresset 'to satisfy me in cypher' with details of Sophia Dorothea's 'ruin'. 'Amours are tragical in these parts', he added in allusion to recent events in Saxony. He assumed that Augustus had 'cleared the debt of 30,000 Rixdalers he had left to him two years ago at play', since Stepney supposed the Count's 'corpse by this time is in the common shore'.

Not that this was any matter of regret to Stepney, who had known Königsmarck 'for a dissolute debauché, whom I would always have avoided'. Moreover, 'if he had been so black as we think he is, his fate (be what it will) is not to be pitied'. Nor did Cresset much doubt the Count's lot, informing Shrewsbury that he could 'rest assured that at Hanover ... we value Machiavelli above the Gospel'.[4]

Stepney had been told that Aurora 'raves like Cassandra and will know what has become of her brother'. The Hanoverians replied 'like Cain' that they were not her brother's keeper; so she turned to her brother's employer for satisfaction, and to some effect.

On 14 August Stepney reported that Augustus had instructed Bannier to 'demand him [Philipp] vigorously', while Wittgenstein, who had been sent from Hanover to 'mitigate' Augustus, courteously told our hero to butt out. He maintained that the Saxon 'ought not to concern himself for a person who was actually in the Hanover service', having been paid just before he went missing. Nor had the Count taken leave of his regiment or Ernst August. 'All which ceremonies being omitted', Königsmarck was 'liable to be punished as a deserter, if he were yet to be found'.

A week later Wittgenstein had an audience with Augustus, in which the Hanoverian envoy protested that Ernst August 'knows not what has become of the person', while to the question whether Königsmarck 'was alive or dead, no positive answer could be given'. Augustus seemed 'very moderate after this answer, as if he doubted not the truth of what had been offered'. However, he hoped that Ernst August would 'give him notice', as soon as he should 'learn any tidings' of Königsmarck. Stepney believed that here 'the affair will end, without causing any breach betwixt the two Electors'.

However, this was not the end of the affair: on 11 September Stepney alerted Shrewsbury to a Saxon threat. Bannier had warned the Hanoverians that if Count Königsmarck 'be not forthcoming, and that suddenly', Augustus would be forced 'to proceed to extremities, and may discover what may amaze the whole world'.

William III was fed up with such posturings. It was made clear to Stepney that it was in the national interest that Augustus should keep his nose out of the matter. Blathwayt instructed the envoy to obtain an audience with Augustus or his ministers and ram the point home.[5]

On Monday 17 September, the day he left Saxony, Stepney met

with Augustus, who 'was very gracious in the short audience I had with him'. Finally the envoy 'touched gently' on the matter at hand. William hoped that the Elector was satisfied with Ernst August's assurance, 'that he knew not what is become' of Königsmarck, and he trusted that Augustus 'would forbear pressing that affair any further, lest it should occasion a coldness betwixt two allies'.

To this Augustus 'answered smiling', that if the Count had transgressed, then he should have been 'delivered up into the hands of justice', but ''twas hard, a man should be spirited away, so as never to be heard of more'. Ingenuously Augustus maintained that, since Königsmarck 'might have fell into the hands of some private persons', he could do no less than press Ernst August to order 'strict enquiry' into the Count's fate, 'without giving any offence thereby' to his Hanoverian counterpart. Stepney accepted that Augustus was now withdrawing from active interest in the affair, not only because 'raising Lazarus is no more practicable in our days', but because in 'all he said he was so moderate' that it seemed redundant 'to urge the matter any further'.

Whether the whole escapade had been 'do-it-yourself' diplomacy by Augustus, or whether Schöning too had kept matters on the boil, cannot be established satisfactorily. However, the old plotter was definitely involved in the next matter to concern Stepney, as the glory-seeking Elector of Saxony turned his eyes to the command in Hungary.

Chapter 10

'Upon another scent'
Augustus and the command in
Hungary 1695

In the sure knowledge that he would be returning to Dresden, Stepney left Saxony on 17 September 1694, after a stay of almost a year. During the rest of the month he performed various tasks in North Germany. These included briefing Robert Sutton, Lord Lexington (1661–1723), who would be England's envoy in Vienna in the years 1694–97; William had commanded Stepney 'to give his lordship the best information I can on the Imperial court'.

In October Stepney was assisting Blathwayt in Holland. It was here that he received a ring from Augustus, as a reward for his role in the treaty negotiations. It is not clear exactly when Stepney reached England, although he was penning letters from Whitehall in mid-December. It is possible that by then George had received compassionate leave, since his 'good old mother' had died at the beginning of November.

On occasion Augustus had intruded into his thoughts. From Celle Stepney had written that 'the Elector of Saxony plays fast and loose and shifts so often, that we know not what he would be at'. In London he informed Shrewsbury that Augustus was 'a young, vigorous, active and bold prince, whose ambition and warlike inclinations' would prompt him to make the next campaign in person, 'for fear he should not have many more seasons to signalize himself'. In the same letter, Stepney wondered whether William might 'be inclined to dispose of the late Elector's Garter in favour of' Augustus.

Nobody was prepared to re-enact the ordeal of the Garter, and Augustus's gift of Polish horses remained unreciprocated. Stepney did win one round, though. Again he pestered Shrewsbury for promotion, arguing that the Saxon court was certainly 'the proudest and most expensive' of any in Germany, where it was impossible 'to converse freely with the Elector without entering sometimes into part of his pleasures'. Nor could one 'live with credit among' his ministers, 'without keeping a table and treating frequently'.

His importunings – or his abilities – were finally rewarded. In January 1695 Stepney received new credentials, this time as minister to the courts of Saxony and Hesse, 'which I am very satisfied with', he told Lexington.[1] Now it was time for the contented envoy to return. Following a hazardous journey, Stepney reached Dresden on 20 February 1695. He had missed Carnival by a fortnight, unlike Augustus and Philippe Plantamour.

'SI OCCUPÉ AUX DIVERTISSEMENTS'

On 8 January 1695 Plantamour reported that His Electoral Highness had not yet returned from Leipzig, and the word was that, health permitting, he would go hunting for several days before arriving in Dresden. Whether or not he butchered a few more animals on the way, Augustus arrived in his capital late on 10 January. Preparations for Carnival were in full swing, 'mais on dit que les Comediens que nous attendons de Paris ne veulent point venir icy'.

Despite the lack of Gallic gags, Augustus determined on a good time, especially when dressing up. 'M. l'Electeur s'y fit distinguer ... par la grande magnificence des ses habits', wrote the Frenchman on 15 January. On 21 January Augustus suffered 'une grande douleur de tete'. He got rid of his hangover by wandering round the town with his entourage, dressed as a Venetian noble. That night he played cards until four the next morning, and found himself feverish and confined to bed the next day.

Count Harrach arrived from Vienna on 26 January. It was not the right time for business: 'On est si occupé aux divertissements du Carnaval qu'on ne songe presque a autre chose'. Perhaps the fun-loving Austrian knew that. Moreover, he would have been in time to see, on 28 January, a magnificent and expensive failure.

Behind the Electoral Palace a large enclosure had been constructed, into which lions, tigers, panthers and other wild animals were introduced. Although it was intended that the beasts should tear each other to pieces for the edification of mankind, they went on strike instead, refusing to move. The introduction of dogs helped a little. These went for the wild boars to whom they were used, as well as their handlers, but wisely declined to attack the big cats. But without their intervention, despite all the cost and trouble, 'il n'y auroit pas eu la moindre effusion de sang'.

On 31 January Augustus broke off from organizing the festivities to hold an audience with Harrach, at which a new project was mooted. In return for sending Saxon troops to Hungary instead of the Rhine, Augustus was offered the command of the Imperial army there, on the same terms as those previously exercised by 'Blue Max', the Bavarian Elector Maximilian II Emmanuel (r 1679–1726). Perhaps stimulated by the proposal, on 5 February Augustus turned up in a 'spot the king' parade attired as Alexander the Great. To no great surprise, it was our hero 'qui a remporté le premier prix'.

Two days later, it was up to Olympus for the grand finale of Carnival. Gods whipped up horses, which drew goddesses in chariots around Dresden, before they retired to the riding school and tilted at each other, in lists lit by 'une infinité de Cierges', until ten that night. Then the gods banqueted, after which came dancing and games, with an electoral edict forbidding any man from retiring before 6 a.m. Augustus finished the frolics by playing tennis dressed as Mercury. It is not known whether such garb gave him speed around the court.

He certainly eluded Stepney for a while, 'For in six days that I have been waiting', the envoy grumbled to Shrewsbury, 'I have not been able to obtain an audience from the Elector', who was 'too intent on his pleasures to allow one moment to business'. To Blathwayt he moaned that Augustus's 'time is chiefly taken up at tennis and visiting the Countess of Königsmarck'. Yet, as usual, Augustus had ambition as well as pleasure in mind.

'IF THE ELECTOR MAY BE PERSUADED'

In December 1694 Augustus told the Prussian ambassador that he had no intention of serving in the coming campaign as a 'volunteer' under Lewis of Baden, as had his brother in 1693. Instead he proposed an independent Saxon–Brandenburg command on the Rhine in 1695, led of course by himself.[2]

Stepney's instructions of 15 January were designed to thwart just such plans. William fully approved of the Imperial proposal to send most Saxon troops into Hungary, 'if the Elector may be persuaded to it', while withdrawing the disciplined Prussians from Hungary for service on the Rhine. Such consent was conditional on there being no extra expense for England's monarch.

If any Saxon troops were to be sent to Flanders, Stepney was to ensure that they 'be not commanded by any professed creature of Schöning's', or by anybody else 'whose zeal for the public good be any wise doubted of'. The envoy was also 'to dissuade and discourage' Augustus from heading Saxon forces in the west. The Elector or Schöning, 'with whom you are to keep up a civil acquaintance', might command only in Hungary.

While travelling to Saxony, Stepney told Lexington that he could see no reason why Augustus 'should be so good a Christian to ruin his army against the Turks'. In his view, quite the contrary would occur: Augustus would 'be firm to send none of his troops but to the Rhine, will go with them himself, and take Schöning with him (if he be in a condition of crawling)'.

However, once he reached Dresden, he was rapidly disabused. Stepney reported that when the command in Hungary had first been mooted, Augustus had made the usual objections about Hungary being the 'Churchyard of the Germans', and that 'it would be a mere sacrifice to send his men thither'. But now, according to Harrach, an expedition to 'le Cimetière des Allemans' was quite on the cards.

There were four reasons for this change in Stepney's view. The first was Augustus's 'active temper which will not let him lie still, while there is an opportunity of exerting himself', coupled with 'an impatient desire' he had 'to signalize himself by some noble action before the war ends'. Second came the fact that there was no 'sphere for his activity' on the Rhine, since Lewis of Baden refused to surrender the command. Given that it was impossible to bring these two 'to a right understanding', it was 'wholly impracticable' to expect 'a junction' of Saxon and allied troops in this area.

Third, Augustus was attracted by 'the vanity of commanding an Imperial army', and this might 'by degrees reconcile him to this project' in Hungary. Lastly, Schöning, although he seemed 'old and infirm which does not promise a long life', had his own reasons for directing his protégé's ambitions to the south, despite any fears that his sovereign's health 'should be impaired in that unwholesome climate, or that troops shall rot'.[3]

At length, on 26 February, Augustus received the English minister and they dined together. Stepney remarked that Augustus 'seems dissatisfied at the freedom with which (he hears) Prince Lewis discourses of him and his troops'. The rest of their talk was about the state of England since the death of William's wife, Queen Mary, the previous December. Beyond this Stepney could only comment that Augustus's health 'begins to be restored, and he takes true method to settle it, for at table he drunk no wine'.

It is interesting to observe that Augustus actually made some attempt to obey his doctors' orders. Although mineral water would never be more than a passing fad, he had also agreed to take a cure at Carlsbad later that year (C11).

AS THE WATERMEN DO'

Now Stepney lent his support to the efforts of Harrach and Schöning to have the Saxon army march south. 'We are therefore upon another scent', he told Stratford, 'and rather than let good troops lie useless, we are endeavouring to have them pass into Hungary' under Augustus's command.

Yet it was not that simple. As Stepney recognized, Augustus was under strong countervailing pressures to decline the 'project of Hungary, which all mankind here (except Schöning) is against'. His mother, wife, mistress and favourites opposed it, 'because of the tenderness they have for his person'. The privy counsellors objected, because they foresaw 'nothing but ruin to their troops, and the greatness of Mr Schöning', which they feared more than anything else. However, the final decision was down to Augustus. And here we can only speculate as to why he was avoiding decision at this juncture; 'for as yet he balances whether he shall accept that command or not'.

That Augustus knew 'very well how to dissemble' is quite evident; indeed, he considered it a necessary virtue in a prince.[4] Now he 'industriously' avoided Harrach over the terms of command in Hungary. When Harrach, Ham and Stepney together tried to corner him, he flew through them 'like lightning, or as if he ran the gauntlet', to avoid 'speaking to us or hearing what we would say'. He seemed to be deliberately confusing the poor envoys about his intentions, by behaving 'as the watermen do, look one way and row another'.

Possibly the sybarite hoped that he might simply be left alone to have a good time with Aurora, causing the Hungarian project to collapse from inattention. 'His day is spent in the tennis-court (he even dines there)', Stepney carped, 'and his evenings with his mistress'. On 1 March 'he drunk four bottles of Rosasolis[?] to his shame, and has been forced to keep his chamber ever since'. He was 'a lost man'. Here the Briton was just wittering, for soon Augustus was flying past him 'like lightning'.

Perhaps Augustus expected the Hungarian project to fall through and had only intimated that he would consider it 'upon a false assumption'. This was that the English and Dutch governments would veto it, on the grounds that the Rhine was the 'most natural station' for the Saxons. When such a veto was not forthcoming, Stepney anticipated that Augustus might force the plan to founder by adhering rigidly 'to the demands he has made' of Vienna, 'on purpose to get loose if they be not complied with'. Stepney also suggested that Schöning had flown the Hungarian kite 'to make us lose time by this amusement', with the result 'that our Saxons may neither serve in Hungary or anywhere else'.

What seems most likely is that his dissimulation was a calculated political act. Not only did Augustus want the Hungarian command, but he was confusing and stringing out the issue in order to get the best possible terms from Vienna. If this was the case, we can only guess whether such tactics were his own or Schöning's. Most likely they came from the combination of the two, with Augustus playing the dissembling front-man while Schöning schemed backstage.

'HUNGARY IS NOW IN THE CRISIS'

If Augustus had all along desired to wriggle out of the Hungarian campaign, he had a perfect opportunity to do so on 15 March, when a courier arrived from Vienna bearing the Emperor's response to the Saxon's terms. There were sufficient key differences between the proposals of the two courts for Stepney to contend that 'the project of Hungary is now in the crisis'.

Augustus wanted to exercise the supreme command in Hungary on the same terms as had 'Blue Max', with the power to engage in battle or siege without reference to Vienna. The Emperor insisted that such decisions be referred to a council of war (Kriegsrat), which would be under his control. Whereas Augustus was offering 8000 men for a campaign or two in return for a subsidy of 400,000 dollars, Vienna expected much more for its money. The Emperor sought 12,300 troops, including the elite of the Saxon army, to serve 'as long as the war shall last with the Turks'. As Stepney drily observed, it had already lasted 11 years and 'may linger out as much more'.

The envoy didn't expect Augustus to 'embark on so uncertain a bottom', particularly as the Emperor had also fallen very far short in the terms that he was offering Schöning. That this was a crucial element in the whole deal was now clear. Harrach admitted that 'by the Emperor's orders', he promised Schöning 'several advantageous conditions for himself', if he would use his influence upon Augustus 'by disposing him to hear favourably the proposition of Hungary'.

Now the Austrians were welching on their part of the bargain, by repudiating the terms Schöning had stipulated, and which he believed he had been promised. In effect, they told the old soldier that he should be well satisfied with the status quo. It was enough that Vienna permitted him to serve Augustus as a Saxon fieldmarshal, 'without mentioning his *Revers*'. He could hardly expect them to grant him 'equipage, appointment or patent as fieldmarshal to the Emperor'.

Augustus could well have raised two electoral fingers to the Emperor at this juncture, had he wished to kill the Hungarian venture stone-dead. Nobody suggested that it was a point of honour that he return to the negotiating fray, although he may well have felt this himself. Nor did he appear downhearted at Vienna's proposals. When Stepney spoke with him on 17 March he was 'in a very good humour', at least until the diplomat, under instruction, brought up the matter of the disgraced Count Friesen. Stepney 'easily perceived what I said had soured him'.[5]

On 20 March Augustus, Knoch, Gerßdorff, Bose and Haxthausen were due to meet with Harrach to consider the Hungarian project. Given the self-interested attitude of these ministers, Stepney anticipated that they 'will be sure not to christen this child', because they knew Schöning was 'the father of it'. If the original attendance had been adhered to, then 'throwing it out of doors' might well have been the plan's fate; but at the last moment, Schöning joined the meeting.

Of course, this was quite illegal, being tantamount to 'annulling his *Revers* by tacitly consenting to his having admittance into civil affairs'. Stepney cited article five of the 1694 Austro–Saxon Treaty to support his view. In this Augustus had expressly promised, 'out of respect to the Emperor', not to make use of Schöning 'so long as this war lasts, either in civil or military affairs, without the knowledge and approbation of his Imperial Majesty'.

Since the Elector had been playing a lot of tennis, this was presumably a political score of '15-all'. Leopold had broken his word over Schöning; so Augustus did the same, and demonstrated the depths of his 'respect to the Emperor' in the process. In any case, article five had already been infringed, by Harrach treating directly with Schöning simply to get the whole project off the ground. But since Schöning had 'now changed batteries out of spite', by wangling attendance at the meeting and *publicly* flaunting his involvement in Saxon affairs, Harrach in turn 'shifts his sails'.

Having finally disentangled himself from a mixed metaphor, Stepney explained the extant position. Harrach had got round the matter of the Saxon insult by a simple expedient. He had provided the Saxons with a written protocol of the current Imperial position and indicated a readiness to accept from them a written reply; but without seeking to know if Schöning had 'a hand in it or not'. One more exposition of the timeless principle that the flexibility of diplomatic codes can always provide a way, if the will is there.

All this was just as well, since Schöning's would seem to be the only hand, other than that of his sovereign, in the Saxon response. On 23 March Stepney reported that Augustus and Schöning had been 'locked up' together, considering Harrach's latest offer. Vienna now accepted that the Saxon contingent would be provided solely for two years. It also acceded to a complement of only 8000 troops, so long as this force included the elite units, numbering around 2300. However, there were no Austrian concessions regarding Augustus's terms of command, nor on Schöning's status.

'THE BETS CHANGE'

Stepney was uncertain what would happen. Early on 25 March, which was Easter Monday, he wrote to Lexington in Vienna, comparing the negotiations to 'a match of cock-fighting', where 'the issue is so doubtful and the bets change so frequently in so short a time'. Yet before that day was out, he was telling his correspondents that 'the tables are quite turned', and 'we now talk of Hungary as a thing certain'.

It is difficult to divine what had happened that day to transform doubt into certainty. The only item which might account for it is the rumoured view of Augustus that, when he reached Vienna as commander, 'he shall have eloquence enough to prevail with the Emperor' to give Schöning his patent 'before the beginning of the campaign'. This may have implied that Augustus intended to blackmail Leopold, by refusing to proceed to Hungary if Schöning was not made up to an Imperial fieldmarshal.

Perhaps Stepney was now also giving added weight to the belief that Schöning would remain behind as Stadthalter or viceroy while Augustus was in Hungary, and would have 'the direction of the Electorate as absolutely as if he were Vice-Elector'. This certainly contrasted with his earlier view, that without Schöning 'at his elbow' in Hungary, Augustus would 'not be able to undertake any great action or enter into deep reasonings on war affairs'.

It is impossible to say who decided that Augustus should venture into Hungary alone, while Schöning was left minding the electoral 'shop'. Certainly the latter was now old and infirm. Perhaps Augustus needed his most trusted adviser at home during his absence. Possibly our hero sought the freedom to be his own man, far from any restraining hands. But the general's position in Dresden would be quite invidious, once Augustus was fighting the Turks. Stepney hardly exaggerated in alleging that Schöning and his family were threatened 'with no less than a massacre' if Augustus 'should come to any misfortune' in Hungary.

Whether or not Hungary was 'a thing certain', on 27 March Augustus 'returned an answer to Count Harrach's composition', which was sent at once to Vienna. While the Saxons awaited the Austrian response to their terms, they presented Stepney with a problem too.

'MASTERS OF OUR PURSES'

Despite the fact that Saxon troops would not be marching to the Rhine, Augustus still wanted to receive the British and Dutch subsidies agreed upon under the 1694 treaties (p 91). As usual, there were money problems in Saxony, and the English had the reputation of being 'good paymasters'.

Not surprisingly, Whitehall saw things very differently. In the first place England, unlike the Empire, was not at war with the Turks, but only with Vienna's other enemy, France. Moreover, there was talk of William acting as mediator between Leopold and the Porte. In addition, any involvement in the war in the east might also have a derogatory impact upon Britain's 'Turkey-trade, which is of great consequence to our nation'. However, the greatest objection of the English to subsidizing Augustus in Hungary was that there was nothing in the 1694 treaties obliging them to do so. The best that they would offer was a compromise.

In mid-March Shrewsbury informed Stepney of William's thinking with regard to Saxon forces. For those going to Hungary, the King flatly refused 'any part of the subsidy agreed on'. Yet since this force comprised only 8000 of the 12,000 troops, which Dresden had agreed in 1694 to send to the Rhine, William was prepared to subsidize the remainder pro rata, so long as they were actually sent west against the French.

Stepney was prepared to negotiate for this residual force after Harrach had completed his own treaty with the Saxons. He told Shrewsbury that 'as we have very honestly held his child at the font, we hope he will not smother ours, when it comes to be christened'. The Austrian attitude is not clear, although noticeably they placed no pressure upon Augustus to supply his 'constitutional' contingent of troops against France. Augustus thought the Emperor should be 'fully satisfied' with the 8000 men being sent to Hungary.

Moreover, the Saxons were *not* prepared to hire out their 'surplus' troops to William. As Stepney told Lexington, the Elector refused to 'send one man' to Lewis of Baden, 'who had a trick of cutting off our Saxons' ears and noses, and hanging up our criminals', while ignoring the jurisdiction of Saxon courts martial.

It is doubtful that this was the real reason. Rather, the remainder of Augustus's army, some 7000 men, was being retained in the

Electorate 'pro bono publico in omnes eventus'. In other words, as Stadthalter Schöning might need a strike-force in case of trouble.

So, in the final analysis, Augustus simply tried it on: he endeavoured to obtain the entire English subsidy of 100,000 dollars, without sending a single man to fight Louis XIV's armies in 1695. Nor did the Austrians try to dissuade him, since they would have to make up any shortfalls of British cash. As Stepney disdainfully expressed it, Vienna behaved 'as confidently as if they were the absolute masters of our purses'.

Something had to give, which it did when Stepney and the Dutch envoy Ham were summoned to a conference on 11 April. As Stepney reminded Shrewsbury, this was 'the first we have assisted at, since the ratifications of last year's treaty'. The meeting also provided the first *formal* notification to the Maritime Powers that in 1695 the Saxons would be marching to Hungary and not to the Rhine. Not surprisingly, the envoys adhered strictly to the letter of the law.

They argued that the Saxons could not dispose of the 12,000 men which they were committed to provide by treaty without the consent of William and the Dutch States. But should the latter consent to allow 8000 Saxons to go to Hungary instead, they expected to be 'eased of' their subsidies, since such monies were now required to fund replacement troops to be sent to the Rhine. Moreover, because the 1694 treaty obligated them to pay only for troops which were employed against France, the Emperor alone must subsidize the Saxon troops in Hungary, since he alone 'was to reap the advantages of this succour'. Finally, they told the Saxons 'plainly they were not to expect one penny from us for these 8000 men'.

The Saxons now contended that if they received no subsidies from the Maritime Powers, then they were released from membership of and obligations to the Grand Alliance. Stepney loftily reminded them that the Elector of Saxony was not a member of that union simply in order that he might receive subsidies. He was there as a confederate, 'who was willing to join his best endeavours towards reducing the unbounded power of France to due limits'. Indeed, 'it was only the French custom to allow subsidies of inaction'.

Despite and because of their stand, Stepney and Ham found themselves 'being only witnesses at Count Harrach's treaty', when the Austrians and Saxons signed their agreement on 13 April 1695. 'In short', fumed Stepney, 'Mr Ham might as well have been in Berlin [his formal posting] and I in London for what we have done'. Certainly the two envoys had been dealt with by 'unhandsome methods'.

As to the Austro–Saxon treaty, Vienna had conceded no new ground. It was agreed that the Saxons should begin their march to Hungary the day after ratifications were exchanged. Augustus was

free to recruit his 8000 men, at the Emperor's expense, from anywhere except Leopold's hereditary territories. The Saxon ruler had
command of the entire Imperial army in Hungary, on the same
terms as had 'Blue Max', save that he required permission of the
Emperor's Kriegsrat before engaging in siege or major battle.

For Schöning, who had set up the whole operation, there was
nothing. As before, Augustus might use him as his own fieldmarshal
in Hungary, 'whose command is to reach no further than our
Saxons'. But according to Harrach, 'the door was shut' on any possibility of his holding Imperial rank.

In summation, neither Augustus nor Schöning gained anything
that Vienna had not been prepared to yield. Short of the usual
Saxon delaying tactics before arriving in the field, or *in extremis*
resigning his command, Augustus had no cards to play in order to
wheedle further concessions out of Leopold. Presumably he learned
lessons from this treatment, and there is no doubting that he would
soon become the most dangerous opponent of the Habsburgs within
the Empire. But such were ambitions for the distant future. The near
future dangled the prospect of glory in Hungary. The present could
be devoted primarily to pleasure.

Chapter 11

'At last got out of their nests'
Preparing for Hungary 1695

'THE ELECTOR AND HIS CATTLE'

On 11 April 1695 Harrach gave a dinner for 'the Elector and his cattle'. Early on 14 April, the herd was due to move on to Leipzig, where the spring fair began next day. When Stepney and Ham went to court to wish him well on his trip, Augustus 'industriously avoided' the envoys who had refused him subsidies.

On his return journey from Leipzig, Augustus took leave of his mother in Lichtenburg, before arriving back in Dresden on the night of 25 April. 'He came on horseback without any servants', Stepney told Lexington, 'and so much incognito that the guards never stood in their arms, and immediately he went to the tennis-court to refresh himself'.

As to the future, Augustus was leaving for Carlsbad soon, taking with him 'his ordinary mistress Klengel, his extraordinary one Königsmarck, and will find a third there ready to his hand, Mlle Altheim'. Satisfying this 'lease of w——, I leave to his constitution', the envoy concluded pruriently, 'but I fancy he has more work upon his hands than he can turn himself to'.[1]

It is difficult to assess the relationship that Augustus had with Aurora von Königsmarck and Eleonore von Klengel at this time. Obviously he ran them in tandem, as he often did in his liaisons. Neither of them was a 'live-in' mistress. Stepney attests that he visited Eleonore as if ashamed of his feelings. Plantamour told Vernon in February that to placate his wife, Augustus had banned her from court, but he specified that 'Mlle Klengel ... passe toujours pour sa Maitresse'. As for Aurora, she spent the winter of 1694–95 in a hotel, where Augustus visited her. There can not have been many assignations, since he was frequently out of Dresden at this time (p 88).

Even when Countess von Königsmarck and Augustus got together, it may have been an odd affair. The memoirs of Haxthausen's son describe how these two often romped with each other like children. That they also indulged in sexual play goes without saying, but this stage may have been reached quite late in the day. As for the great seduction scene at Moritzburg, which is the most memorable part of von Pöllnitz's tedious tome, the evidence suggests that it never happened.[2]

Aurora publicly partnered the Elector at Carnival. There is an unflattering print of her at the *Götteraufzug* ('cavalcade of the gods') of 7 February, described by Plantamour (p 101). It shows a podgy punk-haired Aurora playing herself as the goddess of the dawn, and a rather manic-looking being (Augustus as Apollo?) whipping up the horses. Overall, despite her brains and independence, there is little evidence that Aurora's role was other than an adornment.

'A MAN AT CHESS'

On 26 February Stepney informed Blathwayt that his intentions with regard to Schöning were 'to keep up a civil acquaintance (as you have instructed) and stop there'. For he reasoned that the general's 'design in caressing me' was chiefly to make 'people believe he is well with His Majesty'. When Lexington apparently sought to upset this cosy relationship, Stepney sent him a courteously forthright reply on 8 March: 'If anybody ought to declare openly and positively against Sch——, I had rather your lordship should do it, than I, who am here as it were under his paw'.

It seems that Lexington, like others, was also putting pressure upon Stepney to do something for William's satrap Friesen. That Count, having brought back the Garter, had resigned his Saxon commissions and re-entered William's service. Subsequently, he had ignored all summonses to Dresden to explain himself. Augustus's suspicions had certainly been fuelled by Schöning, who held Friesen and Haugwitz to be most responsible for prolonging his ordeal in prison; that both men were also connected to 'the Family' seems hardly coincidental.

Stepney told Lexington that he could do nothing to help Friesen. Accepting the command of Schöning's guards regiment 'is the greatest crime alleged against him'. However, it was quite likely that 'there may be others kept in reserve, when they shall have brought him into the snare', such as Friesen's 'negotiation at Vienna and his practices with the Countess [Billa] during the last reign'. All or any of these charges 'may be very uneasy if not fatal to him', now that Schöning was back in power. Yet, despite his pessimism, on 17 March Stepney spoke to Augustus about Friesen 'when he least expected it', and quickly appreciated that the subject 'soured' the Elector (p 105).

In mid-April Schöning encouraged Stepney to join Augustus when he left for Carlsbad, dismissing fears of the latter's disfavour with talk of 'a young headless prince'. This led Stepney to write of 'the poor Elector', whom Schöning 'plays and moves with as much ease as one may do a man at chess'. There is no indication as to why Stepney should be invited to the Bohemian baths, although continuing Saxon interest in English subsidies may well have been on the agenda.

At the end of the month Schöning again pressed Stepney to visit Carlsbad. As for his own plans, he related that Augustus was 'urgent with him to go for Hungary'. However, before he could agree, 'he must first see what effect the bath has on him', and crucially, 'whether the Emperor will enable him to serve his master usefully and creditably'. This was an obvious reference to the annulment of his *Revers*, which Harrach was now hinting might follow if Schöning did *not* go to Hungary.

That was Schöning's problem; Stepney's was Friesen. The envoy assured Vernon that he intended to 'move all springs in favour' of the Count before Augustus set out for Carlsbad on 3 May. He soon thought better of it, after consulting with Haxthausen, who was Friesen's 'best and most powerful patron'. The Grand Chamberlain assured Stepney that Augustus was still 'incensed' at Friesen's refusal to return to Saxony and advised him not to raise the matter.

At the end of April Augustus sent Haxthausen to Vienna. To ensure that the Imperialists did not diminish the Saxon's status any further, he was charged with regulating 'the manner of the Elector's reception, after the ceremonial that was observed with the Elector of Bavaria'. Certainly the Imperial court attempted to ensure that Augustus's prior stay in Carlsbad would be to his liking.[3] On 29 April the Saxon Hofstaat left for that destination, and two days later Aurora and Schöning followed, he 'in a litter' escorted by a large retinue.

That Mayday afternoon Stepney and Ham had 'a sort of audience of congé' with Augustus. Most of the conversation, he apprised Lexington, consisted of 'a great deal such stuff' which 'we are forced to say to princes who love flattery'. Augustus asked Stepney 'what course I meant to steer', and they 'parted better friends than I expected'. Indeed, two weeks later Stepney received from the Elector a ring worth £100, which was more than he anticipated 'after having withdrawn our subsidies'.

On 2 May Augustus took his own leave of both Eleonore and Eberhardine, who had recently arrived in Dresden from her self-imposed exile near Torgau. The following day Augustus travelled to Carlsbad.

Stepney did not follow him, but sent Plantamour instead. On 5 May the Briton supped with Eleonore and her daughter. The Dowager Electress was leaving for the spas near Koblenz on the morrow.[4]

Stepney informed Lexington on 10 May that Augustus was in a good humour at Carlsbad, although Mlle Altheim 'has not kept her word in going hither'. Whether this lady recoiled from being one of a harem, or simply objected to whatever term covers the next rung up from troilism (if that was in prospect), remains unknown.

Stepney also referred to reports of coldness between the Elector and Schöning, based upon the discovery of letters showing that the general had never intended to venture into Hungary. Whatever the truth of this matter, it must be remembered that Schöning had suffi- cient enemies to fuel any number of slanders.

On 12 May Augustus celebrated his twenty-fifth birthday in Carls- bad. Presumably he enjoyed himself, although Stepney implied that he might be bored. 'He has there his brace [Aurora and Eleonore], and his billiard-table'; however, a man 'cannot always hold out at the first of these sports, and the other is too trifling for a hero, who has glory in his head'.

He wrote more seriously to Blathwayt on 17 May, that he had no idea how long the Elector might remain in Carlsbad. His stay would be determined by the movement of Saxon forces. Augustus could not go to Vienna and 'loiter three weeks before his troops have so much [as] got into the hereditary countries'. Such a prospect would 'be very uneasy to him'. Meantime, Harrach was trying to accelerate the advance of these same troops to Hungary; he certainly had a job on his hands.

'THE REPUTATION OF SHARPERS'

When ratifications to the Austro–Saxon treaty were exchanged at the beginning of May, there was no agreed march-route to Hungary for Augustus's troops. The Austrian proposal, as outlined by Stepney, was that both horse and foot 'march straight to Budweis (České Budějo- vice) in the heart of Bohemia'. From there the infantry were to tramp to Linz, 'where they embark on the Danube and fall as low as Buda[pest]'. The cavalry were to split into two at Budweis, one group passing through Moravia and the other Lower Austria.

The Imperial court 'pretend to use this method, not to harass our Saxons by too tedious a march, but the truth is, we have the reputa- tion of sharpers'. Therefore the Austrians had decided that the her- editary lands should not suffer typical Saxon depredations. However, Vienna's plans, effectively making the Saxons 'march in a triangle

114

instead of a straight line', were not conducive to their early arrival in the field.

There were two other factors making for delay. First, through Austrian inefficiency, it took another fortnight finally to agree a march-route. In consequence, it was not until 14 May that Saxon forces were actually ordered to move to the frontiers of Bohemia. Second, these troops could not converge upon their destination simultaneously. Some were near the frontier, while others were as far afield as the Silesian borders, Thuringia, and Lusatia.

Obviously, the speediest solution would have been simply to deploy the requisite number from the most proximate units; but this would have offended against current military policy. Schöning had emulated the Brandenburg practice, 'by making an equal draft out of every company', wherever it was stationed. The advantage of this policy was that 'every company is kept in being', for the purposes of recruitment and replenishment of losses.

All in all, Stepney could not see a rendezvous of Saxon forces in Teplitz occurring before 10 June, and he doubted that they would be in Buda before mid-July. 'So that after the manner that our Saxons manage matters', they were likely to be of as little use 'to the Emperor this year on the Danube, as they were last year to Prince Lewis on the Rhine'. However, the Habsburgs too deployed some weapons from the arsenal of delay. For if the Saxons 'loiter more than they ought', Leopold would have plenty of opportunities 'to mortify them, when he has got them safe into Hungary, by slow payments and such-like methods, which are never wanting at Vienna'. By late June Stepney was reporting that Saxon officers in Bohemia were 'complaining of hard usage already, and that the soldiers begin to desert apace'.

'OVER TO CARLSBAD'

On 18 May Blathwayt had instructed Stepney to pursue again the matter of Friesen's pardon. It was not a mission he relished: 'Friesen, his family, and his affair make me quite mad', he erupted to Matt Prior. 'It is the way of the world, the more service you do a man, the more he expects'. Moreover, both Friesen and Ham had represented Stepney 'as a creature of Schöning's': he 'who never did me any harm', in fact 'has shown me many civilities, and done me some services'. It was an interesting snapshot of the role-reversals which had occurred since the halcyon days of 'my good friend Friesen' and Schöning the 'snake'. And why was Stepney always the patsy in this matter? Ham had 'never opened his mouth' on Friesen's behalf, he groused to Blathwayt, while 'my paw is made use of to pull out the chestnuts'.

Nevertheless, the diplomat had to obey orders. Since the 'Friesen affair' could only be aired effectively in an interview with Augustus, he 'judged it most convenient to step over to Carlsbad'. Arriving in the Bohemian town on 27 May, Stepney had an audience with the Saxon ruler on 30 May.

The Elector remained adamant; he was still angered by a man who had 'thrown up his commission in so indecent a way' and had declined to appear before his sovereign to explain himself, despite 'two peremptory citations'. Nor was Augustus happy with the Habsburgs. He told Stepney 'in great passion', that the Imperial court 'used him very scurvily with their chicane'. And since 'they treated him so ill while he is on this side of Vienna', he had every reason 'to expect worse treatment when they have got him into Hungary'.

Naturally, it was not all woe. Stepney continued his letter with a description of a greenhouse, built for Augustus at the cost of 1000 dollars, 'wherein he gives the ladies a masquerade' on 6 June. It was 'an Italian invention, with retirades, couches and all other conveniences which make love easy'. The Elector had sent to Dresden for six wagon-loads of mirrors and lustres to furnish it.

It was anticipated that Aurora would play Diana the goddess of hunting, and the other ladies present her sextet of nymphs. 'I know not as yet to whose turn it may fall to play Actaeon', wrote Stepney in jaunty reference to the hunter transformed into a stag by Diana; 'but before the night be over horns will be grafted, which I take to be the main design of the entertainment'.

The envoy had a chance to check this point when both he and Harrach attended the masquerade, which lasted until 5 a.m. on 7 June. Stepney described the event as 'well-contrived and perfectly well executed'. Initially there were 'some hard words' between Aurora and Augustus, but by the end of the night 'they came to a right understanding'.

Augustus supped with Aurora on 7 June and they lunched together the next day. 'Countess Königsmarck was the favourite till the last minute', Stepney gossiped to John Robinson in Stockholm (p 197). 'The Elector supped with her just before parting' and 'you may easily guess what they did betwixt meals'. Although Stepney claimed not to 'envy the choice he has made', he still 'thought it charitable', once Augustus had left Carlsbad, 'to comfort the afflicted', and found Aurora's 'black eyes not thoroughly dried'.

Prior to playing the gallant, Stepney had doubled as a diplomat when meeting with Augustus on the morning of 8 June. The Elector 'was dressed half-Moor and half-Turk', with diamonds 'to the value of above 500,000 dollars' spangling 'his arms, collar, and turban'. He went out of his way 'to show me them distinctly'. Augustus was taking them all with him to Hungary, 'for he thinks himself under no obligation to lay up for a successor'.

This glittering figure gave no ground upon the Friesen affair. Augustus 'persisted firmly' in his view that the former must 'first give an account of his conduct'. In the meantime, he told Stepney, he hoped that William would not let Friesen serve him, until the Count had fulfilled his duties in Saxony.[5]

Stepney had fulfilled his. With the sound of Augustus's esoteric French ringing in his ears, the envoy withdrew from the presence of this exotically attired sovereign. They would not meet again for three years, by which time our hero would have made himself also King of Poland.

Augustus left by coach for Pilsen (Plzeň) that evening, en route first to Prague and then to Vienna, where he proposed making his ceremonial entry on 15/25 June. Soon after, Schöning, surrounded by 'a greater cavalcade than his master', headed for Dresden in the company of Aurora. The envoy mused that 'the Elector has reposed the two mighty trusts, his mistress and his government' upon the veteran plotter.

However, such matters were no longer Stepney's concern. He had ensured that 'our Saxons are at last got out of their nests' and had delivered up his Elector to Lord Lexington in Vienna. Now he could move on. Blathwayt had ordered him to leave for Frankfurt, 'the centre of Germany, where he would be readiest for any call'.

With Carlsbad 'lying out of the road of all correspondence', Stepney travelled to Leipzig to despatch his final letters from Saxony, arriving there on 14 June; ten days later he set out for Frankfurt. He reached his destination on 1 July 1695, which was 11 July in the New Style calendar in use in western Germany, to which we now convert for the remainder of our story.

From his various postings Stepney would keep a watching brief upon the young Saxon. Although Augustus was out of sight, it proved harder for Stepney to put out of mind this restless ruler, whose mercurial personality had engaged his attention for nearly two years.

117

Chapter 12

'Able to do nothing'
Commander in Hungary 1695–96

From Dresden Stepney had provided a brief pen-portrait of Augustus for the new Secretary of State for the North, Sir William Trumbull. 'He is of middle stature', narrated the envoy, and 'of a vigorous constitution, if he would not destroy it by excessive debauchery'. He could 'pass for the strongest, most adroit and indefatigable prince in Europe, for all bodily and warlike exercises'.

The Saxon Elector's 'inclinations and education lead him to soldiering', he continued. Although he was 'the last of his branch (having no children nor hopes of any), he has a restless ambitious spirit which hurries him to the field', in case he should be 'surprised with a peace' before he had a chance 'of signalizing himself, which hitherto he has not omitted'. Obliged by his brother's death to stay at home in 1694 and receive homage, as well as 'to lay the foundation of government', Augustus now 'returns to his old inclination, and scorns to languish in his residence'. That year he hoped to come 'hand to fist with a Grand Vizier'.[1]

It was a fair summary of the man with whom he had spent so much time: around five feet nine inches tall and solidly built;[2] blue-eyed with chestnut hair; incredibly strong; having no legitimate heir; a military glory-seeker; ambitious, but always ready to give himself over to pleasure in the shape of any debauch. It neglected any assessment of his political growth under Schöning's tutelage, his extravagance or his charm, but overall it was a fair resumé.

Certainly, this 'restless ambitious sprit' sought to come 'hand to fist' with the Turkish commander. Yet the other side of Augustus, the hedonistic seducer, had to be accommodated first. Pleasure remained to the fore. It diluted ambition and ensured that Augustus grappled with others first.

'I long to hear how you like my Elector and what women he likes best', Stepney gushed to Lexington in June. His lordship apparently

119

obliged, since on 12 July Stepney responded that 'I am sorry my Elector can find no better pastime with you than dancing and tennis'. He had hoped that Augustus would 'leave that sauntering life and buckle to business when he got into the Emperor's eye'. Now Stepney fancied that 'he'll take a billiard-table and tennis-court with him to the camp'.

As July progressed things remained much the same, save that Augustus was now embroiled with a new mistress. This young lady was related to Harrach and to Count Leopold Lamberg, the favourite of the Emperor's elder son Joseph.[3] Yet, despite the fact that she would remain Augustus's primary paramour until 1701 (p 218), we know neither the age nor the Christian name of the Lamberg lass. She enters the mistress list under her more commonly known title of Countess Esterle.

'You will have found my Elector to be just the man I described him to you', Stepney prattled to Lexington on 23 July. 'Mlle Lamberg is a pretty creature, and I hope may make him forget his Königs-marck'. Retreating into the history of such matters, Stepney related that the Imperial family 'bawded for the Elector of Bavaria to engage him to the bonne partie', all 'to the prejudice of their daughter'.[4] Since Augustus was commanding on the same terms as 'Blue Max', Stepney approved of him being catered for in like fashion.

The same day that Stepney wrote this, he nonchalantly visited Eberhardine, who had arrived in Frankfurt with her sister on 15 July, hoping to see her father. She appeared well after taking the waters at Ems. On the night of 23 July, Stepney was invited 'to merry-making with her in a garden where we supped'. Two days later the Margrave of Bayreuth arrived, and Stepney returned his attention to the other man in Eberhardine's life.

He told Blathwayt on 26 July that Augustus had a list of personal grievances against the English crown. He had 'expected his brother's Garter, but it was never offered him'. He had presented William with Polish horses 'and no compliment has been returned'. Moreover, the King protected Friesen, whom Augustus 'calls his rebel'.

But this was all too serious for the flippancy of Stepney's current lifestyle. On 7 August he was telling Blathwayt that Prince Charles of Neuburg (p 134) had regaled him with 'a great many of the Elector of Saxony's amorous adventures at Vienna, for it seems he has laid about him there wonderfully'.

'DILIGENT MARCHES'

The mighty Saxon did not perform so wonderfully in Hungary; in truth, the campaign of 1695 is generally held to be a disaster. What is debatable is how much of the blame for this shambles should attach to Augustus. Moreover, to say that his campaign was conducted in Hungary is somewhat misleading for the contemporary reader, since then the term applied to the 'historic Hungary' that had existed before the Turkish conquest and would totter on until 1918. Besides its incontestably Magyar lands, this Hungary encompassed Slovakia and tracts of the present-day states of Croatia, Serbia, Romania and the Ukraine.

Although parts of the former Hungarian kingdom remained unconquered by the Habsburgs, and Magyar insurrections against Austrian rule were endemic, since 1683 the Imperial armies had wrested the bulk of the realm from the Turks. The two major obstacles to their further advance were Turkish occupation of Belgrade and Temesvar (Timişoara). As a result, during Augustus's two campaigns in 'Hungary', such action as there was occurred in northern Serbia and south-west Romania, in an area bounded by the rivers Tisza, Danube, Mureş and Timiş.

Augustus was also hemmed in by controls. Five senior Imperial generals, headed by Schöning's old foe, the venerable and cautious Fieldmarshal Caprara, formed a travelling Kriegsrat. To ensure that the Emperor's will be done, the function of this council of war was to sanction (or stifle) any major initiative by the army's young commander. Augustus listened to this body, and it is reasonable to suggest, as does Haake, that the culpability for the errors of the 1695 campaign should be apportioned between Augustus and the Kriegsrat, with Caprara being most to blame for the major blunders.

Augustus only left Vienna on 28 July. Travelling down the Danube, he joined up with his army of 50,000 near Futtak (Futog), west of Novi Sad, on 10 August. Further to the east, on the River Mureş, were 10,000 more troops under Fieldmarshal Veterani. The chief objective of the campaign was the capture of Temesvar. For this purpose a large arsenal with heavy artillery had been prepared at Lippa (Lipova), which also stands on the Mureş.

The Turks moved first. After a feint east of Novi Sad, their main attack was launched east of Belgrade. The Kriegsrat decided to shadow this assault. Hugging the rivers Tisza, Aranca and Mureş, the Imperialists marched north and east. Compromises in the Kriegsrat begat delays, during which, in a fresh advance, the Ottoman armies stormed Lippa on 7 September and blew up the magazine. With Upper Hungary open to the Turks, Augustus pressed east. The Turks retreated, but also mounted a new attack near Novi Sad, and Augustus marched west to cover it.

En route he learned that a Turkish attack was planned against Transylvania. On 20 September the Saxon split his forces, sending the infantry with a cavalry screen westwards to support the Danube garrisons at Petrovaradin (east of Novi Sad), while he led the Imperial cavalry eastwards to join Veterani in the defence of Transylvania. The problem was that, having ordered the latter out of fixed positions on 13 September, Augustus had neglected to inform him of his subsequent moves. Moreover, the Turks had captured one of Veterani's riders and his current plans. They fell on his isolated corps at Lugos (Lugoj), east of Temesvar, on 21 September and massacred over half of his force. Veterani was among those whose heads were lopped off on the field.

Having learned of this disaster, Augustus pushed on down the Mureş, reaching Deva on 3 October. As Stepney later wrote, 'his diligent marches toward Deva has made the Turks quit the design they had of forcing their way into Transylvania'. Yet, although this door was bolted, the Turks had long since trotted back to base. The campaign was over for that year. Augustus left his army on 11 October and was back in Vienna by 22 October.

That same month, Stepney told Under-Secretary John Ellis (p 264, n 6) that 'my Elector is returning to Saxony full of shame and regret that he has been able to do nothing'. Later he reported that Augustus was 'so far resolved to try his fortune on another campaign', that he had already offered the Emperor his remaining troops 'on what conditions he pleases'. This was an exaggeration, it was Leopold who tendered the command of the next campaign to Augustus. If it suggests anything, it probably indicates a desire by Vienna to bind Saxony tighter in support of Imperial objectives, just as Bavaria had been tied during 'Blue Max's' years of command in Hungary.

Augustus was hardly in a hurry to leave Vienna in 1695. 'I perceive the Elector of Saxony passes his life so agreeably with you, that he has no thoughts of house and home', Stepney burbled to Lexington in late November, 'and I hear he likes campaigning so well, that nothing less will serve his turn than your attacking Belgrade next summer'. The last point was probably just rumour; the former was not. The wife of the Austrian general Count Rabutin helped relieve the tensions of the campaign. This might explain why Rabutin would figure as one of the sternest critics of Augustus's two-year stint in Hungary.

'NOTHING FOR ME TO NEGOTIATE'

Following six months as 'an itinerant envoy' in Germany and the Low Countries, at the end of 1695 Stepney was appointed envoy extraordinary to various princes on the middle and lower Rhine. It was hardly onerous work: 'I am half-drowned with glasses of ceremony, and have lost my hearing by continual drums and trumpets', he nattered to Ellis from Düsseldorf.

On 20 January 1696 he was told 'to prepare to go forthwith to Dresden, as soon as you shall receive His Majesty's instructions for that court'. The issue that prompted Stepney's possible return to the Electorate was the prospect of obtaining Saxon troops for the Rhine in the 1696 campaign. Whose initiative this was remains unclear.

If Dresden was the prime mover, then one can only speculate upon motive, while any deal would relate solely to troops 'surplus' to the 8000 already committed to Hungary for 1695–96. Possibly Augustus's financial state led him to show interest in the earlier English offer of subsidizing his 'spare men' pro rata. It may also have been a means of pressurizing Vienna, who were equally attracted by the chance of recruiting more troops from Saxony. Perhaps once again Schöning's *Revers* and Augustus's terms of command were part of the bargain.

Stepney was clear-headed enough after his experiences at Dresden. Any new mission to Saxony depended upon 'how the Elector may think fit to dispose of his troops', he remarked to Trumbull on 12 February. 'If he resolve to send them to Hungary, there will be nothing for me to negotiate at Dresden'.

Writing to Lexington on 20 March, he referred to Augustus's 'sudden flight to Vienna'. Stepney is our only evidence for this trip, and it must have been brief, since Augustus was back in Dresden, meeting with representatives of his States, from late March to April 1696. However, assuming that this 'sudden flight' took place, its purpose was presumably an attempt to interest the Imperial court (and Lexington?) in surplus Saxon troops.

Vienna quickly took 4000, concluding an agreement with Augustus that March for a total contingent of 12,000 Saxons in Hungary for each of the next three years. Despite this, we can infer that Dresden was still trying to hire out men to the English as well. And Augustus would have had yet other soldiers for sale, since he and Schöning had worked to increase the overall strength of the Saxon army to 20,000 in 1696.

For on 21 April Stepney wrote to Lexington from Frankfurt, referring to Augustus again offering troops against full (not pro rata) subsidies. Three days later he thanked his lordship for his (untraceable) letter of 14 April 'and the fine proposition' he had received from Augustus. 'If the French had their swords at our throats, the Elector could not have offered more Jewish terms'. In any case, Stepney adjudged the matter at an end, telling Trumbull that he had 'left all hopes of our having any Saxons this year on the Rhine'.

'THE SAME WANT OF EVERYTHING'

On 14 April 1696 Lexington's 25-year-old cousin, secretary and name-sake Robert Sutton penned a circular letter to various correspondents: 'On entend de Saxe que les Troupes, que cet Electeur doit envoyer pour renforcer celles qu'il a deja en Hongrie, sont en mouvement'. It was now certain that there would be 12,000 Saxons in Hungary, and no more French from young Robert.

'Finding that all my correspondents understand Englisch [sic]', he wrote on 25 April, 'I am glad of this opportunity of delivering both you and myself from my barbarous French'. He then turned to current plans for delivering Christendom from the barbarous Turks. 'The four thousand [extra] Saxons engaged by the last treaty will be timely in Hungary'. Even Augustus seemed willing to get on with the campaign that year: 'General Rose is preparing the Elector's baggage here [Vienna], that he may not be obliged to make a long stay here after his arrival'. A week later Sutton noted that Augustus was expected in the Imperial capital that night, 2 May.

In his letter to Blathwayt of 12 May, the elder Sutton was less sanguine. 'The generals are all going to the rendezvous near Buda, and the Elector goes the end of next week', related Lexington. Most people believed 'that they will undertake some siege, either that of Belgrade or Temesvar'. But the ambassador feared that it would all end like the previous year, 'for we have the same generals, the same factions and disunion, and the same want of everything'.[5]

On 19 May Sutton junior reported to Ellis that Augustus 'is gone post to review his troops'. These were marching from their quarters in Upper Hungary 'towards the rendezvous in Buda'. A week later Lexington informed Blathwayt that Augustus had left Vienna on 22 May for Buda, 'where the whole army already is, and the siege of Temesvar is actually resolved'. He still feared failure, because the preparations were 'but slenderly made', and some of the generals were 'so inveterate, that they would rather the whole business should miscarry than that Caprara, who commands again, should succeed'.[6]

The younger Sutton chronicled Augustus's arrival in Buda on 24 May. Next day he crossed the Danube by a bridge of boats and reviewed the Saxon infantry, which he saw exercised on the 26th. It is not clear when Augustus left Buda, but he led his army across the Tisza at Szeged on 12 June. From there they marched south-east to camp near Csanad (Cenadg), between the rivers Mureş and Aranca. Other forces covered Petrovaradin and Transylvania. The task of the main army was, as Lexington had said, to besiege and capture Temesvar.

124

However, as his lordship had also opined, there was 'the same want of everything'. Short of troops, artillery, money and above all gunpowder, Augustus's army did not break camp until 30 July, and Temesvar was only beleaguered on 3 August. 'I am promised a journal of the siege', Stepney announced to Ellis. If he ever received such a document, it would prove to be an abridged version.

On 4 August the unsporting Turks crossed the Danube west of Belgrade. For Augustus the issue was whether to hold the invaders with a defensive line, while continuing the siege, or to send the whole army against them for a major battle. The Saxon preferred the former strategy, even preparing a plan for storming the fortress, but Caprara's opposition eventually prevailed.

When the Turks were held, the fieldmarshal was initially overruled and the besieging force opened its trenches on 12 August. However, a renewed Turkish advance won Caprara the day. Although only 50 metres from the citadel, the siege of Temesvar was called off. On 19 August the heavy artillery was returned to Arad and the entire army of 38,000 moved south-westwards, marching between two parallel tributaries of the Tisza, the Bega and Timiş rivers.

Two days later they made cavalry contact with the Turks north-east of Pardany. Then, on Sunday 26 August 1696, the two armies finally had what Stepney termed 'a brush together'. The battle by the Bega commenced late in the day, at five in the evening. The left wing of the Imperialists took heavy casualties, while in the centre and on the right flank they had the better of the action. As night fell, the fighting stilled. The next day the armies lined up for round two, but neither made a move. The want of food and forage gave added incentive for both sides to retreat to existing fixed positions.

Augustus assessed his losses at 3000 dead and wounded, which he contrasted favourably to Lewis of Baden's record in Hungary, contending that the latter often wrote off 6000 troops merely on a march. In a letter to Ellis of 5 September the younger Sutton was vague about casualties, but he reckoned that 'upon the whole it is but too plain we are come off the worst for it'. One week later he reported that 'all that write from the army' maintained that 'the Imperialists had given the enemy an entire rout had they not wanted daylight'. Such a view was hardly surprising; yet the fact remained that the Turks had only taken 4000 casualties. Hence it is hard to come up with any other result for the battle than a score-draw.[7]

'The poor Elector of Saxony is beat about like a shuttlecock', remarked Stepney, with reference to Augustus being compelled to lift the siege of Temesvar. The envoy believed that 'he will leave the army in a huff and make the best of his way to Dresden'. He was correct in one respect: having brought up his army to cover any further Turkish sallies across the Danube, on 13 September Augustus suddenly left it in a considerable tizz. But he travelled to Vienna, not Dresden.

He was traduced and his honour was impugned. The story was circulating that he had been plastered on the day of the battle, and had ordered his forces into action against a decision of the Kriegsrat. Whether Augustus was drunk in charge of an army is impossible to say; the Saxon maintained that he'd been too busy that day to eat, let alone imbibe, while none of the English envoys even hint at the rumour. As to who was responsible for attacking the Turks on the Bega, there seems little reason to dispute our hero's contention that the Kriegsrat was unanimously in favour of such action.

Augustus completed his self-defence with a blistering attack upon the state of the Imperial armies, which he handed personally to Leopold on 1 October. The Emperor replied in his own hand 12 days later, accepting the criticisms, promising rectification and confirming his confidence in the Saxon. He offered him the command once more in 1697, replaced Caprara with his best general, Eugene of Savoy (1663–1736), and undertook to prepare for the siege of Belgrade, as Augustus had proposed. In short, he hardly treated the young Elector as an inept inebriate.

'LEAD IN THE PENCIL'

Somewhat mollified, Augustus stayed on in Vienna and would remain there until late November 1696. In normal circumstances, it would hardly be surprising for Sutton to report that 'the Elector of Saxony is still in town'. His main mistress Countess Esterle was there; so was his great chum Joseph, the Emperor's womanizing elder son. However, for Augustus these were not normal times: in the summer he had lost two important advisers, while in the autumn his first uncontestable progeny came into the world.

In June 1696 Haxthausen died, and on 28 August he was followed into the grave by the 55-year-old Schöning. We know nothing of Augustus's emotional reaction to their deaths;[8] the administrative details he tidied up from Vienna. In late October Stepney reported that Augustus had 'disposed of the employment vacated' by the dead men. Pflug (p 90) became Grand Chamberlain, while Frau Schöning received a pension of 3000 dollars for life.

On 7 October 1696 Eberhardine proved Stepney and others wrong, by bearing Augustus's only legitimate child. The new Kurprinz took his father's name, Friedrich August. Three weeks later

Aurora von Königsmarck emulated the Electress's deed: in the Imperial city of Goslar (south of Brunswick) the Countess gave birth to Moritz Hermann, who as Maurice de Saxe would later become one of Louis XV's most famous commanders. Aurora's genes were still in evidence in the nineteenth century; her great-great-grand-daughter was the French novelist George Sand, one of whose lovers was Chopin.

Aurora had left Dresden in April 1696. It is still uncertain why she and Augustus split up; von Pöllnitz's coarse contention that it resulted from body odours seems implausible. Stepney claimed that Aurora left because Augustus 'bestowed a greater share of his favour' upon Countess Esterle; this too seems unlikely.

In February 1696 Aurora was gaily refusing to shun the 'sweet yoke' of love in her court production of the opera-ballet *Das Musenfest*. It is hard to believe that she, who had joined the harem at Carlsbad, would free herself from 'das süße Joch' simply because of her lover's affairs. More convincing is the argument that it was one particular dalliance that caused her to flounce out: that which Augustus conducted with Fatime, a young Turk brought up in her household as a Königsmarck clone.[9]

Initially Aurora seems to have kept the birth of her son a secret. The Lutheran priest in Goslar merely registered that a refined gentlewoman had given birth to a boy christened Moritz. Soon the whole town council knew, which meant that Liselotte got to hear of it. She wrote to Sophie about that 'wonderful creature', the 'shameless' Aurora, who got the mayor and syndics to witness her 'bastard'. Germany was certainly different 'in her day'.[10] However, she was rather impressed by Augustus's feat: for ages people had said that he could not have children; so he'd brought two sons into the world at one go, just to show that 'there was lead in the pencil, after all'.[11]

Augustus did not seem much worried one way or the other; there were far more pressing matters to concern a glory-seeker. Early in November Augustus dined with Lexington in Vienna and brought up a little matter that the English had neglected. As his lordship reported to Blathwayt, the Elector 'gave me to understand that he wished to have the Garter', and hoped the ambassador would intimate this to William. Lexington inquired 'whether I ought to give him hopes of it, when he comes back, if he speaks to me of it again'.

Blathwayt replied at the end of the month that 'His Majesty allows your lordship to give him hopes of it', if the matter was raised again; however, it was to be made clear to Augustus 'that it is not intended he should have it immediately'. He must earn it first, 'by a hearty engagement in the common cause, of which there is great likelihood since the death of Schöning'.[12]

127

It is not clear whether the exotic combination of Garter and stick was ever waved before Augustus's jaded gaze. By the time that Blathwayt's instructions arrived, he was back in Dresden. At the end of December 1696 Stepney dutifully chronicled the Elector's return, and that Frederick III of Brandenburg had gone to visit him in Saxony. On the first day of 1697 the envoy informed Trumbull that Augustus had written to William in his own hand to announce the birth of the Kurprinz.

Such was hardly news; while, predictably, what *was* new in Augustus's life was not imparted. Amongst the clichéd Latin phrases that passed for inter-monarchical correspondence, there was no mention of his latest scheme. Augustus had decided to bid for the crown of Poland.

'My greatest ambition is glory'
King's ransom 1697–1702

Chapter 13

'Whoever bids most'
Purchasing the Polish crown 1697

'INCAPABLE OF GOVERNMENT'

On 17 June 1696, the last in a series of heart attacks terminated the life of King Jan III Sobieski of Poland at the age of 67. He had reigned since 1674, but the deeds that had earned him renown throughout Europe were now a distant memory.

In September 1683, forming the right wing of the liberating Christian army, Sobieski's Polish cavalry had charged from the slopes of Kahlenberg to end the siege of Vienna and put the vast Ottoman army to flight. For some time thereafter Sobieski was a household word. In England engravings bore the motto: 'Great champion of the cross whose glorious name/Outshines all heroes in the book of fame'.[1]

Yet by March 1688 Sobieski, now virtually a footnote in that book, was telling the Polish Senate that 'future generations will wonder in astonishment' that following 'such resounding victories, such international triumphs and glory, we now face, alas, eternal shame and irreversible loss'. For Poland now found itself 'without resources, helpless, and seemingly incapable of government'.[2]

Ineffectual government was indeed the besetting sin of the Republic or Commonwealth (*Rzeczpospolita*) of Poland–Lithuania, which next to Muscovy was then the largest state in Europe. It was epitomized by the dictum that 'Poland subsists by anarchy' (*Polska nierządem stoi*). Ruled until 1385 by its founding dynasty the Piasts, the lands of the Polish crown (*Korona*) then joined with those of the Grand Duchy of Lithuania in a personal union under the Jagiełło dynasty. When this became extinct in the male line in 1572, the Republic's crown went up for auction.

The players in this roup were the major powers of Europe, their client-states and factions of Poland's nobility, the *szlachta*. Comprising some seven to ten per cent of the Republic's population, the dominant interest of the szlachta was to retain their extensive range of privileges. These, herded together under the umbrella concept of 'Golden Freedom' (*aurea libertas*), constituted a liberty to line their pockets with gold; first by selling their votes during royal elections, and thereafter by running re-greased palms over the creaking wheels of Poland's sophisticated and decentralized governmental machinery.

If it conformed to the interests of the szlachta that the wheels should go round, they could and did revolve. If it served their aims that the central state mechanism should grind to a halt, then the nobility had all manner of sophisticated legal and parliamentary devices to produce such an outcome.

They had the Statute of Nihil Novi, which prevented the king from introducing any new laws without their consent. Further restraints upon the king's powers lay in the Henrician Articles, which bound *all* Polish monarchs, plus the Pacta Conventa, which was the specific agreement extracted from each individual king. Sworn at his coronation, it was an electoral manifesto to which the ruler could be held far more accountable than the promissory notes of contemporary democracies. Overall, as in Hungary, the nobility of Poland sought to produce a king 'whose plaits they could hold in their hands'.[3]

In the bicameral Diet (*Sejm*) other procedures could be utilized. The upper house or Senate was composed of lifetime royal appointees representing central and local government and the church. The lower house, the Chamber of Envoys (*Izba Poselska*) comprised delegates of the dietines (*sejmiki*), which were provincial assemblies dominated by the stooges of the great magnate clans. Through the Liberum Veto any envoy could invoke the principle of unanimity (*nemine contradicente*), and with a shout of 'I deny' (*veto*) or 'I do not allow it' (*nie pozwalam*) he could shatter the proceedings of a Sejm. A handful of złoty tossed to some client of a magnate, or later to some tool of a foreign power, could terminate Poland's entire legislative and financial programme.

Although all nobles were equal, some were more equal than others. As in Hungary with its 'sandalled noblemen', a sizeable element of the szlachta had only their status and rights to mark them out from their low-born fellows. The 'nobles in clogs' were objects of derision. Without land, wealth or education they tied themselves to the interests of the magnates (*magnateria*): the wealthiest szlachta families and clans, who controlled the latifundia in the south and east of the Republic and dominated its chief lay and clerical posts.

Both Poland and Lithuania vaunted a Grand Chancellor, Vice-Chancellor, Treasurer, Grand Marshal and Court Marshal. Likewise each had an army, commanded by a Grand General (*Hetman wielki*) and a Field Commander (*Hetman polny*). The incumbents of these 14 posts were lifetime appointments made by the king. Until death allowed him to supplant such notables with his own placemen, a monarch could merely propitiate their powers. Little wonder that Stepney adjudged Poland's king to be 'not so much a sovereign, as a companion or at most the head of their nobility'.[4]

However, to see the Polish king as impotent is hardly correct. The szlachta fetish of insistence upon their rights (with little or no reference to duties) originated in and was maintained by their fear of absolutism. And there was always a potential for such an outcome in the powers which the monarch retained.

Ordinary Diets lasting for six weeks were called at least every two years, while an Extraordinary Sejm lasted only two weeks. Not only did the king set the agenda of these assemblies, but there were long periods between such sessions when he determined policy, assisted only by the Senate Council. Although royal decrees technically had to be approved by the next Sejm, effectively they could represent a political *fait accompli*. Moreover, in foreign policy the monarch's prerogatives were far greater than in the domestic sphere.

Even this fleeting survey of the Republic's intricate constitutional set-up shows that the Polish crown was no sinecure, but thorny with frustration. Following his victory, Liselotte was not alone in wondering why Augustus had not been content to live out a quiet life as Elector of Saxony. Instead he had frivolously mortgaged his future happiness by becoming King of Poland, where he would be sovereign in name only. For unaided he could never make himself absolute ruler of that 'interesting and fickle (*unbeständige*) nation'.[5]

Her observations were pertinent; yet, before we consider why Augustus should have taken the path he did, it is well to remember that he was never the sole candidate in the field. Poland's crown of thorns tempted a number of masochistic princelings to raise their aspiring brows above the parapet of a quiet life.

'PRETENDERS TO THAT CROWN'

'The King of Poland is dead, and there are already several pretenders to that crown', Sutton wrote soon after Sobieski's demise. Of course, most candidates had been gearing themselves up for entry into the race throughout Sobieski's long illness. But, since the Polish constitution precluded election of a successor during the reigning king's lifetime (*vivente rege*), there was now an interregnum, dominated by the Interrex, who became Poland's *de facto* ruler.

In 1696 the Interrex was the Cardinal-Primate of Poland, the Archbishop of Gniezno, Michał Radziejowski (1645–1705). A skilful and slippery politician, the Cardinal when younger had lived for many years in Paris. There is little doubt that he favoured France in this latest round of the Bourbon–Habsburg tussle over Poland's crown; less distinct at the outset was the identity of Louis XIV's 'favourite son'.

Initially it was the Emperor's preferences which seemed clearer. On 30 June 1696 Lexington told Blathwayt flatly that Leopold had 'declared for Prince Charles of Neuburg'.[6] This young man was the brother of the Empress Eleonore and was also married to a member of the important Radziwiłł clan of Lithuania.

Writing five days later from Düsseldorf, Stepney was more cautious. While believing that Prince Charles would 'put in for a candidate', he warned that 'he has neither an head for government nor a purse to promote his pretension'. Of course, if Leopold stood by him 'with money and interest, much may be done'; however, the envoy considered that the Emperor was 'already engaged' to another relative, namely Sobieski's eldest son James (Jakub), who was married to the Empress's sister. But none of this guesswork altered Stepney's golden rule for the Polish election: 'whoever bids most stands the fairest to be anointed'.

There were other major contenders in this beauty contest. The wealthy Prince Livio Odescalchi was the nephew of a former Pope. Leopold's long-serving commander Lewis of Baden had also tossed his baton into the ring. Initially he won the support of the Elector of Brandenburg, who hoped by such a deal to plonk his predatory paws upon a chunk of Polish Prussia. 'Blue Max' of Bavaria was a reluctant runner; his second wife Teresa was the daughter of Sobieski. But he lacked finance, and his eyes were currently fixed upon the greater prize of the Spanish succession, where the son of his first marriage promised to be a major beneficiary. The young Duke of Lorraine was another German contender with Polish connections, but although he was a nephew of the Emperor he hardly set any eminent pulses racing.

Then there was Sobieski's French-born widow Maria Kazimierza, better known as Marysieńka (1641–1716). She opposed her eldest son's claim to the throne because of James's marriage to a Habsburg. Instead she made her own bid to serve as the power behind the throne, not only by backing the claims of her second son Alexander, but also by dangling her hand for remarriage to the Crown Grand General Jabłonowski.

But once Louis XIV made known his candidate and, more importantly, sent over some ready cash to his hard-pressed envoys, native contenders dropped back in the running. The Cardinal-Primate distributed Louis' loot, mostly within his own needy circle, and then asked for more. Versailles, still engaged in the costly Nine Years War, was reluctant; so was their candidate, Louis' cousin the Prince of Conti. He being another with 'proclivities', according to the indefatigable Liselotte, it was unlikely that life away from the French court held any great appeal.[7] Nor was Conti involved in the campaign to make him king; the whole affair was managed by Louis and French diplomats in Warsaw.

It was the skilful work of the latter, plus the francophile tendencies of Radziejowski and his cohorts, that made Conti the clear frontrunner as election day approached. 'We hear the Prince of Conti's affairs go on very successfully', Sutton told Ellis on 22 June 1697. And 'there appears no redress', unless the Emperor could be 'persuaded to abandon all other thoughts' and not only endorse Lewis of Baden but 'open his purse too; though if he should, 'tis ten to one he finds it empty'.

But Leopold had little interest in Lewis of Baden, nor had he now any need to trawl through his straitened treasury. Austria was backing a new candidate who was spending his own money like water. Little wonder that Sutton could report that 'the gentry never appeared in such numbers at any former election'; the bouquet of boodle was never so pungent. That the Englishman should have missed Augustus's entry onto the scene is less surprising. Even in Warsaw there were those who were equally unsuspecting: an anonymous diarist of the election devotes one reference to Augustus. On Wednesday 26 June, the day of the first ballot, he recorded a 'rumour' that the Elector of Saxony was also competing for the Polish crown.[8]

However, Augustus had not been altogether invisible. Certainly, he always intended to enter the contest late, when other candidates had exhausted their resources. Yet this was merely one move in the skilful and cynical election campaign that he waged over several months. He had committed himself to winning the Polish crown since December 1696. Such ambition had been sparked by a dream.

In this case the original dream was not a fantasy of Augustus. However, it led him to a prophecy which he did adopt as his own; and a scaled-down, though more sober, version of it informed his ambitions until his death. Yet he always remained realistic enough not to treat the revelation as self-fulfilling; it had to be worked for. Capturing the Polish crown demanded more than divination: besides an army, it entailed dollars, diplomacy and duplicity.

'CETTE IDÉE CHIMÉRIQUE'

Augustus returned to Dresden from Vienna on 27 November 1696. Having met the Elector of Brandenburg and enlightened his fellow-rulers about the birth of his heir, in mid-December Augustus found himself in Torgau, a town on the Elbe north of Dresden. One night, while prowling about its castle, he discovered a painting of a man being attacked by lions and defended by tigers. He inquired about the picture, and was told that it represented a dream that was explained in an old book of prophecies.

Intrigued, Augustus obtained the tome later that month, and in it he discovered a prophecy that could not fail to fascinate him. This foretold that a Saxon prince of half-Danish blood called Augustus would be elected King of Poland in 1696. Later this same Augustus would become Holy Roman Emperor and, with the help of a Württemberg prince who had once served as a Danish field-marshal, he would conquer Hungary, the Ottoman Empire and even part of Asia, and would thereafter establish his throne in Constantinople.

This was all too much for a young prince steeped in Saxon superstition, who was a fan of Nostradamus and had little if any religious zeal. The 1696 date for the Polish election was unfortunately out by a year, but this was a small matter. That Augustus went out of his way to hire a Württemberger in Danish service will become evident. The attempt to make his House of Wettin heirs to the German Empire was also to feature in his future plans. However, conquering the Turkish Empire and setting himself up in Constantinople went by the board, following his failure to wrest Moldavia from the Ottomans in 1698 (C14).

In short, Augustus adapted the prophecy to political realities. The revelation spurred him into action; thereafter, events had as much influence upon his policies as the words of soothsayers. Moreover, there were other factors prompting him to seek the Polish crown, which the prophecy simply rationalized.

First was the unheralded competition between the lay Electors of the Reich to attain the status of monarch. Augustus had long known that Frederick of Brandenburg sought to become King of Prussia. George Louis of Hanover was slated for the English throne, while 'Blue Max' was eyeing both Poland and Spain. In such circumstances Augustus, the protagonist of the House of Wettin, which had once ranked next to the Habsburgs in the Empire's affairs, could hardly remain a mere Elector.

Second, the frustrations of Hungary, with its command by Kriegsrat, impelled Augustus towards a sphere of action where he could play an independent role, while the treatment he received in these years exacerbated his animus towards Vienna. Moreover, Poland also held economic attractions. By the standards of the day Saxony was a major manufacturer, yet it lacked important commodities which underdeveloped Poland could provide. The latter, in turn, could act as a market for Saxon exports.

But paramount among Augustus's motives was his yearning to score his name in the pages of history. The abstraction of fame remained the spur. 'My greatest ambition is glory', he pronounced late in 1697, 'and I will strive for it until the end of my days'.[9]

Striving for the Polish crown began almost immediately. In late December 1696 and again the next month, Augustus addressed the financial implications of his bid for that throne. Doubtless some of that cash went on Carnival. In February 1697 Augustus paraded through Dresden garbed as the Sultan leading his Janissaries; an intriguing display by a prince who nominally remained commander of the Imperial armies in Hungary.[10] Perhaps it symbolized that henceforth Augustus would be acting against Habsburg interests.

Such was certainly the focus of his diplomacy. In early February Augustus sent his Livonian general Rose to Rome, in an effort to win over both Pope Innocent XII and Louis XIV to his candidature. To the pontiff Augustus promised his conversion to Catholicism, a prerequisite for any King of Poland. To Louis' ambassador there, Cardinal Forbin, he proposed an alliance against the Habsburgs.

In April 1697 Augustus upped the ante: he offered to withdraw Saxon troops from Hungary and, if Louis paid him the requisite subsidies to maintain 20,000 men, to use them to attack the Emperor in Bohemia or Silesia. All that he asked in return was that Louis drop his support for Conti and back him instead. But the French would not bite; Forbin later reported that it had been made clear to Rose that Versailles was too committed to change policy, and he dismissed Augustus's ambitions as 'cette idée chimérique'.[11]

A back-stabbing agenda did not prevent Augustus from showing his face in Vienna, nor did he look particularly threatening to the Imperial court. 'The Elector of Saxony has hurt himself by a fall at hunting and goes upon crutches', Stepney yarned to Trumbull on 1 February, 'which I do not tell you for news, for this prince is never without bruises and plasters'.[12]

This gave our hobbling hero good cover. In the spa town of Baden, south of Vienna, he made contact with his cousin Duke Christian August von Sachsen-Zeitz (1666–1725), who was now Bishop of Raab (Sopron). The latter had converted to Catholicism only in 1691, and Stepney claimed that 'about four years ago' Augustus had been 'ready to fight a duel' with him 'for having changed his religion'. In March 1697 the Elector wanted his relative to help him make the same transition.

With his diplomacy, slush fund and conversion under way, Augustus made his first test of the Polish waters through a 30-year-old soldier. In later years Jakob Heinrich Flemming (1667–1728) would become Augustus's most important adviser, but in 1697 he was merely the colonel of a Saxon dragoon regiment.[13]

Born in Pomerania, Flemming spoke fluent Polish and French, and after studying law in Germany and Holland he had entered the Prussian army. In 1688 he took part in William III's landing in England and even found time to attend a few lectures at Oxford. Five years later he entered Saxon service as an adjutant to John George IV; he kept the post under Augustus.

On learning that Flemming would be visiting Poland to see his cousin, who was married to the Castellan of Chełmno, Jan Jerzy Przebendowski, Augustus summoned him to Vienna in April 1697. After lecturing the colonel on the prophecies of Nostradamus, the Elector finally disclosed his objective. Like others, Flemming thought his sovereign was leaving it too late, since the Electoral Sejm opened on 15 May; Augustus replied that his tardiness was intentional. Flemming was also deeply perturbed by the prospective conversion. Only when Augustus presented him on 17 April with a signed undertaking that no member of his family or court, nor any subject, would be obliged to renounce Lutheranism did Flemming agree to undertake the mission.[14]

In late April Flemming travelled to Warsaw, where he revealed Augustus's plans to Przebendowski. After some vacillation the Pole took up the cause and introduced Flemming to Radziejowski and other leaders. The Cardinal wrote a letter to Augustus on 24 May, promising to serve his interests once he received personally from Augustus clear testimony of his conversion to Catholicism.[15] Leaving Przebendowski as campaign manager, Flemming returned to Vienna at the end of May.

At this time too, given French coolness, Augustus turned to the Imperial court. It was only politics, after all. He informed Leopold and his Vice-Chancellor Count Kinski of his intention to convert to the true faith and compete for the Polish crown. The Austrians hardly begged him to stay on as commander in Hungary instead. Whether they expected Augustus to win in Warsaw is debatable, but at least they now had a vigorous and attractive candidate to back against Conti.

'UN ROYAUME VAUT UNE MESSE'

It was now time for Augustus to deal with the religious issue. Becoming a Catholic hardly threw him into spiritual turmoil. As a young Saxon nobleman later couched it, Augustus could only have changed

138

his religion if he had had one to swap in the first place. Since at the time of his conversion he was at best an agnostic, Augustus did not then trade faiths; he merely adopted one ('er nahm nur eine an').[16]

Stepney judged his policy similarly. Augustus 'is made King of Poland at the expense of his religion, which was never very great', he remarked in July 1697. To Ellis he wrote starkly that the Elector was of the 'opinion that "un royaume vaut une messe"'.

Later Augustus would show his contempt for Catholic rites in many ways: wrapping his rosary around his dog's neck, so that it could attend mass with its master, was but a mild example. Yet as a ruler, he remained acutely aware of the political weight attaching to a public aura of faith. In his 'Regel pour la posterrité', he advised his son to be neither a bigot nor a hypocrite, but to display to the people a genuine devotion, which they expected of their ruler.[17]

The Saxon's formal conversion took place early on 2 June 1697 in his cousin's house at Baden. One account portrays Augustus with tears in his eyes; they were probably induced by laughter. Although he received communion according to the Roman rite, that was more or less all. The Bishop of Raab signed a woolly 'attestation' of his cousin's abjuration of the Lutheran faith and his profession of the Catholic. However, the document was neither dated nor witnessed, nor did it bear Augustus's counter-signature.[18] It is even possible that the prelate lent to the charade solely his signature and seal, with the Elector himself furnishing the bland Latin text later. The two cousins may well have been in collusion. Raab was known for his grasping ways in collecting benefices. Currently he wanted a cardinal's hat, and Augustus certainly put in a good word for him later. Moreover, he ostensibly fell ill with chickenpox on the day of the 'conversion', which permitted him to be unavailable to those querying his less-than-watertight 'attestation' until after the election.

There is no doubt that Augustus had every intention of denouncing this document, or merely 'reverting' to Lutheranism, if he was not elected King of Poland. There was no point in stirring up his States and subjects over the volatile religious issue otherwise. He said as much in his letter to Radziejowski of 4 June, referring to the weighty considerations ('les grandes raisons') that prevented him from making a public conversion before he knew the election result.[19]

Flemming took this letter and the 'attestation' with him when he returned to Warsaw in mid-June. There he managed to confuse matters further, by claiming that Augustus had become a Catholic two years before when visiting Rome. Although some writers still adhere to 1695 as the date of Augustus's conversion, it is doubly incorrect, since his only visit to the Holy City was in early 1694 (p 71). Not surprisingly, many now shared Forbin's view that 'l'ab-juration est si suspecte'.[20] Radziejowski used this argument on 25 June, in an attempt to invalidate Augustus's candidature on the eve of the election.

Augustus's supporters were equally muddled and prevailed upon the Papal Nuncio in Warsaw, Bishop da Via, to rule upon the 'attes-tation' and whether Augustus was a Catholic. Da Via was familiar with the Bishop of Raab, having conducted his conversion in 1691 when serving as Nuncio in Cologne. On 27 June, the crucial day of the election, he penned a *testimonium credulitatis* which validated the content and signature of Raab's 'attestation', and by implication con-firmed that Augustus was of the true faith.[21]

There is little doubt that the judgement by this young though experienced prelate helped Augustus. Whether this was a deliberate act is another question. It is hard to believe that da Via was unaware of the 'stop Conti' movement among the foreign ambassadors. 'Choose the Elector of Saxony, or even the devil himself', the Bran-denburg envoy rasped at the Poles, 'just don't elect Conti'.[22] Off-stage noises came from the Muscovites too, with Tsar Peter's threat that relations with Poland would suffer if they elected a Frenchman: by definition an ally of the Turks, with whom he was at war.

According to the Imperial ambassador, the only thing that would prevent disaster befalling Poland, and bring wavering Conti suppor-ters over to Augustus, would be an unequivocal assurance by the Nuncio that the Saxon was a good Catholic.[23] Possibly da Via pro-duced his *testimonium credulitatis* to save the Poles from themselves and blunt the prospect of civil war and/or Russian invasion. He was certainly accused of partisanship by Louis and by Conti's Polish sup-porters, and subsequently withdrawn by an irate Pope.

It is unlikely that Augustus sent da Via any thanks. He had by then already purchased considerable support. He was also an attractive candidate to some Poles because of his reputation as a commander, however ambivalent this might be. For the Republic still had scores to settle with the Turks and their Tartar allies.

But buying up the szlachta electorate was only part of the battle. A good vote here gave the Saxon legitimacy, but it is doubtful that he expected it to be made unanimous. Even before the double election of 27 June Augustus was preparing to settle the matter by force. Yet his moves were masked by so much secrecy and disinformation that Stepney was prompted to tell Ellis that he was aware of 'no man living, that is so perfect in the art of dissimulation' as the Saxon. Money, men and mystery were the ultimate keys to his success in Poland.

'FLEECING HIS COUNTRY'

It was massive bribery that most popularized Augustus with Poland's noble electorate. In order to find such funds, he bled, peddled and pawned his lands and chattels. It presented no emotional problem. Most German princes played with their realms like toys – save Prussia, which played soldiers instead. For a self-confessed addict to the greater glory of himself and the House of Wettin, the territorial integrity of Saxony was no more sacrosanct to Augustus than would be that of Poland in later years.

His profligacy was evident from the first budget that the young Elector levered out of his States on 1 April 1695, after that assembly had sat for over four months.[24] The sums that they then voted their ruler were, according to Stepney, 'more than was ever allowed to any of his predecessors in their greatest wars and exigencies'.

In terms of hard cash, or more precisely solid gold, Augustus was to receive 18 tuns of that metal valued at RT 100,000 a tun. Of this huge sum of 1.8 million dollars, half was for 'the extremity of the war' against France. The remainder went 'towards paying old debts' and helping Augustus out 'in his domestic expenses, for which his ordinary treasury is not found sufficient'. Not mincing words, the envoy described it as 'fleecing his country', since it was 'more than our little land can bear'. However, Augustus did not think so; he felt short-changed. 'The Elector would have screwed them up to three tuns more', Stepney observed, 'but even his own Privy Council showed it was impossible for the country to bear any greater burden'.

While extortionate, this levy was at least legitimate. However, as Flemming pointed out, Augustus was quite prepared to fill his till by 'unlawful means' (A2). From Dresden Stepney filed a few examples of such fiddles, which he described as 'all dangerous stories to write'.

First, he was 'assured by very good hands the Elector has melted down a very good collection of medals, which have been handed down by his ancestors'. From this gold Augustus's minions had produced 30,000 double-ducats, and disguised their master's responsibility by having 'them stamped as if they had been the coin' of his grandfather, John George II. Then there were the 'light movables', the electoral jewels, which travelled with him to Vienna. Finally, Stepney mentioned a common practice: imprisoning the most rapacious officials, and ransoming their freedom against a cut of their ill-gotten gains.[25]

Shortly after Augustus became Elector, the cell-door clanged shut upon Ludwig Gebhard von Hoym (1630–1711), Saxony's former Treasurer (*Kammerpräsident*). He was accused of tampering with the coinage (*Münzfälschung*), which may have been the model for

141

Augustus's meltdown. Stepney said that Hoym was worth between 600,000 and 700,000 dollars, and the asking price for his freedom was rumoured to be about half that sum. He was finally released after paying 'compensation' (*Bußgeld*) of RT 200,000.

On the 'poacher turned gamekeeper' principle, Augustus restored Hoym to the treasury and his other posts and let him loose on a reform of Saxony's tax and administrative system. Yet this was never likely to produce the requisite sums. Strapped for cash, Augustus had a sale.

The long-disputed Lauenburg went for 1.1 million guilders to Hanover, which for another RT 600,000 also acquired the county of Mansfeld. The Duke of Sachsen-Gotha paid half a million guilders for Borna, and Frederick III snipped Quedlinburg for a mere 300,000. A whole raft of minor offices were knocked down to other takers. It is likely that they represented bargains, given the usual inability of governments to price public assets properly.[26] Pawning his jewels with the Jesuits in Vienna raised another million guilders for our hero.[27] Then there were voluntary and compulsory loans and taxes.

To put a global figure on this sell-off is impossible. It would seem to be over £1 million at then values, probably far more. The sums disbursed in bribes to the szlachta and prelates, and in back-pay to the soldiers of Poland–Lithuania, seem to be well in excess of this. Yet this was only the beginning. When he travelled to Poland in July, the Saxon was carrying over 800,000 guilders as a slush fund; this soon went. That same month he demanded that Hoym send him RT 200,000 at once, and twice that amount by the next post.

Given such circumstances, two points will bear emphasis. Whatever disasters Augustus's ambitions inflicted upon Poland, he did not operate unaided or unsupported. He bought and retained the backing of segments of the szlachta *throughout* his reign. Nor could the Poles blame him for corrupting their political system; an indigenous elite had already done that job only too well. He simply took advantage of a ready tool.

Like their master, Flemming and his aides operated with loads of ready cash, since there were many electors. For over a month in May and June 1697, the Wola Field west of Warsaw, the traditional venue for elections, came to resemble a cross between pre-Thatcher British strike meetings and pre-TV American conventions, with the whole conducted largely on horseback.

Were there really 100,000 mounted szlachta there on 25 June, as da Via claimed?[28] There could have been, first charging around their open-air polling-station, then marshalled behind the standards of their families and clans. Straining to hear the speeches and promises of the campaign managers for the various candidates, picking up rumours, discussing delegation strategy; much had a familiar political ring.

Radziejowski presided and called the first 'vote' on 26 June. The delegations of Conti and Augustus were ordered respectively to the right and left of Wola. There seems little doubt that the Frenchman's supporters predominated, but Augustus's adherents refused to accept that this represented a Conti victory. Eventually the Primate acceded to demands to postpone a proclamation until the next day. It was a fatal mistake.

Everyone stayed in the field, the Cardinal napping there in his coach, while others were more wakeful. Augustus's team plied the starlit szlachta with brandy, plus the promise of a thaler apiece for voting their appreciation. The non-French diplomats finally united behind the Saxon, and James Sobieski released his residual vote to him. The astute Przebendowski utilized the scribes of the Jesuit College to render Augustus's electoral programme into Polish.

By the morning of 27 June many of Conti's supporters had defected to Augustus. All sorts of figures are bandied about regarding later electoral alignments. The Saxon now either had an overwhelming majority behind him, or was still in the minority, or the votes were about even. It hardly matters; the szlachta electorate was fatally sundered and neither side would withdraw to make the decision unanimous.

Making the best of a bad situation, Radziejowski simply proclaimed his man Conti to be king and, ignoring the objections from Augustus's backers, led his followers to Warsaw for the traditional Te Deum. Shortly after, those remaining in Wola heard the Primate's deputy, the Bishop of Brześć Kujawski, pronounce Augustus to be king. This was followed by another Te Deum sung in the open air.

It was a double election. Poland had two kings: one poncing around Paris, the other ensconced on the Polish frontier with his army. The sword would decide; Augustus's blade was already drawn and far closer to the Republic than any French rapier.

'THE ADVANTAGE TO BE CROWNED'

Augustus had reappeared in Dresden in mid-June. On 23 June Plantamour reported that the Saxon was expected to return soon to Vienna. This was a reasonable surmise, since publicly at least he was still commander in Hungary. Yet it could also have been the product of disinformation, scattered by Augustus and his agents to keep others guessing about his next move. There was considerable ignorance even in his Electorate.

On 22 June Augustus finally informed the Saxon Privy Council of his intention to bid for the Polish crown; he did not bother to enlighten his States. That same day he left Dresden for Görlitz in the Imperial province of Silesia, joining his troops there on 24 June.

Plantamour had received a long letter from Dresden which gave differing reasons for this march: to ward off a Polish attack on Silesia or Brandenburg; to support Lewis of Baden in Poland; to extort money from Lusatia.[29] The idea that Augustus was cantering off to buttress his *own* claim to the Polish crown did not merit suggestion; either it had not registered, or it had been suppressed.

On 3 July Lexington told Blathwayt that Augustus was in Breslau (Wrocław), where he had received a Polish deputation, 'and the great Embassy, with the crown, is following as fast as possible'.[30] Three days later Augustus was on Polish soil in Tarnowskie (north of Katowice). On 22 July the first Saxon troops arrived there. The next day he received a delegation of his supporters and paid them off.

On 27 July Augustus was a few miles further east in Piekary Śląskie, at the shrine of the Blessed Virgin Mary. Here he publicly professed his Catholic faith. Yet it hardly involved any fervent denunciation of Lutheranism; what Rome damned, rejected and anathematized, Augustus echoed in general terms.[31]

A few days later he arrived in Cracow (Kraków), where on 15 September he was crowned King Augusta II of Poland. Countess Esterle was one of the spectators at the ceremony. She would have seen Augustus faint during its progress. Was it the weight of the Sarmatian coronation robes? Or the burden of guilt catching up with a ruler who had abandoned his people and their religion in his quest for glory? It may even have been a premonition of his later diabetes.

There was no serious opposition to Augustus's enthronement. Although the French envoys had informed Louis that his nominee was elected, the Contiist camp in Poland crumbled. Louis too appeared indecisive. The French had already been humiliated once. Radziejowski 'has bubbled them of their 80,000 dollars', wrote Stepney gleefully, 'and has only sung them a Te Deum for it'. Eventually, in what was more a gesture than a policy, Louis sent a reluctant Conti, with a squadron of ships, a few troops and inadequate funds, to stake his claim.

A fortnight after his rival's coronation, Conti's flotilla anchored uneasily near Danzig (Gdańsk). His presence hardly led to an upsurge in Polish support for the Frenchman. Those few that meandered over to the little harbour at Oliwa drank with him, took his money and promised forces that never came. Conti had the aura of a usurper.

Augustus had 'the advantage to be crowned, which is no small matter', Lexington sensibly observed.[32] Finally, the King of Poland invoked possession. With nine-tenths of the law and most of the military muscle on his side, Augustus sent his cavalry against the French intruders and dispersed them. On 9 November Conti sailed away, never to return. 'It looks very much as if the Poles had only sent for the Prince in order to extract money from him', concluded Liselotte in disgust. 'They are a treacherous and greedy people, even worse than the English'.[33]

At least she did not accuse the latter of any involvement in Conti's discomfiture, since their only role in these Polish affairs had been that of ignorant spectators. On 3 July Lexington wrote of 'the surprising news' of Augustus's election, and swore that Vienna 'never knew one word of it till 'twas done'. It was a fatuous judgement, but in putting his lordship down Blathwayt betrayed a different blindness.

The Polish election had 'very much surprised the world, and is like to give it no less trouble', but Lexington would 'never be able to persuade the King or anyone here' that the Emperor and Count Kinski 'were ignorant of the Elector of Saxony's pretensions' from the outset. It was all 'an intrigue of the Jesuits, very well carried on, but not without the privity of the court of Vienna'.

Stepney saw no Jesuits, but still viewed Augustus's election as 'of vast advantage to the Emperor'. He thought it 'certain this young vigorous King will push on the war' against Turkey 'as far as it can go'. And it was 'the prospect of prosecuting this Holy War' that made the Imperial court 'give in to this intrigue'. Stepney boasted, fairly, that he knew Augustus and Saxony 'as well as any Englishman can know them', and unless he was much mistaken, Augustus would 'prove a tyrant to his subjects' and 'a troublesome neighbour' to Brandenburg's ruler, 'who had better a Frenchman King of Poland than this prince'.

Blathwayt could not avoid one dig at Lexington. 'And now His Electoral Highness or Majesty has changed his religion', he purred, 'I suppose your lordship will not make any overtures to him of the Garter, which no popish prince has in this age been willing to accept of'.[34]

This cruel loss of a strip of ribbon had hardly been uppermost in Augustus's mind, as the crown of Poland brushed his brow. He could now receive the plaudits of his fellow monarchs. Even if they bore him no Garter, the English would join in the felicitations. And it fell to one George Stepney to tender them.

Chapter 14

'The intestine broils of the kingdom'
At the court of King Augustus 1698–99

'THE BEST TERMS HE CAN'

After leaving Saxony, Stepney had, in his own words, served as 'a sort of military envoy to the electors and princes of the Rhine'. In July 1697 King William made him one of eight Commissioners for Trade and Plantations at £1000 per annum. Returning to England in September, George 'stuck near five months' at his desk job and 'thought no more of rambling'. That was until he was offered another mission.

On 11 January 1698 Stepney was appointed envoy extraordinary to Elector Frederick III of Brandenburg and other princes in Germany. He arrived in Berlin on 14 March. En route he had reflected that the 'promotion' of Augustus to the crown of Poland was likely to have occasioned 'night thoughts' for Frederick. But the Saxon hardly seemed in threatening mode.

Letters from Danzig of 22 March informed Stepney that Augustus was still in that town and 'so well diverted' that he intended to stay there longer, 'notwithstanding the disorders that reign in Poland'. On 7 April Augustus was joined there by his father-in-law for 'a hard drinking bout', prior to their setting out for Warsaw on 10 April. Poland's new King was heading for his capital to attend the Pacification Sejm opening there on 16 April. Stepney feared that 'it will have as little success as the other assemblies have had of late'.

Since Stepney had to follow Frederick to (ducal or East) Prussia, he inquired of Vernon, who was now Secretary of State, 'what commands His Majesty may have for me with the King of Poland, while I am in that neighbourhood'. Vernon sent him credentials for meeting Augustus, together with a homily. 'I hope you will find him in peaceable profession, for we have no need of disturbances on that side'. The failing health of the King of Spain was 'like to find us work enough'.

Berlin was currently 'the common thoroughfare to all passengers

147

who go to and from Poland', Stepney told Vernon on 19 April. They reported that Radziejowski 'continues obstinate' and had sent couriers to France to encourage Conti's return. All this was despite Augustus trying 'to gain him', even toying with the possibility of reimbursing the Cardinal for the 200,000 dollars 'which his Eminence pretends to have advanced for the French party'. Stepney could not foresee 'the issue of the unhappy division in that kingdom', but it seemed that Augustus was 'preparing against all accidents'.

The Sejm which convened on 16 April solved nothing. It was 'so thin, and soon at an end'. Meantime, the Primate and his adherents were 'now holding the assembly of *Rokosz* or malcontents near his palace at Łowicz. However, it was the general opinion that 'this last effort will prove a weak one', and that their confederacy will 'now fall to pieces', everyone making 'the best terms he can'. So it was to prove, and Augustus too would cut the best deal he could.

'AN HAPPY MONARCH'

Elector Frederick III, 'my little gentleman' as Stepney dubbed him, left Berlin on 23 April and arrived at Königsberg (Kaliningrad) a week later. Stepney followed, quitting Berlin at the end of April. Judging matters to be in a 'tolerable state at Warsaw', he left Danzig in early May, and travelled to the Polish capital 'to pass the compliment of felicitation on the new King of Poland'. Stepney reached Warsaw on 16 May and stayed there about ten days, sending Vernon several lengthy despatches upon current Polish issues.

The first news he received was that, some hours prior to his arrival, an accommodation had been signed between Radziejowski's adherents and Augustus's commissioners. As Stepney observed, there were three contributory factors assisting the conclusion of this treaty: the pressure put on the Cardinal-Primate by the papal nuncios in Warsaw; some 5000 Saxon soldiers ordered into the suburbs of the capital; and a straight bribe for Radziejowski, in the shape of Augustus recompensing him for his 'losses' in opposing the new King.

Now Radziejowski led his followers into church 'and first made a speech in commendation[?] of the Elector of Saxony'. This was followed by 'acclamations Vivat Augustus Rex Polonica, and ended in Te Deum', which the Cardinal intoned '*in pontificatibus*, as if the King had been but that very minute elected'.

Stepney went on to report upon Lithuania, which was in a state of virtual civil war between the followers of the dominant Sapieha family and the lesser gentry, led by Ogiński. Stepney emphasized that

148

Augustus had thrown his weight alternately behind both factions. Fanning the troubles in the Grand Duchy suited him on sound 'divide and rule' principles and also gave him an excuse to maintain his German forces in part of the Republic.

Meeting Augustus on 19 May 1698, Stepney was pumped for further information upon the English attitude towards peace with Turkey. The envoy stuck to his position of being there solely to convey the congratulations of his monarch to Poland's sovereign. Yet, as he later reported, he was unable 'to persuade the young vigorous King to hear of peace', and if Tsar Peter should 'hold out with him, I make no doubt that he will carry on the war for this campaign and another'. On 12/22 May the envoy watched the qualified personal submission of the Primate to Augustus. It was our hero's twenty-eighth birthday.

Stepney's last major letter from Warsaw was on 26 May and he was in Königsberg by 8 June. 'I am got out of Sarmatia safe and sound', he recounted. 'I like both the country and the people as well as most I have seen'. He had attended a Senate meeting in Warsaw, listening out for 'the little scraps of Latin which were sometimes intermixed with their Polish eloquence'. But he had not received a present from Augustus. More Polish eloquence uttered 'excuses that there was nothing good enough for me at Warsaw', so they had sent to Breslau for 'pieces of value', and that 'a handsome remembrance should be sent after me'.

During his stay in East Prussia, Stepney deliberately absented himself from the meeting between Augustus and Frederick at Johannisburg (Pisz), which lasted from 4 to 7 June. However, he left a record of its farcical proceedings, as the two sovereigns played out the politics of ceremony, with the Elector endeavouring to enthrone himself upon an armed chair. Aside from this 'triomphe de fauteuil', there was a more sober aspect to the meeting. This concerned Prussian occupation of the Polish port of Elbing (Elbląg), which Augustus had 'sold' to Frederick, but whose takeover he was obliged publicly to resist by the Sejm.

Convinced that with the submission of his opponents, Augustus was 'now likely to prove an happy monarch', Stepney returned to Berlin. Soon he was reporting upon preparations for the Saxon's late summer campaign against the Turks.

Augustus had promised in his Pacta Conventa to place his forces at the disposal of the Republic, both to recapture Kamieniec Podolski on the Polish–Turkish border and to subjugate the Ottoman dependencies of Moldavia and Wallachia. In reality he intended to turn the latter into hereditary Wettin dominions. He was certainly not in favour of an early peace with Turkey, as were the Empire and

149

Venice, Poland's allies in the Holy League. Only Russia supported him, because the young Tsar Peter sought to break the Turkish–Tartar hold over the Crimea and ultimately gain access to the Black Sea.

These two inexperienced sovereigns met in south-east Poland at Rawa Ruska from 10 to 13 August 1698 (p 163). After Peter left, Augustus held a council of war in Lwów (Lemberg) to discuss the possibility of besieging Kamieniec. But disease broke out amongst his forces, and there was open hostility between its Saxon and Polish components, leading to acts of violence among the troops. The only battle with the nominal enemy, at Podhajce on 8–9 September, resulted in the Poles being worsted by the Tartars, and Augustus's 'prophetic' commander, the Duke of Württemberg (p 136) quitting his service to return to that of Denmark.[1]

Following this less than glorious campaign, Augustus returned to Lwów. He was in Warsaw for a Senate meeting in November; from there he travelled to Brest-Litovsk to be 'splendidly treated' by Prince Radziwiłł. Stepney did not note Augustus's move to Grodno, where on 1 January 1699 he held his first fateful meeting with Patkul (p 165). Then it was back to Warsaw, another Senate meeting and the hope of a little fun between the crises.

'A VERY CONSIDERABLE POINT'

On 13 January Stepney related that Flemming, now lieutenant-general, had of late marched three regiments of Saxons between the Sapieha and Ogiński forces, to produce a sort of peace in Lithuania. In Whitehall Vernon was impressed by the way that Augustus had 'managed the factions' in the Grand Duchy and wished 'we knew as well how to govern our parties here, and make them subservient to the public good'.

For Augustus it was a breathing-space. 'The King of Poland turns all his thoughts to diversions', sighed Stepney. He was preparing 'the merriest Carnival ever known in Poland, and 'sending about for virtuosos and comedians'. As late as 6 March the envoy could report that all business was on hold in Warsaw, continually postponed 'by the divertissements of the Carnival, which suit more with the King's genius than business or deliberations'.

But business eventually had to be faced. The Peace of Carlowitz had been signed with the Turks by Austria, Venice and Poland (but not Russia) on 26 January 1699. Thanks to Sobieski's capture of some Moldavian forts eight years earlier, there was something for the Poles to trade against the return of Kamieniec and other parts of

150

Podolia. Augustus had hardly been instrumental in achieving this restoration of the *status quo ante*, but he took such plaudits as were on offer.

The Senate meeting of 17 February resolved that each senator should congratulate the King 'for the advantageous peace with the Turks concluded under his regency' and also for 'the success His Majesty has met with hitherto, in quieting the intestine broils of the kingdom'; to ensure 'the entire suppressing whereof', it was agreed to call a Sejm in the summer. However, the peace treaty also exacerbated a problem for Augustus: that of his German forces stationed in the Republic.

In April 1698 Stepney had noted that Augustus had with him 6000 German auxiliaries. These were 'not properly in the service of the Republic, but the King's, who contracts for them in his own name' and provided for 'their subsistence as Elector of Saxony'. Augustus was then also negotiating for another 4000 German and Danish mercenaries. These 10,000 auxiliaries, plus the 22,000 Saxon troops which 'he has already on the frontiers', were the linchpin of Augustus's power as King of Poland. Conversely, the Poles remained 'apprehensive that their liberties may suffer' from the presence of 'so formidable a body of foreigners'. Once peace was signed with the Turks, the ostensible grounds for the presence of this 'considerable German army' in Poland were undermined.

'I believe the King of Poland must think likewise of disbanding', Stepney told Vernon in February 1699. The Starost of Podlachia was 'very clamorous' against the Saxons quartered there, while the Lithuanians were 'more noisy than ever for having all foreigners dismissed out of their duchy'. By mid-March the envoy was reporting that the presence of Saxon troops 'cause[s] great disorder, and if not suddenly disposed of, may occasion a new confederation and rebellion'. On 8 April Stepney noted that Augustus had promised 'to dismiss all except 6000 men'; but in the Briton's view, this would not 'satisfy the Poles', who had already 'begun to cut to pieces such foreigners as they find straggling in small parties'.

Inevitably Radziejowski was involved. His reference in a letter to 'the scum of heretics which overrun Poland' was, in Stepney's view, 'a trumpet for another *Rokosz*' designed to drive out the Saxon troops. In response Augustus played 'a desperate game', intending 'to camp his little Saxon army round about Warsaw' for as long as the latest Sejm should last. He hoped thereby 'to influence their counsels, and at least secure his person'.

In an endeavour to calm the situation, Augustus ordered seven regiments of Saxons, together with his mercenary forces, to march from Poland on 15 May. Stepney still doubted whether this would be enough to 'content the Poles, and put them in a humour of going on with their Diet'. In any case, there would still be between 8000 and 10,000 German troops left in the Republic, which Augustus hoped to retain by quartering them upon crown land.

The Sejm opened on 16 June 1699, with 4000 Saxon troops posted 'in and about' Warsaw. Not until 1 July was the Marshal or Speaker chosen; 'He is the King's creature', Stepney asserted. However influential this appointment, Stepney could later report that 'after many contestations' in the Sejm, Augustus appeared 'likely to gain his point, in keeping up a good part of his troops under the name of guards'. When the Sejm finally closed on 31 July, Augustus had been permitted to retain 6000 Saxons in Poland–Lithuania, with this force maintained at the Republic's expense. These troops would be the nucleus of the army which would soon attack Riga. In more ways than one, our hero had gained 'a very considerable point'.

'A VERY OBLIGING INVITATION'

Stepney deduced that Augustus 'intended to make his Electorate a visit' as soon as the Sejm was at an end. He noted that the King was obliged to ask the consent of that assembly to leave the Republic's territory, 'unless he will run the risk of abdication'. This provision of the Polish constitution was not hollow; it was invoked against Augustus when he was 'dethroned' in 1704 (p 205). But in 1699 permission was speedily granted, probably because a fair few of the Republic's hierarchy intended visiting the Leipzig Fair along with their sovereign. His retinue for this excursion included the younger Sobieski brothers, a pack of Sapiehas and Countess Lubomirska (p 218).

Following 'a small fit of fever occasioned by too violent exercise', Augustus put off his return to Saxony. Finally he left Warsaw on the evening of Tuesday 25 August, arriving in Dresden on 2 September 1699 'incognito and without any manner of attendance'. He 'went directly' to Eberhardine's apartment, 'whom he surprised very agreeably'. She, like his subjects, had not seen the Elector-King for over two years.

Six days later the Saxon States assembled, 'and after the proposition made to them', Augustus left them to deliberate, while he spent a fortnight at the spas of Teplitz. Here he 'diverted himself with many frolics', as Stepney rather inevitably recited. After that he was off to the Michaelmas Fair at Leipzig, which commenced on 11 October. Stepney understood that 'great preparations are making' for Augustus's reception there. The envoy had also heard that, in contrast to his own visit in 1693 (p 45), 'several princes and some electors intend to repair thither'.

This was enough for Stepney to plan a journey to view the 'very great splendour' promised. Although Blathwayt disapproved of him dropping in on Augustus, the younger man had this covered. The Electress Sophie Charlotte had received 'a very obliging invitation' to visit the Princess of Anhalt at Oranienbaum, and 'has engaged me to go along with her, which honour I cannot decline'.

Nor did he. Having spent a few days with the Princess of Anhalt, Stepney travelled to Leipzig.[2] 'We are at the height of mirth here as far as this country can afford any', he regaled Ellis on 17 October. 'No less than thirty-six princes and princesses already, and more a-coming'.

He told Blathwayt that 'nothing can be more obliging than the civilities' shown by Augustus to Sophie Charlotte. 'He would have waited upon Her Highness in ceremony, but she declined it'. So Augustus 'came in disguise with three or four attendants only, and in the same manner has been twice at supper with her', where Stepney too 'had the honour to be admitted'.

On 24 October Eberhardine returned Sophie Charlotte's visit. Augustus too put in an appearance 'with all his lustre', coruscating with diamonds 'at least to the value of two millions of crowns'. This Stepney found 'surprising after the presents he has made before and since his coronation'. Later that day Sophie Charlotte, the Princess Dowager of Anhalt and her daughter Henrietta left Leipzig. Along their route they met Augustus, 'who pretended to ride out with a design to hunt, alighted, and took place in the coach with them', keeping them company to Oranienbaum. There he 'lay that night and the next', before Sophie Charlotte and Stepney left for Berlin on 26 October.

What was he up to? Was Augustus trying to seduce the Electress of Brandenburg – or Henrietta? Or had he joined the party to talk diplomacy with George Stepney? For the envoy told Blathwayt that he had held 'frequent conversations' with the King of Poland.

He found Augustus 'very much changed to his advantage'. Stepney considered that his problems in Poland had 'abated much of his volatile temper' and brought 'his frolicsome humour' to a 'moderate pitch'. His conversation was 'very easy and agreeable and polite, to a greater degree than I have formerly observed'.

'I shall not at present entertain you with a recital of his amours', wrote the diplomat teasingly to his mentor. He compared them in variety to those of Henry VIII and Charles II. 'His choice is not very nice', opined Stepney, 'and the whole covey' of Augustus's mistresses were 'so well-disposed, that they dance and converse together without any appearance of animosities' and 'make no difficulty of coming into the Queen's [Eberhardine's] presence'.[3]

After taking his leave of the Brandenburg Court, Stepney crossed to England late in December 1699. He was back at work as a Commissioner for Trade by the end of the month and century. When Augustus began his disastrous war against Sweden in February 1700, Stepney was desk-bound and remote from the scene. There was no English envoy in Vienna or Moscow, let alone Dresden or Warsaw. London's nearest representative to these explosive events was Plantamour, who was holding the fort in Berlin after his friend and employer had left.

However, the English were hardly alone in being caught unawares by the predatory attack upon Sweden mounted by Augustus, Frederick IV of Denmark and Tsar Peter. This alliance had been welded together in utmost secrecy by the remarkable Livonian Johann Reinhold von Patkul. If the resources and determination applied to the project had matched the greatness of the egos involved, Augustus might well have succeeded in his ambitions, with history remembering him very differently. Instead, he was condemned to spend a third of his life struggling against the consequences of this one crass act. That he came out of it at all is a tribute to his tenacity and political skills; that he got involved so fecklessly in the first place is testimony to the weaker traits of his complex character.

Chapter Fifteen

'The chief promoters of this present war'
Patkul, Tsar Peter and Augustus 1698

'THE UNHAPPY INSTRUMENT'

'I understand Patkul (the unhappy instrument of these disturbances in the north) has been lately here incognito', reported Stepney from Vienna in December 1702. Nine months later Dr. John Robinson, then in Warsaw, observed that 'Mr Patkul, a gentleman of Liefland [Livonia], and one of the chief promoters of this present war, is come hither from Muscovy'.[1]

These appear to be the sole allusions in the British archives to the doings of that singular Livonian, Johann Reinhold von Patkul (1660–1707), during his 'active' period in the years 1698–1705. Later, there are some references to the *cause célèbre* of his imprisonment by the Saxons, his handover to the Swedes and his barbarous execution (C21–23). But Patkul's frenetic activities in those crucial eight years had a far greater impact upon events in Europe than his brutal but deserved end.

It is hardly surprising that there is but this brace of sightings of Patkul. Not only was England unrepresented at Dresden, Warsaw and Moscow throughout most of this period; even more than at the time of the Polish election, dissimulation was the name of the game. Augustus and Tsar Peter, together with the Danish king, Frederick IV (r 1699–1730), plotted a surprise attack upon the Swedish Empire with a secrecy that was remarkable for those days. The crucial role of transforming these edifying regal designs into concrete plans and treaties was played by Patkul, a professional conspirator living the last quarter of his life under a Swedish death sentence.

In this sense the two English assessments are apt. Patkul was merely an 'instrument' in the orchestrations of others; he was only one of the 'promoters' of the Great Northern War of 1700–21. Other descriptions of him as a 'firebrand' also presume the existence of a political 'tinderbox', which he simply helped to ignite. Yet an isolated exile, representing at most certain aspirations of the German-speaking

barons of his Baltic homeland, could never have kindled such a con-
flagration on his own; any more than Gavrilo Princip 'began' the First
World War. Patkul's importance lay in his burning hatred of Sweden
and his zeal, courage, willpower and intelligence, all of which he skilfully applied in leading a prial of kings down a route which they had
already half travelled.

Hatred, injustice, ambition and arrogance were the forces that
impelled Patkul towards his role of 'freedom fighter'. In a later world
he would have posed as president, general secretary and commander
of 'the Livonian National Liberation Front'. Sometimes he appeared
to be its only member as well.

We can assign him 'freedom fighter' status at the outset of his
career, as long as we remember that any concept of a 'nation' referred at this time only to the elites which monopolized political and
economic authority in Europe's 'states'. Patkul sought solely the 'liberation' from Swedish rule of the Ritterschaft, his own Germanic bar-
onial and knightly 'class', who were the former rulers of Livonia. He
had no interest in the rights of its Latvian and Estonian peasant
masses, because it no more dawned upon him than upon his privileged brothers elsewhere that such a herd of human misery should
have 'rights'.

If he began as a 'freedom fighter', he converted en route, like
many paragons who have trekked that road, into a political 'fixer'.
The programmatic ideal degenerated into the pragmatic spiel.
Secrecy, free-wheeling and double-dealing, 'principled' deceit and
ruthlessness were the main weapons in his political armoury. Patkul
originally utilized them as means to an end; but by the last years of
his life they had, as again so often happens, become ends in themselves.

The politics junkie, who must fix an opponent or a 'situation' in
order to 'fix' himself, is an overt feature of the detritus of democ-
racy. But such operators, spinning one more intrigue, dabbling in
another louche deal, are as old as politics and thereby as old as
mankind. Tagging Patkul with the label 'fixer' is entirely apposite, for
he offered a service to make political events happen.

For a while he was crucial to the needs of the 'big boys'. Augustus
and Peter were of necessity operators themselves, but Patkul could
help with both the 'big idea' and the political slog. Moreover, the
'big boys' were to some extent just that: still a little green, untutored,
distracted by big girls, booze and 'frolics'. Yet they had what Patkul
neither had nor ever could have: legitimate supreme authority over
states and the resources of such entities. In the final analysis they
could use power in its violent form; the option of force was with
them, and without it the Swedish Empire could not be humbled.

By the end Patkul forgot who he was: an exile enriched and empowered beyond expectation. His turbulent mood-swings, acerbic tongue and vitriolic pen brought him many enemies. Allowed a dynamic role by both Augustus and Peter, with a fabulous range of powers and responsibilities, he abused his status and contributed mightily to his own fall. His apologists seek to encapsulate his fate as determined by the whims of three kings: Augustus who betrayed him, Peter who abandoned him and Charles XII who ordained his ghastly death. This is a rather one-sided view of Patkul's nemesis.

In 1705, with no authority other than his 'reputation', Patkul sought to fix up a Swedish–Russian peace, to Augustus's detriment. This was as much a betrayal as that by the Saxon, when he finally handed Patkul over to the tender mercies of the Swedes in 1706. Likewise, hiring out Peter's troops to the Emperor in 1705 showed as much disdain for the Tsar's position as Peter initially expressed for his imprisoned envoy.

Patkul's ultimate hubris was his first. Whatever his ambitions, and no matter how great his sense of injustice, he was by any interpretation a Swedish subject. As such he intrigued with his sovereign's enemies, he helped plan and execute their assault upon his King's realms, and ultimately he brought devastation upon his homeland. Years before his death, Livonia's liberation had been sacrificed in his hunt for another fix; by the end it was as sacrosanct to Patkul as is the venerable fragility of a granny battered for her pension by a dope-head.

When Patkul's own head went onto the block, it was the merited fate of a traitor; one whose egotistic vision had condemned myriads of innocents to their less publicized annihilation. Civilians and soldiers, Balts, Ruthenes, Poles, Russians, Swedes and Saxons, they fell by the hundred thousand beneath the hooves of the four horsemen who trampled for two decades over their lands. This was the legacy bequeathed by the Livonian 'freedom fighter' and fixer, together with his royal co-producers. Against it, Patkul's broken and quartered torso ranks as a speck of dust.

'THE BOSOM OF CHRISTENDOM'

Despite his un-Germanic name, which might have derived from an Estonian or Lettish property held in feu, Patkul's forebears, like most of the Livonian nobility, came originally from Westphalia. Members of the German knightly orders (Ritterorden) that colonized Prussia and the Baltic lands, they had dwelt in Livonia for some 300 years. They saw themselves as frontiersmen of the German

Empire, defending Catholic and, later, Protestant civilization from the barbarians: the Orthodox Russians, the Lithuanians and the various native peoples.

Riding in tandem with the dispossession and harshness born of colonization came civilization, founded on the trading nexus of the great Hanse towns of the east Baltic. Riga, at the mouth of the Düna (Daugava or Western Dvina) river, dominated the scene. But others like Reval (Tallinn), Mitau (Jelgava) and Dorpat (Tartu) were centres of commerce, education and industry.

It was Tsar Ivan IV (r 1533–84) who shattered this settled and privileged Teutonic world. 'Ivan the Terrible' was the first of many Russian maniacs, which that great people has inflicted upon Europe since the end of the fifteenth century, when Muscovy broke the yoke of Tartar occupation.

Insulated by that experience from even the mildest flirtation with the Europe of the Renaissance, landlocked Muscovy developed in a cocoon and grew up still swaddled, as did its infants. With little fresh cultural air to breathe or free space to move in, her people clung to despotism as one more orthodoxy of life, to be imbibed as much as excessive alcohol and to remain as unchallenged as her pious, illiterate church.

In 1558 Ivan declared war upon the Livonian Order, pushing, like his successor Peter, for the sea; both to control the outlets for his trade and to waft a little air into his reactionary realm. Missionary worlds collided as the German 'frontier' met the backwoodsman. Unable to stem Muscovy's hordes, the last Grand Master of the Order opted to keep Livonia 'in the bosom of Christendom under the sceptre of His Majesty, the King of Poland'.[2]

The Russian hold upon the Baltic coast proved tenuous. Under Polish and Swedish military pressure it was relinquished, and Muscovy itself fell apart in the 'Time of the Troubles' (1598–1613). Meantime in Livonia, Polish promises of native German hegemony ('eingeborene deutsche Obrigkeit'), with extensive privileges in law, language, religion and administration for the Ritterschaft, gave way to the Catholic Counter-Reformation and Polonization of offices. In consequence, the German knights' next call upon salvation was directed at the most proximate Lutheran power, the kingdom of Sweden, which under its remarkable Vasa dynasty had broken away from Denmark in 1523.

When the Grand Master accepted Polish suzerainty over Livonia, the northern town of Reval had placed itself under Swedish protection in 1560. From 1570 to 1595 the Swedes fought Muscovy to extend this first outpost of empire to the whole of Estonia, and in the process expelled the Russians from their conquest of Narva in

1581. By the 1617 Peace of Stolbova and later the Peace of Kardis of 1660, Sweden acquired all of Ingria (the province east of Estonia) and further territory in Eastern Karelia. She now controlled the entire coastline of the Gulf of Finland. Conversely, Muscovy was denied any direct access to the Baltic, at least until she could wrench it from Swedish hands.

However, because Estonia was viewed legitimately as a constituent part of Poland's newly acquired province of Livonia, and also because of a contested dynastic union between Poland and Sweden, the interests of these two states also clashed. Once Muscovy was pushed back inland, Sweden, led by its great monarch Gustavus Adolphus (r 1611–32), was free to pursue its objectives in Livonia. Punctuated by truces, the struggle with Poland continued until the Swedes overran almost the entire province in 1625–26. Thereafter, Gustavus's armies intervened crucially in Germany during the Thirty Years War (1618–48).

'NO MIDDLE WAY'

Many Livonian nobles joined the Swedish King there, among them the young Friedrich Wilhelm von Patkul. In 1632 he returned to his estate in Livonia, where he became a leading representative of the Ritterschaft, as well as an officer in the Swedish army. In the late 1640s he married his second wife Gertrud. A feisty semi-literate daughter of another noble family, Gertrud could ride, shoot and breed. She bore Patkul's father eight children in ten years.

In 1655, as part of the 'Deluge' (*Potop*) of multiple invasions that nearly drowned Poland, renewed war broke out between her and the invading Swedes. The conflict spread into Livonia, and the Patkuls fled before the Polish armies into Wolmar (Valmiera). In that besieged town, plague broke out amongst the defenders and carried off all eight Patkul children.

When Wolmar fell, Friedrich Wilhelm was a broken man. Soon he was a prisoner too, arrested for treason by the returning Swedes. The charge related to an oath he had sworn to the Polish victors after Wolmar surrendered. He was shipped off to gaol in Stockholm. Swedish penal policy, already enlightened, allowed Gertrud to join him. On 27 July 1660 she delivered Johann Reinhold von Patkul into the world. He began life, as he would leave it, in a Swedish prison.

Friedrich Wilhelm was released a few months later. He fathered three more sons before dying in 1666. Despite this and the family's straitened circumstances, Gertrud contrived a good education for her boys. Like Stepney, Johann Reinhold was naturally bright and grew into a gifted linguist, fluent in German, Swedish, French and Latin. Later he read the Bible in Greek. Even at an early age he evinced an interest in politics, history and theology. In 1677, two years after his mother's remarriage, he left Livonia to study in Germany.

He attended courses in Kiel and other universities, broadening his interests into law and also learning to fence. Endowed with his mother's prickly temper, he would fight several duels during his life-time. In 1680 Patkul returned to Livonia to take over the running of the family estate, and continued his law studies from books. In 1687 he moved to Riga and joined the provincial militia as a captain. His high rank was determined by the transient favour of the Swedish Governor-General.

It was in Riga that Captain Patkul first became embroiled in poli-tical activity, and the issue was the so-called 'Reduktion' of noble estates. To help finance Swedish involvement in the Thirty Years War, both Gustavus Adolphus and his successor Christina had mortgaged crown lands throughout the Swedish Empire to the nobility, who proceeded to exploit them as their own. Now the crown wanted these estates back to provide it with a source of revenue, and the non-noble members of the Swedish Riksdag ratified royal wishes.

In Livonia the argument concerned not only property rights as such, but also the authority of the Swedish parliament to legislate in the Ritterschaft's affairs. The German barons contended that sover-eignty resided in their own assembly, the Livonian Landtag, and that the Swedish King Charles XI (r 1660–97) had confirmed their privi-leges in 1678. It was this dispute that would drive Patkul down the road to exile, treason and death.

Impecunious monarchs tend to suffer from amnesia. Charles ignored all deputations and petitions from this irksome elite, which refused to admit that they were vassals of the Swedish crown. Even-tually in 1689, when five-sixths of estates had returned to crown own-ership, he commanded the Ritterschaft to send two delegates to Stockholm to negotiate. In February 1690 the Landtag chose Patkul and the 50-year-old Baron Gustav von Budberg to undertake the mission. In October they left for Stockholm.

Our knowledge of what transpired there owes most to Patkul's account, and that irascible and moody man, with his penchant for fantasy and his often soaring style, cannot be deemed a reliable or impartial witness. There was certainly no compromise on the Reduk-tion policy, and the Swedes seemed less than impressed by justifica-tions for the continuing sovereignty of the Livonian Landtag. Whether or not Patkul's unyielding rhetoric dashed hopes of a com-promise, the Swedes saw him as the obstacle. 'With Patkul there's no middle way', one Swede advised his King. 'Therefore we should either try him quickly and lop off his head, or promote him to colonel and give him a regiment'.[3]

Following Patkul's return, the Landtag reconvened in Wenden (Cēsis) in March 1692. Their proceedings, particularly a petition to Charles penned by Patkul, were deemed to threaten rebellion. The Landtag was dissolved and Patkul and other Livonian leaders were summoned to Stockholm. Patkul, who had already fled to Courland, demanded a safe-conduct (*Geleitbrief*) from the King. Upon receiving one the Livonian returned in May 1694 to Stockholm, where the following month he and his comrades came before a Swedish tribunal.

In such a brief account, it is hard to convey fully the issues of this obscure trial, which revolved around such concepts as monarchical absolutism and natural law, but also involved specific charges against Patkul of *lèse-majesté*, undermining military discipline, and desertion. In the final analysis the Swedes wanted Patkul to stop causing problems in Livonia. Whether they had decided already upon his execution is unclear. Patkul did not wait to find out; using or abusing his safe-conduct, he fled from Stockholm to Courland in November 1694.

Next month the Swedish court condemned him to lose his entire property, his right hand (which had written the words offensive to his sovereign) and his head. His co-accused also received death-sentences, which were later commuted to six years in gaol. As Charles XI lay dying in 1697, his mother extracted from him a pardon for these Livonians; nothing was said about Patkul. Whether, if he had not fled, he would merely have been taken out of circulation for a time like the others, will never be known.

Obscure too are Patkul's movements in 1695–97, as befits a man on the run in fear of kidnap, assassination or deportation. Some reports place him in England, Italy, France and Poland. We do know that he left Courland in summer 1695, and that he was in Leipzig and Halle later that year, apparently resuming his earlier interest in theology. In 1697 he may have served in the forces of the Landgrave of Hessen–Kassel. Thereafter, using the alias Fischering, he was near Lausanne on the estate of the powerful Brandenburg minister Danckelmann. Why the latter should have protected Patkul is another mystery. The Livonian left Switzerland in early 1698.

Later that year he was in Berlin and other parts of Brandenburg. Here he heard the call; it might have been destiny speaking. In fact the impetus came from Flemming, and the catalyst was the first meeting between Augustus and the Tsar of Muscovy in summer 1698.

'BONDS OF FRIENDSHIP'

Tsar Peter I (1672–1725) came to the throne of Muscovy in 1682. Until 1696 he was co-ruler along with his older half-brother Ivan. Although the regency of his exceptional step-sister Sophie ended in 1689, Peter did not fully assume the reins of power until five years later.

The young Tsar was a brutally handsome epileptic, standing six feet seven inches. Intelligent, self-educated and hyperactive, Peter, like his fan Stalin, was a cruel and cowardly modernizer of a retarded state. 'He is a ruler both very good and very evil at the same time', wrote Sophie of Hanover after their meeting in 1697, 'his character is exactly the character of his country'.[4]

Inheriting a desultory war against Turkey and its minions the Crimean Tartars, Peter used the campaigns of 1695–96 to test his embryonic navy and capture Azov at the mouth of the Don. But access to the Black Sea, as to the Baltic, was still denied him. There was no military effort against the Ottomans in 1697, for that March the towering figure of the Tsar travelled 'incognito' to Western Europe, under the auspices of Muscovy's 'Grand Embassy'.

Peter's ambiguous status led to many ticklish problems of protocol for his hosts. However unintended, the worst breaches came at Riga, which were exacerbated when Swedish sentries quite properly challenged the phantom giant as he casually sketched the walls and ramparts of the fortress. From that point on, the 'insult' to his Tsarish Majesty would provide – to Peter at least – a fig-leaf of legitimacy for his future aggression against the Swedish Empire.

For six weeks Peter stayed at Pillau (Baltiysk), near Königsberg, observing the outcome of the Polish election. Despite the presence of his rag-bag army of 60,000 on the Lithuanian frontier, it is doubtful that Peter intended to invade the Republic. He merely made clear that he belonged to the 'anyone but Conti' school. The presence of the louring Muscovite host was more effective in helping to restrain support for Conti following the election. Peter later claimed that Augustus owed his throne to him; but this was after the first blush of their mutually two-timing alliance had deepened into embarrassment. Nor was it true; Augustus owed his throne to his own efforts.

After visits to Brandenburg, Holland and England, Peter returned to the continent in May 1698. His main objective now was to shore up the faltering alliance against Turkey. In September 1697 Eugene of Savoy, Augustus's successor as commander in Hungary, had scored a signal Imperial victory over the Ottoman armies at Zenta (Senta). Following this the Sultan sued for peace. Both Vienna and Venice were interested in a settlement that permanently recognized their extensive conquests. However, the Tsar and Poland's new King remained committed to war, since their current gains ranged from non-existent to minimal.

On 10 August 1698 the two callow monarchs met at Rawa Ruska, north-west of Lwów. It was the very first encounter between rulers of Muscovy and Poland. 'I cannot begin to describe to you the tenderness between the two sovereigns', gushed one of Peter's entourage, as the Tsar embraced Augustus.[5] It was a foretaste of the future; Poland would become familiar with bear-hugs from her mighty neighbour.

The reason the two men so took to each other at the time was that they behaved like a pair of regal lager louts. Having exhibited their prowess as drinkers and muscle-men, they turned their fuddled heads to future prospects, should peace with Turkey be imposed upon them. The favoured candidate for a thorough 'duffing-up' was the Swedish Empire. This was simply random thuggery; there were no concrete plans as to how Sweden should be 'sorted'. That would require Patkul's brand of sophisticated *Realpolitik*.

On 13 August Peter left Rawa for Moscow to deal with the mutiny of the Streltsy. To aid the Tsar's justice, Augustus handed him the sword with which he had recently hacked off a stag's head with one hefty blow. Peter gave the King his own in exchange.[6]

In September Peter was back in Moscow, proudly flaunting the Saxon's sword and thereby demonstrating, as an attendant diplomat put it, that 'the bonds of friendship' between them were 'stronger and closer than the Gordian knot and could never be cut by any blade'.[7] Comparable resistance was hardly forthcoming from the necks of his miserable Streltsy captives.

The Streltsy (*strelets*: 'archer' or 'musketeer') were an admixture of standing army, palace guard, police and traders. Quartered mainly in the capital, they had become a Muscovite version of the Praetorian Guard or Ottoman Janissaries. Peter had first encountered a Streltsy rising in May 1682. The ten-year-old Tsar had cowered with his mother and half-brother while these king-makers scoured the Kremlin for the objects of their hatred, before tossing their victims onto upturned spears and mincing them with axes.

Peter's revenge in autumn 1698 was sweet; it was also vile, even by the barbaric standards of Russia. The sniffy comments of foreign envoys, whose states practised such butchery merely to a lesser degree, are worthy only of scorn. Nevertheless, the picture of Peter roasting and decapitating some of these powerless rebels is not an edifying sight.

Yet when the carnage was over, so too was any future military threat from Russia's old order. The armed forces that would eventually eliminate Sweden and Poland as powers were the product of

Peter's reforms. Their awesome might was hammered out in the crucible of protracted war. Not that a lengthy struggle had entered the minds of three rapacious kings and a vengeful Livonian noble when they conspired together to destroy the Swedish Empire; it should have been a walkover.

Chapter Sixteen

'To make war on Sweden'
Patkul, Augustus and Peter 1699–1700

'THE FEAST WE HAD PREPARED'

In May 1698 Patkul was in east Brandenburg, visiting the estate of his countryman and near-namesake Otto Arnold von Paykul, who had left Livonia at 15 and was now in the Saxon army. Paykul's near neighbour was Fieldmarshal Flemming, an uncle of Augustus's bagman in Poland. When the Livonians visited the older Flemming, either by chance or design his nephew was also present. Young Flemming listened to Patkul's bilious anti-Swedish rhetoric and noted the latter's query as to the chance of him receiving both pension and protection from Augustus.

That October Flemming invited the Livonian, who was currently in Berlin, to meet with his King. Patkul complied, and his first encounter with Augustus took place in the Lithuanian town of Grodno on New Year's Day 1699. For some 90 minutes they discussed attacking Sweden, and Patkul was invited to prepare a paper upon the subject.

He left Augustus a memorandum the next day; it is doubtful that he drafted it overnight. In Warsaw on 7 April, Patkul presented the Saxon with a more refined version. It now bore the ornate title 'Unsanctioned reflections concerning the scheme to make war on Sweden' ('Unmaßgebliches Bedenken über das dessein Schweden zu bekriegen'). Patkul's presumptuous thoughts only required the sovereign's fiat; there is no indication that Augustus withheld his approval.

In contemporary terms, Patkul was a one-man self-appointed 'think-tank', and his Machiavellian document was but one of many 'position papers' that he wrote. With his interminable, *machtpolitische* memoranda, Patkul comes over as a very modern man. Long before Marx, Freud and Veblen, this clever, lonely, erratic exile was hinting that the world was barely worth living in without a *Weltanschauung*. Politics was for professionals; the average untutored specimen, he claimed, was like 'an ape with a pocket-watch'.[1] Prised from such gauche grasp, the use of power could likewise be made into a precision instrument.

What he offered Augustus was a recipe for conquest. There was to be none of the fanfare of a declaration of war. Livonia would be taken by means of a decisive surprise attack (*coup de main*, *Handstreich*) launched against Riga; about whose defences this former captain in the Swedish army was hardly uninformed. Given Ritterschaft touchiness, only Teutonic troops, Saxons or German mercenaries, were to be used at the outset. This avoided another problem too; for Augustus could not employ the Crown and Lithuanian armies without the Republic's approval.

Patkul warned Augustus against insufficient diplomatic preparation for his strike against Sweden. He had to take into account the interests of other powers and either bring them onside or neutralize them. Patkul proposed all manner of ploys to deal with the Maritime Powers, France and the Emperor; Brandenburg was to be kept neutral, at least, by recognition of Frederick as King of Prussia, when he finally made this expected move to upgrade himself.

Denmark, in constant conflict with the Swedes over the Øresund and the Holstein-Gottorp question, would be in Augustus's camp. So would the Tsar, once he had made peace with Turkey; for had he not already proposed war at Rawa Ruska? ('Selbst die proposition zu dem Kriege gethan'.) However, Patkul voiced concern about the alliance with Peter. It had to be made clear to the Tsar that, although they would support his gaining a 'firm footing' ('fester Fuß') on the Baltic, this could only be in Ingria and Karelia. Even then, Augustus must somehow ensure that Muscovy did not commit its 'usual' atrocities or limit freedoms in these lands.

What concerned Patkul most of all was the need to exclude Peter and his armies entirely from the territory of his 'Fatherland', in which he included Estonia. They must ensure 'that he did not devour the feast we had prepared for ourselves, by snatching Livonia from under our very noses'.[2] Patkul knew about Peter's interest in Narva. This Estonian town stood on the west bank of the river of the same name, which constituted the frontier between Estonia and Ingria. He warned Augustus that if Peter took Narva, he could threaten central Livonia and capture all of Estonia almost before such news reached Warsaw.

But if Peter was not to have Livonia, who was? Its previous 'owner' was Poland; yet it is debatable whether Augustus had promised in his Pacta Conventa to reconquer the province for the Republic. Naturally, that would not stop him from using Polish lands as a springboard for his invasion, while wearing his other hat, crown or cap as Elector of Saxony. As to who was in a position to transfer the title-deeds of Livonia, this was of course Johann Reinhold von Patkul. Together he and Augustus went through an elaborate charade.

In January 1699 Saxon troops in Lithuania moved into winter quarters in Polangen (Palanga), a port on the Baltic coast of the Duchy of Courland, which was a Polish fief. That same month Patkul and Flemming travelled to Mitau, the capital of the duchy. In mid-February Patkul was reported to have journeyed secretly to Riga. There he obtained from the Ritterschaft a so-called *Instruktion*, which contained a number of conditions; the first being the maintenance of the Lutheran religion in Livonia. This document also appointed Patkul as plenipotentiary of the Ritterschaft in future dealings with Augustus. He was empowered to negotiate on their behalf not only the terms already contained in the *Instruktion*, but whatever else he judged 'to be best for our Fatherland'.[3] In short, it gave Patkul the power to dispose of Livonia as he deemed fit.

There seems little doubt that Patkul himself was the author of the *Instruktion*. That in itself was not abnormal, since he had drawn up most of the documents that gave any substance to the aspirations of this querulous band of barons. But had the Ritterschaft actually authorized the powers which he had arrogated to himself? It seems unlikely. The *Instruktion* was not signed by anyone, and although it bore the Ritterschaft seal, this meant little. One might even doubt whether Patkul went to Riga. Not that he lacked courage, but it would have been foolhardy for him to risk capture at this juncture.

Possibly he just betook himself to the home of his relatives in Courland, who had sheltered him upon earlier occasions, and there drafted the *Instruktion* and sealed it himself. At best he may have received visits from some other 'extremists', since he returned to Mitau in March with a letter for Flemming ostensibly written by old Budberg, his fellow-delegate in 1690. Whatever the truth of these details, of one thing there is no doubt. Patkul represented only himself and at most a few cronies; in no way did he possess the legitimate authority to dispose of Livonia's future.

It is impossible to say whether Augustus knew this or, if he did, whether it influenced him. He may have been under Patkul's spell, or entranced by the Torgau 'prophecy', or just sharing a dream-world with the Livonian. Perhaps he was too distracted by events in Poland to attend to the consequences of his involvement. Alternatively, he may have merely been stringing Patkul along. Whatever his state of mind, on 24 August 1699 the King of Poland, who was renowned for his 'dissimulation', signed a formal agreement (*Kapitulation*) with the self-appointed 'plenipotentiary' of the Livonian barons.

If there was a surreal quality about the signatories, it extended to the contents of the *Kapitulation*. This document promised the Ritterschaft an aristocratic and agrarian paradise; virtually every ancient and existing right they had enjoyed was guaranteed. On the other hand, pro-Swedish and commercial Riga was to be deprived of any independence and placed under the sovereignty (*Hoheit*) of the barons on their estates.

More tangible was the future status of the province. Although Livonia was to become a fiefdom (*Lehn*) of Poland, a secret article ensured that it would remain a hereditary fief of the Elector of Saxony, whether or not he was also King of Poland. Augustus could now tag 'Duke of Livonia' onto his tally of titles, while the Ritterschaft would be ruled by a German prince. All that was needed to produce this blissful outcome was an alliance capable of crushing Swedish power.

'SI CE COUP MANQUE'

Although Saxony and Denmark had signed a mutual defence treaty in March 1698, this was not adequate for the aggressive needs of the two states. In May 1699 one Herr von Wallendorf (alias Patkul) was sent to Copenhagen to make the appropriate soundings.

On 8 August Flemming summoned a conference in Warsaw to consider the mechanics of the strike against Riga. It was decided to send Patkul and Major-General Georg Karl von Carlowitz to Moscow, in order to urge Peter to mount a concurrent attack in Ingria and Karelia. In August 1699 Patkul formally entered into Saxon service, effectively as a Geheimrat. When Augustus left Warsaw for Dresden in that month (p 152), both Flemming and Patkul journeyed with him. The Livonian was but briefly in Dresden. Early in September 1699 he and Carlowitz were travelling the long road to Moscow.

In the meantime, King Christian V of Denmark had died, thereby necessitating a renewed ratification of the Danish–Russian treaty by his successor, Frederick IV. It would soon be forthcoming, his ambassador in Moscow, Poul Heins, assured Peter. For Augustus's Danish cousin was eager for war with Sweden, in order to gain control over the Øresund and sole authority over Schleswig. On 25 September 1699 Frederick concluded a treaty of aggression with Augustus. It contained the first concrete specification of a date for the Saxon invasion of Livonia – January or February 1700.

By now Moscow was filling up with diplomats. A major Swedish embassy had arrived in July 1699 to renew the 1660 Treaty of Kardis on behalf of their young King Charles XII. When signing the treaty, Peter salved his conscience by not kissing the cross to indicate its sanctity, claiming that he had already done so at his accession (when he was a minor). The visitors did not press the point. Augustus too was blithely lulling the Swedes. Yet before their delegation left Moscow Peter had sealed secret pacts for joint aggression against the Swedish Empire, with both Saxony (21 November) and Denmark (3 December).

Before doing so he had to plough through a memorandum from Patkul. The Livonian sought to turn Peter's interest towards trade with Asia, in an endeavour to minimize his interest in the Baltic. This was unrealistic: Peter did not simply share older Russian urges for access to the sea, he was a navy man and seafarer. The first Tsar to sail on salt water, he skippered ships and even built them. It was not a question of whether Peter intended to have a port upon the Baltic, but rather of how much of its coastline would content him.

He talked openly of taking, or rather taking back, Narva and other areas. Narva was in Estonia. Depending upon whose 'history' one read, it was 'traditionally' part of Livonia, or an 'ancient' Russian town. Obviously the sword would settle title-deeds in the end. Yet it was also the case that the provinces allocated to Muscovy (Ingria and Karelia) had no worthwhile ports. Although the Tsar would ultimately build in this area something more than an anchorage, at St Petersburg, it is unlikely that such a grandiose scheme filled his head in 1699. At that time he was looking for something extant, and Narva was the obvious prize. Yet, when he spoke of other Baltic ports, was he already eyeing Tallinn and Riga, which had *never* been part of Russia?[4]

Whatever Peter's plans, in the treaty signed between Saxony and Muscovy on 21 November 1699 Augustus undertook to buttress Peter only in his recovery of Ingria and Karelia. In support of this, he promised to mount a diversionary attack upon Riga, for which task the Tsar would send Russian auxilaries to assist the Saxon.[5]

Both powers agreed to try to bring Brandenburg into the war against Sweden and to make no separate peace. To Augustus fell the task of involving Poland. However, the most important point, the date of the Russian attack against Ingria and Karelia, remained unspecified. Although Peter hoped to be in the war by April 1700, the thirteenth and final article of the treaty expressly reserved his position: he would not make war on Sweden until he had made peace with Turkey.

As an edifice of tripartite aggression, the interlocking treaties rested upon a rather rickety foundation. All depended upon the success of the Saxon surprise attack upon Riga. If it failed, it would spell calamity for their other plans. Only Heins appears to have expressed such doubts. 'Si ce coup manque', reflected the Danish ambassador, 'ce seroit un grand malheur pour les mesures a l'avenir'.[6]

'AT ANY COST'

In November 1699 the Saxon troops in Polangen moved into the north Lithuanian province of Samogitia, establishing their headquarters at Joniškis, directly south of Riga. Lieutenant-General Flemming commanded the force. His deputy was the Livonian Major-General Paykul. Also there was Patkul, with the rank of colonel.

Flemming was absent when the first attempt on Riga was made. Nor is it clear in which century it occurred: the dates of Christmas 1699 and early January 1700 are both given, which might simply reflect the difference between old and new style calendars. Nor do we know whether the move was authorized by Augustus or merely allowed by Paykul, at the urging of his headstrong countryman Patkul. Was it the classic 'missed opportunity' or a debacle spawned by disobedience?

In any event, several hundred Saxon soldiers, disguised as Latvian peasants, waited overnight to cross the frozen River Düna on sledges. The plan was that they rush the fortress gates, overpower the watch and seize both citadel and city. Such a coup would have put Augustus in virtual control of Livonia.

However, not for the only time in the history of Germany's *Drang nach Osten*, the troops were inadequately kitted out against the winter. A few sheepskin coats from the local peasantry might have helped. Instead, most of the waiting Saxons suffered frostbite, and the venture was abandoned. Indeed, it was a double failure, in that all element of surprise was now lost. Count Eric Dahlberg, an astute septuagenarian and Governor-General of Livonia since 1695, learned of the abortive coup. His response was to strengthen watches and patrols.[7]

Exactly what was happening in Saxony is not clear. The picture that we do have is not particularly edifying. Flemming seems to have delayed his return to the Livonian front for two reasons, neither of which should have impinged upon the duties of the man entrusted with the critical capture of Riga. First, he reportedly married a Lithuanian princess of the Sapieha clan and spent some time on his honeymoon; then he was used as a diplomat, to negotiate a treaty with Brandenburg.[8] This hardly had the result of bringing the Prussians into play: the cautious Frederick expressly reserved his position as to whether he would fall in with the plans of the anti-Swedish

170

alliance. Ultimately, he opted to sit back and see what happened ('stille setzen und zusehen').[9]

If Flemming's behaviour lacked urgency, he was presumably taking his lead from his master; and Augustus's conduct was unforgivable. It smacked more of a gambler, staking his all on one card, than of a ruler, considering the interests of his realm in a statesmanlike fashion. And it was mired in hedonism: crucially in this instance, the realization of his ambition succumbed again to pleasure.

When the element of surprise was lost, Patkul evidently assailed Augustus with another memorandum, inquiring whether or not they should persevere with their venture. There were only two alternatives, pronounced Augustus in January 1700: either they could proceed 'at any cost' ('a quelque pries que cla soit'), or they could just let things drop. The latter was out of the question, because others were involved and Saxony was deeply entangled in commitments; therefore they had to continue.[10]

Soon afterwards he ordered Flemming, once he had signed the treaty with Brandenburg, to leave immediately for his command and capture Riga. His general did not get much else. Augustus bombarded him with platitudes: everything was in God's hands; 'I trust things go well'; be strong-hearted; 'I have given mature consideration to your problems'. Following this twaddle came a few tangibles: 'I will certainly produce some money for you'; Livonia was stripped of troops; and before reinforcements arrived from Sweden, Augustus would be there with the remainder of his army.[11]

Why did he not take overall command himself, and lead the rest of his troops to Riga straight away? The Russians thought it was because he was too interested in having a good time in Dresden.[12] Certainly Augustus attended Carnival, and a goodly part of a RT 100,000 loan from Denmark was lavished upon festivities and a French troupe playing comedy in Dresden. Only the dregs went to the needs of the miserable unpaid Saxon soldiery. More money for Augustus's military needs was eventually procured from his States, which met from September 1699 to March 1700; to get it, Augustus had to agree to concessions in other areas. Once this was settled, Augustus left for Warsaw, arriving there on 24 March.

Meanwhile, a new war had greeted the new century. It would last for 21 horrendous years; yet it commenced upon a small scale. Flemming left Berlin on 2 February and reached his headquarters in the middle of that month. On the night of 21/22 February 1700, Flemming launched the Saxon invasion of Livonia, without a declaration of war. His troops soon overran Swedish outposts, but they were inadequate for a full-scale siege of Riga; nor did he have the requisite heavy artillery, since they had banked on the coup.

171

Huffing and puffing with frustration would not bring down the walls of that great fortress, so the Saxons addressed themselves to easier targets. Having taken the small fort of Kobron on the left bank of the Düna, Flemming launched an attack on Dünamünde on the Baltic, to cut off Riga from the sea. The stronghold was valiantly defended by a battalion of Finnish troops, and in their initial attack the Saxons lost 1000 men, including Major-General Carlowitz. Dünamünde finally fell on 24 March, and Flemming flatteringly renamed it 'Augustenburg'.

Following this, Flemming and Patkul proceeded to Warsaw to obtain reinforcements and big guns. They got a Te Deum instead, while in May the Senate Council refused to permit the Republic's participation in this 'Saxon' war. A few thousand pro-Sapieha volunteers turned up, but that was all. And although hostilities between Denmark and Sweden had commenced in Holstein in mid-March, there were no Russian auxiliaries for Augustus; Peter had still not signed an accord with the Turks. Muscovy's message therefore remained the same: no peace in the south, no war in the north.

Nor had the Saxons received any assistance from their fellow-Teutons in Livonia. The Ritterschaft were *attentiste*, when not overtly hostile. The idea of becoming the vassal of Catholic Poland held no appeal. Their passive response to Flemming's insipid manifesto, with its 'justification' of the Saxon attack, revealed the bankruptcy of Patkul's position. The niggling knights of Livonia would not lay down their lives for the liberty that he had 'negotiated' upon their behalf.

Ironically, the only sector of society to support the Saxons were the non-Germans (*Undeutschen*). The Latvian and Estonian peasantry rose in rebellion; not against the Swedes, but against their hated Livonian lords. It took Saxon troops several weeks to suppress them.

In June the bold Baltic barons compliantly autographed Dahlberg's denunciation of Patkul. The venerable boss of Livonia told the Landtag that his King would not rest until the 'traitorous and perjured Patkul' ('der verraehterischer und meineydige Patkul') had been dragged to the gallows.[13] The prospect for any waverers was clear. After the usual prattling amongst themselves, the entire Ritterschaft, Budberg included, cravenly stigmatized their former champion, then galloped back to their estates.

Such freedom of movement existed because in May Swedish reinforcements from Finland had driven Flemming's force back into Lithuania. It was but a temporary reprieve for the defenders: in the summer of 1700 a Saxon and mercenary army, anything between 15,000 and 24,000 strong, returned to Livonia.

'THE HARMONY OF THE ARTILLERY'

In mid-July the 30-year-old King of Poland led his troops in a flamboyant display more suggestive of a pageant than a campaign. Preceded by white-shirted heralds with rods in their hands, Augustus cantered off to war in full finery. Sumptuously attired in armour, astride a brown-and-white piebald, he headed a gaudy throng of courtiers who came to witness his conquest.

With troops and batteries established upon the river sandbanks opposite Riga, and something like the requisite siege cannon in place, the great city was now beleagured. Augustus was present on 27 August 1700 when, to the ritual accompaniment of kettledrums, the first of 15 great bombs was blasted at the fortress. Three days later the salvo was repeated, and again in early September. Yet when the smoke finally blew away, Riga appeared little damaged and the defenders distinctly unimpressed. The Saxon army, which stood poised to storm through the city's breached walls, now melted away.

News had arrived that the Danes had left the war (p 179). On the other hand, the Russians had still not entered it. Augustus was alone and exposed. The accompanying French ambassador, du Héron, offered his mediation. He pranced off to Riga to be lavishly entertained by Dahlberg. The city hardly seemed on the verge of starvation. Héron negotiated a truce. The siege was gradually broken off, prisoners were exchanged, and via French good offices Augustus sounded the Swedes on terms of peace.

It appears that in the meantime, even heavier guns were brought up, but they were never used. Around mid-September this artillery was dismantled and shipped back to 'Augustenburg'. Then, in search of a few limp laurels, Augustus turned his armies on Kokenhusen (Kekava), south-east of Riga, and captured the fort. It was intended as a bridgehead to ensure communications with Courland and Lithuania.[14]

Leaving 600 men there as garrison, in late September Augustus withdrew the remainder of his army into winter quarters in Courland and Lithuania, and himself retired to Warsaw. Riga stood unscathed, a mockery of his ambitions and a douche upon his pleasures. Even when it finally fell, it involved him in another farce played out against the thunder of guns.

In November 1709 the Tsar's all-conquering armies surrounded Riga. It was Peter's turn to fire the first bombs: 'I thank God', he gloated to Augustus, 'that I myself have been enabled to set under way our revenge on this accursed place'.[15] Russian forces finally took the city in July 1710.

At that time Augustus was in Marienburg (Malbork) in Royal

Prussia, along with the then British envoy George Mackenzie. He decided to commemorate Riga's fall, even though he expressed himself 'better pleased to've seen it continue in the hands of the Swede'. Notwithstanding such reservation, 'the court was in gala and the appearance magnificent enough'. After assisting at a Te Deum, Augustus 'was pleased to give a splendid entertainment' to the attendant Muscovite generals.

The 'ancient' castle in Marienburg was 'not much in repair' and had deep cracks in its walls. As Augustus was dining, the celebratory salvoes of the Saxon cannon opened up; and so did the masonry. In one wall 'the rent widened so visibly and such quantity of sand fell down from the gape' that both diners and servants fled in fear. With 'the fright so general', the King of Poland 'thought it advisable to make immediately cease the harmony of the artillery'.[16]

Along with Riga, every inch of Livonia and Estonia was bagged by Peter in 1721 under the Treaty of Nystad; while fully one-third of Augustus's life was squandered in dealing with the consequences of his rash, inept and immoral assault upon the city. He believed that he could whisk it away from Sweden's young king and bask thereafter in the tarnished glory of his deed. For Augustus had no conception of the nature of Charles XII of Sweden in consequence, a startling revelation awaited him and all the courts of Europe.

Chapter Seventeen

'But by the ruin of my foes'
Charles XII strikes 1700–1702

'THE SWORD DOES NOT LIE'

On 5 April 1697 Stockholm was shrouded in a snowstorm. As the blizzard raged, Charles XI died following a dogged battle against stomach cancer. He had come to the throne as a four-year-old in 1660. A warrior like his father Charles X, his losses had been safeguarded by the triumphs of Louis XIV, which had made the Swedish monarch 'arbiter of Europe'. Domestically he was one of that continent's most absolute rulers: the 1693 Declaration of Sovereignty (*Suveränetets-förklaring*) had transformed him into 'an all-commanding sovereign King', responsible for his actions 'to none on earth', and with the authority 'to rule and govern his realm as it seemeth him best'.[1]

In May 1680 Charles married 20-year-old Ulrika Eleonora, youngest daughter of Frederick III of Denmark. The job-description accorded with that of her sister Anna Sophie, Augustus's mother: 'Madam', the King stiffly informed her, 'we have taken you that you may give us children, not advice'.[2] Ulrika complied, breeding like a sow and supplying seven infants in under eight years, before expiring aged 33. Of this litter, only a trio remained alive when her husband died four years later. Two were daughters; the sole survivor of five sons was Charles, born on 17/27 June 1682.

Ascending the throne as Charles XII, Sweden's new King was not yet 15, some 12 years younger than his Saxon cousin. Like Augustus, he inherited marked traits from both parents. Unlike him, in Charles's character the virginal outweighed the venal. His mother endowed him with intelligence, truthfulness, piety, a love of justice and self-control. From his father he took the Vasa temper and will-power, and emulated his proclivities for hunting, break-neck riding and soldiering. Like his forebear, he too would detest diplomacy and diplomats. Mingled with this aversion was a distrust of France. Charles XI declined to sport 'a French knife', as he termed the rapier; his son matched him and added a refusal to speak French, which he understood perfectly, as he did German and Latin.[3]

Qualms about France did not entail the absence of her envoys from Stockholm, and it is to Count Guiscard that we are indebted for a portrait of Charles, penned shortly after his seventeenth birthday. 'The King of Sweden is of tall stature', remarked the diplomat, and 'very handsome', with 'fine eyes and a good complexion'; but as for his 'very strange style of dress', Versailles vogue it was not. Charles wore a small wig, a plain stock without cravat, flat-soled shoes and a 'very tight jerkin of plain cloth, with sleeves as narrow as our waist-coat sleeves'. From the skimpy belt looped around this coat hung 'a sword of extraordinary length and thickness'.[4]

Yet Charles would always be original and something of a minimalist in sartorial taste. Abandoning wigs in favour of the close-cut *Schwe-denkopf* was hardly detrimental to the prowess of Sweden's warriors. His trademark uniform of blue multi-buttoned tunic, black cravat, buckskin breeches and high boots drew frequent comment.[5]

He continued to carry his remarkably long and broad sword. It was not Excalibur, but it still represented literally and metaphorically the guiding principles of his life. 'The sword does not lie' ('Värjan ljuger inte'), 'the sword does not jest', he would say. 'The sword makes the best conditions, it always means what it says'.[6]

These words were simply variants upon the concept that might is right; yet Charles also considered himself righteous. He lived an upright life and expected others to adhere to the same code. 'This young King', Robinson advised Stepney, 'has very great *fonds* of honour and integrity in his own heart, and is apt to be shocked at the want of it in others'.[7]

Tsar Peter expressed the same view 20 years later, when Charles was safely in his grave and Russia's triumph over Sweden was vali-dated by the Treaty of Nystad. There never was 'so perfect a man and hero as brother Charles', but 'he was too great to rule over men'. Because 'he was a man of his word, and honourable, he looked that all should be so'.

In this, as the Tsar implied, Charles was naive and literally unworldly, since all men are inherently flawed. They apply power in the pursuit of objectives, and this is met by countervailing power serving contrary aims. Such is the essence of politics. Unless life is to be conducted as constant warfare for the attainment of uncorrupted ideals, politics requires compromise between the diverse aims of imperfect men. Soiling his hands in making such adjustments was part of a sovereign's task. 'Therefore', concluded Peter, 'that man comes off best in ruling over other men, who is aware of human weakness in himself'.[8]

But Charles *was* uncompromising. He was wronged by those who had wantonly attacked him, and he was prepared to use force ruthlessly, but justly, to right this wrong. 'I have resolved never to engage in an unjust war', he proclaimed to his Senate, 'but on the other hand, never to conclude a just war but by the ruin of my foes'.[9] There was no room for trade-offs or negotiated settlements in this doctrine; therefore it heralded continual warfare to attain his ideal. Means and ends were matched in the time of Charles's triumphs; yet after the Swedish army was destroyed at Poltova in 1709, he still sought the same ends with virtually no resources.

It is this period that demonstrates more the measure of this amazing man, although it offers no simple conclusions as to his character. Was he simply deranged, deluding himself that he was carrying out God's will? Did he believe that right was might? Was Charles the ultimate idealist and hero of history, who, rather than accept any injustice, literally fought on to the end of his life against overwhelming odds, clenching that great sword of truth? Was he now some incarnation of Mars, unable to conduct his life save through unceasing warfare, which had evolved from a means into an end? Was he the most irresponsible of rulers, prepared to see 'Sweden shed her last drop of blood as a libation to Charles XII's caprices'?[10]

Such questions can also be posed about his early career; but history does not ask questions of the victor, as Hitler comprehended so well. The Führer may also have empathized with the King's invasion of Russia and the Götterdämmerung of the Swedish Empire. Then there was Charles's all-powerful status within his realm: his formal accession to the throne saw the installation of Sweden's most absolute monarch. At his coronation in December 1697, he demanded the oath of allegiance from his Estates before, not after, the event. He planted the crown upon his own head and omitted to swear the royal oath. Charles XII had no obligation to his subjects, other than what he would grant of his own will; but the duties of his vassals were absolute. 'The King's word is our law', explained one of his officers.[11] In this terse phrase he spoke for the nation.

Charles believed that 'a soldier will be happier if he avoid the possession of a wife'.[12] There were no women in his life, nor was there wine. This was Aurora von Königsmarck's Olympian judgement upon him too: 'Enfin chacun des Dieux discourant à sa gloire, / Le plaçait par avance du temple de memoire: / Mais Venus ni Bacchus n'en dirent pas un mot'.[13]

Some wine had passed his lips during the mad days of the 'Holstein frenzy', after Charles first came to the throne, when he seemed intent upon squandering Sweden's entire treasury upon his pleasures. But he made the reverse transition to Augustus and replaced this French frippery – literally – with small beer.

Whether or not Charles was homosexual is irrelevant, save for those seeking to contradict the fallacious view that history is forged solely through heterosexuality. For what it is worth, Liselotte, that understandably jaundiced witness, while prepared to assert that William III amongst others was so inclined, completely exculpated the Swedish King. In fact, her worry was that Charles had been 'so badly hurt' in a riding mishap (p 193), 'that he is no longer any use for marriage'.[14]

Rather, Charles had no use for marriage; he was an ascetic wedded to his sword. The many descriptions of his spartan ways evoke a man more fitted for the monastic cell than for any majestic court. In another age he would have graced a knightly order, and even in his own he was a crusader. Possessed of 'more than supernatural courage', as Peter fairly phrased it, to his soldiers he was 'un étendard vivant' on the battlefield, and an impossible standard off it. He wolfed down his plain food in silence, then rode alone for miles and hours. Perhaps it purged his natural urges; possibly it removed him from the pressure to make decisions.

That he thought long and hard about his moves is undeniable. He might listen to advice, but only he called the shots. 'The moon in silence goes her way, and heeds no yelping curs' was a line by his countryman Stiernhielm that he was wont to quote.[15] Then, after the long pregnant silences and bouts of lassitude that marked his behaviour during the Great Northern War, came the bursts of frenetic activity. 'Our Lord', averred Charles, 'is ever on the side of him who boldly accomplishes that which he has to do'.[16]

God was on the side of the bold battalions, no matter how big they were. Charles would demonstrate this, in turn, to each of the three kings who had been so rash as to attack his realm. Augustus, Frederick and Peter had unleashed a force that is impossible to blank out of the pages of history. Whether mad, sublimely moral, or both, this incredible figure was now propelled onto the forefront of the world's stage, to act out his Homeric life.

'BY MEANS OF OUR LAWFUL ARMS'

Charles learned of the Saxon invasion of Livonia on 17 March 1700, and of Danish moves in Schleswig-Holstein two weeks later. 'It is strange that both my cousins want war', he mused, before stiffening with resolve. 'So be it', Charles vowed. 'We have a just cause, and

God will help us. I will deal first with the one, after that will be time enough to talk to the other'.[17]

Effectively organized by military districts, the Swedish army was ready to leave Stockholm by early May. 'Everywhere there were great multitudes in the streets', recalled a subaltern, 'and at the windows weeping'.[18] Such tears would be but a trifling down-payment upon the torrents undammed by Swedish losses over the next 20 years.

Charles dealt first with his Danish cousin. Under cover of the fleets of the Maritime Powers, acting as guarantors of the 1687 Peace of Altona, the Swedish army made a lightning invasion of Zealand (Sjæl-land) in the summer. With Swedish and German forces overcoming the Danes in Holstein too, Frederick IV sued for peace. The Treaty of Travendal of 18 August 1700 took Denmark out of the war.

The following day Russia entered it. A 30-year armistice with the Turks had been signed in Constantinople on 14 July, but the news only arrived in distant Moscow on 18 August. On 19 August came the ukase of 'the Great Tsar'. Owing to 'the many wrongs' of the Swedish King, and 'especially' because the Tsar 'suffered unpleasantness' in Riga, 'his soldiers shall march in war on the Swedish towns'.

It was pathetic stuff, but at least 'the Great Tsar' had the courtesy to declare war, unlike Charles's cousins. More realistic grounds were provided by the stated objectives of the war: the capture of Ingria and Karelia, 'which by the Grace of God and according to law' belonged to Russia, and were 'lost during the Time of Troubles'.

The trouble this time was that Peter would in fact be invading Estonia and directing his armies against Narva. Following the declaration of war, Peter penned a letter to 'his dearest brother, sovereign, and neighbour' Augustus, expressing the hope 'that Your Majesty will not see other than profit' from it.[19]

More likely, Augustus judged that he would never see Narva, when the spoils were divided. With Denmark out of the war, no Russian help against Riga, and now Peter aiming at Narva, the Saxon too looked to his own interests. As we have seen, he broke off the siege of Riga, but at the same time strengthened the garrisons of the captured forts of Kobron, Kokenhusen and 'Augustenburg' in order to maintain his lines of communication. Then he pulled his main army back across the Düna to winter in Courland and himself retired to warmer quarters in Warsaw.

From there Augustus bombarded Peter with requests for aid and openness about his future intentions, while at the same time he pressed Louis XIV to arrange an armistice between himself and the Swedes. The French King obliged; like the Maritime Powers, he was looking for allies in the looming War of Spanish Succession, and both Sweden and Saxony had potential. He did not want to see their armies decimated or deadlocked in some trivial dispute on the wrong side of Europe.

Charles, however, was unimpressed when the French 'communicated the King of Poland's terms'. In early October he stressed that, without 'full restitution' by Augustus for his 'unjust and faithless invasion', he intended 'to obtain right and satisfaction by means of our lawful arms'.[20]

Initially, Charles was attracted by the idea of invading Saxony directly, seeing it as the speediest way to bring Augustus to heel. Two things dissuaded him, and sent him instead to the eastern Baltic: first, the opposition of the Maritime Powers, who kept Denmark quiet and desired no ructions in the Empire, their main source of mercenaries; and second, the Russian declaration of war and attack upon Narva. 'If once the Tsar gets a place on the Baltic, he'll stick to it come what will'.[21] This prescient view of Chancellor Oxenstierna remained germane when the Swedish army landed in the north Livonian port of Pernau (Pärnu) in October 1700.

There Charles learned of Augustus's withdrawal from Riga and the more pressing needs of the besieged Swedish garrison in Narva. Following only five weeks of preparation, Charles marched some 10,000 of his 'brave blue boys' towards the north Estonian town. For the time being, cousin Augustus was off the hook.

The proximity of the Swedish army was too much for the Tsar's volatile courage. A Saxon general observed Peter 'confused and half-mad, wailing and draining glass after glass of brandy'.[22] Finally, using the miserable and specious excuse of pressing engagements elsewhere, 'the Great Tsar' fled from Narva a few hours before the enemy arrived.

On 30 November 1700, in a blinding snowstorm, the King of Sweden and his troops hurled themselves against the Russian army of 40,000. Losing one-fifth of their own small force in dead and wounded, the Swedes inflicted between 8000 and 10,000 casualties upon the Muscovites. Besides these, the bag of prisoners outnumbered their potential guards, and the men, though not the officers, were bundled across the River Narva and pointed back to Russia.

From Stockholm, Robinson wrote of 'our young hero's prodigious victory'.[23] It stunned the courts of Europe. There was a new King on the block, and he was little more than 18. He had not led the army that day, for he was still an apprentice; but he had played an incisive role in the plan of attack and thereafter had been where he would remain – in the thick of the fighting. As the official account of the battle related, Charles went 'where the fire was hottest and the fighting sharpest', hazarding himself to 'all the perils to which the meanest soldier was exposed'.[24] To Hedges, the latest Secretary of State North, the King of Sweden appeared 'to be an extraordinary man, as well as a great prince'.[25]

The war could have ended there, with the Danes whipped, Peter's army shattered and Augustus, isolated and buffeted, suing for peace. The miserable life of 'Carlos the Bewitched' had finally come to an end on 1 November 1700, and the envoys of the various protagonists in the upcoming War of Spanish Succession were buzzing around Stockholm soliciting Swedish favour. To Oxenstierna, such circumstances suggested ending 'this present lean war' and 'making His Majesty the arbiter of Europe'. But if this meant a deal with Augustus, then Charles would have none of it. 'It would put our glory to shame', he objected, 'if we were to lend ourselves to the slightest treaty or accommodation with one who has so vilely prostituted his honour'.[26]

An unworthy foe, more whore than king, Augustus was to be ruined, not rewarded with diplomatic table-talk. He had yet to feel the 'lawful arms', the avenging sword of truth, wielded by Charles XII. This righteous man, whose good book was replete with tales of overweening monarchs toppled from their thrones by the servants of the Lord, was ready with his wrath. In the coming years, Augustus would relentlessly suffer the dire consequences of having fired that ire.

'AFTER SUCH A GREAT REVERSE'

For now, the Saxon enjoyed a false sense of security in distant Warsaw when, after Narva, Charles put his army into winter quarters in Estonia. Meanwhile, the loser in that battle sent his emissaries to the Polish capital to inform Augustus of 'a certain unexpected and unhappy event'. Augustus responded later in December; spurning euphemism, he quizzed Peter as to what he planned to do 'after such a great reverse'.[27]

The upshot was that the two young sovereigns met again for three weeks in February and March 1701, in the north Lithuanian town of Birsen (Biržai). Despite some heavy carousing, they did manage to produce an agreement. However, the Treaty of Birsen of 9 March was a virtual Diktat by Augustus, the sole member of the anti-Swedish coalition whom Charles had not yet defeated.

The Tsar reaffirmed that when Sweden's Baltic Empire was partitioned, both Estonia and Livonia would fall to the Elector-King. Peter's other obligation to sustain the alliance was to furnish Augustus with heavy subsidies and 20,000 Russian infantry. It was the beginning of the substantial supply of 'men and money' from the Tsar to his ally, a policy which ultimately worked greatly to Peter's advantage.

Augustus's gains at Birsen were soon offset by a string of misfortunes. On 25 March there was a fire in the Electoral Palace at Dresden. The first letters that William Aldersey received in Hamburg 'gave but very little hopes' that 'any part of it was saved'. Later he could report that 'about a third part' was incinerated, with the loss in the royal apartments of 'several costly hangings and beds with other rich furniture'. Overall, the damage was estimated at RT 400,000.

April 1701 yielded a crop of rumours that Augustus was dead. But on 29 April Aldersey received letters from Warsaw dated the 17th, which related that the Saxon was 'ill of a fever and has been let blood thrice in one day'. By 3 May he was reportedly 'somewhat better', and by 6 May 'well recovered, though he does not stir abroad for fear of a relapse'. A fortnight later Augustus was up and about. Plantamour forwarded a letter from Warsaw, which described how 'il fait construire un grand Batiment pour sa retraitte et pour son divertissement'. He was probably pouring Peter's money into the project, since 'le Czar a déjà envoyé au Roy 85,000 Ducats de la somme qu'il luy a promise'.

By now Swedish forces were congregating in Estonia, preparatory to marching south 'to undertake something' against Saxon units 'drawing together on the other side of the Düna in Courland'. Three days later, on 27 May, Aldersey added that rumour had it that Augustus 'designs to go in person to the army', if there was no likelihood 'of coming to an agreement with Sweden'.

There was none. As Aldersey informed Ellis on 31 May, Augustus 'would hear in no wise of any indemnization to Sweden for the hostilities committed' in Livonia, nor would he make any agreement without Peter's concurrence. Conversely, Charles had continued to ignore all French efforts to broker peace, leading Guiscard to remark sardonically that the Swede apparently feared he 'might run short of enemies'.[28]

On 17/28 June 1701, his nineteenth birthday, Charles left Dorpat and marched his army of between 15,000 and 18,000 men through stifling heat to Riga, where he arrived on 18 July. But he would not be facing his cousin in battle. 'The King of Poland has quitted the design he had' of 'marching in person against the King of Sweden', reported Stepney, owing to the 'violent fall he had lately from his horse (which bruised his shoulder and almost broke his neck)'. Forced to carry his arm in a sling, our hero could only wait in Warsaw for the outcome of the engagement.

Entrenched upon the high ground behind the left bank of the

Düna was a Saxon army of 9–10,000, commanded by Fieldmarshal Steinau (until 1699 another 'prophetic' Württemberger in Danish service). Also in the line were some 4000 of the 20,000 Russians sent by Peter. Although outnumbered, Steinau's fortified position was strong: 'if the Swedes even numbered 100,000', contended a subordinate, 'it would be impossible for them to cross successfully'.[29]

'Impossible' seemed not to figure in Charles's vocabulary. On 19 July 1701, by dint of imaginative pontoons and raw courage, the Swedish infantry got across the Düna. If their cavalry reserves could have been ferried across in time, then the Swedish triumph might have been decisive. As it was, casualties were quite light. Charles lost some 500 dead and wounded, against 2000 killed and captured Saxons and Russians. The injured Steinau withdrew his remaining forces towards Kovno (Kaunas) in Lithuania, but was not pursued by the exhausted Swedes.

Thereafter Charles consolidated. A Swedish force occupied Mitau, the capital of Courland. Other measures taken in that duchy suggested that Sweden intended its long-term incorporation into her empire. Early in September Charles took up winter quarters not far from Libau (Liepaja) in western Courland, while his troops mopped up the remaining Saxon resistance behind Swedish lines.

Although Steinau had voluntarily evacuated Kobron and Kokenhausen, a tenacious Saxon garrison, short of wood and salt and ravaged by illness, held out in Dünamünde, the short-lived 'Augustenburg'. When the besieging Swedes finally took the fort on 22 December 1701, only a handful of several hundred Saxons remained in a condition to surrender. Charles was impressed by their fortitude, and other Swedes by the artillery that they had captured.

So was Stepney in Vienna. He had seen this 'train of such infinite consequence' in Saxony, and 'it may pass for as good as any prince in Europe is master of'. Transporting it down the Elbe, 'round about to Danzig' and then to Courland, cost over 140,000 dollars. 'It was intended for the beauty and defence of Riga', when that city was taken, but was now likely to be 'the ornament and trophies of the arsenal at Stockholm'.[30]

'IF I COULD TRUST HIS WORD'

Soon after the inconclusive battle on the Düna, Charles decided to concentrate upon the total defeat of Augustus before invading Russia. As part of his programme he adopted Oxenstierna's idea that the 'suggestion ought to be made to the Poles that they might get rid of their troublesome warlike King'.[31]

Receiving prevaricating and inadequate response to his proposals (p 189), Charles marched into Lithuania in January 1702, ostensibly at the invitation of the Sapieha faction there. Stopping and starting, yet rebuffing all ploys by Augustus and the still non-belligerent Republic to prevent his southward advance (including a bizarre episode involving Aurora), the Swedish King eventually led his army into Warsaw on 25 May.

His logic was simple: the logic of power. If the Poles thought it compatible with their neutrality to let Augustus use Poland as a base, then consistency demanded that they concede Charles the right to seek out his enemy on the Republic's territory. And if the Polish leaders sought peace, then their option was clear-cut. In conference with the wily Radziejowski, Charles demanded that he convoke an Electoral Sejm to allow the Poles to dethrone Augustus, promising that 'I will never grant the Poles peace till they have elected another king'. 'He still continues in his dethroning humour', observed Stepney, 'and I do not see who can hinder him'.[32]

Augustus tried. On 16 May he had decamped with the crown jewels to Cracow. It was in this direction that Charles led his army in mid-June. Finally, the two cousins clashed directly for the only time on 19 July 1702 at Kliszów (between Cracow and Kielce). Here a Swedish army inferior to the Saxons in cavalry and artillery imposed a serious defeat upon Augustus. The Swedes lost less than 1000 of their 12,000-man force, while a quarter of the 16,000 strong Saxon army were dead, seriously wounded or prisoner. They had not been much helped by the Poles, who had demanded the place of honour on the right of the line. Arriving late, the Crown Army had fluttered over the hill, wafted their lances at the Swedes and then melted away.[33]

Augustus, who according to Voltaire's account thrice led his men in a charge, escaped at the last moment and retreated as far east as Lwów. Charles moved on to Cracow, taking that city at the end of July. Next month Augustus proceeded westwards to Sandomierz, and from there attempted to rally the szlachta of eastern Poland. In September 1702 he returned to Warsaw (p 190).

But now he was less ruler than fugitive, his writ running only where he and the remnants of his army were *in situ*, or subjects remained loyal. Elsewhere his sovereignty was challenged and fractured, not only by the Swedes, but by the endemic anarchy of Poland's nobility. Yet, if Augustus ruled from the saddle as a hunted man, he was at least fortunate enough to be in an immense country, where he could somewhere go to ground away from his pursuers; with the final option of sanctuary in Saxony.

His supporters were less fortunate. In October, 2000 Swedes under

Stenbock moved into Red Russia and the Volhynia to exact and destroy. Marauding 'torch in hand', Stenbock followed 'the compass of disobedience' to the Carpathians. Charles, recovering from a broken leg (p 193) as his army marched north along the Vistula, encouraged him. 'I see you are giving the Polacks a hard time', he remarked, adding that 'it will do them no harm'.[34]

Conversely, it did Charles little good. As the main Swedish army advanced into Lublin at the end of 1702, Augustus quit the capital and transferred his forces behind the Vistula-Bug rivers. This set the pattern for four years, as the two monarchs minueted around the vast Commonwealth, never again to face each other personally in battle.

Charles could not bring the war to an end. 'I would give Augustus peace immediately, if I could trust his word', he told his new Chancellor Count Piper in August 1702. But as soon as peace was made, 'and we are on our march towards Muscovy', the Saxon would 'accept Russian money and attack us in the back', and Sweden's task would be 'even more difficult than it is now'.[35] So the only solution remained for the Poles to dethrone their King and elect a more amenable (and pro-Swedish) successor.

Yet this was the very policy that stimulated Augustus into continued resistance. He could not go back to being a mere Elector, particularly as his peer in Prussia had crowned himself King in January 1701. So what Swedish officials dubbed 'that cursed Polish dethronement' committed their country to the east, and Charles knew it, and probably relished it. 'We shall be fighting this side of the water for many a year to come', he had predicted in 1701.[36]

It was to be a long test of wills and treasuries between the two sovereigns and their suffering domains. And it was into this imbroglio that an English envoy was pitchforked in January 1703. On this occasion it was not George Stepney, although he had done much to set up the mission. Ironically, it was his very familiarity with Augustus that debarred him from undertaking it.

Chapter Eighteen

'In a lucky minute'
The origins of English intervention
1701–02

'THE PEACE OF EUROPE'

On 20 March 1701 England's new envoy extraordinary to Vienna received his instructions from William III. The object of George Stepney's latest mission was 'to cultivate the friendship' already existing between England and the Empire 'and to make if possible, a stricter union and alliance for the preservation of the peace of Europe', which was again threatened by 'the overgrown power of France'.

Such wording could have come straight out of the previous century. The focus too was the same: William III versus Louis XIV, the Maritime Powers versus France, in the struggle for the control of Western Europe. There was no reference to the fact that war had already broken out in the east of the continent; a war that would ultimately influence Europe's destiny far more than the stalemate of the pending War of Spanish Succession. But such ignorant downplaying of events in Eastern Europe, in the capitals of the west, is hardly a historical novelty.

Stepney was also to inform himself 'of the dispositions of the several princes of the Empire, in relation to the present affairs'. William wished to know which would support or oppose him in his latest bout with Louis, and which 'intend to stand neuter'. It was solely in this context, in his role as Elector of Saxony, that Augustus initially figured in the Briton's mission. Not only was Stepney *not* accredited to Augustus, but the British displayed a growing frustration with the mercurial Saxon. 'The King fears we shall never hold Proteus', wrote Blathwayt to Stepney, 'and that he will continue to turn himself into a thousand shapes and slip from you'.

Stepney arrived in Vienna on 1 May 1701 and made his first reference to Augustus on 25 May. He reported him offering 20,000 Saxon troops to the Empire, after his war with the Swedes was finished, in exchange for the district of Glogau in the Imperial province of Silesia. Stepney found it 'hard to guess what he aims at'. Yet the target seems obvious: a 'Silesian corridor' linking Saxony with Poland would allow Augustus to shuttle both troops and trade between his realms, without reference to Vienna.

Some days later Stepney reported upon the Sejm that had convened in Warsaw on 30 April. It proposed that Augustus should send away his Saxon troops and make peace with Sweden. The representatives adjudged that the Republic was not involved in the war, since their King had attacked Sweden in his capacity as Elector of Saxony. Radziejowski offered to mediate and sent a letter to Charles, to which the Swede would respond in August 1701 with a demand for his cousin's dethronement. Other than that, the Polish leaders retreated into their surreal world, ignoring the pressing military necessities, which no amount of constitutional niceties could replace.

'THE TWO ROUGH KINGS'

Unknown to the Poles, there was another potential mediator around, namely England's Secretary of State for the North, Sir Charles Hedges. He appeared to be acting upon his own initiative when he wrote to Stepney on 28 June 1701, the day Charles marched for Riga. Hedges told the envoy that William had given no directions for 'composing the war' between Charles and Augustus, but 'seems inclinable to make that step'. If he did, and Stepney had 'a mind to be employed in that business', Hedges would 'propose it and promote it' all he could. As he understood the terms of peace, 'the King of Sweden will insist upon having all his places restored to him', since he refused to recognize Augustus as 'a lawful enemy, being assaulted by him without any provocation or warning'.

Replying on 16 July, Stepney thought the time was 'far from being ripe' for such intervention. He considered that 'the two rough Kings must exchange blows, before they can be brought to an agreement'. Moreover, the allies must ensure 'their being disposed to be really our friends, before we endeavour to part them'. For if one or both of Charles and Augustus should later 'fall into the interest of France, it had been better for us to have left them to exercise upon one another'.

Stepney claimed to have 'business enough', without this new role alluded to by Hedges; yet he was clearly interested. He suggested that it would be November before a meeting could be fixed, and recommended Danzig or Breslau (the latter but four days from Vienna) as a site for negotiating a settlement. Moreover, his proximity would save William the cost of sending out a special mission. Then came the clincher: that Stepney had 'the advantage of being better known' to Augustus than 'anybody else that can be employed', having been 'three times at his court as Elector and King'.

Hedges was impressed by this response. He replied in early August that it 'confirms me much in my opinion of your fitness above others' to mediate a peace between the 'two northern Kings, when things are ripe', should it be 'in our interest to do it'. He conceded that 'several circumstances' mentioned by Stepney had not occurred to him when he first mooted the project, 'which I did upon the general notion of your apparent dexterity in negotiating affairs of a like nature'.

However, it was the military dexterity and political ham-handedness of the Swedish monarch which would most effectively stymie mediation. On 19 July the Swedes scored their points victory on the Düna, following which Charles stiffened his terms for any settlement. In early August 1701 he wrote to Radziejowski from Bautzen (Bauska) in Courland. Responding to the Primate's offer of mediation, Charles demanded that the Poles should dethrone their King. He was to adhere stubbornly to this policy. Not for nothing did the Turks later dub him 'iron head' (*demir bache*), while Augustus during his campaigns against them had rated merely as 'iron hand' (*demir delhe*).

When Stepney learned of this letter, he observed 'how roundly' Charles expressed his intention to dethrone Augustus. But for now the issue was deflected. Radziejowski delayed his prevaricating response to Charles until October, and the Swedish army marched no further south in 1701. However, on 14 December Stepney reported that Charles had sent another letter to the Poles, 'more severe, pressing for an answer, and demanding once more their concurrence towards dethroning their King'.

On the 22nd day of that month a new Sejm commenced in Warsaw. The deputies demanded not only that no Saxon troops be allowed to return, but – in a surge of Sarmatian vindictiveness – that all Saxon officers and ministers 'be likewise obliged to quit' Poland. However, once Charles crossed their borders in January 1702 the Polish position changed, and Augustus was permitted to bring back his Saxon forces to defend the Republic. The Crown Army was also mobilized for this purpose, although constitutionally Poland–Lithuania remained at peace with Sweden (and at Kliszów would hardly epitomize belligerence).

Augustus needed little encouragement. Stepney reported that he had 'gone roundly to work'. An army supposedly 20,000 strong was to assemble at Lützen near Leipzig on 25 April 1702. However, rumours that Augustus 'may take a ramble thither, to assist in person at the general review' proved false: instead the Saxon army came to him via Silesia, making its usual 'ravage' of the land en route.

After this force was defeated at the regal punch-up of 'the two rough Kings' at Kliszów in July, Augustus retreated first to Lwów and then to Sandomierz. He left Sandomierz on 2 September 1702 and 'marched away with his Saxon forces towards Warsaw, where he arrived the 8th in the evening'. In the Polish capital, it was bizarreness as usual. Augustus was 'attended in his residence' by officials and envoys, 'as orderly as if there was no enemy in the kingdom'. By October hunting and comedies were again on the royal agenda.

Stepney, however, also contended that the King of Poland had sent 'submissive letters' to the Swedes, of which the Republic's ministers were in ignorance. This, along with a conversation that the envoy held with his Swedish counterpart, led to a resurrection of the proposal for an English peace mission, with Stepney offering to lead it. It seems quite likely that he felt a need to make himself appear 'essential' to the new administration in London, since his position had been undermined by the fall of his long-time patrons.

'DIFFICULT TIMES'

The see-saw party politics of England intruded upon Stepney's career from the moment when Hedges was dismissed in December 1701. Vernon moved over from the southern department to replace him as Secretary of State North, while Lord Manchester took South. Then in March 1702 William III died following a fall from his horse, to be succeeded by his sister-in-law Anne.

The Queen's first ministry saw the appointment of her favourite, John Churchill, Earl (and later Duke of) Marlborough (1650–1722), to the post of Captain-General, while Lord Sidney Godolphin (1645–1712) returned to the role of Lord Treasurer. These two men, later joined by Robert Harley (1661–1724), would dominate England's affairs both at home and abroad, during the War of Spanish Succession. This conflict formally commenced in May 1702, with declarations of war by the Empire and the Maritime Powers upon France and Spain.

In the lower ranks of officialdom place-men changed places too. Marlborough took Stepney's friend Adam Cardonnel to Holland as his military secretary, leaving his predecessor out of the in-crowd. 'I find myself in all appearances so far released from a foreign attendance, and even thoughts of foreign affairs', the redundant Blathwayt informed Stepney in March. Pertinently, he added that he was also 'out of the way of being able to do you service'. A month later, Vernon told Stepney that he and Lord Manchester were 'to make room' for the returning Hedges and Lord Nottingham. 'All I understand of the reason for it is, that a party will have it so'.[1]

But Stepney had no intention of making room himself: he had 'recourse to a more than ordinary patron', by going directly to the top man. Writing to Godolphin on 10 May, he noted that he was unknown to Anne and feared 'lest my being absent and a stranger should turn to my prejudice'.

Stepney ran quickly through his curriculum vitae. He had dedicated to William 'the best years of my life', fully one-third of which had been spent on twelve missions 'in this wild Empire' (C4 n1). These found him 'marching with auxiliaries', as well as 'drinking and negotiating with German princes'. Then he came to his main concern, his 'sheet-anchor'. As a remuneration for services rendered, William had made him a Commissioner for Trade, as a 'support in the difficult times of tallies and tickets', when payments were irregular and fell 'much short of what was designed'. As extra insurance Stepney delved into his cellar, and on the last day of 1702 Godolphin rewarded him with 'an abundance of thanks for the best Tokaj that I have ever seen in England'.

'A TICKLISH PIECE OF WORK'

Perhaps Stepney had quaffed a glass or two himself, before he wrote to Hedges on 20 September 1702 to promote his mission to Charles. Prior to Kliszów he had remained far less sanguine. In June there was Austrian pressure upon Anne 'to interpose for an accommodation of affairs in the north'; so Hedges decided that 'this juncture' seemed to be 'a fit time' to press Charles to settle 'matters with Poland'.[2] Stepney demurred, still being of the opinion 'that the animosities are too great to be decided otherwise than by blows'.

Certainly Kliszów saw the 'blows', but it hardly dispelled the 'animosities'; so why should Stepney now see a 'window of opportunity'? Because Augustus was writing 'submissive letters'? These cost him nothing and lacked any agreement to surrender his crown. Because Charles was 'receiving daily complaints' of Muscovite devastations in Livonia and therefore 'may at last hearken to overtures of peace'? On the contrary, Charles was coldly indifferent to the suffering of his subjects there.

Stepney was clutching at straws. He offered no solid grounds for suggesting that his mission might be successful. He appeared simply to will its success, and his masters in London, who were desperate to recruit Swedish and Saxon troops for their war against France, went along with him. Once Stepney not only effectively lifted his 'veto' upon earlier proposals, but also tendered his own insubstantial terms, the mission took on an unreal life of its own.

Stepney's reasons for proposing his mission seem mainly selfish. He doubtless wanted to conform to Ellis's wish that he 'be among the blessed peace-makers'. Perhaps he shared Under-Secretary John Tucker's assessment of his talents, that 'what is possible to be done, you will do'. Yet he also wanted to make a splash, and to show how essential he was to the new masters in London.

Nor was money far from his thoughts. In November he confessed to Ellis that 'my main view (next to doing a good work) was to hook in my arrears', while 'if I succeed, I have a fair pretence to the allowance of a plenipotentiary, or at least an augmentation'.

There was also an element of being 'his own carver'. Stepney wanted to control his mission. He saw it as 'a hattering business', suitable for one who worked alone. 'I would desire to be left to my own judgement', he told Tucker, 'not to set out till it appears the conjuncture is favourable'.

This was ludicrous. First he deemed the situation to be favourable enough to propose his mission; now he wanted to stall it until the situation was favourable. It was more like poking entrails than diplomacy. Given the initial false premise that Charles was ready to make peace with a crowned Augustus, the 'conjunctures' were never right. Stepney was obliged to veer and tack in his subsequent analysis. Ultimately, he was mightily pleased to be shot of the mission; yet he was very skilful at having it accepted in the first place.

He told Hedges that neither Charles nor Count Piper could speak any language other than Swedish or German, which 'will make it a hard matter for you to find a man capable to treat with them tete a tete'. This was not true, and Stepney knew it.[3]

'I am not very fond of a jaunt to Poland', the envoy alleged, 'having already more than satisfied my curiosity, by a turn I took to Warsaw'. However, if it was deemed useful that he went, while Charles was only five days' journey away from Vienna, 'I offer my service'. And such was simply for the greater good; 'no interest of my own tempts me' to make these proposals. Stepney's only satisfaction lay in performing 'a considerable piece of service in a lucky minute, which ought to be watched and laid hold of'.

In other words, anyone might be sent on this mission; it did not have to be Stepney. Hedges should feel free to appoint some other multilingual and altruistic diplomat, who had visited Poland and was currently resident close to the Swedish King. There must be plenty of them in Queen Anne's service. Yet, after reviewing the competition, Whitehall plumped for Stepney.

On 15 October 1702 Hedges wrote to him from Bath. 'Your going to the King of Sweden is approved and your despatches are preparing'. Nottingham, the other Secretary of State, informed Stepney that he might soon expect his credentials, made out as the envoy wished, 'one with and the other without a character, and therefore you are to prepare for that journey'.

'Nothwithstanding the rigour of that season', Stepney replied nobly, 'I shall put myself in a readiness to execute what commands I shall receive'. To Hedges, he conceded that 'to catch and fix' Charles was 'a ticklish piece of work'. However, 'some step must be made to convince him that he was not neglected'.

This was another strand of the 'lucky moment' thesis and was equally fatuous. Charles was not sulking in his tent because he was neglected by fawning envoys sent by self-interested states. He loathed the company of diplomats, and he was perfectly capable of promoting Sweden's interests by dint of his own resources. Up to now, the effect of his blade had been far mightier than any opus from an envoy's quill. While Charles saw a role for agreements, the stroke of a pen might only ratify what he was forced to attain by strokes of his sword. And so long as Augustus posed on Poland's throne, the sword stayed unsheathed.

Although not sulking, Charles was in his tent, laid up by the leg he had broken in a riding accident on 30 September. His absence sparked rumours, doubtless stoked by Augustus, that he was dead. Another canard had it that Marlborough had blundered into a French patrol and been captured; and his imprimatur was essential to the success of Stepney's project.

'I here send you Her Majesty's instructions when you go to the King of Sweden', wrote Hedges on 27 October, 'by which you will find you are to observe whatever my Lord Marlborough shall direct you'. We need not detail the content of these instructions, since Stepney did not go on his mission. In brief, he was instructed to procure peace, to bring Sweden into the Grand Alliance and to treat with Charles for a portion of his army to serve as mercenaries against France.

Stepney replied on 18 November 1702 that he was still wondering whether it was 'seasonable' to see Charles. Strangely, the 'lucky minute' had still not arrived, and only Stepney could divine its delicate 'conjunctures' and 'seasons'. He also pointed out that, if he was to mediate, he needed credentials to Augustus as well, 'were it only out of decency upon coming into his kingdom'. Moreover, he wondered about the Tsar's position, 'with whom, I understand, the King of Sweden is not willing to treat on any account whatsoever'. He also wanted his instructions to permit him to return to Vienna, as and when he saw fit, without awaiting further orders; otherwise 'I may be in danger of being led about to Liefland [Livonia] or God knows where'.

These were all important caveats. It is an indication of the sloppiness of the initial proposals and their acceptance in London that they were not considered earlier. What did receive scrutiny, however, was Stepney's association with both Vienna and Augustus.

On 24 October Cardonnel told him that Marlborough 'believes you as proper for the business as any person whatsoever'. But he considered that Stepney's 'coming from the Court of Vienna may be a great obstacle to your negotiation'. Certainly, there was no reason for Charles to feel any warmth towards an Emperor who allowed Augustus to ferry his forces from Saxony to Poland through Silesia.

By now Stepney was almost ready to accept the fact that his mission would be vetoed. He told Tucker on 19 November that he was waiting for Marlborough's instructions 'if my journey holds, but I am apt to believe the contrary'. Too many people saw him as 'too partial for the King of Poland', because of his 'familiar acquaintance of old with that disorderly prince'. He claimed to 'care not three farthings' whether he went to Poland or not, 'and shall be indifferent whoever does this piece of service – provided it be done'.

On 1 December 1702 Stepney received Hedges' letter of 14 November. This informed him that, 'some objections being made in Holland against your going to the King of Sweden', a final decision was being deferred until Marlborough's return to England. Stepney replied that he already knew about these 'objections' and was satisfied to be 'dispensed from that uncomfortable commission'; particularly as Charles seemed less inclined to come to an agreement than in September! 'There were thoughts of sending me on a short errand', Stepney wrote glibly to Halifax in late December, 'but I am willing to believe those thoughts are now over'. His assumption was correct; as Ellis worded it, 'some other person will be sent upon that errand'.

'A long train of miseries'
King on the run 1703–1707

Chapter Nineteen

'Wholly at a stand'
The failure of mediation 1703

'SOME OTHER PERSON'

The 'some other person' who was burdened with Stepney's 'jaunt to Poland' was Dr John Robinson (1650–1723), England's minister resident in Sweden.[1] A Yorkshireman of humble birth, but a future Lord Privy Seal and Bishop of London, Robinson was an Oxford graduate and, until 1686, a fellow of Oriel College. A decade later the married, though childless, clergyman was made a Doctor of Divinity. In later life, a contemporary depicted him as 'a little brown man of grave and venerable appearance', but 'of good sense, and very careful in his business'.

Robinson had first gone to Sweden in 1680 as chaplain to the English embassy. Save for a couple of brief sojourns in England, he had served in Stockholm ever since, rising from secretary and agent to his present rank. He spoke fluent Swedish and knew German, French and Latin as well. Like his fellow envoys, he had often been driven to the verge of financial ruin by a tardy Treasury.

In January 1702 he had told Stepney of his wish that William 'would give me leave to return to England and a parsonage in London, the Dean and Chapter of Canterbury have offered me'. One year on, such a dream was even more remote when, as the legatee of Stepney's caprices, he was obliged to undertake the other's 'disagreeable errand'. Ellis fancied that 'Dr Robinson will give nobody thanks for putting him upon the execution of it'.

Yet his first reference to the whole affair, in a letter to Stepney of 27 December, was perfectly restrained. He mentioned that Cresset had nearly got the job, but had excused himself. Stepney too was lucky 'to have missed that uncomfortable fatigue', particularly as there were 'so small grounds to hope for success' from the mission.

'I am in pain for you', Stepney replied on 20 January 1703. Perhaps tinged with guilt, he worried how Robinson would manage in Poland during 'this hard weather', and 'how a campaign life will agree with one of your sedentary temper'. He promised the older man 'a volume of transactions which I had gathered for my own use'.

Not that Stepney thought them of much relevance. Although once believing that Augustus would somehow 'get out of the briars', he now reckoned that he 'will be out of the saddle before you reach the Goth', who was pressing for 'dethronization more than ever'. Repeating this view to Ellis, he added pointedly that Augustus's 'successor may not be so much in the interest of the allies as my mad friend has been'.

References to the two monarchs were more dignified in the instructions given to Robinson in December 1702.[2] Robinson was to prevent any disturbances of the Treaty of Travendal (p 179), and to seek a stricter union and alliance with Charles. He was to impress upon the Swedish King that 'a peace in the North' would contribute to the defeat of Louis and to invite him to provide the allies with 12,000 troops.

Robinson was also given credentials to Augustus, 'which you will make use of as you shall find occasion, if you discover you are like to do any good in the matters you are sent upon'. If such propitious circumstances should arise, Robinson was to seek an audience with Augustus. If peace should somehow break out, he was to parley for a Saxon contingent of 8000 men. Overall, Robinson was to try and enlist 20,000 units of cannon-fodder from the two kings 'upon the best and most reasonable terms'.

'A SORT OF LAPLAND-AUDIENCE'

Leaving Karlskrona on 13 January 1703, Robinson landed five days later in Stralsund, then part of Swedish Pomerania. He hoped to reach Danzig in a few days, but, as he quipped to Hedges, 'I am now in a country, where the wagoners in their sphere, are as sovereign as their princes'. And of the two warring princes striving for control of Poland, the Saxon was far more accessible to Robinson. Charles was still in winter quarters in the castle of Jabowice near Lublin, while Augustus was in Marienburg, a few miles south-east of Danzig.

While Stepney had marketed his muddled mission, his 'mad friend' had left Warsaw on 28 October 1702 and travelled north-west to Thorn (Toruń), a 'pretty well-fortified and garrisoned' town further down the Vistula. Augustus disappeared from Thorn around midnight on 7–8 November, attended only by five courtiers, and returned there 'after his ramble' on 21 November. According to Plantamour, he had been to Saxony, for the sole purpose of visiting a young alchemist he held in the fortress-prison of Königstein.[3]

There is no indication that our hero returned laden with home-made gold. He was, however, still weighed down with self-made troubles; so the appearance of Dr Robinson in Danzig was not an opportunity to be missed. In February 1703 a Scottish officer in Saxon service contacted Robinson to tell him that Augustus would be pleased to see him, 'but did not insist on it'.

The qualification was a relief to Robinson. 'I must make excuses', he told Hedges, 'and resolve not to see him or his ministers, that I may not render myself unacceptable elsewhere'. After ducking an audience with Augustus, Robinson left Danzig on 21 February and pressed on to Warsaw. Reaching the capital on 1 March, the envoy evaded another conclave, this time with Radziejowski, and headed for Lublin. He arrived there on 9 March.

Charles was exhibiting his usual dislike of diplomats. 'He will have no foreign ministers about him at this time', Piper told the Briton. To counter this, Robinson adeptly used the ploy of being in the vicinity 'as a letter carrier rather than as a minister', informing the Swedes that he bore missives from Queen Anne as well from Charles's sisters. It seemed to work, for on 11 March Robinson could report that Charles 'will give me an audience tomorrow morning'.

On 12 March 1703 a brusque interview took place between the 52-year-old envoy and the 20-year-old King. By any standards it was, in Stepney's words, an 'odd rencontre'. Charles was already marching north when he permitted Robinson his 15 minutes of freezing fame at 'a sort of Lapland-audience'.

As he travelled towards the Swedish camp that day, Robinson espied 'the Goth' at the head of some Swedish cavalry. Leaving his carriage, the cleric stood in a frozen field, garbed in 'a very large robe with the furs turned outwards, a great fur cap in my hand, and a very sorry periwig on my head'. With Charles 'sitting on horseback bareheaded', giving 'great attention to what I said in Swedish', Robinson skilfully rattled off certain of his instructions.

Charles 'made no reply to this harangue', save to consent to Robinson's request that he be permitted to remain some days in the Swedish camp. The best that the envoy could get was to learn from Piper that Charles would entrust 'his interests in Her Majesty's hands preferably to any other, whenever such interpositions shall be reasonable'. On 21 March he took his of leave of Charles and returned to Warsaw.

'BUT LITTLE VIOLENCE'

Robinson arrived in the capital only shortly before Charles, who reached Praga, then a little village lying on the east bank of the Vistula opposite Warsaw, towards the end of March 1703. The Swedes then entered into negotiations with Radziejowski in April. These talks again produced no solution to the question of dethronement, even though Charles is somewhat generously attributed with showing 'flexibility'.

This apparently revolved around his considering the possibility of Augustus being succeeded by his six-year-old son, with a preference for the lad to declare his loyalty to the Protestant persuasion. Besides profaning Poland's constitution, such 'concession' hardly altered his basic objective. 'Should I stay here 50 years', he reiterated, 'I would not leave the place till I have dethroned the King of Poland'.[4]

If the Poles thought that they could prevaricate upon this issue, because their King still possessed countervailing power to Charles, the latter soon disabused them. Leaving Praga on 28 April, the Swedish army marched north-east and crossed the Bug two days later. On 1 May 1703 'the Goth' administered his annual thrashing of the Saxons and their calamitous commander at Pułtusk, a small town on the River Narew. From Steinau's force of 3500, over 1000 were killed or taken prisoner; the Swedes, 3000 strong, lost less than 20.

Charles now moved down the Vistula. On 25 May he invested Thorn, a predominantly Protestant city with 6000 Saxon defenders. However, the Swedish bombardment had to await the arrival of heavy siege artillery from Livonia, and only began in mid-September. There was a certain irony in the Siege of Thorn, besides the fact that it was conducted with Saxon artillery. 'Many of the bigoted Poles', wrote the Anglican Robinson sourly, 'instead of being concerned for the place', saw it as 'a judgement on both, that a Protestant army and a Protestant town are endeavouring to destroy each other'.

In fact casualties were light. 'Here at Thorn the business has been done with but little violence', Charles enlightened his sister after the town capitulated in October 1703.[5] Nearly 5000 sick and hungry Saxons were added to his bag of prisoners. Augustus's army had now dwindled to 4000, facing a Swedish force at least six times that strength. But at least Charles's five-month involvement in Thorn had given the Elector-King (as well as the distant Tsar) some respite and room for manoeuvre.

'LABOURING FOR PEACE'

After Pułtusk Augustus had moved south to the now vacant Lublin. There he assembled an Extraordinary Sejm, which met from 19 June to 12 July 1703. This body excluded delegates from the pro-Swedish area of Wielkopolska, who in turn established the Confederacy of Środa, which Charles took under his protection. Poland was lining up for civil war.

On 12 June Robinson and the Dutch envoy left Warsaw, 'to wait on the King of Poland'. On the morning of 14 June they met with Augustus in Lublin. Addressing him in French, Robinson warbled the usual felicitations and assurances of esteem and friendship on behalf of his sovereign. Augustus muttered the appropriate responses, then talked up his deeds in favour of the common good.[6] He maintained that he had 'these two years been labouring for peace in these parts', but since cousin Charles could not be 'persuaded to a treaty, it became necessary for him to take other measures'. Despite this, he assured Robinson that he would 'still retain a peaceable disposition'. Overall, the Briton 'found great reason to be content with the favourable reception' he had encountered.

The envoys returned to Lublin on 24 June. That evening Augustus 'received us in a garden, and discoursed very openly with us upon the situation of affairs here'. The next night Radziejowski arrived in Lublin; on 27 June the envoy was present at a debate in the Sejm, 'wherein the Cardinal was used with all indignity imaginable'.

From what he 'heard and saw' at Lublin, Robinson concluded that 'the design of dethroning the King of Poland has had a quite contrary effect, and entirely confirmed to him the affections of his people'. He had not heard a word 'spoken to him, but with the greatest veneration, and high contestations of zeal for his service'. Despite that, it was with no high hopes that the English, Dutch and Imperial envoys presented the Polish proposals to Charles.

Meantime, the Lublin Sejm gave Augustus control over the Lithuanian as well as the Crown Army. It also resolved that the latter should be enlarged and placed entirely at his service. Finally, this body gave Charles six months to give tangible proof of his desire to make peace; otherwise the Republic would declare war on him. Unsurprisingly, Dr Robinson concluded that 'the transactions of the Diet at Lublin' had only 'increased the suspicions and distrusts on the Swedish side'.

Warsaw being currently free of Swedes, in August 1703, our harassed hero moved there, where he was joined by Patkul, who arrived from Russia in September.[7] Opining that he was 'in considerable credit' with the Tsar, Robinson defined Patkul's mission as 'to prevail with the King of Poland to continue' the war, and to 'engage the Republic' in it too. To assist his powers of persuasion, Patkul was said to have brought with him 400,000 ducats and promises of more Muscovite 'men and money'.

201

Robinson thought that, before deciding upon his response to Patkul, Augustus would wait for the Swedish reply to the last Polish peace proposals, advanced by the allied ambassadors. Should there be 'any tolerable hopes of peace', he would decline the Livonian's terms. It was a forlorn hope, for in September the Swedes rejected the Polish proposals 'as insufficient, without making any other overture'.

'MEASURES TO THAT END'

Things were now 'wholly at a stand', Robinson told Hedges on 29 September, and he did not see 'what more can be asked of the King of Poland'. The envoys had been called into Augustus's presence that evening, since he 'desired to know our thoughts' upon the existing situation. Lamely, they could only reply that they must report home and await further orders; that was, unless the Elector-King had fresh proposals to tender. He did not. Augustus saw no choice but to change tack; there would be no more 'Mr Nice Guy'.

'His Majesty answered he would make no more offers'. The next overture must come from Charles, declared the Saxon, 'and he would now only think of taking his measures to that end'. It was time for him to behave 'more vigorously than hitherto'.

In other words, Augustus was committing himself to the new reality. The only serious prospect of peace required him to assent to his dethronement. His only hope of keeping his crown was, in effect, to act as a mercenary. He would have to accept the junior role in his alliance with Peter and fight the war on behalf of the Tsar, far from Muscovy, with Russian 'men and money'.

For much had changed since Augustus called the shots at Birsen, in the aftermath of the Russian debacle at Narva. For more than two years Augustus had been the sole Swedish quarry, suffering defeats on the Düna and at Kliszów, Pułtusk and Thorn. Conversely, Peter's revitalized armies had won a major victory over the Swedes in Livonia (at Hummelshof in summer 1702) and picked off the Swedish garrisons in Ingria and Karelia.

Since May 1703 Peter had been building that mighty monument to himself, his policies and his conquests at St Petersburg on the mouth of the Neva. Currently his hordes were laying waste Estonia and Livonia, with the Swedes pushed back into the coastal fortresses and Dorpat. There was nothing that Charles could do about it, at least until he was free to invade Russia; and this he could not even contemplate while Augustus, down but still not out, lay in his rear.

The new agreement between Augustus and Peter, the Treaty of

Warsaw signed in October 1703, was therefore tailored to the Tsar's interest: that the war against Charles be fought in Poland, while he consolidated his great project on the Neva. The treaty committed the whole Polish Commonwealth to alliance with Russia. This was something that far surpassed the previous local agreements which Peter had made with Lithuanian factions.

In return for this and for promises both to make no separate peace with Charles and to pursue him should he turn against Russia, Augustus would receive an annual subsidy of 300,000 roubles to create a new army in Saxony, plus 12,000 Russian troops. Whether he would still collect Livonia and Estonia as his share of the spoils was unknown, since the new treaty was silent upon the matter; it would seem unlikely. In any case, Augustus was probably content just to be given the chance to hang on to his thorny crown.

The allied envoys tried to produce the same result by further negotiation. On 27 October they met Augustus at Otsot on the east bank of the Vistula, 'where His Majesty is less exposed to any sudden excursion of the Swedes'. Expecting the fall of Thorn to be followed by a new move against himself, Augustus had withdrawn to Otsot from Warsaw on 17 October.

Robinson now made another attempt to persuade Charles to desist from the 'chimerical security' of dethronement in favour of 'other practicable terms of peace'. In early November he traipsed over to the Swedish camp near Thorn with his latest proposals. Piper did not think it 'advisable at present to lay these matters before the King'. Robinson hovered for eight fruitless days, remarking sardonically that 'care was taken to keep me from being oppressed with too much company'. In mid-November he returned to Warsaw empty-handed.

Augustus was no longer there. By now, becauses of further alienation of his subjects on account of the Russian alliance, the Confederacy of Środa had been joined by the Prussian palatinates. Lacking any power-base in the north and west of his kingdom, in November he and Patkul left for Jaworów, to the west of Lwów.

From Warsaw Robinson observed to Stepney that he did not think it fit for 'ministers that are addressed to both Kings to follow, nor of any use to stay here'. So he expected to 'draw nearer the seaside', and wait there 'either for something to do, or leave to return home'. Early in December Robinson travelled to Danzig to involve himself in British commercial interests in that port.

Possibly he also hoped to be near Charles, who had entered winter quarters in Heilberg in Ermeland, with his main forces deployed around that bishopric and in Elbing. Brandenburg could hardly miss his warning not to get involved. Meantime, General Rehnskjöld and ten regiments headed south to harass Augustus's supporters throughout the winter.

Augustus was still in Jaworów on 15 December, but spent Christmas in Cracow. On 27 December he headed for Saxony, arriving home on the last day of 1703. We know little of what he did there; perhaps he just sought some vacation from the vexations of Poland. Yet his current problems were but small, compared to those he would soon confront.

Cardinal Radziejowski now felt strong enough to summon a General Confederacy in Warsaw. Shorn of Augustus's supporters, it was not a national assembly, and overawed by Swedish force it was hardly an independent body. This mattered little in terms of the reality of power, for Augustus was about to lose his throne.

Chapter 20

'A scission is likely'
Poles apart 1704

'DRIVEN TO THIS EXTREMITY'

'An assembly is to be held next week at Warsaw under the direction of the Cardinal-Primate', reported Robinson on 12 January 1704. At this gathering 'the enemies of the King of Poland promise themselves a new king will be declared', and all the serious money was on James Sobieski.

This meeting of the self-styled General Confederacy opened with an address from the embittered Radziejowski. With customary opacity, the Cardinal referred to Augustus's recent withdrawal from Poland to Saxony, and to a general desire for some agreement to bring peace. Another speaker was more forthright, candidly proposing that the election of Augustus be set aside. They were 'driven to this extremity', he railed, 'by the treatment their representatives had received at Lublin, and by the excesses of the Saxon troops'.[1] Many days of debate followed.

In Danzig, Robinson learned of events through letters sent to him from Warsaw. He noted that 'the assembly is not numerous', and with 'none appearing at it from the King of Sweden' it had 'produced nothing' and adjourned. Things changed when the General Confederacy reconvened on 30 January. Now Swedish officials, headed by the soldier-diplomat Arvid Horn, were on hand to 'open His Majesty's mind to that assembly'.

Once they had reiterated that Charles 'will not on any terms desist from the dethronization', a number of confederates pressed 'the Cardinal to declare the throne vacant', on the grounds that Augustus was 'out of the kingdom'. However, other delegates expressed 'no less zeal for maintaining their King on the throne, so that a scission is likely to happen in that assembly, and increase the confusion'.

Stepney informed London that the Swedes had exhibited 'several letters of dangerous consequence to the liberty of Poland', which had been 'writ some time ago by the King of Poland to the King of

Sweden', and delivered by Aurora von Königsmarck (p 184). These disclosed that Augustus had offered to surrender parts of the Republic's territory in exchange for peace. How influential these missives were upon Radziejowski, compared to the brooding presence of Swedish dragoons, is a moot point. But, as Horn laconically phrased it, the combined pressures 'gave his Eminence the spur'.[2]

On 14 February 1704 'the Most Serene King Augustus' was adjudged by the confederacy 'to have disregarded our laws and rights, and to have thereby freed us from our obedience'.[3] In plainer words, Augustus had forfeited his throne. However, he had lost neither his political skills nor his ruthlessness. His response was simple: in today's parlance he simply 'took out the opposition'.

'VIOLENCE BY HALOES'

Patkul planned the operation, Augustus ordered its implementation, and, by strange coincidence, George Stepney, returning from Berlin to Vienna after a sojourn in England, was a virtual eyewitness of his 'mad friend's' move. On 2 March he sent a long despatch to Hedges from Breslau, the Silesian capital, describing 'an incident of remark' which occurred on the afternoon of 28 February not far outside the city.

Since his father's death James Sobieski had lived on an estate in Ohlau, some 15 miles from Breslau. The Emperor had allowed him to reside within his domains, not out of any personal fondness for the francophile prince but 'in consideration of his lady', who was the sister of the Empress. James appears to have been a man of regular habits, his 'usual method' being to travel into Breslau from Ohlau 'every post-day' and return home in the evening. Just as in our time, such routine behaviour made him an ideal target.

Between three and four o'clock, while journeying home by coach with his younger brother Constantine, James was ambushed by some 40 Saxons, 'mostly officers'. The troopers 'made him alight after he had fired one pistol, and set him upon a horse in his silk stockings'. Stepney wrongly supposed that the two Sobieski brothers were 'gone the straight road' to the fortress-prison of Königstein, 'the general rendezvous of all wretches who fall under the King of Poland's displeasure'. He also mentioned that a strongbox 'with Prince James's papers of consequence' had been found in the coach, and "'tis thought very large discoveries may be made from thence of intrigues both with Sweden and France'.

The envoy reflected upon the possibility that the Saxon might now also eliminate Radziejowski. In his view, Augustus was 'desperate' and would use any means 'to destroy those who were resolved to ruin him', and if 'he must fall, 'twill be like Samson with a general destruction'. From all this, Stepney concluded that he 'has yet some hopes of securing his hold'. But this also depended upon 'how this accident may operate' with Charles and the confederates in Warsaw.

There was also Leopold to consider. By his wanton act of kidnap upon foreign territory, Augustus had violated the 'law of nations', that small body of restraint which sovereigns permitted to police these forceful times. His Imperial Majesty, however, did not even issue a reprimand; there were reasons for such partial behaviour.

The Emperor had his hands full with the French, Bavarians and Hungarians. He could not afford to alienate an ally, no matter how dubious his pedigree. Augustus had contributed a force of 8000 Saxons to the Imperial army in 1703, and his troops would be needed again in coming campaigns. Furthermore, in January 1704 the Elector-King had recognized Leopold's younger son Charles as King of Spain,[4] and issued a proclamation forbidding his Polish subjects to aid Rákóczi's rebellion in Hungary.

Possibly, the failing Leopold was just too used to Augustus treating the Imperial province of Silesia as his own backyard, as he marched his troops between realms with impunity. He may have appreciated, as did the Pope when issuing his tepid 'condemnation', that the kidnap was a desperate act by a desperate ruler.

Moreover, Augustus was Catholic, anti-French and a legitimate King; why should the zealous Leopold favour his opponents? Not only was Charles a Lutheran monarch; he showed an unhealthy interest in the status of the Emperor's Protestant subjects in Hungary and Silesia. As for the potential usurper of the Polish crown, James Sobieski was 'known to be French in his heart', contended Charles Whitworth (C20 n18), then deputizing for Stepney in Vienna. Despite this, James was still his brother-in-law, and Leopold acted privately upon his behalf.

It was initially thought that the Sobieski brothers had been murdered. Eugene of Savoy told Whitworth that he doubted 'whether they were still alive', since he could not imagine that Augustus would 'commit such an act of violence by haloes'. Later Stepney reported that the princes were in Pleissenburg castle in Leipzig, where they were treated 'in the best manner possible'. Despite alleging that James had planned both to kidnap and to poison him, Augustus was offering to return the brothers, if the Emperor would answer for their behaviour. But Leopold refused to see the Polish ambassador.

There were also widespread fears that Augustus's desperate act of bravado would induce an infuriated 'Goth' to throw himself upon either Silesia or the Saxon sanctuary. However, invading Saxony was nowhere on Charles's agenda at this time; when rumour of the kidnappings first reached him, he seemed genuinely nonplussed. 'If it be true there is no remedy', he admitted to Horn, 'and we must find another way'.[5]

While in Warsaw Robinson noted that, despite the general condemnation of Augustus's deed, there was no publication of a state of interregnum. The confederates insisted upon first opening negotiations for the proposed treaty with Sweden, 'being desirous ('tis supposed) to see what other demands' Charles would make, 'before they actually declare the throne vacant'.

However, such delaying tactics left Charles cold. 'Whether or not the interregnum exists is nothing to me', he said with disdain. 'If it exists, it does not affect me in any way, and I do not trouble myself about it'.[6] Instead he concerned himself with finding a new candidate for the Polish throne. Alexander, the third Sobieski brother, declined the honour, arguing plausibly that Augustus would murder his siblings should he accept. Whereupon Charles turned instead to the leader of the original Šroda Confederacy, the *voivod* or palatine of Posen (Poznań) Stanisław Leszczyński (1677–1766).

'IN THE KING'S FAVOUR'

After ordering the kidnap of the Sobieski brothers, and thereby forcing Charles to find a new 'pretender' to his throne, Augustus returned to the Republic. 'The King of Poland has left Cracow, and most of his Polish ministers have left him', recounted Robinson wryly in mid-March. 'The Czar seems to be his chief dependence'. Letters from Warsaw dated 31 March reported that Augustus 'was about Casimir' on the Vistula. There was no news of 'the approach of the Muscovite forces', but financial assistance 'to the sum of 200,000 crowns' had arrived from Peter, 'and good supplies of that kind from Saxony also'.

In early April the missives reaching Robinson mentioned an engagement between 'some of the King of Poland's troops, and a party of Swedes under General Rehnskjöld'. The former were forced 'to give ground, and retire over the Vistula, leaving three or four field-pieces and some few men behind them'. Charles XII's correspondence confirms that such a skirmish took place, but we can be less sure of Augustus's purpose in undertaking it. Was it simply a chance encounter between enemies unaware of each other's presence? Was he trying to overawe the General Confederacy by force? Certainly it was a feeble blow; but Augustus currently deployed little in the way of military muscle.

Soon he had even less. On 23 April Robinson reported that a 'misfortune has happened in the King of Poland's camp'. In a fire in a village on 11 April, 'forty of the King's officers and servants, some of good note, were burnt', and Augustus lost horses and baggage 'to the value of 60,000 crowns'.

Since his military efforts were faring none too well, Augustus switched to the 'constitutional' tack to foil his enemies. In early May the General Confederacy in Warsaw had finally agreed they would elect a new king on 19 June. Augustus countered by calling for a Sejm to meet in Sandomierz on 16 June. Soon Robinson was reporting 'a great confluence of deputies' there, who were 'forming a confederation in the King's favour'. On 27 May the loyal nobility established a General Confederacy of the Crown, its members more commonly styled 'Sandomierzanie'.

In Warsaw the election of a new king was postponed first to 26 June and then indefinitely. At the same time the Swedes were reported marching on the capital. To Robinson this meant that 'all hopes of ending the war', other than by 'a fatal extremity on one side or other', seemed to be 'quite lost'. In Warsaw the confederates now simply meandered, with Radziejowski 'using all means to defer' fixing a date for the election. Nor had 'they yet agreed whether they shall choose a stranger, or a native'.

But Polish procrastination was no longer of consequence, since the only mind that mattered was made up. Charles had made his choice; he had selected Stanisław Leszczyński to be Poland's new and native king. As Patkul predicted, this was 'the finest stroke that the King of Sweden could have imagined for ruining his interests in Poland'.[7]

'THE NEW ELECT'

At the beginning of June 1704 the Swedish army marched south from Ermeland 'for one of our customary pleasant excursions', to use Charles's waspish phrase.[8] It halted in Błonie just west of Warsaw at the end of the month. 'The Goth' had come to puppeteer the election of his protégé, although he left the mechanics of the process, as well as an army corps and the requisite slush fund, to Arvid Horn.

Charles's candidate was hardly chock-full of charisma. In fact it was Leszczyński's simplicity and dubious honesty that allegedly appealed to the spartan King of Sweden. 'A man with no money and no merit', quipped a Polish deputy. 'A tall handsome prince wearing Polish costume', detailed Stepney, 'but inclinable to fat' and 'not remarkable for energy'.[9]

He hardly needed it, for the Swedes would provide the zeal, along with everything else. However, the main objection to his becoming King of Poland was, perversely, that he was a Pole. Radziejowski was not alone in contending that any 'native' or 'Piast', other than a Sobieski, would not last on the throne for six weeks.[10] Not even Charles, in a long interview with the Cardinal in Warsaw, could convince him to nominate Leszczyński.

'Sire, he is too young', protested the Primate. 'He is much about my own age', Charles riposted tartly. 'I would rather be buried alive than consent to proclaim such a candidate', said the Pole. 'Your Eminence may spare yourself that inconvenience', parried the attendant Horn, before explaining that the ambitious Bishop of Posen had consented to 'do us that kind office'.[11]

And so it came to pass. At midday on 12 July 1704, a crowd gathered in Wola Field, but much of it was not Polish. Horn, conspicuous on horseback, 'together with a great many other Swedes', was there and 'used great threatenings', recorded Robinson. Horn conceded that he was seen in the company of several hundred Swedish troops, who were deployed 'at a good musket-shot's distance' to encourage the electorate 'to speak the right language'.

Not a single palatine was in Wola save Leszczyński. The only high official present was Benedict Sapieha. The sole prelate in attendance was the presiding Bishop of Posen, somewhat the worse for wear following a few drams with Horn. When the bishop asked the electoral throng if they would have Stanisław Leszczyński to be their king, the sole dissent came from some Podlesian deputies. But the more numerous gentlemen of Great Poland released their caps from greased palms and threw them into the air with the traditional cry, 'We will! We will!' Some Swedes joined in the chorus; 'I did not spare my throat either', recalled Horn's secretary.[12]

With Stanisław acclaimed as King Elect, the motley electorate repaired to Warsaw. There the Bishop of Posen preached the inaugural sermon in an almost empty cathedral, while Swedish troops loosed off salvoes outside. This was part of the shape of things to come. So was another matter, to which Robinson alluded shortly after the 'election'.

He gave credence to a report that Charles had 'solemnly promised the New Elect to maintain the crown upon his head, at the hazard of his own', and never to abandon him 'so long as there is a man in Sweden that can bear arms'. Events would prove Robinson's intelligence to be only too tragically correct; so, too, his prediction that electing Leszczyński in Augustus's stead was a 'choice, which 'tis judged, will involve Poland in a long train of miseries'.

'WALKING ABOUT THE COUNTRY'

Having seen to the election of his puppet, Charles marched out of Błonie on 19 July 1704, heading an army of more than 25,000 men. Behind him in Warsaw he left Horn and 1000 troops to hasten the arrangements for Stanisław's coronation, and a Swedish–Polish commission charged with working out a preliminary peace treaty. To the west he sent three cavalry regiments, both to protect Wielkopolska from the ravages of Augustus's partisans and to cover Poznań, which was held by a small Swedish garrison.

On 6 August Robinson noted that Augustus had left Sandomierz for Lwów, in order to meet up with Russian forces of 16,000 foot and 3000 Cossack horsemen. It was in this direction that Charles was now heading; marching south along the west bank of the Vistula, he reached Sandomierz on 5 August. From there the Swedes followed the San to Jarosław, where Augustus was now supposedly camped. Proceeding east, Charles advanced upon Lwów.

The Augustan strategy – pincering the Swedes between forces deployed to both their west and east – fell apart when the Swedes beat Saxon troops under Schulenburg near Poznań in August. With the luckless Steinau also unable to pierce the Swedish defences from the west, Augustus was compelled to rely on his own small Saxon units and the undisciplined Russian forces in the east. With neither the quantity nor quality of troops to take on Charles in a set-piece battle, the best he could do, in Patkul's caustic verdict, was 'to keep the Swedes walking about the country'.[13]

In truth, the fighting east of the San was no stroll but a merciless guerilla war, and the local population suffered between two ruthless kings to the political benefit of neither. At length the Swedes stood before Lwów. Its fall would show Augustus's impotence even in an area of his most loyal support. The 'Lion City' declined to roar, and surrendered with little loss of life in early September. There was no looting; instead the city had to disgorge a cash bounty of 300,000 dollars to fund Charles's subventions to the 'New Elect'.

However, the 'Ex-Elect' was nowhere to be found, for the simple reason that he was once more in his capital. While that stern sentinel Rehnskjöld awaited him at Jarosław with 12 regiments, Augustus had turned north in the direction of Brest–Litovsk, then west to Lublin, at the head of 3000 Saxons, thrice that number of Russians and sundry Poles. Then leaving his infantry to follow, he sped along the Vistula with his cosmopolitan cavalry, arriving in Warsaw in early September. The city which had hosted his dethronement now awaited his displeasure.

Robinson, still in Danzig, reported on 6 September that Augustus was attacking Warsaw Castle. Within the citadel were Horn and some 500 Swedes under bombardment from red-hot cannon-balls, until they surrendered and became the first substantial bag of prisoners that Augustus had taken. The similar-sized Swedish force stationed at Latowice, west of the capital, was less fortunate; after capitulation to the Cossacks, most of its members were cut down.

On 10 September Robinson recorded that Augustus had 'with great difficulty, and not without giving the Cossacks some discontent, hindered them from plundering' Warsaw, which 'in lieu thereof' had to pay up RT 500,000. Other accounts say that the Cardinal's palace and the houses of the confederate gentry were pillaged. But few were at home: Radziejowski had fled to Danzig and Stanisław to Rehnskjöld's camp, while the Bishop of Posen was removed to Rome, to be dealt with by the Pope 'for having abetted a prince who had been put on the throne by the arms of a Lutheran'.

All in all, since the capture of Warsaw was Augustus's first experience of holding the advantage against Charles during 'the torrent of his misfortune', he was not unduly punitive.[14] But further north-east Peter was, when he conquered Dorpat in July 1704 and Narva in August. The latter's fall sent Stockholm into panic and the Tsar into ecstasy, as he crowed to Augustus about revenging the battle 'where four years ago our arms were disgraced'.[15]

Charles's response to his opponents' victories was swift, as was the speed of his march. After leaving Lwów, his 'army kept more (unofficial) fast-days in a month', recalled an officer wryly, 'than others might do in a century'.[16] Hastening north via Rawa Ruska and Lublin, by 20 October Charles and his cavalry drew bridle 20 miles east of Warsaw.

Unfortunately for him, Augustus was on the west of the Vistula, which was in full spate, and the Elector-King had burnt everyone's boats. From his headquarters west of Warsaw in Wyszogrod, Augustus sought to hold his capital for as long as possible, both to cover Poznań, where a Polish–Russian force under Patkul was besieging the Swedes there,[17] and to allow a new Saxon army under Schulenburg to reach him.

But on learning of Charles's attempts to ford the Vistula south of Warsaw, Augustus withdrew on 28 October. Racing south-westwards with 3000 cavalry, he circled north and west of Łódź before heading south-east for Cracow. Augustus finally left Cracow for Dresden in late November 1704. He passed through Breslau on 27 November, his journey noted by Whitworth, who was travelling to his new post in Moscow.[18] For the next two days the road was full of Augustus's guards and retinue, 'who came out of Poland in small parties, the better to avoid interception by the Swedes'.

For Charles, once across the Vistula, but thwarted again by his elusive cousin, had instead pursued Schulenburg's lumbering infantry, who were retreating towards Silesia. Charging across western Poland with six cavalry regiments at the astounding rate of 40 miles per day, Charles closed the gap on his prey. On 7 November Schulenburg was forced to stand at Pünitz (Poniec), very near to the Silesian frontier; but after a brief skirmish, the Prussian soldier of fortune led his troops away in the dark.

For the first time, Charles moved into Silesia, as far as Glogau on the Oder. However, his quarry was gone. To vent their frustrations and avenge their comrades slaughtered at Latowice, the Swedes massacred 3000 unhorsed Cossacks and regular Russian infantry whom they found in the area. Then, sending his main forces into winter quarters in Royal Prussia and Wielkopolska, Charles and his elite Brabants occupied Rawicz, a small town on the Polish side of the border with Silesia. Augustus was now bottled up in his Electorate; and if Peter wanted to send forces across Poland to aid him, then Sweden's King would be only too pleased to receive them.

'LEFT TO SHIFT FOR HIMSELF'

Following the major allied victory over Franco–Bavarian forces at Blenheim in August 1704, the state of play in the Great Northern War once more became an issue for the powers embroiled in Western Europe. The allies were now less concerned with unrealistic expectations of Swedish and Saxon contingents for their armies than with their recurrent nightmare that Charles might invade Saxony. If the threat became a reality, such an operation would assist only the French.

Robinson addressed this unease in several despatches sent from Danzig to Whitehall in 1704. Swedish officials had told him that, while any 'incursion into Germany' would not be undertaken 'with a direct intention to favour France', this had nothing to do with Habsburg sensitivities. For only 'the interest of Sweden' would 'move His Majesty to do anything for the Emperor's preservation', Vienna having done 'much to estrange his affections, but nothing to gain them'.

This was hardly an exaggeration. Leopold had constantly offended Charles, through complicitously allowing Augustus free rein in Silesia for supply and transit of his troops. Then there was the small matter of the kidnap of the Sobieski brothers. Moreover, the staunchly Lutheran Swede was displeased by the Emperor's treatment of his Protestant subjects in Silesia.

213

Although Robinson contended that Charles was surrounded by men who were 'entirely addicted to France', he also conceded that the King was pursuing solely Sweden's interest. He pointed out that Charles considered himself abandoned by the allied guarantors of the Treaty of Oliwa, which sanctified Sweden's possession of Livonia. Being 'left to shift for himself', Charles was 'resolved to leave them to do so too' and simply to concentrate upon accomplishing 'his own great design here', without bothering 'who gains or loses by it'.

Therefore all was subordinate to Charles's 'prevailing passion' of toppling Augustus from his throne. Swedish officials emphasized 'that their master will not give over pursuing him, till he be turned out of all and lodged in a cloister'. While it is hard to envisage Augustus in such an establishment, unless it was a nunnery, Robinson's assessment of his prospects in Poland paints a direly realistic canvas.

'For it is too sure he is not loved by his Polish subjects', all of whom were 'extreme weary of the war' and eager 'to see an end of it'. Many were his 'open enemies', while even more were indifferent and would be 'glad to be rid of him without dishonour'. Those that adhered to him were of 'a very wavering and precarious fidelity', mainly sticking by Augustus because of 'shame only, that a foreign power should dispose of the throne of Poland'. So, given the right circumstances, even the most faithful would be ready to abandon him and conclude an agreement to 'preserve their country', and their even more valued 'private fortunes', from ruin. Since this war was not 'a national, but merely a personal quarrel', it only required their consent to 'the King of Poland's dethronization to end it and their miseries'.

However, Robinson saw problems in supporting such a policy, which would end in a Swedish–Polish peace favourable to Charles. In the first place, there was 'the great discontent' it would give Tsar Peter, upon whom 'by that means the whole force of Sweden, and probably of Poland also, would so much the sooner fall'. Secondly, the 'sudden downfall' of Augustus would simply 'make room for the New Elect'. And with Stanisław sporting an uncontested crown, 'there will be so much the sooner upon the throne of Poland, a zealous favourer of France'.

Robinson was therefore opposed to 'the destruction' of Augustus, arguing that 'whatever his other miscarriage may have been', he did not deserve 'to receive his ruin from the hands of the allies'. In his view it was 'more safe' for the allies that Charles 'should find employment here for a long time, than that he should suddenly gain his point'. The Tsar beavering away in St Petersburg, his armies rampaging through Livonia and Estonia, could hardly have expressed his own wishes better.

For Augustus it seemed that the immediate future would be all about self-preservation. Charles was on his borders, the Emperor was wavering, Peter was waging war by proxy and the French and English saw him as no more than a pawn. Both Polish and Saxon subjects opposed his war, money was short, and his love life was causing problems. 1705 did not promise to be a happy new year.

215

Chapter 21

'His crown is not worth any longer struggle'
Stand-off 1705

'A MORE POTENT RIVAL'

This was the year that Augustus fell in a big way; for from all we know of the relationship between our hero and Countess Cosel, it is hard to believe that he ever loved a woman more than he did her.[1] Typically, this did not consign him to the outlandish state of monogamy; and it was equally inevitable that the route to her arms was strewn with major affairs, which seeded a minor scattering of his progeny.

On 23 November 1701 Stepney composed a private letter to Hedges, entitled 'The secret history of the King of Poland's amours'. It is unfortunately nothing of the sort, although it does provide some detail about Augustus's womanizing to supplement what is revealed by other accounts.

Stepney began by gossiping about the end of the relationship between Augustus and Aurora von Königsmarck in 1696 (p 127). According to the envoy, Aurora had laid up some money and purchased a home in Silesia, where she had lived 'in retirement for these two years'. Other sources suggest that this dwelling was bankrolled by an admirer. Yet whether or not this was her primary abode at the turn of the century, Aurora was no recluse and had frequently visited Saxony since splitting up with Augustus.

She and her sister helped entertain Tsar Peter, when he passed through Dresden in June 1698 on his way to meet Augustus at Rawa Ruska. It is likely too that Aurora, Eleonore von Klengel, Countess Lubomirska and Countess Esterle were all part of the covey of past and present paramours gathered around Augustus in Saxony in late 1699 (C14 n3). But whether the last-named was still chief mistress at that time is a moot point.

Augustus had met her as Mlle Lamberg in Vienna in 1695 (p 120).

Dipping his quill into mellow venom, Stepney now wrote that 'in order to preserve her reputation with the cloak of matrimony', the gallant Saxon 'engaged Count Esterle a Bohemian, by a portion of RT 50,000, to take her to wife, without having anything of a husband but the name'. The Count also acquired some Saxon offices and was 'allowed to travel wherever he pleases'. All of which reads more authentically than the caricature of a brain-dead and cuckolded husband in von Pöllnitz's saga.

'In the meantime the lady followed the King and his fortune into Poland', where she played 'the chief part in his good graces, though her sovereignty has not always been absolute'. Countess Esterle was at Augustus's coronation in September 1697. The following year, when the Elector-King marched off to battle the Tartars in south-east Poland, he left her behind in Warsaw, where she gave birth to a boy on 1/11 August 1698. If this was Augustus's son (for she counted Flemming amongst her other lovers), then he did not recognize the fact.

The Countess accompanied Augustus to Saxony and Teplitz in the late summer of 1699. Presumably she returned to Poland with him before his forlorn foray against Riga in 1700. 'At last, it seems, a more potent rival has dispossessed her', narrated Stepney the following year. But rather than bear 'that mortification', Countess Esterle pouched the jewels worth £40,000 which Augustus had bestowed upon her and, 'without taking leave of the King or anybody else', made her escape from Warsaw and was last reported to be somewhere in the neighbourhood of Vienna.[2]

Her successor was Ursula Catherina von Boccum, Countess Lubomirska (1680–1730), whose relationship with Augustus probably commenced in 1699.[3] Of French and Lithuanian blood, Lubomirska was a niece of Cardinal Radziejowski and married into an important magnate clan. Mordantly Stepney noted that, as 'a blessed preferment', her husband was named ambassador to Turkey. Yet although Ursula was an intelligent young woman and doubtless attractive (her portrait dates from her later years), there would appear to have been a high political content to her affair with the King. Certainly her charms and excellent riding skills were insufficient to lull Augustus into fidelity.

Ursula shared her lover with Fatime (p 127) at least. A year younger than Lubomirska, the Turk presented Augustus with his second acknowledged bastard (Friedrich August, Count Rutowski) in June 1702. Lubomirska produced the third (Johann Georg, Chevalier de Saxe) in August 1704, and a week later was raised to the rank of Imperial Princess. Augustus apparently patched up relations with her and the Lubomirski clan just before he left for Dresden in November. Perhaps he intended returning soon to Poland, and to Ursula, now Princess of Teschen. However, in Saxony there waited the woman who, as Countess Cosel, was to become Augustus's most famous mistress.

Anna Constantia von Brockdorff was born in Holstein on 17/27 October 1680 into a family of minor nobility. Her father, a soldier, not only turned Constantia into an excellent rider, but taught her to shoot with pistol and carbine, as well as to fight with the sword. After serving as a lady-in-waiting to the eldest daughter of the Duchess of Holstein-Gottorp (the latter another sister of Augustus's mother), Constantia married in June 1703.

Her husband was the Saxon privy councillor Adolph Magnus Hoym (1668–1723), the son of Augustus's 'fund-raiser' in 1697 (p 141). The younger Hoym was also involved in finance: as director of the General Excise Authority (*Generalakzisekollegium*) he oversaw Augustus's tax plans. Hoym was also involved with another woman, who lived and worked in the same house as his new bride.

Not being the submissive type, when Hoym refused to evict his shadowy lover Constantia withheld conjugal relations. In response, Hoym threatened her with divorce. This blissful situation still pertained, when Augustus arrived back in Dresden at 2 a.m. on 30 November 1704.

Constantia had been presented to her sovereign when he was last in Saxony in 1703, so he may already have notched her on the four-poster as a forthcoming attraction. Then, one week after his current homecoming, the Hoyms' house in the town centre burned down. Fearing that an inferno might again engulf the capital, Augustus hastened to the scene. He found instead a calm and authoritative Constantia, still attired in court dress, directing the extinction of the flames.

Perhaps, like many philanderers, Augustus needed and indeed secretly desired a 'strong' woman. He certainly got one with Constantia, who was raised to Reichsgräfin as Countess Cosel in 1706. Although the years 1705–07 are not those of her greatest power, when she 'ruled' in Saxony–Poland as an uncrowned queen, they are the years when she and Augustus began their turbulent affair. It would bring them three children and her great wealth. Later the turn of politics would cast her down: three years after Cosel fell from power in 1713, she was condemned to house arrest in the castle at Stolpen. This would be Constantia's appalling fate from 1716 until her death in 1765.

'UNDERHAND DEALING'

Augustus's fate was to be distrusted: 'The King of Poland is capable of any underhand dealing', Stepney conceded to Lord Raby

(1672–1739) in January 1705. However, he could not believe that Augustus had offered 'to join with Sweden in dethroning the King of Prussia'. He reminded the new and often credulous English envoy to Berlin that such 'suggestions are artfully scattered to cause distrust' between the Prussian and Polish monarchs.

If anything, the boot was on the other foot: the Prussians and the Austrians were perfectly willing to see Augustus deposed from his Polish throne. 'This King should be cashiered', snapped the Brandenburg minister Ilgen. 'So let him damn well fall', growled Kaunitz, the Austrian Vice-Chancellor, 'then we'll all know where we are for once'.[4] 'There is of late a remarkable change in the language of the Imperial ministers, in reference to the King of Poland's affairs', concluded Robinson in March, 'it seeming now their opinion, that his crown is not worth any longer struggle'.

Needless to say, Augustus was himself deeply embroiled in machinations. Upon hearing of his return to Dresden, Raby had reported that Augustus 'designs to make a great change in the regency there, for most people are dissatisfied' with the Stadthalter. This was Prince Anton Egon Fürstenberg (1656–1716), the Munich-born Catholic who had suceeded to Schöning's old post in December 1697.[5]

In 1705 Augustus made an initial stab at reforming and centralizing the administration in his Electorate. Influential upon his thoughts was a pamphlet entitled *Portrait de la cour de Pologne*, published anonymously the previous year. Its author was a young Saxon nobleman, Johann Friedrich von Wolfframsdorff, who sought a more dynamic and absolutist internal and foreign policy. With its attacks upon the dead hands of the Saxon aristocracy and the Habsburgs, it was almost as if Schöning had clambered out of his tomb.

Augustus's 'memoirs' (A1) and his advice to his son ('Regel pour la posterrité') would both seem to date from 1705. So does a third document, 'Project in fahl das Haus Estraich absterben sohltes', which stemmed from his abiding interest in the Wettins' succeeding to the Imperial throne, should the Habsburgs die out in the male line, as seemed at the time a distinct possibility. Augustus proposed that the German territories of the Reich should elect the new Emperor (who could be himself or his son). The Habsburgs' hereditary territories he could acquire for his house through the marriage of his heir.[6]

He probably wrote the 'Project' in the wake of Leopold's death in May 1705. Augustus then became Reichsvikar of the Empire, overseeing its affairs until the coronation of his friend the King of the Romans as Emperor Joseph I (r 1705–11). Despite some accounts which place him at the coronation, Augustus was not in Vienna. Visits to Carlsbad and Teplitz in June and July 1705 were his only forays outside of Saxony that year before he returned to Poland. At the spas he was attended by both Patkul and Constantia.

Patkul held the purse-strings to Peter's funds, and the impecunious Augustus was obliged to flatter the Livonian to obtain his allowances. Patkul was reluctant to shell out, since he knew full well that when the Saxon secured such advances, 'money meant for Mars veered off towards Venus'.[7] For Aphrodite's enticing arms, outstretched in love, still tapered off into ample hands with upturned palms.

Constantia's divorce only became final in January 1706, yet by the end of 1705 she had procured a promise that Augustus would wed her and make her Electress and Queen when Eberhardine died. Meantime she settled for a pension of RT 100,000 and Augustus's gift to her of the Pillnitz estate. It all seemed strangely reminiscent of an earlier affair. And although Augustus did not try to murder his wife, the Cosel liaison shattered the last parts of her heart.[8]

'GOING THROUGH WITH THE WORK'

There seems little doubt that both Augustus and Peter attempted to broker a separate peace with Sweden in 1705. Peter negotiated through Patkul and members of the Brandenburg government. Augustus used Arvid Horn (p 212), freed on parole, as his go-between; although Aurora also glided into the act. Yet, if Augustus thought Charles would let him remain upon his throne, he was very much mistaken. As Robinson reported in March, 'the King of Sweden adheres unalterably' to his intention of 'going through with the work of dethronization', and would not hear of 'any other terms of accommodation'.

Like Robinson, Cardinal Radziejowski remained in Danzig. From there he prevaricated over the coronation of Stanisław throughout the spring and summer. Augustus was more direct: he obtained a papal bull which forbade Polish bishops, under pain of excommunication, from participating in the coronation. However, as Robinson noted in late July, the Cardinal did 'not seem much affected by the Pope's menaces'.

Augustus tried to balk the ballots of the Coronation Diet with bullets as well as bulls. Robinson received letters from Warsaw dated 31 July which mentioned a 'skirmish' that day between Augustan units and 'a strong party of Swedish horse'. It had lasted some hours, and losses were 'said to be near equal'.

In fact, Augustus had sent virtually all the troops that he could muster within the Commonwealth to disrupt, if not disperse, the Coronation Sejm. In consequence, a Saxon–Polish force some 10,000 strong, led by his Livonian general Paykul, fought for about six hours against 2000 Swedish cavalry. The Swedes took about 400 casualties and Paykul's command perhaps 2000.

Paykul himself was captured. In theory he was a Swedish subject who had committed high treason, although he had entered Saxon service before Augustus's sneak attack upon Riga. There was some sympathy for pardoning him, particularly since he was also renowned as an alchemist, who could turn base metal into gold, and such talents would have provided a welcome boost to Stockholm's parlously depleted treasury. But Charles's response resembled the Red Queen's: he rejected his sister's pleadings, because 'the matter is of so grave a nature, that I may not yield to you'. So, 'for the sake of example', off came Paykul's head near Stockholm in February 1707.[9] There was little doubt thereafter what would be the fate of the arch-traitor Patkul. Yet that was the future; for now Charles was king-making. To that end he marched his main army into Błonie in August 1705.

Folowing several postponements, on 4 October the great day finally arrived for King Stanisław I and Queen Charlotte. True, they were to be crowned in Warsaw and not the ancestral city of Cracow. Moreover, Augustus still held the coronation regalia. So Charles ordered new diadems made; not from gilded tin, as some jibes have it, but of gold and diamonds.

Who was to lower these coronets upon the Leszczyński brows? Legally only the Cardinal-Primate had that right. Yet although gravely ill, Radziejowski set such conditions that Charles turned instead to the next ranking prelate, the Archbishop of Lwów, to perform the task, and promoted him Primate when Radziejowski died on 13 October.[10]

Swedish troops took pride of place in the coronation procession, while Horn and his henchmen hogged the royal dais during the subsequent banquet. Nobody was under any illusions as to who was the real King of Poland. Upon hearing the news, the Tsar, with mock ceremonial, crowned his jester King of Sweden.

'HIS HAPPY RETURN'

'There is no more relying on that prince than on a broken reed'. Stepney's trenchant verdict upon Augustus was written in October 1705 and referred to the dim prospect of recruiting Saxon troops against France. Nor had Tsar Peter seen many of that commodity in *his* war. Other than Paykul's ill-fated force, which was decimated at Warsaw in July, there was only a promise of troops from Augustus.

In early April Whitworth reported on a despatch sent by Patkul from Dresden. The Livonian told Peter 'that a design hath been formed by the King of Poland which has already cost him 500,000 crowns' and could not fail to procure 'their great and sure success' against Charles XII. For now, Augustus wished 'to be excused from explaining his mysterious project' and 'only entreats the Czar not to engage the Swede or undertake any other operation' before Augustus himself arrived in Lithuania to give Peter 'a full account'.[11]

Augustus certainly took his time arriving. The delights of Dresden, the charms of Constantia, events in Vienna, statecraft in Saxony, health problems, all kept (or excused) him from hastening back to Poland and another round of war. He left Silesia only in early October. From there Augustus journeyed incognito with just a few companions to the small Lithuanian town of Tykocin (south-west of Grodno), which he reached on 1 November 1705.

Whitworth, while pleased at the prospect of being able to converse again in German when Augustus arrived at Grodno, also invoked the Lord's 'mercy upon all weak heads and stomachs'. Not that the young envoy would be bringing a bottle to any Augustan booze-up, since Tsar Peter had cleaned him out of wine. Just 'one royal visit in an afternoon', he grouched, 'drunk me up all the stock I had laid in for the whole campaign'.

Peter travelled from Grodno to meet Augustus, and Whitworth paid his respects on 12 November. The following day Augustus reviewed the combined Saxon, Lithuanian and Muscovite cavalry, which was concentrated in Tykocin. Thereafter, Augustus returned with Peter to Grodno, where on 23 November he presided over a Senate Council, which congratulated him 'on his happy return'. Joy indeed! For some bigwigs it was just like a birthday, given the number of sinecures to be 'doubly supplied' by Poland's two kings.

Whitworth could not help noticing how Augustus 'shows a wonderful complaisance and moderation on every occasion'. However, the envoy thought that the Russians were 'not over assured' of Augustus's 'inclinations'. As for Peter, he'd simply had enough of the war; Whitworth saw him as 'more earnest than ever to treat with Sweden'. The Tsar was 'weary of this way of living and begins to be in an ill state of health'. Moreover, his 'dominions are exhausted of men to recruit [to] his armies, and drained of money' to pay subsidies to Augustus. In short, Muscovy was running out of 'men and money'.

On 19 December 1705 Peter quit Grodno for Moscow. Whitworth noted that in his absence he had 'left the command of his army to the King of Poland', from whom the Tsar's Scottish fieldmarshal Ogilvie 'is to receive his orders'. And Augustus would be giving quite a few commands in the New Year; for in Dresden, that same December night, Patkul was arrested, while at his headquarters near Warsaw the young King of Sweden was preparing to advance to the east.

'UNEXPECTEDLY ARRESTED'

In Dresden on 15 December 1705, Patkul, still the Tsar's general and ambassador to Saxony, concluded a treaty with the Imperial envoy Straatmann. Under its terms the survivors of the Russian troops placed under Patkul's orders in 1704, whom he had subsequently led into Saxony (C20 n17), would enter the Emperor's service for one year.

While there is no doubt that these men had been shamefully neglected in Saxony, and that Patkul had provided for their upkeep from his own resources, it would seem that he never received unambiguous permission from Moscow to transfer them into Vienna's pay. And although Patkul 'offered to find out several pretences for delaying the [treaty's] execution, till the Czar's pleasure should be further known', this does not alter the fact that he wilfully disobeyed Moscow's orders by signing the treaty in the first place.

There was also the larger question of whether either Patkul or Moscow had any jurisdiction at all over these forces. In other words, could these soldiers be hired out or otherwise disposed of without Augustus's agreement? As Stepney observed, the Russian troops had been made over to the Elector-King 'by solemn treaty for all the time that the war in Poland should last'.[12]

Patkul's negotiations with Straatmann were hardly secret; in Vienna they were 'the ordinary town-talk'. Therefore the Regency Council, which governed Saxony in Augustus's absence, most probably had forewarning of the treaty. It seems likely that their fear of how Augustus or Peter would react to it was their main reason for arresting Patkul, always assuming that they acted without higher instruction.

While many factors made the Livonian unpopular, such as his acid tongue, overbearing ways, access to funds and engagement to the wealthiest heiress in Saxony, none of these in isolation would have justified the furore sparked by the arrest of an allied ambassador. Even Patkul's role in the Russian–Swedish negotiations conducted in Berlin earlier that year could not be cited as grounds, at least until the Saxons got their hands on his papers.

On 19 December, as Whitworth reported later, Patkul 'was taken out of his bed about eleven at night by a Saxon officer'. Having been 'unexpectedly arrested by the Regency of Saxony', he was 'carried prisoner to the castle of Sonnenstein'. Saxon penal policy was less enlightened than Sweden's: 'His bed was not allowed him, nor his servants to attend him, no one was permitted to speak with him, pen and paper refused'. Yet the 'most aggravating' thing was that he spent five days 'without seeing a bit of bread'. However, other accounts aver that it was Patkul who refused food, for fear that Augustus would have him poisoned.[13]

From Moscow in early 1706 Whitworth provided the 'best account' of events that he could gather. Patkul had initially complained to the Tsar and his foreign minister Golovin that 'the Muscovite forces in Saxony were in a perishing condition'. When he proposed that these troops should be hired out to the Empire, Moscow responded that if the Saxons had no use for these soldiers, Patkul should 'use the best means to reconduct them home into Russia'. If that was not possible, he could 'begin a treaty' with Vienna, 'but not conclude anything till further orders' had been sent.

Once he reached Grodno, Augustus had 'complained of the instructions, and procured positive orders' from Moscow for Patkul 'not to conclude' with Count Straatmann. 'But it seems not wholly relying on them, he sent private directions' to the Regency Council in Dresden, that if Patkul 'should go on', they should 'immediately put him under arrest'. However, Augustus denied that 'the proceedings against Patkul have been by his direction'. But then, he would, wouldn't he?

The Russians were at a loss how to react. On the one hand they disapproved of Patkul concluding a treaty 'contrary to instruction'. On the other, they resented 'this act of violence committed on their minister without their knowledge', particularly as the Livonian was not permitted to seal his own papers. The Saxons did this, which was worrying for Moscow, since Patkul 'had all the Czar's affairs which related to Germany in his hand'. Among them were several documents 'concerning their negotiation at Berlin, which they are not willing should come to the King of Poland's sight'.

Early in 1706 Augustus wrote to the Tsar, 'excusing what has passed', and blaming some of his ministers, who 'through an indiscreet zeal, and without his knowledge, had thus apparently violated the law of nations'. This did not prevent him from secretly endorsing the action of these same ministers, or ignoring Peter's requests that Patkul and his papers be sent to Moscow.

But by then both monarchs had more pressing matters on their minds. Charles had decided upon a winter campaign, and within months the Swedes had scattered their foes like chaff. Now there was nothing to prevent 'the Goth' from violating the Saxon refuge.

Chapter 22

'His coming into Saxony'
The shattered sanctuary 1706

'NOTHING BUT BAD LUCK'

On 8 January 1706 a Swedish army of between 18,000 and 20,000 men left Błonie. 'My soldiers have enjoyed their winter quarters in summer', declared their enigmatic King, so it was 'only right that they should take the field in winter'.[1] Covering nearly 200 miles in 16 days (five being rest-days), by 24 January the Swedes stood on the south bank of the River Niemen opposite Ogilvie's force in Grodno.

Six days later Augustus left that town at the head of some 5000 Saxon cavalry and Russian dragoons. By 5 February he was in Warsaw, where he waited for a further body of horsemen to join him from the south, which brought his force up to around 8000. With it he intended falling upon the rear of Rehnskjöld's army of about 12,000, which was quartered west of Poznań.

To his west, from Silesia, Rehnskjöld anticipated the advance of a considerable 'Saxon' army under the command of Lieutenant-General Johann Matthias von der Schulenburg (1661–1747). This was Augustus's 'mysterious project', which had cost him so much money and was designed to procure 'great and sure success' by crushing Rehnskjöld between two armies. After that the victorious Saxons would take Charles too from the rear, while Ogilvie held him at Grodno.

Schulenburg's force is variously computed as between 16,000 and 22,000 strong, with a cavalry component of 2000–5000. One-third of his infantry was Russian, and other units of the foot were battalions comprising French, Swiss and Bavarian deserters and prisoners of war. According to Stepney, this army consisted mainly 'of troops newly raised'.

But there was no victory for Augustus. He was at Kalisz, some four days' march away, when Schulenburg and Rehnskjöld clashed at Fraustadt (Wschowa), near the Silesian–Polish border, on the

227

morning of 14 February. It was another disaster for our hero, and a bloody one.

Stepney's account, based upon letters from Silesia, was sent to London on 20 February. He described how the Saxon left wing 'began the attack with some success, but their horse being soon routed, the foot suffered extremely, being abandoned in a plain'. The Muscovites 'made a valiant defence and orderly retreat' for over an hour; but finally they were 'so warmly plied, that hardly any of the 6000 escaped', since Rehnskjöld had 'resolved to give them no quarter'.

The Saxons 'shifted something better by retiring to a village'. The Swedes surrounded it and set it on fire, and seven or eight battalions surrendered there. In all, 'the whole body of foot' was lost with all its baggage and artillery: perhaps 7000 infantry died and 6000 to 8000 became prisoners. However, only 100 of 5000 cavalry and dragoons were slain 'upon the spot'; the rest had fled.

Raby sent his own version of events that same day, along with a copy of Rehnskjöld's letter, to his wife. 'Nous n'avons perdu de nos braves Soldats qu'un fort petit nombre', wrote the Swede of his light losses of 400 dead and 1400 wounded. 'Dieu m'a specialement conservé', he added, 'ayant eu un cheval tué sous Moy'.

Schulenburg lost more than a horse shot from under him. Raby reported that he was held responsible for the disaster, in 'that he would take it upon him to attack the Swedes, when his King was with 6000 men within four days march of him'. The expectation was that 'his best fate will be keeping M Patkul company in prison'.[2]

After Fraustadt, Augustus retreated south-eastwards from Kalisz towards Cracow. Peter was 'now absolutely disgusted at the repeated misfortunes of his ill-fated ally', contended Whitworth. Despite 'all the money he had given the King (which is near 1,600,000 roubles) he had brought nothing but bad luck', while Muscovy was 'drained of men and money'. The Tsar was 'resolved to shut up his purse-strings'.

In the east Charles tried to engage Ogilvie in Grodno, but the weather thwarted him. At the beginning of April the Scot led the remains of an army depleted by privations southwards. By the time Charles could cross the thawing Niemen, Ogilvie had a four-day start. Struggling through the Pripet marshes, the Swedes pursued their foes as far as Pinsk, which they reached on 4 May. There Charles called off the chase, and the Muscovites staggered on to Kiev. Although Peter's main army was saved, the Russians had 'abandoned all Courland and Lithuania with the same precipitation as they took possession', noted Whitworth.

Charles stayed at Pinsk until early June 1706, both to rest his troops and to harry Augustus's supporters. Then his army tramped south-westwards to Łuck, the capital of Volhynia, a region almost untouched by war. Arriving there in mid-June, the Swedes replenished themselves and their horses from the abundant grain stocks; for their next trek would be lengthy.

'REASONS BOTH OF WAR AND POLITICS'

Charles 'had forborne several times to invade Saxony, when all the reasons both of war and politics should have engaged him to it' and despite 'having destroyed their army and having the country at his mercy'. This was how the Swedish ambassador in Berlin expressed matters to Raby in April. Possibly he was preparing the political groundwork.

Following the allied victory over the French at Ramillies in May 1706, the envoy returned to the issue of removing Augustus as a player. He argued that it was in England's interest to recognize the puppet Stanisław instead, since as King of Poland he 'could not be able to do anything to disturb the allies'. If Augustus remained upon the throne, then once the Swedes withdrew 'he'd begin his old play again, for he was a prince that would not be quiet'. He would revamp 'his old project' of making the Polish throne hereditary 'and joining Saxony to it'. Then Augustus would marry his son to Emperor Joseph's daughter, and if 'the Austrian family should be extinct' in the male line, 'by this match his son might pretend to the greatest part of the hereditary country and to be chosen Emperor'. Then, concluded the envoy, Augustus 'would be more to be feared than the French King and have as great (at least) a power'.

Whether or not the Swedish sovereign endorsed such political arguments, he had settled by now upon a solution by the sword. On 17 July 1706 Charles marched out of Łuck. Having crossed the Bug and the Vistula he teamed up with Rehnskjöld's force north of Łódź on 16 August. A week later he forded the Warta. Passing full circle through his old base of Rawicz, Charles led his army across the Oder at Steinau (north-west of Breslau) on 2 September, and four days later the Swedes entered Saxony.

'Their march goes straight to Dresden', hazarded Stepney from Vienna. Eberhardine fled to her father's, while Augustus's mother and son left for Magdeburg. The few Saxon troops remaining in the Electorate melted away into Thuringia. The general population, recalling Swedish ravages from the Thirty Years War, were on the move too, with their effects.

'This attempt in Saxony is only to put a speedy end to the war in

Poland', maintained the Swedish envoy in Vienna; Charles had no intention of disturbing the Empire, 'provided they do not molest him in his present undertaking'. Stepney hardly anticipated any Imperial interference with the activities of the Swedish King. For 'as near as I can perceive, the princes on all sides are in awe of the lion' and fear that the slightest 'remonstrance' might provoke him 'to fall upon them'. Ironically, only Augustus would be molesting the Swedes, and he was desperately trying to avoid just such an outcome.

'SAXONY SHOULD BE PUT OUT OF CONDITION'

After Fraustadt, Augustus retreated to Cracow; we know little of what he did there. On 24 April the visiting Plantamour (now in Augustus's service) told Raby in Berlin that 'the King diverts himself very well'. He was 'under no apprehensions of the Swedes', and had more of the Polish nobility with him 'than before the unfortunate battle of Schulenburg's'. He also retained 6000 men in Saxony and at present had no fear of a Swedish invasion of his Electorate.[3]

In late July Whitworth reported that Augustus had retired from Cracow to Hungary. On 18 August the envoy told London that the Elector-King was marching towards Grodno with the Crown Army and 7000 Saxon horse, a 'good part whereof, he has insensibly drawn from his Electorate by small troops' since Fraustadt.

In fact Augustus was currently about 80 miles east of Grodno, in Nowogródek. His close adviser (Referendarius) Georg Ernst Pfingsten left that town on 16 August bearing a letter to Charles. This expressed the Saxon's wish that the two cousins might fully reconcile their differences.[4] Besides this missive, Pfingsten carried a set of principal and subsidiary instructions (*Haupt- und Nebeninstruktion*) for use at a conference with Swedish representatives. These made clear that the surrender of the Polish crown was only to be agreed to as a last resort, in order to prevent the invasion of Saxony. If the negotiations broke down, Augustus expected the Regency Council to defend the Electorate by all possible means.[5]

Pfingsten only reached Dresden on 1 September; given a Swedish army on the march in western Poland, this was probably not excessive. But it also meant that Augustus's negotiating position was already shattered. When the Saxon Privy Council met on the morning of 2 September, the Swedes were crossing the Oder and only a few days off from invading Saxony. Moreover, the panic and disorder in the Electorate precluded any possibility of armed resistance.

Charles was in possession of Augustus's letter on 4 September, two days before he crossed the Saxon frontier. His answer would come better from the sword of an occupying power, than the pen of a negotiator. Therefore, it was not until 12 September that the Swedes consented to receive Pfingsten and the Geheimrat Anton Albrecht Baron von Imhoff at Charles's temporary headquarters in Bischofs-werda, about 20 miles east of Dresden. This proved to be the one and only 'negotiating' session.

The Saxon plenipotentiaries received their powers from the Privy Council and not from Augustus. It made little difference to the Swedish terms. Their first and unalterable condition remained Augustus's renunciation of the Polish crown, and his recognition of Stanisław as the legitimate King of Poland.[6] All attempts by the Saxons to evade this point shattered against the rock of Charles's obstinacy.

The Saxons endeavoured to obtain a Swedish withdrawal from the Electorate as a quid pro quo for accepting Augustus's abdication. They argued that Saxony could not sustain such a large force, particularly the numerous Swedish cavalry, and generously suggested Brandenburg as a more congenial site ('dort gebe es fette Quartiere'). However, they were foiled here as well. As a Swedish diplomat phrased it, occu-pation of the Electorate would be the very means whereby 'Saxony should be put out of condition for the future to assist King Augustus with men and money'. Occupation would also increase pressure upon Dresden to ratify and execute the peace treaty.

Once Pfingsten and Imhoff had conceded abdication and occupa-tion, they capitulated down the line: on Patkul's handover, the release of the Sobieskis and abrogation of Augustus's treaties with the Tsar. Satisfied with the results, Charles removed his brooding pre-sence from Bischofswerda the next day, and on 15 September he crossed the Elbe at Meissen. Six days later he reached the castle of Altranstädt, situated a few miles west of Leipzig, where he would maintain his headquarters throughout the Swedish occupation.

On 24 September 1706 the two Saxon plenipotentiaries arrived there. Together with Piper and Cederhielm for Sweden, and two shadowy representatives of King Stanisław I of Poland, they signed the 22 articles of the Treaty of Altranstädt.[7] For the moment its pro-visions were academic, since strict secrecy had successfully shrouded the negotiations.

Charles had not wanted any publicity to interfere with his subjuga-tion of Saxony. Nor had Augustus courted it, since his position was far more precarious. He had ostensibly made peace with his Swedish cousin and voided all treaties with his ally Peter. Yet currently, he was surrounded by thousands of Russian cavalry, who under his leader-ship were aiming to destroy a Swedish army.

'A SIGNAL VICTORY'

Progressing south-west from Nowogródek, by 17 September Augustus was at Brest-Litovsk 'waiting for thirteen regiments of dragoons, which the Czar has promised him'. This force, under Menshikov, and Augustus's own cavalry joined together at Lublin, which town they left on 1 October. 'The King of Poland has passed the Vistula with an army of 30,000 men', reported Robinson further on 13 October, 'and is marching towards the frontiers of Silesia, where 'tis supposed the King of Sweden may meet him'. Charles was of course in Saxony, but a Swedish army under Major-General Mardefeld was stationed in Kalisz (west of Łódź).[8]

On 15 October Augustus was in Piotrków (south of Łódź), where he was located by Pfingsten, who bore a Swedish safe-conduct and a copy of the Treaty of Altranstädt for his sovereign to ratify. Fearing that an attack upon Mardefeld would jeopardize the treaty and cause Charles to wreak havoc in Saxony, Augustus sought to delay the further advance of his army. He also gave Pfingsten a letter for the Swedish general, informing him of the treaty, and urging him to leave the way free by retiring to Poznań.

Carrying Augustus's ratification, Pfingsten began his return journey to Saxony on 20 October. He did not personally deliver his King's letter to Mardefeld, but handed it to the Swedish resident in Breslau, with the result that it arrived late. However, the general did receive a message from Augustus's Grand Marshal Pflug on 21 October. This was Mardefeld's first intimation of the peace treaty and, not surprisingly, he was wary of the invitation to retreat. Only on 24 October did he receive his first communication from Charles, confirming the existence of the treaty and granting permission to withdraw.

However, it was now too late to retreat. Mardefeld's small force of a little over 4000 had a large infantry component, with several battalions formed of German, Swiss and French troops captured at Fraustadt. Beyond that he enjoyed only the dubious support of between 9000 and 10,000 Polish cavalrymen who were adherents of Stanisław.

His foes, who had resumed their advance westwards on 22 October, numbered around 35,000, comprising some 6000 Saxons, 20,000 Russians (half being irregulars), and the remainder pro-Augustus units from the Crown Army. Composed exclusively of cavalry and dragoons, this host had cut off Mardefeld's lines of retreat. The Swede had no choice but to make a stand outside Kalisz.

Whitworth later recounted that Augustus 'was against hazarding an engagement', but was overruled by Menshikov, 'who alleged that

232

having marched so far to come within a mile of the enemy, he was resolved not to go back without looking him in the face'. Whatever the truth of this, there is no doubt that Augustus, sword in hand, took part in the Battle of Kalisz. It began in the late afternoon of Friday 29 October 1706 and was over in three hours.

Robinson reported that 'the provident Poles immediately took to their heels', while the Swedes 'made a very stout resistance, and thrice repulsed their enemies'. Mardefeld's troops were defeated only when Augustus's second line subjected them to withering fire. Some 500 Swedish cavalry escaped towards Poznań, and others got away elsewhere. Some 1800 'Swedes' surrendered, and their dead were around 700. Mardefeld lost all of his artillery and supplies. Russian casualties may have been as low as 400.

According to Whitworth's despatches, the Saxons 'seized on all the booty for themselves', and although they had captured only seven Swedes in the battle, Augustus demanded 'that all the prisoners should be consigned to his custody'. Menshikov at first refused, but later yielded. Ostensibly Augustus sought a prisoner exchange, while in fact he simply released the Swedes.

Ignorant of developments, English diplomats thought that the Saxon would use Kalisz to his advantage. On 5 November Robinson was in Frankfurt on the Oder. From there he relayed accounts of the battle, which had been brought to his companion, the Danish ambassador, 'by a gentleman the King of Poland had sent express to carry the news of this victory to Berlin and elsewhere'. The envoy thought that his triumph at Kalisz was 'like to be of considerable advantage to King Augustus, if he lay hold on the occasions this successful blow offers him'. Writing from his new post at the Hague, Stepney concurred.[9] He conjectured that such 'a signal victory over the Swedes' might make Charles 'more reasonable in his proceedings and demands than he has seemed of late'.

The contrary was the case. Pfingsten had delivered Augustus's ratification to Charles by 2 November. The subsequent news that his cousin had assisted the Russians in destroying a Swedish army awakened all the worst fears of Augustus's duplicity. Charles was on the point of tearing up the treaty and devastating Saxony, when a missive from Augustus arrived. In it the Saxon apologized for Kalisz and apparently provided such a convincing explanation for having to take the action he did that Charles accepted it and let the treaty stand. He also wrote 'a very kind letter with his own hand to King Augustus'. However, to unmask the other before the Russians and to obviate any further chicanery, Charles ordered his diplomats to publicize the Treaty of Altranstädt in the courts of Europe, which they did on 16 November.

'UPON NO PRINCIPLE'

When it was published, the treaty evoked both consternation and indignation. Given the secrecy with which it was originally negotiated, this was hardly surprising. Robinson, who arrived in Leipzig on 12 November, referred to 'a peace very unexpectedly concluded in these parts'. The Dutch alluded to 'the sudden peace in Poland'.[10] Stepney judged that both kings had 'kept their secret very faithfully'. For neither Vienna, Hanover, nor Berlin 'knew anything of this agreement, till the moment it was published everywhere by the Swedish ministers'.

Raby deemed it 'one of the most extraordinary treaties that was ever made'. He was amazed that Augustus had 'given up his crown so tamely'. Stepney riposted that 'all King Augustus's actions are unaccountable, because he is used to go upon no principle'. Scornfully he assured other correspondents that 'the King of Poland does not deserve that any mortal should espouse his cause, since he himself has so meanly abandoned it', and 'nothing can happen to him that he has not richly deserved'.[11]

'I have never heard of anything more shameful than the peace which King Augustus has signed', Liselotte fumed to a relative. 'He must have been raving or drunk to accept such terms. I couldn't believe he would be so cowardly, and I blush for our nation'.[12] Whitworth referred scathingly to 'conditions so dishonourable for his person, so disadvantageous to his best ally, and so ruinous to his own country'.

As the opprobrium rolled over Augustus, Charles appeared to be moderation itself. In early October he urged the Hanoverian envoy to 'assure his master' that he would do nothing 'to disturb the peace of the Empire', or offend 'the princes of Germany, except the Elector of Saxony'. Soothingly Piper explained that Charles's 'design was only to hinder King Augustus from drawing succours of men and money' from Saxony, and thereby 'bring the war in Poland to an end'.[13]

To Robinson, Piper dwelt upon Charles's 'great care to avoid anything that might be of prejudice to the common cause'. He had 'accordingly deferred entering into Saxony for two years for that reason'; only undertaking it when 'the allies had gained such a superiority over' France that 'his coming into Saxony could not be of any prejudice to them'.

Not that anyone in the Empire intended to argue; Raby observed that Joseph, 'by his occupation in Hungary, is in an impuissance to do anything against the Swedes'. As for Brandenburg, 'this court dread extremely the Swedes', since Frederick's 'countries both here and in Prussia are mightily exposed at present'. Augustus was on his own.

'GROVELLING IN THE DARK'

After Kalisz, Augustus journeyed to Warsaw. He had some serious 'dissembling' to do. Having at once written apologetically to Charles, on 30 October he composed an awkward letter to the Tsar. In Whitworth's translation from the German, there is first a reference to Kalisz as 'this great and glorious victory'. But now Augustus expected that Charles 'will be provoked to revenge this disgrace, by entirely ruining my poor country with fire and sword'. To carry on the war Augustus needed fresh foreign troops, which in turn required Russian subsidies. 'Give me these marks of your friendship', he implored Peter, in his latest craving for the narcotic of 'men and money'.[14]

Augustus appears to have remained in Warsaw for most of November. Letters from the Polish capital recorded that on 20 November, he had 'published a declaration which was fixed upon all the public places', promising to 'venture his life to maintain himself upon the throne'. Four days later Robinson noted that Leipzig had been 'filled with apprehensions' that Augustus had been 'persuaded not to stand to the treaty so lately made and ratified'. However, the envoy deemed it more probable that 'the King of Poland has no thoughts of breaking the treaty', and that appearances to the contrary were designed 'to finger a good sum of money, expected from the Muscovites, before the secret break out'. The Prussian envoy to Dresden endorsed this view, telling Raby that the Saxon ministers anticipated Augustus arriving in Dresden on 6 or 7 December, and that 'he stays this long in Poland to receive some money from the Czar before he leaves him'.

Whether the Tsar actually dropped some more dollars into the Augustan ocean is not clear. He did send to Warsaw 'an officer to compliment him upon his victory near Kalisz'. Nor is it certain that the Russians actually knew about the Treaty of Altranstädt at this juncture, and confronted Augustus over it. However, during his stay in Warsaw 'many shifts and changes' were made 'to get safely away after the peace was known'. Finally, according to Raby's further account, after a courier arrived with an urgent message from Saxony, Augustus, Pflug and a few guards 'went away on a sudden'.

Our hero left Warsaw before dawn on 30 November. On his departure, the Russians told Whitworth, 'he left a letter on his table'. This informed his Polish supporters that 'he was only gone into Saxony to entice the Swedes out of that Electorate', but that he 'would never forsake them or their interest'.

Augustus is variously reported as travelling next to Cracow or Lublin, before doubling back and crossing through Silesia. Stepney detailed Augustus passing through Breslau on 5 December. Raby later wrote that he stayed some days in Silesia at the house of a Count Nostitz, 'which still kept people in doubt, as if he would not come into Saxony till he had better terms from the Swedes'.

Was he actually trying to renegotiate the Treaty of Altranstädt from a distance? Certainly, Berlin credited the possibility. 'We are all here still grovelling in the dark to find out the bottom of King Augustus's design', wrote Raby on 11 December. 'For 'tis unnatural to think he would quit his kingdom to save his hereditary Electorate, and in the same treaty leave it entirely at the mercy of the Swedes'.

'UNITED IN AFFECTION'

On 15 December Robinson referred to 'certain information' that Augustus 'has for some days been on German ground, but his ministers here seem not to know at what place His Majesty is'. The scene was set for what Stepney dubbed an 'extraordinary interview', which saw apparent reconciliation between the two cousins and foes, after a war that had cost so much blood and treasure. Yet by other standards it was also an end to a personal quarrel, which had contained elements of a duel, a hunt, a sport. One had triumphed, but the other wished to show himself to be a really good loser, albeit still a loser.

Robinson registered Augustus's arrival in Dresden on 15 December. The next day he left for Leipzig; on the way he 'was struck by a horse on the outward part of his right thigh'. He reached Leipzig, 'whither he came incognito' on the evening of 16 December, accompanied by Grand Marshal Pflug and some domestics. There he lodged for the night with one of the signatories of the treaty, Baron Imhoff.

On 17 December Augustus turned up at Charles's quarters in Altranstädt. The Swedish king was not at home – he was probably out riding – so the Saxon plodded round to Piper's abode instead. He was just leaving there at about one o'clock, when Charles 'came also thither in great haste, and made but two steps up a pair of stairs of twelve'. Augustus had only 'just got into the entry before Count Piper's chamber, when the King of Sweden met him'. There 'mutual embraces passed' between the cousins, that 'showed great affection on both sides'.

Augustus spoke 'and the retort[?] was made in gestures extremely civil'. Then, with Charles 'pressing King Augustus to go before him', they went into Piper's apartment. Since the doors were left open, it soon 'filled with a crowd of spectators'. The two kings remained there for 'about three hours, which was mostly spent in general conversation'. Around four o'clock, after Augustus had accepted Charles's invitation that he 'lodge that night at his quarters', the two monarchs 'went thither, the King of Sweden giving the other his own horse and the right hand [pride of place] all the way'.

On arrival they had a supper, which ended at 7 p.m. This was a lengthy repast for Charles, who was renowned for wolfing down his food. 'He continues his former diet, eats very fat meat and drinks nothing but small beer', explained Robinson, and "tis very seldom that he sits half an hour'. After this banquet, Charles conducted the Saxon 'into his own bedchamber, a lodging being provided for him elsewhere'. The two kings remained there some two hours, their discussions punctuated by 'great marks of confidence and familiarity', as was noted by 'several that took the boldness to look through the windows'.

One of these bold spirits was Robinson's secretary, who 'chanced to be present' but could not hear what was said. Another was the Swedish student Alstrin (C17 n5). 'Augustus appears as the gallantest cavalier that could be found', he remarked, 'of an exceptionally fine figure and somewhat big'. He observed how the Saxon and his own sovereign 'sat side by side like a handsome knight and a peasant-lad new-listed', who 'kept his eyes downcast with rustic shyness'.[15]

Others saw not the appearance but the effect. Robinson considered that the meeting had dispelled all doubts 'concerning the late treaty of peace', with both camps 'overjoyed at the happy success of this interview'. It was also 'very favourable' for Augustus, of whom the Swedes spoke 'with the greatest respect'. The crusty Rehnskjöld announced that 'he could well be content that should be the last day of his life', now that he had seen 'those two great Kings met together and so well united in affection'. Robinson supposed that Augustus's 'conversation will have won much upon the King of Sweden, as it remarkably does upon all he converses with'.

The two sovereigns met again early next morning; after which, to remind Augustus who was actually King of Poland, Charles paid a visit to Stanisław. Around midday our hero left Altranstädt for Leipzig, intending to stay at his usual residence there. The kick from the horse appeared to ail him, 'and having stood much yesterday and this morning', he appeared to be 'in great pain'.

He was well enough, however, to receive Charles, who returned the Saxon's visit on 21 December and stayed for over an hour. He was the only other monarch that Charles ever met. 'King Augustus now stays at Leipzig', he told his sister. 'I have been in his company a few times. He is merry and droll. He is not tall, but of compact build; a little corpulent also. He wears his own hair, which is quite dark'.[16]

'HIS OWN COUNTRY'

In pain or not, Augustus appeared well enough to scheme. On 21 December Robinson received his Grand Marshal. Pflug informed the envoy that Augustus's 'great concern for the common good of Europe, was one of his motives for making the late peace'. Doubtless remaining po-faced, Robinson did not enquire about the other motives. However, when Pflug hinted that his sovereign was ready to supply the allies with Saxon troops, Robinson and his Dutch counterpart asked him to provide more detail about this offer.

Returning on 22 December, Pflug told the envoys that Augustus had 'between 12 and 15,000 men, of which a good part is cavalry'. He was offering them all or as many as were wanted, 'for the service' of the Maritime Powers, and for as long as 'they may have occasion for them'. Through his minion, Augustus insisted 'upon no other conditions', save that the troops 'be entertained as usual while they serve, and restored when they shall be no longer needed'. Otherwise he left it entirely up to Queen Anne and the States-General, 'whether they think fit to give him any subsidy for that assistance or not'.

Augustus sought a different generosity from Charles, whom he visited again on 23 December. Robinson was told that at this meeting, the Elector would 'try to procure his subjects' ease, in respect of the contributions that are still expected from them'; the Saxon position being that these monetary exactions should cease entirely at the end of 1706. He did not get his way. Whether from pique, or a desire to fritter some more of Saxony's wealth before it all vanished, Augustus left at once for Dresden, promising to return to Leipzig in a week.

Yet failure to budge the Swedish King merely confirmed the *de facto* situation. 'For the present', observed Charles, 'it is I who am Elector of Saxony'.[17] Stepney thought so too, remarking how Charles 'affects to do the honours in Saxony, as if it were his own country'.

Robinson opined that whensoever the Swedes quit the Electorate, 'they will leave it very bare'. In support of this view, he noted some very creative accounting. The Swedish levies for January and February 1707 had been reduced by a quarter, and those for the next two months by a half. On the other hand, the four exactions for September–December 1706 had been raised by 50 per cent, from 500,000 to 750,000 crowns per month. Perhaps the Swedes too wanted to grab as much as possible as speedily as possible, before Augustus squandered the rest.

On 24 December it was Robinson's turn for an audience with Charles, who he thought was 'grown taller and more spread' than when he last saw him in 1703. He noted too that the King was 'less difficult than formerly to permit his courtiers' and officers' ladies to be with their husbands', but 'himself does not yet show any attachment for the sex'. The substance of their talk revolved around Robinson conveying Queen Anne's gratitude that Charles had 'attained his ends' in Saxony, while 'in his great wisdom' he had also managed 'to prevent the inconveniences his friends and allies had reason to apprehend'.

Otherwise it was business as usual. The Imperial ambassador, Count Harrach, murmured to Robinson about the allied interest in getting their hands on Saxon troops. The problem here was that Augustus had specifically excepted Vienna from his offer. In turn, Harrach intended excluding him from the Polish throne.

Having noted a three-day sojourn of Stanisław and the three Sobieski brothers with Charles, Harrach offered the following view upon the 'agnition' of King Stanisław. Since the allies would have to recognize him as Poland's King, it was best that 'it be done *de bonne grace*, and without much loss of time'. Robinson said nothing to this, although he later reflected that 'Poland seems like to fall into greater confusion than ever'.

'Greater confusion than ever'! Such words might well have dusted the lips of Augustus, as he came back to Leipzig on the last day of 1706. Priming himself for a less than idyllic New Year was becoming something of a habit.

Chapter 23

'To please the King of Sweden'
Occupational hazards 1707

'CESSION OF HIS TROOPS'

Charles had a considerable agenda in Saxony. His primary task was to refit and reinforce his army for the coming war against the Tsar. However, he was determined to leave behind him a secure rear, which meant the complete execution of the Altranstädt Diktat by Augustus, and its guarantee by the allies. This required Augustus to recognize his dethronement and Stanisław's accession and to surrender Patkul and the Russian troops in Imperial service to Charles.

The troop question created tensions with Vienna, as did the aspirations of the Silesian Protestants.[1] Whatever was said by the Swedes, there remained the suspicion that the Brabants might still march not east, but west into the Empire. Robinson kept an eye on this matter, and also negotiated for a Saxon contribution to the allied armies. This the Swedes were perfectly willing to grant; the further removed the Saxon army was from their backs, the better they liked it.

On 18 January Robinson learned from Piper that Charles had approved Augustus's 'design to make cession of his troops to the allies'. And soon, at Dresden's request, the allied envoys were endeavouring not only to obtain Saxon prisoners of war from the Swedes, but also to muster the units still in Poland. During the proceedings came hints that Augustus might actually have the odd condition to attach to his 'unconditional offer' of Saxon troops.

Augustus preferred to keep his 'offering' as a united contingent, Robinson informed Marlborough on 22 January, 'but if it be found necessary to divide them he will not be against it'. Such concern for the composition of his forces was indeed gracious of the Elector, given their current decomposition. On the Rhine there were already 1500 Saxons. In Dresden there were 12 battalions, some 4000 infantry in all. Two more battalions were in Cracow castle; 'mais le plus vieux pied est en Suede', wrote Pflug to Robinson, and these prisoners were 'au nombre de 7 a 8m hommes'. As for cavalry, there were some 6000 in Poland and Saxony, with other units scattered around Silesia, Thuringia and Prussia.

Augustus had other conditions. He wanted Vienna to have no influence upon his 'offering'. Robinson referred to 'the aversion the King of Poland shows to transact with the Emperor for all or any of his troops'. And, given that his old rival Prince Lewis of Baden was dead, 'he was desirous to take the command of the army of the Rhine'.

Then in early March, at a meeting between Pflug and Robinson, the previously optional 'subsidy' was converted into a dire necessity, because of the financial burden of upkeeping the Saxon cavalry. As the Grand Marshal explained, 'things have happened otherwise, than was first expected', and as matters now stood, 'the troops cannot be made mobile without some assistance'.

Robinson was unimpressed. He correctly assessed that Augustus would 'let fall much of these demands', since there was no chance that he could 'dispose of his troops elsewhere'. Nor could he keep them for his own purposes, 'the charge being above his present ability'.

Stepney negotiated the treaty with the Saxons in the Hague. It was signed in April. Under its terms, 3390 Saxon foot and 1125 horse were taken into the pay of the Maritime Powers and destined for the Rhine. 'The 70,000 crowns that are to be given, to put them in a condition to march, must be speedily paid', Marlborough emphasized to Godolphin, 'for the troops can't march till one month after the payment'. The Lord Treasurer replied in mid-May that he was remitting funds 'for the march of the Saxon troops', but without 'much hopes of their coming time enough to be of use to you in this campaign'.[2]

'TO PENETRATE HIS DESIGN'

'We are now very curious to know what piece of work the Swede will cut out for himself', wrote Stepney from the Hague in November 1706, 'and wish his odd fancy may lead him towards Muscovy. At least we should suffer there very little, whoever gets the better'.[3] By next month the seeds of doubt had been sown. While admitting that Charles had not 'hitherto acted directly against the allies', Stepney remarked that 'the most intelligent people here seem a little uneasy, lest he should be tempted to make an ill use of his power at this time'.

Robinson disagreed, informing Whitehall on 22 December that 'I can not from any hand discover, that the King of Sweden hath other design but to prosecute the war against the Muscovite'. Similarly, in January 1707 Sweden's ambassador in Berlin assured Raby that all Charles's 'preparations were designed against the Czar'.

But the concerns remained; so Marlborough volunteered to visit Charles, to try to 'penetrate his design'.[4] His trip was approved, and on 27 April the Duke met Charles in Altranstädt. He noted that despite their temperate conversation, which Robinson translated, the King's eyes flashed at each mention of the Tsar's name, while the table in his room was decked with a map of Muscovy. Although hardly conclusive, Churchill was confident enough to write to Godolphin of the time when Charles would 'march through Silesia in his way to Poland'.

Naturally, Augustus could not be kept out of the act. The Duke reported that on the evening of 27 April, he 'sent a gentleman to make me compliments, and to let me know that he is come to Leipzig on purpose to speak to me'. At their meeting on 28 April Augustus intoned the requisite 'many repeated assurances of his respects' for Queen Anne, as well as 'his strict adherence to the interests of the allies'. Thereafter, he moaned about 'the great hardships and extortions he had suffered from the Swedes'. The Saxon wanted the guarantor powers to make Charles rebate some allegedly overpaid tribute. But Churchill advised him not 'to offer at anything at this juncture', that might give Charles grounds 'to delay his march out of Saxony'.

However, Marlborough did assist with one matter. Since Augustus's remaining troops were 'a greater burden to him' than he could cope with, 'at his desire I have pressed the Court of Vienna to take three or four thousand horse into their pay'; this from a King who was but recently refusing the Imperialists a single soldier.

The Duke met Stanisław too and pleased the Swedes by treating him like a king. On his return trip he also called upon the Prussian monarch. 'This journey has given me the advantage of seeing four kings, three of which I had never seen', Marlborough told his wife. 'They seem to be all very different in their kinds. If I was obliged to make a choice it should be the youngest, which is the King of Sweden'.[5]

'KING AUGUSTUS'S PROCEEDINGS'

On New Year's Day 1707 Augustus called upon the King of Sweden, and the next day Charles reciprocated his visit. Since 17 December they had now met six times. The Saxon's charming dissimulations were perhaps beginning to pall, while Charles's visit to Stanisław on 3 January indicated that the pressure was still on. 'The violent passion that the two Kings showed at their first meeting is quite cooled', mused Raby. 'Now sorrow is much in Augustus's face and neglect much in t'other's'.

On 19 January Robinson reported upon the vexation of the Swedish court 'at the great slowness of the Saxons in executing the treaty'. As a result, they had given the tardy Teutons 'a list of eight points yet wanting'. All of these had been acknowledged and promised by Dresden in a new agreement signed that month, 'except the articles of the extradition of General Patkul, and the delivery up of the Muscovites'. While both were 'plainly stipulated' in the treaty, Robinson explained that 'King Augustus avers it was promised him, the former would not be insisted on'. But then he would hardly say otherwise.

Raby wrote in similar vein two days later: Charles 'was no ways satisfied with King Augustus's proceedings', for he had not yet notified 'to any court his abdication of the crown of Poland', nor requested the Maritime Powers to guarantee the treaty. Then there were the several intercepted letters he had sent since the peace was concluded, all encouraging Peter and Augustus's Polish supporters 'never to own' Stanisław. Berlin was also 'mightily embarrassed' about how to reply to Augustus's letters to King Frederick I, since in them he gave himself 'not only the arms of Poland but all the titles'.

By 9 February Robinson was recording 'more of a stiffness and coldness in the Swedish ministers than heretofore'. Doubtless Augustus felt the chill too, since he 'has now with him his Queen and the Prince'; the Saxon had summoned them from Bayreuth in January. Eberhardine had refused to come to Leipzig while the pregnant Constantia was there. This led to a violent row between Augustus and his mistress, during which he struck her. Eventually Countess Cosel stormed off to Dresden, and Augustus went home to mother in Lichtenberg. He was there when he received news that Constantia's son had come into the world stillborn. He hastened to Dresden to be with her, not returning to Leipzig until 3 February, where Eberhardine arrived with his sole legitimate child the next day.

Having posed briefly as husband and father, Augustus left Leipzig on 12 February. Three days later he presided over a great hunt at Liebenwerda (north of Dresden). However, the chief guest was absent. Robinson reported that Charles 'did not think fit to be present at the hunting, which King Augustus invited him to'.[6] So, after a sulky stay at Torgau, Augustus decamped to Dresden on 24 February.

Robinson thought 'it will be indifferent' to Charles, whether

Augustus 'be near to him or not', since most matters concerning 'the execution of the treaty are already done'. The two items outstanding remained the extradition of Patkul, and whether Augustus could 'style himself King of Poland in writing to other princes, and they give it to him in their letters'. Moreover, Charles demanded that his cousin answer a letter that he had received from King Stanisław. In the envoy's view, this last had 'no other difficulty besides the aversion' Augustus had 'to him that has supplanted him, which I suppose will be overcome'.

Overcoming his aversion to ceding his throne and surrendering Patkul were major problems for Augustus. Yet, surprisingly, Robinson could report, after an audience in Dresden on 28 February, that 'His Majesty appeared very easy in all parts'. Either he was punch-drunk, or life with a recovered Constantia was good.

'PAID WITH INGRATITUDE'

In September 1706, Whitworth recorded that the Tsar had made 'several very earnest instances' to Augustus for Patkul's release, 'but hitherto without any effect'. Indeed, the Saxons now kept the Livonian 'more close than ever' and had imprisoned his cook and other servants in Königstein for having smuggled out several letters which Patkul had composed 'in his justification'.

Patkul had the strength to pour out more screeds, since he was now eating; in fact he was gourmandizing. Amazing fare entered the prisons of Sonnenstein and later Königstein, to which he was transferred in September 1706. A boar's head, 300 oysters, wine, butter and white bread reached Patkul's cell in January 1706. The May menu sampled geese, capons, crabs, salad and artichokes. In June salmon, eels, apricots and cherries were in season at Sonnenstein.

However, the Swedish occupation of Saxony, personified by a vengeful King, doubtless took the edge off Patkul's appetite. Charles had specifically demanded the traitor's handover. It was agreed to by Augustus in Article 11 of the Treaty of Altranstädt. The Saxon might wriggle and temporize, but 'Iron Head' would not be thwarted.

The Tsar was now urging other monarchs to intervene on behalf of Patkul; but Robinson warned that 'no open applications can be made with hopes of success'. The whole 'business must be left to the private means' used by the Livonian's friends to win his pardon. Only if they were successful and 'after the thing is done' would it be time for 'foreign princes' to 'intervene with their thanks', should they 'find it needful to give the Czar that content'.

However, Patkul's friends and their private means were getting nowhere. 'The Saxon ministers begin to be convinced', noted Robinson on 5 March, 'that the extradition of Patkul cannot be avoided on any terms'. Even though 'considerable sums of money have been offered underhand' to Swedish officials to procure a pardon, the latter would not 'for any consideration undertake to solicit it'.

Indeed, not only did they refuse the lavish bribes, but the Swedes apparently countered with threats. On 9 March Robinson reported Dresden's fear 'that the King of Sweden intended to use some severe means to force King Augustus to execute the remaining points of the treaty'. Charles was 'so unalterably set' on having Patkul's head, Swedish officials informed him, that 'no offers whatever, not even of all Saxony, will prevail with him'.

Despite this, and with something less than a kingdom to drop into the pot, Robinson met with Piper on 18 March. He tendered the Swedish Chancellor 30,000 crowns on behalf of Augustus's mother, together with a letter from her to Charles. Piper replied that he wished Patkul 'might be pardoned, but had very little hopes'.

Augustus had very little hope either, despite trying to evade the final deed by forlorn compromises. He offered to guarantee that the Livonian would be held prisoner for the rest of his life. As an alternative, he proposed consigning Patkul to a four-power consortium of the Maritime Powers, the Empire and Prussia. Not surprisingly, Charles resented this proposal 'very highly' and took it 'for a mark of a secret engagement still subsisting' between Augustus and the Tsar.

Augustus was also involved in a half-cocked plan to allow Patkul to escape from custody and ultimately from Saxony. It fell through because our hero, choosing between the wrath of two sovereigns, bowed to the prevailing power of Sweden rather than the distant desires of Peter.

Finally, Charles terminated all prevarications. At midnight on 6–7 April 1707, a Swedish detail went to Königstein, took delivery of Patkul from his Saxon gaolers and carted off their shackled prisoner. They even wrote and signed a receipt for their hapless cargo.[7]

As if unburdened by one surrender, Augustus forthwith made the other. On 8 April he wrote to Stanisław. His bitter, sardonic letter reeks of self-pity and clearly indicates that he was only bowing to *force majeure*. However, it still constitutes his recognition that there was a new King of Poland.

Sir and Brother
We do not consider it was necessary to enter upon a detailed correspondence with your Majesty; but to please the King of Sweden, and that it may not be said that we have been unwilling to satisfy him, we hereby congratulate you upon your accession, and hope

that your subjects will prove more faithful to you than ours have been to us. Everyone will do us the justice to believe that we have only been paid with ingratitude for all our benefits, and that the majority of our subjects have only aimed at our ruin. We hope that you will not be exposed to like misfortunes, and commit you to God's keeping.

Your brother and neighbour,
Augustus, King.[8]

Meantime, Augustus, King, meted out more ingratitude. On 29 March Raby noted that he had sent Spiegel, his favourite *valet de chambre*, to Königstein, 'and 'tis thought that as soon as he dares venture, Imhoff and Pfingsten will keep him company there'. The implication is that Spiegel, like the two courtiers, had some special knowledge regarding the signature of the Treaty of Altranstädt. This may be true, because this shadowy figure is frequently mentioned as a courier for Augustus. However, Spiegel also received Augustus's mistress Fatime as his wife, when our hero decided to marry her off. When this was is unclear, but Augustus had recently fathered a second child on the Turk (p 251), so the differences between King and valet might have had another source.

Raby was right about Imhoff and Pfingsten: on 10 May Robinson reported that the pair were 'taken into custody last week'. They were charged with 'very great malversations in reference to the King's revenue', as well as keeping 'one or more of the blanks' signed by Augustus and 'entrusted to them in order to make the late peace'. The envoy added that the Swedes made 'no reflection on this incident'.

On Augustus's orders the unfortunate duo were brought to trial upon various charges amounting to high treason. Found guilty, Imhoff received a life sentence, while Pfingsten was condemned to death. The former eventually served a seven-year stretch; Pfingsten evaded the axe and died in Königstein after 28 years' incarceration.

'KING OF NOTHING'

'It is unheard of to be King of Nothing', remonstrated Augustus in February 1707; but by April that was effectively his status, no matter how this 'King without a Crown' (*König ohne Krone*) tried to live his former life. In May he had returned to Leipzig to visit the spring fair. There Charles made him another visit, which the Saxon returned on 10 May. These encounters had 'passed with appearances of mutual satisfaction', related Robinson; but only Charles had got his way.

On 9 June, having dined with Eberhardine in Dresden, Augustus 'rid out' to Torgau 'and spent two or three hours' reviewing a regiment of cuirassiers and two of dragoons that were to enter the service of the Maritime Powers. On 11 June he left again for Leipzig, in search of money to make another 6000 cavalrymen 'mobile'.

A few days later, Robinson recorded that the Prussian envoy had returned to Berlin without seeing Augustus. The only explanation that the Briton could offer was that Augustus 'will not admit his credential letters in which the title King of Poland is omitted'. On 20 June Piper had to remind Augustus that he had agreed to this under Altranstädt, and the cavalier chancer was 'at once' quite 'content to renounce' his title again, and zero in to his role as 'King of Nothing'.

But by now he would promise anything, in the expectation that cousin Charles would soon be on his way. The only 'reason that retains the Swedish army in Saxony', declared Robinson in June, was the need for the allies to sign separate acts of guarantee of the Treaty of Altranstädt with Augustus and Charles.

On 6 July Augustus returned to Dresden. But if he thought that he was about to have his Electorate all to himself, he was soon disabused by the depth of Charles's quarrel with the Empire. This was not finally resolved until September and resuscitated all the old fears that Charles might invade the Habsburg realm.

Underpinning this, by implying that Charles might well stay in Saxony beyond 1707, was Robinson's despatch of 27 July. He reported Swedish talk that since Charles had 'waited so long for the guarantees demanded', it was now too late in the campaign season 'to remove from hence'; particularly as Russian forces had 'made such havoc in Poland' that the Swedish army 'cannot possibly subsist there for any time'.

This may well have been disinformation fed into the reverend ear. If Augustus heard it, he seems to have ignored it, as in mid-August he blithely flew a trial balloon. Robinson noted a recent publication asserting the 'right' of the Wettin house to the kingdoms of Naples and Sicily, coveted by the Habsburgs. The alleged author was Augustus's 'Historiographer' writing without his sovereign's assent. In all, opined Robinson, 'there appears nothing that can do King Augustus service one way or other'. The putative 'King of Something' evidently reached the same conclusion: a week later, Robinson mentioned that the Dresden court 'highly disavows the pamphlet'. The envoy thought that the whole matter 'will fall there'.

It certainly did not stop the Swedish departure, which began on 1 September after a year living off Saxon fat. The army which had entered the Electorate had numbered less than 20,000. That which departed was over 32,000 and would be augmented to nearly 44,000 when it met up at Poznań with the latest draft of recruits from Sweden. 'To human eyes these brave, sturdy, well-equipped, well-trained fellows look invincible', crowed the student Alstrin, as he watched these 'pampered men' in their blue and yellow uniforms tramp east.[9]

In the wake of his army, Charles with a few companions paid a visit to other men whose lives had known little of privation over the last twelve months. Whether Charles acted upon a whim, or desired to see Augustus's capital, or simply intended to take leave of his cousin, is not clear. However, after quitting Swedish headquarters, then near Meissen, on 5 September, Charles took the road south-wards along the Elbe until Dresden came into view. 'We might as well ride into the town now we have got so close', he informed his party.[10]

The oft-related story that Charles was 'arrested' by Dresden's 'main guard', and only released when Flemming recognized him, appears to be untrue. As Raby later recounted, Flemming, then on a visit to Berlin, told the tale 'other ways than his secretary writ it'. This version stated that when Charles, posing as a colonel, and his eight companions reached the town, the King 'showed a passport he had signed himself, so that they were not stopped at all at the Grand Guard, but went straight to the palace and met King Augustus there'.

By all accounts our hero was unwell and received his cousin in his dressing-gown. While Charles paid another visit to his aunt, Augustus slipped on some finery, then he showed the younger sovereign the sights, firing off a cannonade in salute when the tourists left. The next day Augustus summoned his advisers. When the Swedes learned of this, Rehnskjöld remarked cynically that the Saxons were now 'deliberating as to what they ought to have done yesterday'.[11]

If Robinson knew of this last meeting between the cousins, his account cannot be traced. In any case, the envoy appeared more concerned with his own departure. Although he remained in Saxony until the end of September, he had already received instructions to proceed to Hamburg to help sort out the latest conflict between Denmark and the Duke of Holstein-Gottorp. Consequently, it was from there that he made reference, almost in passing, to his last meeting with Augustus on 25 September. The Saxon burbled the usual 'great assurances of his friendship and esteem' for Queen Anne and promised her use of his remaining 6000 unemployed cavalry as foot-soldiers.

The dethroned offering the unhorsed aptly summed up the situation of Saxony and its ruler in late 1707. For two years the quondam King of Poland would be an itinerant, dodging between beds and battlefields, dreaming, scheming and waiting: waiting for the spin of fortune's wheel that would eventually rumble from the carnage of Poltova, in the Ukraine, when Peter annihilated Charles's army in July 1709.

'BROKE ALIVE UPON A WHEEL'

On 17 September 1707 the Swedes re-crossed the Oder at Steinau. Before them the Muscovites retreated eastward. Peter, who had spent several months in the Republic, touting a potential third crown of Poland to such as Rákóczi and Eugene of Savoy, left Warsaw in August. It was to be another of his frantic marathons: across Lithuania to Petersburg, and on to Moscow for a flying visit. 'I know nothing that travels more or faster than the Czar', lauded Whitworth, 'except the sun'.[12]

Poland was more like the dark side of the moon. The Cossack and Calmuck irregular cavalry had left there a swathe of slaughter and devastation to confront the advancing Swedes. Charles halted his army at Poznań on 26 September, to collect reinforcements and to ensure that Vienna executed its undertakings towards the Silesian Protestants. He also took the opportunity to settle Patkul's fate.

Having spent the months since his transfer into Swedish custody chained to a heavy stake, then transported in a virtual cage, the wretched Livonian was brought to the small monastery town of Kazimierz (north-west of Poznań) on 9 October 1707. The following day, at Charles's express order, Patkul was sentenced as a traitor to be broken alive on the wheel, then beheaded and quartered.

The local executioner was ill-equipped and inexperienced by sophisticated western standards. Having pulverized Patkul's limbs with 15 blows of a sledgehammer, he was starting on the chest, when the victim crawled to a block and laid his head upon it, croaking the words, 'Kopf ab!' The commander of the Swedish detail granted permission, and eventually the executioner complied, although it took four blows of his axe finally to sever Patkul's head from his shattered body. Thereafter it topped a pole by the roadside.

That aficionado, the Tsar, later wrote that the merciful Swedish officer was cashiered by his King for not ensuring that the victim died in agony prior to decapitation and dismemberment. But we should not judge too harshly: such subtle refinements of the degradation inflicted by humans upon their peers unfortunately linger on into our times, although quartering appears somewhat démodé.

Raby enlightened London that 'poor Patkul' had been 'broke alive upon a wheel, and afterwards his quarters were set up on the road'.

The Swedish diplomat who brought these tidings commented that Patkul's 'sentence and execution was hastened', because they had 'discovered several designs of the Muscovites to set him at liberty'.

Augustus's reactions to Patkul's gruesome death were ambivalent. It seems that he sent a detail to gather up the dessicated dregs after he re-entered Poland in autumn 1709. Was it remorse, morbid curiosity, or simply a desire to dispose of all reminders of his involvement in this affair? According to Voltaire, Patkul's remains were brought in a box to our hero in Warsaw. He perused them in the presence of the French ambassador. 'These are the members of Patkul', he remarked without compunction.[13]

'IMPOSSIBLE FOR HIM TO BE QUIET'

On 26 September 1707, after long bouts of illness, George Stepney died in Paradise Row, Chelsea, of either dysentery or tuberculosis, or a combination of both dreadful scourges. On the night of 3 October this proud commoner was interred 'in great state' in Westminster Abbey, his pall 'carried by two dukes, two earls and two barons'.[14]

There is no evidence that Augustus learned of or cared about the demise of the envoy who knew him as well as any Englishman. He was probably too involved with clambering back onto the European stage. He still had horsemen for hire, and it appeared that they might now climb back into the saddle too.

At the end of October, Marlborough described the prospect of 6000 Saxon horse as 'a very necessary augmentation' for the Imperial army;[15] Raby was more captious in his judgement. On 10 December he warned that the allies must take care how they reconstituted Augustus's cavalry, 'for if he is armed 'tis impossible for him to be quiet, and all his neighbours complain of him already'.

Doubtless his portrait of a regal rowdy owed much to the input of the Brandenburg court; yet it is the same view that we began with, of a 'prince who would not lie still'. Augustus already entertained plans 'to march with the first grass' into Poland, to reclaim his tainted crown. However, the fact that Charles did not even cross the Vistula before January 1708 aborted any such project. 'Stories of King Augustus pretending once more to the crown of Poland seem to be fallen to nothing', Whitworth wrote contemptuously. Then, perhaps, the names 'Kliszów' and 'Fraustadt' still echoed around the Saxon's head.

In love as in war, Augustus at 37 was only down, not out. Despite his amorous and costly affair with that tall, imposing brunette Constantia von Cosel, he had still managed to father a second child upon

Fatime (now Frau von Spiegel) in 1706. This was his fourth acknowledged bastard and the first daughter, Katharina, later Countess Bielinska.

Early in 1707 he nearly gained another son, but Countess Cosel's boy was stillborn (p 244). However, on 26 November that year Henriette Rénard presented Augustus with another girl. Henriette was the wife or daughter of a French wine-merchant in Warsaw; the Saxon had doubtless been a good customer of his. But procreation could hardly have taken place in Poland early in 1707; it must have occurred in the Electorate, under the eyes of the pregnant Constantia. Presumably, Augustus had indulged that manly habit of going off the boil, when his woman was with child, before going off altogether, with one who wasn't.

However, Henriette was no pushover. Even though she lacked rank and status, she demanded that Augustus recognize their child, Anna Catherina; which he did, later raising her to the rank of Countess Orczelska (1707–69). As his favourite daughter, Orczelska gained a certain notoriety of her own, when the Margravine of Bayreuth implied that in 1728 she was indulging in incest not only with Augustus, but with her step-brothers as well. The fact that the King of Poland was then 57, and weakened by diabetes and an amputated toe, did not staunch the fantasies of the young Prussian princess, who thought she was intended to be Augustus's second wife.

Gurlitt, however, makes a more pertinent point about Henriette gaining recognition and riches for her child. If she from her lowly stand could do it, why did not many more mothers of his alleged 300-plus children follow in her footsteps?[16] Is it because the true number of Augustan bastards was between eight and ten – namely, the five that we have detailed, plus the three children of Countess Cosel born outside both wedlock and the time-span of this book: Augusta Constantia, Countess Friesen (1708–28); Friedericke Alexandra, Countess von Mosczynska (1709–84); and Friedrich August, Count Cosel (1712–70)? To these we might perhaps add the offspring of Sophie von Zinzendorff (p 46) and Countess Esterle (p 218).

And if we pass from Augustus's progeny to consider his main mistresses, a very obvious point arises: not one of these ladies stemmed from the Saxon aristocracy. Nor did his chief ministers: Schöning was from Brandenburg, Haxthausen from Westphalia, Pflug from Bohemia, Fürstenberg was a Swabian and Flemming Pomeranian. This was quite deliberate; that small extract of Augustus's 'memoirs' that we possess brooks no ambiguity upon the subject (A1).

He saw the Saxon nobility as a dead hand, holding back the virile Wettin Electors from their true destiny of promoting the glory of their house. However, despite various attempts, Augustus never imposed himself in absolutist fashion upon the Saxon nobles, as did the Hohenzollerns in Brandenburg–Prussia. Even had he done so, he would still have been left with the situation in his second realm of Poland, where shafting the szlachta offered the same prospects of outright success as fornicating with a sponge.

And like the last, Augustus soaked up resources. While his country was bled by Swedish exactions, its sovereign built Constantia a palace and purchased for her Billa's old residence at Pillnitz, which came into her acquisitive hands in December 1707. It is true that, for now, he cavilled at lashing out RT 58,485 on the recently completed 'Court of the Grand Mogul' (*der Hofhalt des Großmoguls*). This, one of several exquisite items crafted for him by Johann Melchior Dinglinger and currently on display in Dresden's 'Green Vault', cost more than Pillnitz. Later, it joined Augustus's hoard; but goldsmiths, unlike mistresses, could be made to wait for their rewards.

He was also short of ready money for refitting his 6000 cavalrymen: the estimate for their uniforms alone was nearly RT 90,000. But it was simply a matter of pleasure's priorities. In September 1707 Raby could report that Flemming 'tells us of the fine liveries King Augustus makes to appear at the next fair in Leipzig, which cost him 50,000 dollars, so little seems that prince to mind retrenching; for all his own and his country's misfortunes'.

With one ambitious eye on Poland, the other beamed hedonistically at the latest vogue, and both scrutinizing almost every woman they saw, Augustus remained true to Flemming's prescription. Among his treasures was a bejewelled figurine of an archer, inscribed 'Mon but c'est la gloire'.[17] Yet the shafts of ambition he targeted upon glory would, almost always, be deflected by his other congenital addiction to pleasure.

Appendix 1

'Connaissance de ses forces'
The 'memoirs' of Augustus (1705?)

On nous (n'a) pas donné la moindre teinture des affaires étrangères ni de ceux de nos propres états par la raison que, le maître régnant, ils ne pussent pénétrer ni être instruits de ses intérêts, pour être assujettis à la direction de leur noblesse et à leur but, qui a été de tout temps de tenir le maître dans une subjection et de ne le pas laisser devenir grand. Ce qu'ils ont soigneusement exécuté ayant tenu le maître éloigné de connaissance de ses forces, alléguant qu'il ne fut pas bon que le maître sçût ce qu'il a, et régnant plus que lui, tenant sa bourse, corrompant son conseil, lequel on (ne) remplissait que des personnes liées comme une chaine de famille à famille qu'il n'y a pas eu moyen de rompre ces liens et esclavages, ainsi que le régent ne porta que le nom de maître et fut gouverné. Du vivant de mon père on le tenait encore dans cette servitude, mais comme un prince d'un bon sens et qui commençait a l'entrée de son règne de régler ses affaires, levant une armée et aimant les guerres (le dernier surtout, ils le craignent de leur maître), ils tâchèrent de l'occuper par des continuelles chasses, auxquelles il avait grande passion, et comme il ne haïssait le sexe, de peur qu'il ne prit une maîtresse, qui ne fut de leur bande, un des premiers ministres fit un engagement d'une de ses parents belles et douces personnes. Par ces deux voies on l'amuse et on lui a empêché de s'appliquer ni d'être instruit pour ses intérêts. Mon frère, qui commençait du vivant de son père à voir toutes ces menées, commençait à son avénement a l'électorat de reformer tout cela, à quoi un feltmarechal Schöning lui assistait en homme de bien, voulant voir son maître véritablement maître et hors de tutelle et l'agrandir. Mais cet honnête homme paya l'aubade; car on fit tout qu'on le mit en soupçon à la cour impériale d'être bon français. Un jour qu'il se servit des eaux, on l'arrêta sur les terres de l'Empereur; il y eut grand bruit, mais nos messieurs s'en réjouissaient internement, dont je peux rendre témoignage, étant prince et me croyant pas assez pénétrant pour voir leurs menées. On se dressait à moi pour détourner souvent mon frère des choses violantes, à quoi il inclinait. Delà j'ai appris leurs beaux sentiments; je sçais jusqu'ils vont, passant pour ce temps-là pour un de leurs objets qu'ils pourraient avoir à leur dessein. J'ai oublié de dire que les états voyant que le maître veut empierrer, ce qui est juste et ce qui lui convient de droit, ils s'y opposent point directement (car vous n'entendrez jamais qu'ils diront non, mais ils cherchent une autre voye à vous traverser), mais (ce) sont les princes de la famille qu'ils font agir, à quoi on songeait à remédier depuis suivant mes mémoires. Mon frère mourut au milieu de la carrière qu'il avait enterprise. On eut grande joie de me voir à sa place, me sçachant d'un humeur plus doux; je n'avais donc ni connaissance ni lecture ni la moindre étincelle de la régence. Tous les coffres étaient vides et des dettes. Je n'avais en but que la gloire des armes et me mettais peu en peine de domestiques, n'ayant fait depuis ma 18. année autre métier ni application.

Appendix 2
'Famous alike for his virtues and his vices'
Flemming's character sketch of King Augustus 1722

QUALITIES

The King would fain be a second Alcibiades, famous alike for his virtues and his vices.

He possesses qualities which are most admirable in so considerable a prince.

A pity it is that he was not reared as a prince should be, but lived with wasters and prostitutes whose outlook he has made his own.

He is polite and courteous as a private gentleman, and nothing exceeds his chivalry to women. Formerly he could not tolerate bawdy talk in their presence, but of late has somewhat relaxed in this regard.

If, instead of trusting too much to his strong consitution, he would live a more temperate life, he would certainly reach a great age.

He is noble, full of sympathy and of heroic courage.

He is envious of the fame of others.

Ambition and a lust for pleasure are his chief qualities, though the latter has the supremacy. Often his ambition is curbed by his lust for pleasure, never the latter by his ambition.

His ambition and his thirst for the world's admiration and applause have sometimes tempted him to shine by displaying his knowledge of trifling matters, whereby state affairs of great moment have often been retarded.

There is joined in him both a capricious disposition and a lively power of perception. His fancy paints the hues of future delights too brightly, while it exaggerates what is disagreeable.

He likes men to tell him the truth, unless it be done in public or with a schoolmaster's air.

His mind easily grasps the whole of a situation and penetrates to the root of the matter.

His knowledge is comprehensive and the extent of his information, by which in his youth he set little store, now gives him satisfaction.

Owing to his defective bringing-up, he has learnt little of the history of the world and repeatedly mistakes the idealism of the historian for historical truth, so that his judgement is often extravagant.

In many things he cannot be persuaded, particularly when he is once resolved. If one does not then yield to his wishes, it makes him irritable and sometimes the more obstinate. He himself, however, often changes both his purpose and his resolution: when the weightiest reasons have failed to move him from a disastrous decision and he is left to act according to his choice, he is sometimes of his own accord converted to what he had before opposed.

His keen understanding prevents him from communicating his cares to others, since he deems it useless to seek in them that consolation which he has failed to find in himself.

He is not malicious, but can be made so.

He is tender-hearted though unwilling to avow it.

He does not lightly forget an injury, but he forgives it. If someone had mortally offended him but were to throw himself at the feet of the prince and acknowledge his guilt, I think he would first treat him with great harshness but soon abate his indignation.

The King is a ruler whose genial and good-natured address captivates the hearts of all who come to know him.

Despite the popularity for which he strives, he stands more than is common upon his dignity. At banquets, though he take no open offence, much displeases him, and though he be deep in his cups nothing escapes his notice.

He likes to jest and does it with a ready wit, teasing his courtiers unmercifully.

TRUSTWORTHINESS

His boundless mistrust seems ill to accord with his keen understanding, since in general the possessor of such is free from suspicion.

He desires that men should have a perfect trust in him.

When it is a question of giving a direct answer or deciding what measures or decisions should be taken, one can be sure of him, but if it be desired to go into matters with more particularity, he is quite capable in all good faith of giving others the lie and going back on

258

his word. This leads many astray who cannot perceive his true character.

He acts as though he were dissembling, but it is clearly only a pretence. Nonetheless it is just this which has done him harm as a statesman, since he would have fared better in his politics had he played a different part with certain persons.

I have already said that he cannot dissemble though he attempts to do so. I should like to add that this transparent hypocrisy springs from his desire to have the applause of all with whom he has to do.

Hence it is that his utterances are often contradictory. Earlier, when he had no permanent ministers, this damaged his repute in affairs of state. He was wont to send envoys to foreign courts with instructions agreeing only in part with those given to others, so that in the negotiations their voices were in conflict, and while in a particular matter an envoy was treating at one court, his efforts were being thwarted by his fellow at another. Since, however, the council has been formed he has abandoned this method of conducting affairs and a uniform policy is followed.

MISTRESSES

Among his pleasures it is gallantry that has most enthralled him. But even here he has not found the bliss of which he boasts. He has had, it is true, sensational intrigues, which in the beginning he pretended to clothe with secrecy, but he is not the daring gallant he would have himself considered. Indeed he has scarcely ever exposed himself to a risk of rebuff. He has had many adventures, and although most of them were very tame, he has always pretended that there were romantic obstacles in his path. He has acted the part of the jealous lover, but in reality he has not been very nice in his intrigues, which have usually been with women who had first been handled by others. In fact, he has not even disdained to consort with public women of the town, sometimes even of the lowest degree.

Often he has spoilt his mistresses and favourites by letting them perceive those weaknesses from which no man is free. For them the consequences have been disagreeable. For after having known the weak side of a prince who far surpassed them in his talents, they assumed a superiority over him and imagined now more than ever that their place was supreme. This madness made them high-stomached and arrogant, and after, when their fellows would not brook it, ridiculous, contemptible and ungrateful to their prince.

Of his mistresses and ministers the most are disappointed in him. His mistresses think he loves them as he professes. In reality he does but hold them for his delight, and since a lust for pleasure is his master passion, he is ready to endure much rather than forgo it. When, however, his mistresses grow overweening and mistake his patience for proof of his affection, then he bids them a prudent farewell.

MEN

It is for this reason that they call him fickle. He behaves in exactly the same way with those ministers whom he has appointed to relieve him of his burdens.

When his confidence lets them think that they are indispensable and they govern more in accord with their humour than with his desire, he allows them to observe his mistrust. Thereby those who have founded their place on his favour are disillusioned. To those ministers, however, who studiously carry out his intentions and found their place not on his favour but on his interests, without regarding themselves as irreplaceable, he gives back his confidence, even after, owing to lying reports or some other reason, it has once been withdrawn.

In a sense he is good-hearted. For example, if someone has won his favour or even persuaded him of his utility, such a favourite is not easily displaced by the envy of others. But if someone who has been of service has fallen out with a fellow then he will give no help to either, but let them fight the matter to a finish without his interference. The less he be involved in the affair, the better he is contented. This strange attitude has often enough driven his mistresses and other ladies to despair, and many times even his ministers.

Since he knows his court well, he fits his talk to the character of his hearers. To one he says what he believes him to think of his fellow, and to his fellow what the latter thinks of the former, so that each finally believes he knows his sovereign's opinion of others but not of himself.

He is persuaded that no man whom he would win to his interest, can withstand him and has often put this to the proof; thereby he has become the dupe of those rogues whom at times he fails to distinguish from honest men, thus affrighting the latter and encouraging the former in their villainies.

He can refuse nothing, particularly if he be trustfully entreated, and therefore is more of service to rogues than honest men.

MONEY

He is generous and openhanded; nonetheless many have thought him avaricious and even his ministers have believed that if they could but procure him money, their own fortunes would be established. In this they would have been right, if avarice had been his master passion, for then he would have striven to conserve his resources. But he needs money in order to give the rein to his generosity, to gratify his wishes and satisfy his lust for pleasure, and thus he values those who procure him money, lower than those who content his desires. Since he is always in need, those who have engaged themselves or been chosen to minister to his necessities, cannot do enough for him, and yet stand lower in his favour than they feel should be their deserts.

He does not require that money be furnished him by unlawful means, but if it be so furnished, its acceptance causes him no discomfort, and if he can put the blame of it on another he feels himself free of all reproach.

OTHERS

Next to gallantry his greatest delight has been in military and civil architecture, and as to his cognizance of this art, there can be but one opinion. Even here however he has never carried anything to completion, because his weakness for universal applause causes him to make such frequent changes in design, that in spite of many and varied commencements nothing is ever concluded.

He loves to give feasts and entertainments, in which he is well versed. As, however, he insists in interfering with the smallest details, his presence hinders many in their work. Further, since he is not equal to every task, confusion often results, and the labour is fearfully increased, both for himself and for those whose province it is.

Notes

Although this work is directed primarily at the general reader, it contains much information for the specialist. To accommodate disparate interests regarding references and notes, and also to compress them, I have endeavoured to tailor a system to suit varying requirements. I trust that those who like their material sourced will find sufficient research guides below.

There is no conventional bibliography. Instead, where appropriate, I have created an 'Overview of Chapter Sources' (OCS) to detail the archival and/or published sources which have provided information for a particular chapter, and on occasion other chapters too. Besides this, within each chapter there are notes, some of which are simply references to direct quotations from published works, while others develop particular points at length. In addition, because so much of the material upon Augustus is difficult to obtain in Britain, I have supplied original (and mainly uncorrected) German and French texts of certain sources.

ABBREVIATIONS USED IN REFERENCES AND NOTES

AM   Additional Manuscripts (British Library, London)
ASG   *Archiv für die Sächsische Geschichte*
DNB   *Dictionary of National Biography*
HVJ   *Historische Vierteljahrschrift*
NASG *Neues Archiv für Sächsische Geschichte und Altertumskunde*
NF   Neue Folge
SP   State Papers (Public Records Office, Kew)
TRHS *Transactions of the Royal Historical Society*

INTRODUCTION

1. Flemming's pen-portrait of 1722 was written in French and can be found in P. Haake, *August der Starke im Urteil seiner Zeit und der Nachwelt*, Dresden 1922, 19–24. There is a translation into English by Raglan Somerset in K. L. von Pöllnitz, *The Amorous Adventures of Augustus of Saxony*, London 1929 (Originally 1734), 281–88. This is reprinted as Appendix 2, but in a reorganized sequence, intended to improve its

coherence. I have not otherwise altered the text. For some reason Somerset inverts 'pleasure and ambition' in his translation, but I have based the title of this book upon the original French.

2. J. Gleeson, *The Arcanum: the extraordinary true story of the invention of European porcelain*, London 1998.

3. Wilhelmina, Margravine of Bayreuth, *Memoirs*, London 1812, is the source of the 'triple-hundred-plus-bastards' tale. Von Pöllnitz, *Amorous Adventures*, recites his litany of the Elector-King's affairs.

4. H. Beschorner, 'Augusts des Starken Leiden und Sterben', NASG 58, (1937), 48–84, is an excellent study of Augustus's illnesses, wounds and death. However, the letters of Stepney and his fellow diplomats make reference to several maladies and injuries not recorded here.

5. Stepney's boast is recorded in context on p 145. As early as June 1692, one of his patrons conceded that 'we have not had for many years, if ever, one of our country that knew more of the affairs of Germany than you do'. Another cynically suggested to George, who died unmarried, that he had 'espoused Germany'. Vernon to Stepney, 30 June 1692; Blathwayt to Stepney, 2/12 August 1694, SP105/82. For a list of his missions, see C4, n1.

The original book that I wrote, was subtitled 'Augustus the Strong and George Stepney 1691–1707'. In it I focussed upon the interaction of their tangential lives in the period commencing with Stepney's first mention of Augustus and concluding with the Briton's death and the nadir of Augustus's life. I also endeavoured to present a picture of Stepney the man, as well as the diplomat.

However, in order to cut a long book by one-third, and to concentrate upon Augustus, I have deleted virtually all of the detail I garnered upon Stepney's character, relationships, love life, travels, financial problems, ambitions, illnesses and death. I have also omitted from the text a number of his reports from Dresden and Warsaw, which I originally intended as appendices.

6. In September 1701, Stepney wrote that he was hoping to succeed the present incumbent as head of the (State) Paper Office (the precursor of the Public Records Office). He sought the post 'not out of any prospect of gain (for I know very well the salary will not maintain two clerks), but a spirit of curiosity, and out of an ambition of making that fairy treasure of use to the public': Stepney to Blathwayt, Vienna, 24 September 1701, SP105/63.

He did not acquire the post and our state archives evaded 'open government'; presumably the salary has improved. Instead, Stepney provided some 40 volumes of 'fairy treasure' (catalogued as SP105/50–89), which now repose in the selfsame PRO. This is the most important collection of Stepney's papers. The other is AM 7058–7079 held in the British Library. There are a few other volumes containing pertinent correspondence in these two archives, plus minor collections of letters in smaller depositories.

However, one other source must be mentioned. John Ellis (1643?–1738) was Under-Secretary in the office of the Secretary of State (p 43) from 1695 to 1705. The 21 volumes of correspondence sent to him, however sporadically, by virtually all British envoys in this period, are also held in the British Library (AM 28896–28916). These tomes contain many letters from Stepney, some of which are used in this work. More importantly, they also hold many missives sent to Ellis by Robert Sutton, Philippe Plantamour and William Aldersley in the period 1696–1702. These letters provide much detail upon Augustus's role in Hungary, the Polish election, the assault upon Riga and the initial campaigns against the Swedes (C12–13,15–17) which is totally absent from the State Papers.

7. I have utilized the following biographies of Augustus:
   K. Czok, *August der Starke und Kursachsen*, Leipzig 1987; K. Czok, *Am Hofe Augusts des Starken*, Stuttgart 1990; F. Förster, *Die Hofe und die Cabinette Europas*, Band 3: *Friedrich August II, König von Polen und Kurfürst von Sachsen*, Potsdam 1836; C. Gurlitt, *August der Starke: ein Fürstenleben aus der Zeit des deutschen Barock*, 2 vols, Dresden 1924; P. Haake, *August der Starke*, Berlin–Leipzig 1927; D. Nodalski, *Wahre Geschichten um August der Starken*, Taucha 1991; G. Pilz, *August der Starke: Träume und Taten eines deutschen Fürsten*, Berlin 1986; H. Pönicke, *August der Starke: ein Fürst des Barock*, Göttingen 1972; H. Schreiber, *August der Starke: Leben und Lieben im deutschen Barock*, Munich 1981.

   H. Beschorner, 'August der Starke und seine neuesten Biographen', NASG 48 (1927), 236–48, uses a review of Haake's *August* to underscore the incomparable contribution of Professor Paul Haake (1873–1950) to any understanding of Augustus's life. Beschorner also correctly analyses how disappointing and 'user-unfriendly' *August* is. Printed in *deutsche Schrift*, its quaint runes cover over 200 pages of text, which are allocated to just three colossal 'sections'. There are no chapters or references, and the reader is confronted unremittingly with monster paragraphs and serpentine sentences. Even allowing for the nature of the German language and the dire fate that it so often suffers at the hands of German academics, *August* is not an easy read. Although it remains the most important and comprehensive study of Augustus, it falls far short of the masterpiece that Haake was uniquely equipped to write.

8. Gleeson, *The Arcanum*, 10. In May 1704, while serving in Vienna, Stepney noted that two German florins, a specie dollar and a French crown 'are generally computed at the same value, and (as the exchange now goes) is all we can get for an English crown'. Stepney to Hedges, private letter, 10 May 1704, SP105/72. Given four English crowns to the pound, there would also be four thalers or dollars to the pound sterling. As far as I can establish, a guilder was the same as a German florin, in which case there would be eight florins or guilders to the pound; although elsewhere Stepney computes ten guilders to the pound.

CHAPTER 1

1. The following is a quick reference to the life-spans and reigns of the four rulers named John George, who succeeded each other as Electors of Saxony in the seventeenth century: John George I (1585–1656) reigned 1611–56; John George II (1613–80) reigned 1656–80; John George III (1647–91) reigned 1680–91; John George IV (1668–94) reigned 1691–94.

2. The bastard half-brother of Augustus and John George IV was Johann Georg Max von Fürstenhoff (1668–1753), whose mother is unknown. One can note that he was born in the same year as the Electoral Prince John George IV; a feat which Augustus would duplicate in 1696 (p 126).

Max became a fortifications expert, and Augustus later made him a major-general.

In SP81/81 there is a ten-page paper entitled 'Etat present de la Maison de Saxe 1679'. From the information contained within it, the more likely date for its concoction is 1682, and it is doubtful that the anonymous author had any direct contact with Saxony. That John George III had 'plusieurs enfan[t]s' is incorrect. That he moderated his drinking when he became Elector, and that he and Augustus's mother intended a formal separation, are both debatable.

3. In 1680, not long before the death of John George II, the French envoy in Dresden penned a portrait of the old Elector. Amongst other matters, it makes clear that Augustus inherited thick eyebrows and a long nose ('les sourcils fort épais, le nez un peu gros et long') from the Wettin side too. Full text in B. Auerbach, *La diplomatie française et la cour de Saxe*, Paris 1887, 406–07.

Besides his love of the bottle, John George II suffered badly from colic. In 1658 a witness related that he kept by his side a young woman presented to him by his wife, 'die sich uff ihn legt, wenn ihn das Grimmen ankompt'. Haake, *August der Starke*, Berlin–Leipzig 1927, 4.

If alcoholism is a genetic disease, then the Wettins were certainly victims. Augustus's great-grandfather John George I was another addict to the bottle, as well as to hunting. Like his son he also loved music. See the lively portrait of him in C. V. Wedgwood, *The Thirty Years War*, London 1966, 59–61.

4. '[B]ehten, lesen und Schreiben, außwendiglernung des Catechismi, tröstlicher kurzer Sprüche der Schrifft, der kurzen Psalmen, und nach Zunehmung deß Alters und verstandes, fleißiger lesung der heyl. Bibel'. J. Richter, *Das Erziehungswesen am Hofe der Wettiner Albertinischen (Haupt)Linie,* Berlin 1913, 261.

5. 'Prinz, Ihr sollt noch Kurfürst werden'. Haake, *August*, 13.

6. The descriptions of John George IV and Augustus are based upon two published extracts from Augustus's 'novel':

(a) 'Diesse beiden brieder hatten nur stehten krieg miet einander und dieweil die natur den ingern mehr forteil vor dehm elteren geben, wahr er schallus; hingegen der ingere misgonte dehm Codrus [John George], das ihn die natur ihm gegenteil ihm zum elteren gemacht'.

John George 'wahr von natur und glietmassen schwag, von gemiette zornig und mellanquollich; sehr grosses belieben, wiessenschaften zu lernen, in welchen er sehr reuchirte'.

Augustus characterized himself, in the role of Pallantes, as a 'frischen Herrn', 'der wenig achttete und in seiner jugen(d) schon zeigte, das er von leibe, gliederen und constitution stark wehr(d)en wierde, von gemiette giettig [gütig], freigebig, nichts anders, als was eine ehrliebente sehl notwendig tuhn sohlte, liebte, geschickt alle exerci(ti)tia zu lernen; hiengegen wohlte er sich zum studiren nicht appliciren, sagend, er wierd nichts als einmahl den degen zu seinem fortkohmen bedierffen, derohalben ihm in der zarten jugent schon das soltahtenwessen eingepflanzet wahr'.

P. Haake, 'Die Jugenderinnerungen Königs Augusts des Starken', (1900) HVJ, NF3, 395–403, ('Haake, *Jugend*'), 397.

(b) 'Der ältere war schmächtig, kränklich, Inclination zu gelehrten Sachen, nachsinnig, dabei aber sombre und sehr jähzornig'.

'Der jüngere aber war von starcker complexion und Gliedern, hat Lust zu allen exercitien, worin er besonders Talente zeigte, Liebhaber vom Jagen, und besonders zeigte große Begierde zum Soldatenleben; er war fröhlich und ließ keine Bekummerniß anfechten, nicht zornig aber leichtfertig, um allerhand Spaß anzustellen; in den beyden Herren regierte auch eine große aemulation von Jugend auf'.
F. A. O'Byrn, 'Ein sächsischer Prinz auf Reisen', ASG, NF VI, (1880), 289–326; 290.
The 'novel' forms part of the youthful autobiographical 'sketches' penned by Augustus in 1690. These 'sketches' are to be found in Locat 3057 of the Dresden archives, together with three documents written by him in 1705, to which reference will be made later (p 220). The 'sketches' comprise eleven sheets, of which four pertain to his 'novel'; three cover the years 1680–88; one describes his affair with Marie Elisabeth von Brockdorf; two relate to his *Kavalierstour* and the 1689 campaign; the last deals with the 1690 campaign. Their structure and contents are analysed in Haake, *Jugend*.

7. Southwell's correspondence on the death of John George II is in SP105/49. The dates of his mysterious mission are in L. Bittner and L. Gross, *Repertorium der diplomatischen Vertreter aller Länder seit dem Westfälischen Frieden*, Vol. 1 (1648–1715), Oldenburg 1936, 197.

8. K. Czok, *Am Hofe Augusts des Starken*, Stuttgart 1990, 34.

9. 'Unser geliebten jüngsten Sohnes Prinz Friedrich Augustens Lbd. in fremde lande reysen zu lassen, damit Sich Se. Lbd. in allen Wohlständigen Fürstlichen Tugenden desto mehr perfectioniren möge'. O'Byrn, 'Ein sächsischer Prinz', 291.

10. For the letters of Liselotte and Sophie in English, see the two delightful volumes by Maria Kroll, *Letters from Liselotte*, London 1970, and *Sophie: Electress of Hanover*, London 1973, plus the collection edited by Gertrude Scott-Stevenson, *The Letters of Madame*, Vol. 1, London 1924.

11. 'Ich kan noch nichts recht von selbigen printzen sagen; er ist nicht hübsch von gesicht, aber doch woll geschaffen undt hatt als gutte minen, scheinet auch dass er mehr vivacitet hatt alss sein herr bruder, undt ist nicht so melancolisch; allein er spricht noch gar wenig, kann also noch nicht wissen was dahinder steckt'. Liselotte to Sophie, 19 July 1687, in Haake, *Jugend*, 400.
'Wie Ihro Liebden hir waren, hatten sie eine artige taille, das gesicht aber war nicht angenehm, hatt gar einen großen mundt; er war schon sehr starck; er nahm ein gross lang undt schwer rohr undt hube es vorn ahm mitt zwey finger von den erden auff, alss wenns ein stecknadel were; niemand konnte es ihm nachthun, nimbt mir also nicht wunder, daß er nun, da er mitt dem alter noch viel stärcker muß geworden sein, einen silbern teller rollen kan. Wenn die Damen hir dießes Churfürsten perfection undt stercke gewust hetten, würden sie ihm greulich nachgeloffen sein'. Liselotte to Sophie, 14 April 1697, in Haake, *August der Starke im Urteil seiner Zeit und der Nachwelt*, Dresden 1922, 6.

12. Haxthausen to John George III, 22 August 1687, in Haake, *Jugend*, 400–01.

13. O'Byrn, 'Ein sächsischer Prinz', 304.

14. 'Kohme in Paris an, divertire mich 6 monat, unterschidene intrigen'. Haake, *Jugend*, 400.

15. 'Ew. Gnaden dürfen mir nur befehlen; wenn Sie ins Feld gehn, so bin

ich schon gestiefelt und gespornt zu Ew. Gnaden zu kommen, denn ich mir das vor das größte Gluck halten werde, meinen Anfang unter Ew. Gnaden zu machen, wie auch von Sie angeführt zu werden'. O'Byrn, 'Ein sächsischer Prinz', 323.

16. 'Paris hat den Prinzen ganz verdorben'. Haake, *August*, 17. This could be rendered more pejoratively as 'depraved' or 'corrupted'.
17. Stepney's letters are in SP105/50.

CHAPTER 2

OCS2: The main sources for this chapter are: Stepney's letters in SP105/50; and J.F. Klotzsch, *Die Liebeszaubereien der Gräfin Rochlitz*, Aus der Handschrift hrsg. von Johannes Jühling, Stuttgart 1914.

Klotzsch completed his original manuscript in 1780, and certain contents understandably remained explosive in Saxony at this time. Having no wish to be a martyr to the cause of historical truth ('Ich fühle keinen Beruf, fur die Landesgeschichte ein Märtyrer der Wahrheit zu werden', p 27), Klotzsch withheld publication of the text in his lifetime. It was sold to the Royal Library in Dresden for 90 thalers and remained there until Johannes Jühling discovered it. His edited version was published in 1914. Doubtless the Great War robbed the work of impact. Amongst Augustus's German biographers only H. Schreiber, *August der Starke: Leben und Lieben im deutschen Barock*, Munich 1981, has made extensive use of Klotzsch's study.

1. Ursula's date of birth is nowhere specified precisely. I have given the year 1651, since Klotzsch, *Gräfin Rochlitz*, 157, writes that she died on 3 July 1713 in her sixty-third year.
2. Klotzsch is ambiguous about Billa's date of birth, giving 8 February 1676 in the text, but correcting this, when printing the epitaph (*Grabschrift*) which John George IV prepared for her funeral, to 8 February 1675. See Klotzsch, *Gräfin Rochlitz*, 35, 93. The accuracy of the latter date is confirmed by Stepney (p 60). The distinction has some relevance when considering her tragic sexual precociousness, which thereby commences at the age of 12 rather than 11. C. Gurlitt, *August der Starke: ein Fürstenleben aus der Zeit des deutschen Barock*, 2 vols., Dresden 1924, 41, cites another contemporary source as favouring the ripe old age of 13.
3. Schreiber, *August*, 18–19, is emphatic that Rudolf von Neitschütz was with his troops at the time of Billa's conception in 1674, although this contention, like all those in his book, is unsourced. Yet even if true, this only establishes that Rudolf was not her father; it does not prove that John George III was.
4. 'Ein Weibsbild das lebenslang ein geil hurerisch Leben geführt ... hat mit Kurfürst Johann Georgen III. öffentlich gehuret und mit diesem die Gräfin von Rochlitz in Unehren erzeuget, diese ihre Tochter aber nachero an ihren Bruder, Kurfürst Johann Georgen IV., verkuppelt und ihn auf Hexenweise in die größte Blutschande gebracht'; Klotzsch, *Gräfin Rochlitz*, 36.
5. Stepney to Blathwayt, Dresden, 29 June/9 July 1694, SP105/54.
6. There is no other indication that John George was responsible for Eleonore's miscarriage; if indeed this occurred, given the events outlined in C4. There were stories that John George's fall from a horse in July 1692

had unhinged his mind; I lend no credence to such tales. John George IV appears to have been something of a psychological time-bomb and was beset by personal and political problems throughout his reign. There was already enough going on in his head, without blaming his problems upon his poor old horse. John George was less forgiving; he shot another(?) steed through the brains (p 80).

CHAPTER 3

OCS3: Stepney's reports from Berlin in 1692 are in SP105/50. Those from Vienna in 1693 are in SP105/58 and 59. The letters of Colt and Schweinfurt to Stepney are in SP105/84. Colt's letters to Blathwayt and King William from Dresden and the Rhine campaign are in AM 9807–9809.

1. K. G. Helbig, 'Kurfürst Johann Georg der Vierte und Feldmarschall Hans Adam von Schöning, 1691–1694', (1872) ASG 11, 351–408; 360.
2. Stepney to Blathwayt, Dresden, 4/14 September 1694, SP105/55. Schöning's French pension is detailed in J. Fayard, 'Attempts to build a A Third Party' in North Germany 1690–94', in R. Hatton, *Louis XIV and Europe*, London 1976, 213–40; 230.
3. S. Baxter, *William III*, London 1966, 225.
4. Some eight years later, when he was envoy extraordinary to Vienna, Stepney made a short tour of Moravia. In Brno, he was lodged by the provincial governor 'in the high castle Spielberg, in the same room where General Schöning was so long a prisoner. The prospect is not inferior to that of Windsor'. Stepney to Blathwayt, private letter, 17 September 1701 (NS), SP105/63. However, this author can attest that Spielberg also contains some extremely grim dungeons below ground.
5. There is no DNB entry for Colt. Baptized on 2 March 1646, which was presumably the year of his birth, he was knighted in November 1684. Colt married three times: see *Burke's Peerage and Baronetage*, 105th edition, 611. William III's instructions to Colt are in SP105/83.
6. In his will, John George I followed a common German practice (notably eschewed by Prussia) and divided his lands between his four sons. John George II inherited the Electorate, while his three brothers became Dukes of Sachsen-Weissenfels, Sachsen-Merseburg and Sachsen-Zeitz. Sachsen-Weissenfels stood to inherit the Electorate if both John George IV and Augustus died without issue (p 81).
7. England's resident in Hamburg wrote that Augustus's 'retirement to this place was on occasion of a quarrel between him' and John George. It was rumoured that he had consulted with the Danes and received 5000 ducats and 'other promises of being put into the inheritance of Saxon-Lauenburg'. Rycaut to Stepney, Hamburg, 26 April 1693, AM 7060.
8. See for example the contemporary rhyme printed in J. F. Klotzsch *Die Liebeszaubereien der Gräfin Rochlitz*, Aus der handschrift hrsg. von Johannes Jühling, Stuttgart 1914, 72–73. Colt told the minister christening the child that he would never propose it. For Stepney's 'rebuttal' see p 48.
9. For the back-dating of Billa's marriage contract with John George, and the text of the contract, see Klotzsch, *Gräfin Rochlitz*, 68, 227–29. That

the October 1691 date might in fact be genuine, see J. H. Kemble, *State Papers and Correspondence 1618–1714*, London 1857, 148–51.

In June 1694, after the deaths of Billa and John George, Stepney reported that the Saxon authorities had found in Billa's cabinet 'a certain contract of marriage, which may be of an earlier date than the marriage with the Electress. But they pretend they have witnesses that can prove this contract with the Countess was posterior to that of the Electress, and was only antedated to make it seem of greater force'. Stepney to Blathwayt, Dresden, 22 June/2 July 1694, SP105/54.

10. Augustus's 1705 'memoirs' are presented in modern French in P. Haake, 'Die Jugenderinnerungen Königs Augusts des Starken', HVJ, NF3 (1900), 395–403; 398–99 and reprinted herewith as Appendix 1.

CHAPTER 4

OCS4–11: Stepney's letters covering events in Saxony are to be found in the four letter-books bearing on his two missions to Dresden in September 1693–September 1694 and February–June 1695: these are SP105/60 (September 1693–May 1694); SP105/54 (June–August 1694 and June–October 1695); SP105/55 (September 1694–June 1695); SP81/87 (sporadic but important letters from October 1693 to May 1695).

OCS4: Much of the scanty biographical information upon Stepney is in SP105/82, a collection of letters sent to him in the years 1686–95. Further details are culled from others scattered throughout his correspondence. There is little to be added from published sources, including his dated DNB entry. The most substantial, though limited, of three articles known to me, is E. K. Halbeisen, 'George Stepney: A Calendar', *Notes and Queries* (August 1930), 93–96, 114–17.

William's instructions to Stepney of 22 September 1693 are in SP105/83.

1. Stepney detailed 12 missions in the Empire in his letter to Godolphin, Vienna, 10 May 1702(NS), SP105/63. His list was: (1) Brandenburg 1692; (2) Vienna 1693; (3–4) Saxony 1693–94 and 1695; (5–9) Electors of Mainz, Trier, Cologne and Pfalz, and the Frankfurt Congress, in 1696–97; (10–11) Brandenburg and Poland 1698–99; (12) Vienna 1701.

   Poland was not in the Empire. Stepney quit Vienna in September 1706, to serve in the Hague. This thirteenth mission proved fatal, with a dying Stepney leaving Holland in August 1707 to pass away in Chelsea (p 251).

2. Cited in H. Snyder, 'The British Diplomatic Service during the Godolphin Ministry', in R. Hatton and M. Anderson (eds), *Studies in Diplomatic History*, London 1970, 47–68; 51.

3. From early 1692 until September 1706, Stepney was under the jurisdiction of the Secretary of State North. The men who held this office, or were sole secretaries in this period were: Daniel, Earl of Nottingham, until March 1693; Sir John Trenchard, March 1693–March 1694; Charles, Duke of Shrewsbury, March 1694–April 1695; Sir William Trumbull, May 1695–December 1697; James Vernon, December 1697–November 1700; Sir Charles Hedges, November 1700–December 1701; James Vernon (again), January–April 1702; Sir Charles Hedges (again), May 1702–May 1704; Robert Harley, May 1704–February 1708.

On the office of the Secretaries of State, see M. A. Thomson, *The Secretaries of State 1681–1782*, Oxford 1932; J. C. Sainty, *Office-Holders of Modern Britain: Officials of the Secretaries of State 1660–1782*, London 1973. For a broader view of the context in which Stepney served, see D. B. Horn, *The British Diplomatic Service 1689–1789*, Oxford 1961. On Blathwayt, see G. A. Jacobsen, *William Blathwayt: a late Seventeenth Century English Administrator*, New Haven 1932.

4. Blathwayt to Stepney, 4/14 September 1693; Vernon to Stepney, 12 September 1693, SP105/82. Stepney to Blathwayt, 16/26 September 1693 and 30 September 1693(NS), SP105/59.
5. Fortuitously, we can identify the two partners in this marriage from a footnote in F. A. O'Byrn, 'Ein sächsischer Prinz auf Reisen', ASG, NF VI (1880), 289–326; 326, which relates that von Haugwitz's daughter, Sophie Louise Elisabeth, married Count Otto Heinrich von Zinzendorff on 7 July 1693.
   A few observations may be in order. If Augustus sired this child, then like his own father he availed himself of 'das Frauenzimmer'. If the child lived, he did not recognize it, unlike his other bastards; although the latter were all legitimized after he became Elector and King. If the pregnancy was of normal span, then the child was conceived very near to the time of Augustus's marriage in January 1693.
6. Stepney displayed a mercurial attitude and considerable intimacy towards this lady. However, although Stepney *was* having an affair with an unnamed married woman in Dresden, it was not with Eleonore.
   'For me, (state affairs apart) I am as happy as the day is long', he told Matt Prior in late November 1693. 'There is a great deal of danger, expense, and adultery in this affair; but the pleasure and vanity is what I never expected to arrive at in the whole course of my life. Lest you might mistake, it will be necessary to tell you I do not mean the Electress; but God damn me, if I am four persons below her.'
   Following John George IV's death, Stepney wrote a poem dedicated, 'Pour la mort de SAE de Saxe a SAE Madame l'Electrice Eleonore', which is in SP105/85. There is no indication that he actually presented it to her.

CHAPTER 5

1. Stepney to Blathwayt, 13/23 September 1693, SP105/59. Blathwayt to Stepney, 8 October 1693(NS), SP105/82.
2. Many years later, Augustus told his son that both John George IV and John George III had considered converting to Catholicism. 'Faites réflexion, mon fils, aux exemples de votre père, de votre oncle et de votre grand-père, lesquels ont voulu se rendre catholiques'. Augustus to the Electoral Prince Friedrich August, 23 July 1712, in P. Haake, 'Der Glaubenswechsel Augusts des Starken', HVJ 10 (1907), 382–92; 384n. At the time, he was pressurizing his reluctant son to convert to Catholicism too; so citing such precedents would be useful, yet not necessarily true.
3. The entry in the *Hofkalender* for 24 February/6 March 1694 refers to: 'S. Ch. D. [*Seine Churfürstliche Durchlauchtigkeit* = His Electoral Highness] unerhörte und gefährliche rencontre mit der Gemahlin wegen Abtretung des Guts Pillnitz an die Gräfin von Rochlitz': P. Haake, *August der*

Starke in Urteil seiner Zeit und der Nachwelt, Dresden 1922, 14. The quota-
tion 'had certainly ... design' is from K. L. von Pöllnitz, *The Amorous
Adventures of Augustus of Saxony,* London 1929 [1734], 16. This author
(pp 15–18) gives the cause of the confrontation to be Billa's persuading
John George that Augustus and Eleonore 'were unlawfully acquainted'.
While such a relationship (with John George 'quoted' as crying, 'I perceive your vile affection for my unworthy wife') is not beyond the
bounds of possibility, his timing of this confrontation is. Von Pöllnitz
dates it as occurring just prior to Augustus's departure for France in
1687, when John George would have been unmarried. He also identifies
Ursula and not Billa as the Countess of Rochlitz.

The possible embellishment of Augustus removing three blades from
his brother's hands is from Sophie of Hanover to Raugräfin Luise, 8/18
April 1694, in Haake, *Zeit,* 14n: 'daß die gansse welt weis, wie daß der
Courfürst von Saxsen Seine gamallin hat wollen ermordern were auch
vol geschehen, wan Herzog Friedrich J. L. nicht 3 Degen nach einander
aus der handt gerissen hätten, da er noch alle finger von zerschnitten
hat.' Augustus's cut fingers are mentioned in several sources, although
the full extent of the wounds is uncertain.

Stepney's account, which was written on 8 June 1694, is the only one
to attribute John George's behaviour to drink and to specify that other
people were wounded in the brawl.

For Augustus often being called upon to pacify his brother, see his
'memoirs' in Appendix 1. For John George drawing his sword on Billa,
see J. F. Klotzsch, *Die Liebeszaubereien der Gräfin Rochlitz,* Aus der handschrift hrsg. Von Johannes Jühling, Stuttgart 1914, 77.

That John George was not always worsted in their scraps is clear from
Stepney to Vernon, 15/25 November 1693. This describes the two brothers fencing, with Augustus receiving 'a thrust in the eye with a stiff file
which threw him on his back, and had like to cost him his eye; but by
the applications that were made he is perfectly restored'.

CHAPTER 6

1. 'Vergangnen Mitwoch ist die Gräfin von Rochlitz, nachdem sie 9 tag an
   den platern granck gelechen, gantz unvermuht gestorben, denn sie ganz
   außer gefahr geweßen. Sie ist aber auf ein Mahl vernunft, sprach- und
   hörloß geworden und so von 9 uhr des Morgens biß den antren Morgen
   nach 7 ist sie gelechen ohne einige bewechung, da sie den munt uf
   gethan und so verschilen. Es ist ein mechtiges exempel, allwo man die
   Wunter Gottes genuch erkennen kan'. P. Haake, *Christiane Eberhardine
   und August der Starke: eine Ehetragödie,* Dresden 1930, 18.
2. Stepney does not appear to have completed his *relation galante,* despite
   continuing to collect material. For example, he told Blathwayt on 14
   August that he had twice met with Eleonore of late. The former Electress 'kept me up two or three hours telling me old stories and some
   particulars of the disorders of the late reign, which I would never have
   learned from anybody else. She has given me leave to wait upon her frequently, which I shall do, on purpose to render my *histoire galante* more
   complete'.

3. Several published accounts assert that John George *did* plant one or more fateful kisses upon Billa's diseased lips.
4. A somewhat simplistic judgement of John George's policy towards France (C3). John George told Colt in February 1693 that 'it was equal to him whether he was a slave to the Emperor or France'. J. H. Kemble, *State Papers and Correspondence 1618–1714*, London 1857, xiiin.
5. J. F. Klotzsch, *Die Liebeszaubereien der Gräfin Rochlitz*, Aus der handschrift hrsg. Von Johannes Jühling, Stuttgart 1914, 86, asserts that Billa's body was covered in green and yellow spots. The doctors contended that these were the result of convulsions and the application of Spanish fly. In this case, it was not a matter of the aphrodisiac qualities of the Lytta or Cantharis, to give the blister-beetle or Spanish fly its medical name; rather a preparation of cantharides, made from the insects' dried bodies, had been used to produce blisters upon Billa's. Klotzsch further contends that her corpse *was* opened, but no trace of poison found.
6. Klotzsch, *Gräfin Rochlitz*, 88–89, 229–33, provides a more detailed account of Billa's funeral based upon contemporary accounts. Many quotations from the Bible were produced, ostensibly as funeral texts. Nahum III vv 4–6 was a popular choice: 'And for all the countless harlotries of the harlot, graceful and of deadly charms, who betrays nations with her harlotries, and peoples with her charms. Behold, I am against you, says the Lord of hosts, and will lift up your skirts over your face; and I will let nations look upon your nakedness and kingdoms on your shame. I will throw filth at you and treat you with contempt and make you a gazing-stock'.

CHAPTER 7

1. See G. Scott-Stevenson, *The Letters of Madame*, Vol. 1, London 1924, 99; L. and M. Frey, *Frederick I: the Man and his Times*, New York 1984, 28–37; B. Auerbach, *La diplomatie française et la cour de Saxe*, Paris 1887, 409.
2. However, suspicions persisted. On 2 April 1695 Stepney told Prior that Eberhardine had invited Schöning's wife to supper, and that the latter ate nothing for fear of being poisoned. Augustus later accused James Sobieski of planning to kidnap or poison him, with the context suggesting the exact obverse (p 207). When Augustus's ministers arrested Patkul, he refused food for several days, for fear that our hero would have him poisoned (p 225).
3. For quotations from Augustus's 'memoirs', see Appendix 1.
4. On the other hand, as Stepney put it, Grand Marshal Haugwitz 'keeps his charge'. Beichling also survived, and for a time prospered under the new Elector. 'Beichling est honnete homme', proclaimed Augustus. 'C'est dommage qu'il est entré dans cette famille'. K. G. Helbig, 'Kurfürst Johann Georg der Vierte und Feldmarschall Hans Adam von Schöning, 1691–1694', ASG II (1872), 351–408; 395.
5. Klotzsch, *Die Liebeszaubereien der Gräfin Rochlitz*, Aus der handschrift hrsg. Von Johannes Jühling, Stuttgart 1914, 134–35, 234–35. The latter reference is to a clinical contemporary protocol of the items taken from the grave, although unlike Stepney's account, it does not mention any letters.

6. K. L. Von Pöllnitz, *The Amorous Adventures of Augustus of Saxony*, London 1929 [1734], 95, has it otherwise, and devotes a few lines to the execution of Ursula, still erroneously identified as the Countess of Rochlitz.

CHAPTER 8

1. C. Gurlitt, *August der Starke: ein Fürstenleben aus der Zeit des deutschen Barock*, 2 vols, Dresden 1924, 42–44, offers some detail about Carpzov's speeches. Utilizing the original manuscripts, he estimated that the oration delivered at John George's funeral (which he misdates as 9 May) lasted two hours. Carpzov spoke again, at even greater length, during the burial in Freiberg on 5 July.

   Stepney was absent from this leg of John George's last journey, since none of the foreign envoys 'have been invited to this solemnity'. However, he continued to file reports based upon others' information.
2. There is a description of the Leipzig ceremony in K. Czok, *August der Starke und Kursachsen*, Leipzig 1987, 16–17.
3. K. L. von Pöllnitz, *The Amorous Adventures of Augustus of Saxony*, London 1929 [1734], 92–93, depicts Augustus first clapping eyes on Eberhardine, whose 'beauty seemed to him to exceed all that he had seen in his travels', while passing through Bayreuth following his first campaign in 1689. According to this author, she 'had not yet attained the fifteenth year of her age'. Eberhardine was born in Bayreuth on 19 December 1671; so, if their first meeting did take place in late 1689 (and no other source offers an alternative), she would then have been pushing 18.

   Stepney records Augustus and Eberhardine as already betrothed by November 1691 (p 20), which starkly contradicts the detail provided by Paul Haake in his study of their marriage (*Christiane Eberhardine und August der Starke: eine Ehetragödie*, Dresden 1930, 5–18). This has it, that it was not until after the Saxon's fourth proposal in August 1692 that Eberhardine's father, Margrave Christian Ernst, and his shrewd second wife, Sophie Luise, consented to the marriage; while other suitors, particularly from the Danish Court, were also showing interest in Eberhardine's hand at this time.

   In his letter of August 1692, our hero addressed Eberhardine as 'the most beautiful princess in the world' ('die schensten princessin von der wehlt'), who had it 'in her hands to finally make or break the happiness of a most loyal slave' ('enfein sie haben in ihren henden, einen gehorsamsten schlafen glicklich und unglicklich zu machen'). A romantic touch was added in Italian: 'where are you, where are you hiding?' ('dove sei, dove dascondi?'), while lifetime fidelity was promised in French ('toujours le meme'; 'une seule me plait').

   Augustus's realism regarding political marriages and ephemeral beauty, is shown in the 'political testament' ('Regel pour la posterrité'), which he wrote for his son, probably in 1705. He enjoined him to conclude 'marriages of state', not love-matches. 'La beauté se passe, le dégout vient et il ne reste que la femme'. P. Haake, 'Ein politisches Testament Königs Augusts des Starken', *Historische Zeitschrift* LXXXVII, (1901) 1–21; 9.
4. For the von Klengel family, see C. Gurlitt, *August der Starke*, 22–24, and

particularly F. A. O'Byrn, 'Wolf Kaspar von Klengel', *Mittheilungsheft des Königliche Sächsische Alterthumsverein*, XXII (1872), 29–53.

O'Byrn, who was a baron and a chamberlain at the Saxon Court, paints a rather more idyllic picture of the family than Stepney. His detail on Sophie Eleonore von Klengel comes on p 48 of his article. He makes it quite clear that he considers her to be the same woman identified by von Pöllnitz, in his *Amorous Adventures*, 97–109, as Eleonore von Kessel. Some authors treat von Klengel and von Kessel as separate mistresses, but can offer no information upon the former. I have followed O'Byrn in fusing the 'two' as von Klengel. Possibly von Pöllnitz was given the wrong name, or misheard it, when he was told the tales that he embroidered into his 'history'. At least Stepney's account confirms the existence of Eleonore von Klengel as a mistress of Augustus. I have seen no picture of her, although O'Byrn writes that her portrait (as Baroness von Senffertitz) used to hang in the Venussaale at Schloss Pillnitz.

5. H. Schreiber, *August der Starke: Leben und Lieben im deutschen Barock*, Munich 1981, 258, contends (as usual without sources) that Augustus dated Eleonore von Klengel to cover his affair with Billa; in what manner is left unexplained. However, if he ever had anything more than a fling with Billa (if that), it strikes me as exceptionally unlikely that it was still in progress in 1692 or later.

6. P. Burg, *Die schöne Gräfin Königsmarck: ein bewegtes Frauenleben um die Wende des 17en Jahrhunderts*, Braunschweig 1919, 10.

7. Philippe Plantamour was a Protestant refugee from Chalon in Burgundy, who had escaped from France once the persecution of the Huguenots began. Born around 1664, he was Stepney's secretary in the years 1690–99, when he succeeded his master as England's representative in Berlin, holding the post until 1703. After that he entered the service of Augustus, in his capacity as King of Poland, until at least 1706. Stepney described the Frenchman as 'of good parents, and a very pleasant companion'. He was 'very honest, ingenious and capable to serve', and was endowed with 'an admirable French style, and a ready pen for copying'.

Regarding Plantamour's date of birth, we can be no more precise than he himself: 'je suis agé d'environ trente deux ans', Plantamour to Ellis, 7/17 March 1697, AM 28899. I have no idea where or when he died.

CHAPTER 9

1. One of the indictments against Ursula at her trial was: 'Ob sie nicht anfangs den Herrn von Haxthausen durch Zaubermittel zur Liebe ihrer Tochter bringen wollen'. J. F. Klotzsch, *Die Liebeszaubereien der Gräfin Rochlitz*, Aus der handschrift hrsg. Von Johannes Jühling, Stuttgart 1914, 280.

2. R. Hatton, *George I: Elector and King*, London 1978, 48–69.

3. C. Gurlitt, *August der Starke: ein Fürstenleben aus der Zeit des deutschen Barock*, 2 vols, Dresden 1924, 154.

4. Cresset to Shrewsbury, 10 August 1694, SP81/159.

5. The substance of the 'royal command' to prevent further Saxon–Hanoverian friction is in Blathwayt to Stepney, 7 September 1694, SP105/82.

CHAPTER 10

OCS10: Plantamour's letters to Vernon from Dresden are in SP81/87. He may have known English, but all his despatches are written in French. William's instructions to Stepney of 15 January 1695 are in SP105/83, as are Shrewsbury's of 12 March.

1. Most of Stepney's letters to Lexington derive from SP105/55. The bulk are duplicated in volume XV of the Lexington papers, classified as AM 46535, which extends the correspondence to 1697 and is of use for subsequent chapters. A few of Stepney's letters are printed in H. M. Sutton, *The Lexington Papers*, London 1851.

   There is no trace, however, of Lexington's letters to Stepney. Indeed, few of his lordship's letters to anybody appear to survive. Lexington appears to have been something of a 'minimalist' in his diplomatic reportage and in his correspondence generally. The following must suffice as an example: 'I have a thousand pardons to ask you, for being in debt to you for so many letters, but I have this for my excuse; that I have not been a day out of the postwagon, or a stag-hunting with the Duke of Celle, since I left Collen [Cologne?], and which is a better excuse to you, I have had nothing at all to send you worth the postage of a letter'. Lexington to Vernon, Celle, 29 September/9 October 1694, SP80/17.

2. P. Haake, 'Die Türkenfeldzuge Augusts des Starken 1695 und 1696', NASG 24 (1903), 133–54; 136.

3. Sadly, we must exclude one reason for Augustus to accept the Hungarian command, which was suggested by a sardonic Matt Prior. The Dutch States refused Augustus 'a passport for three hundred bottles of Burgundy to come through the [United] Provinces'. Prior intended to notify Stepney of this, 'and possibly it may make the Elector determine his Hungary expedition, that he may drink Tokay [Tokaj wine] *sans passe-port*'. Prior to Lexington, the Hague, 5/15 April 1695, in Sutton, *Lexington Papers*, 74.

   Today the excellent wines of Tokaj are white. However, my impression is that in the seventeenth century they were red and the most favoured in Europe; at least, whenever the frequent wars with Louis XIV disrupted supplies from France.

   Augustus's predilection has already been mentioned (p 9). In November 1703, Stepney's deputy in Vienna observed that the Hungarian rebels were near Tokaj, and 'the rich wines of the neighbouring mountains are like to fall to [their leader Prince] Rákóczi's share, who will probably draw a considerable sum of money for them out of Poland' (where Augustus was now King). Whitworth to Hedges, Vienna, 17 November 1703, SP105/70.

   Stepney made frequent trips to his cellar in search of 'gifts'. At a crucial point in his career, he hauled out a classic Tokaj to send to Godolphin (p 191). However, George managed to replace it in spades during his otherwise disastrous involvement in mediating between Vienna and Rákóczi in Hungary. In late 1704 he bragged to friends how he had been 'drinking Tokaj at the fountain-head, I mean with Rákóczi himself, who has the best in the world, and who gave me a roundlet of the same at parting'. This was now 'safe in my cellar'. Stepney to Huntingdon; Stepney to Cadogan, both Vienna, 26 November 1704, SP105/74.

4. In his 'political testament', Augustus offered this advice to his son: 'Ce n'est pas être dissimulé que de ne pas dire tout ce qu'on pense, ce qui seroit plutôt une imprudence'. P. Haake, 'Ein politisches Testament Königs Augusts des Starken', *Historische Zeitschrift* LXXXVII (1901) 1–21; 6. For Flemming's estimate of Augustus as a 'dissembler', see Appendix 2 under 'Trustworthiness'.

5. William's instructions of 15 January noted that, through Schöning's influence, Augustus 'has proceeded so far as to order Count Friesen to be summoned to appear before a council of war' in Saxony, for having commanded the general's guards regiment. On his monarch's behalf, Stepney was to intercede 'for a person of whose zeal for the common cause we have had long experience'. It was 'very acceptable' to William that Friesen be kept on at the Hague.
There is a long relation by Stepney on Count Friesen in SP81/159.

CHAPTER 11

1. This rendition comes from SP105/55. The version in H. M. Sutton, *The Lexington Papers*, London 1851, 84, lacks the final sentence. H. Schreiber, *August der Starke: Leben und Lieben im deutschen Barock*, Munich 1981, 148–49, corrects 'Altheim' to 'Althan', which leaves this author none the wiser. Given Stepney's earlier description of von Klengel (p 85), I presume 'w——' stands for 'whores' and not 'women'. As to 'lease', it may mean simply 'a contract for renting', but it can also be rendered as 'gathering'.

2. K. L. von Pöllnitz, *The Amorous Adventures of Augustus of Saxony*, London 1929, [1734], 132–37. The Moritzburg episode, replete with Diana the huntress and sundry nymphs, is identical in this respect with the masquerade at Carlsbad described later in this chapter. I would suggest that von Pöllnitz either simply got his location wrong, or more likely, cavalierly changed the setting to one with which he was familiar. If a like event did take place at Moritzburg, then it must be observed that it was unusual for Augustus to repeat a 'happening', since he interfered zealously in every detail of such events and prided himself on his originality (Appendix 2, 'Others'). Of course, it is possible that Aurora was aroused by Diana outfits and bows and arrows, and that the episode was repeated for her delectation.
The larger question hanging over Moritzburg, however, is *when* it could have happened. Aurora arrived in Dresden in August 1694 and her role as Augustus's mistress, or rather one of his mistresses, was at an end by April 1696, if not sooner. If we exclude the times when Augustus was out of Dresden in this period (in Bayreuth, Leipzig, Vienna and Hungary), then the event, much of it occurring outdoors and on water, and with sex as its primary object, can only have taken place in midwinter. In Saxony this is cold enough for brass monkeys to have a problem, let alone....

3. There is a report from Vienna written by one Barnard on 11 May 1695 (NS): 'Des que l'Empereur a apperçu que l'Electeur de Saxe va à Carlsbad, il a ordonné à la Chambre de Boheme de fournir toutes les Choses necessaire pour l'entretien de S.A.E. et de sa Cour pendant son sejour

aux bains, comme aussy nommer un Comissaire, qui aura join que rien luy manque'. SP80/17.
4. It was not a happy trip. As Stepney reported later, she 'had her wagons plundered by snap-hawks [freebooters]' and lost plate and goods worth RT 30,000. Eleonore died on 9 September 1696.
5. Stepney gave this last section in French: 'et en attendant il esperoit que sa Majesté ne se serviroit pas de luy avant qu'il se fut rangé à son devoir'.

CHAPTER 12

OCS12–13: Stepney's correspondence from Holland, Frankfurt and the Rhineland during 1695–97 is in SP105/54, 56 and 57. His letters to Ellis are in the four volumes of the Ellis papers (see Introduction, note 6, above), which cover this period, AM 28897–28900. The three last tomes also include the missives sent to Ellis by Robert Sutton Jr.

OCS12: The information upon Augustus's Hungarian campaigns derives mainly from P. Haake, 'Die Türkenfeldzuge Augusts des Starken 1695 und 1696' (1903) NASG 24, 133–54. Despite its promising title, K. M. Setton's *Venice, Austria and the Turks in the Seventeenth Century*, Philadelphia 1991, manages to avoid any coverage whatsoever of Augustus's two campaigns.

1. Stepney to Trumbull, 24 May/3 June 1695, SP105/55.
2. K. Czok, *Am Hofe Augusts des Starken*, Stuttgart 1990, 55, gives Augustus's height as 1.76 metres and his top weight (in 1712) as 121.4 kilos, a little over 19 stones. His poundage later dropped drastically during the initial onslaught of diabetes. C. Gurlitt, *August der Starke: ein Fürstenleben aus der Zeit des deutschen Barock*, 2 vols, Dresden 1924, 95, details Augustus's girth (*Leibesumfang*) in 1702 as 109 cm, nearly 43 inches.
3. A French agent described Leopold Lamberg as 'a man whose only merit is that he is a good huntsman and an excellent pimp for his master'. D. McKay, *Prince Eugene of Savoy*, London 1977, 94. Later Joseph made him Reichsjägermeister, the post that Augustus's father had also held (p 16).
4. Emperor Leopold I (1640–1705) reigned from 1658 and married thrice. In 1666 he wed Margarete Theresa (1651–73), the daughter of the Spanish Habsburg King Philip IV (whose 30-plus bastards appear to have occasioned less comment than those sired by Augustus). This marriage produced only one surviving child, Archduchess Maria Antonia, who became the first wife of Elector Maximilian ('Blue Max') of Bavaria in 1685. Widowed in 1673, Leopold remarried in that year Claudia Felicitas of Tyrol (1653–76). There were no children of this marriage. On Claudia's death in 1676, Leopold again went straight back into harness, wedding Eleonore of Pfalz–Neuburg (1655–1720) later that year. This marriage produced four daughters and two sons: Joseph (1678–1711), who reigned as Emperor Joseph I (1705–1711); and Charles (1685–1740), who, after a stint as Carlos III, one of the Kings of Spain during the War of Spanish Succession, succeeded his brother as Emperor Charles VI (1711–40). Neither son produced a male heir, a matter which greatly interested Augustus (p 220).

On the reigns of Leopold and Joseph, see J. Spielman, *Leopold I of Austria*, London 1977; L. and M. Frey, *A Question of Empire: Leopold I and the War of Spanish Succession 1701–05*, Boulder 1983; C. Ingrao, *In Quest and Crisis: Emperor Joseph I and the Habsburg Monarchy*, W. Lafayette 1979.

5. H. M. Sutton, *The Lexington Papers*, London 1851, 203.

6. Sutton, *Lexington Papers*, 208.

7. David Chandler, *Warfare in the Age of Marlborough*, London 1976, lists the battle as Olaschin and classifies it as an Ottoman victory. He gives the Turks losing 4000 from an army of 60,000, but provides no record of Augustus's casualties from a 50,000 force. P. Haake, 'Die Türkenfeldzuge, 145–53, mentions Olaus/Olausch/Olasz as a site near to the battleground, but refers otherwise to the battle of Dinyas on the Bega. He gives Imperialist losses of 3000 and explains the reduction of Augustus's forces to 38,000 before the battle.

    Sutton's letter to Ellis of 5 September contains the following line: 'The story of the Elector's killing General Rose, I believe is false'. I haven't an inkling what this refers to; however, the tale was certainly bogus. The Livonian Rose is to be found heavily involved in Augustus's bid for the Polish crown in 1697 (p 137). He must also have led a charmed life; two years later Plantamour reported: 'La nouvelle de la mort du General Rose qui s'est battu en duel contre le Comte de Trautmansdorff a Dresden s'est trouvée fausse'. Plantamour to Ellis, Berlin, 25 November/5 December 1699, AM 28904.

8. Schöning's embalmed body was buried at Tamsel, his estate in Brandenburg, in November 1696. Presumably Augustus could have attended this ceremony had he so wished. Possibly his absence was prompted by fear of exposure to another oration by Carpzov, whose funeral harangue over Schöning's coffin in Dresden had straddled a mere 72 pages in the court chaplain's hand: K. G. Helbig, 'Kurfürst Johann Georg der Vierte und Feldmarschall Hans Adam von Schöning, 1691–1694', ASG 11 (1872), 351–408; 397, 408n.

9. K. L. von Pöllnitz, *The Amorous Adventures of Augustus of Saxony*, London 1929 [1734], 141–42, writes of Augustus never leaving Aurora 'during the time of her illness'. The context suggests that her 'illness' was her 'pregnancy'. In this case it is balderdash to portray Augustus as attentively at hand throughout Aurora's labours; as we have seen, he was absent from Saxony from April to November 1696.

    Possibly the 'illness' was a separate event. According to our fallible muckraker, Aurora thereafter 'retained an almost continual sweat, very disagreeable to the sense of smelling, and which not even the strongest scent could exceed. This unfortunate disease ... at last gave the Elector so great a disgust, that by insensible degrees he avoided his formerly beloved Countess, till having entered into other engagements, he entirely ceased to live with her as his lover'.

    For Aurora's production of *Das Musenfest*, see P. Haake, *August der Starke*, Berlin–Leipzig 1927, 47. Stepney's view is given in his private letter to Hedges, Vienna, 23 November 1701, SP105/64. On Fatime, see H. Schreiber, *August der Starke: Leben und Lieben im deutschen Barock*, Munich 1981, 147–50.

10. Schreiber, *August*, 86; Gurlitt, *August der Starke*, 154–55.

11. 'Mann hatt so lang gesagt, er bekomme keine Kinder, hatt also auff

einmal zwei Söhne daher gesetzt, ce n'est pas y aller de main morte': P. Haake, *August der Starke im Urteil seiner Zeit und der Nachwelt*, Dresden 1922, 6.

12. Lexington to Blathwayt, Vienna, 7 November 1696; Blathwayt to Lexington, Whitehall, 20/30 November 1696, in Sutton, *Lexington Papers*, 226, 230.

CHAPTER 13

OCS13: The most useful work in English on Augustus's reign in Poland is J. Lukowski, *Liberty's Folly: The Polish–Lithuanian Commonwealth in the Eighteenth Century 1697–1795*, London 1991. Background and enlightenment upon this period of Polish history can also be found in: N. Davies, *God's Playground: A History of Poland*, Vol. 1, *From the Origins to 1795*, Oxford 1981; R. I. Frost, *After the Deluge: Poland–Lithuania and the Second Northern War 1655–60*, Cambridge 1993; A. S. Kamiński, *Republic vs. Autocracy: Poland–Lithuania and Russia 1686–97*, Cambridge MA 1993; J. B. D. de Parthenay, *The History of Poland under Augustus II*, London 1734 (this study goes no further than 1700); O. Subtelny, *Domination of Eastern Europe: Native Nobilities and Foreign Absolutism 1500–1715*, Gloucester 1986; A. Zamoyski, *The Polish Way: A Thousand Year History of the Poles and their Culture*, London 1987.

1. R. Przeździecki, *Diplomatic Ventures and Adventures: Some Experiences of British Envoys at the Court of Poland*, London 1953, 142.
2. Zamoyski, *The Polish Way*, 206.
3. Subtelny, *Domination*, 25.
4. Stepney to Vernon, Königsberg, 3/13 June 1698, SP105/51.
5. Liselotte, letter of 1 August 1697, in P. Haake, *August der Starke im Urteil seiner Zeit und der Nachwelt*, Dresden 1922, 6–7.
6. H. M. Sutton, *The Lexington Papers*, London 1851, 212.
7. Liselotte observed that Conti's 'love for his sister-in-law does not prevent his loving his pages as well': G. Scott-Stevenson, *The Letters of Madame*, Vol. 1, London 1924, 209.
8. 'Heute ist ein gerücht entstandten, das der Churfürst von Sachsen auch zur Cron concurriere, von dem keine proposition noch requisition noch briefe gehabt'. This 50-page journal can be found in SP105/88.
9. 'Mein höchster Ehrgeiz ist Ruhm, wonach ich bis an mein Lebensende streben werde'. Augustus to Flemming, 8 November 1697, in P. Haake, *August der Starke*, Berlin–Leipzig 1927, 78.
10. Haake specifies the date 9 February 1697 and the garb of Sultan: P. Haake, 'Die Wahl Augusts des Starken zum König von Polen', HVJ 6 (1906), 31–84; 51. However, K. Czok, *Am Hofe Augusts des Starken*, Stuttgart 1990, 91, states that on 3 February 1697 Augustus was attired as Alexander the Great. This at least symbolized the correct direction for crossing the Hellespont, if he intended to fulfil that part of the prophecy relating to the conquest of the Ottoman Empire. Of course, Augustus had already posed as Alexander the Great on 5 February 1695 (p 101).
11. Forbin to Polignac, 21 June 1697, in Haake, 'Die Wahl', 52n.
12. There is some dispute about the cause and nature of this injury. Stepney

describes it as a hunting accident. Beschorner, 'Augusts des Starken Leiden und Sterben', NASG 58 (1937), 48–84; 49, relates that it occurred in January 1697 during Carnival, when Augustus was tilting in the ring, and his horse fell on him and crushed the second toe of his left foot. This injury, combined with dropping a marble bust on the big toe during his antics in Venice and the later onset of diabetes, would lead to the amputation of the second toe in January 1727.

However, Lexington wrote to Blathwayt on 5 June that Augustus was using the spas near Vienna 'for the curing of his leg, which he wrenched last winter': Sutton, *Lexington Papers*, 266. According to Haake, 'Die Wahl', 57, Augustus was taking the waters to heal a broken thigh ('um einen Bruch des Schenkels zu heilen').

13. On Flemming, see W. Konopczyński, 'Feldmarszałek Flemming', *Roczniki Historyczne*, XVIII (1949), 163–80; H. Pönicke, 'Politisch einflußreiche Männer um August den Starken', *Archiv für Sippenforschung*, 40 (1974) 56, 599–610.

14. Augustus's guarantee of 7/17 April 1697 read in part as follows: 'Gestalt Wir denn auch über dem hierdurch öffentlich und bey Unsern Churfürstl. waaren Worten versichern, daß bey dieser veränderung, die Wir nur allein vor Unsere person vornehmen, sonsten im übrigen weder in Unsern Churfürstenthum und Landen noch bey Unserer Hoffstatt nicht die geringste mutation in der religion erfolgen oder veranlaßet werden solle, Wir auch weder Unsere Gemahlinn noch Unsern Churprinzen noch jemand von Unsern hohen und niedern Bedienten, Unterthanen noch sonsten keinen einzigen menschen, es sey wer es wolle, zu einem gleichmäßigen changement nötigen, sondern vielmehr männiglich in seinen gewißen ungekränkt, so wohl auch den statum religionis et ecclesiarum durchgehends in allen Unsern landen, wie er gegenwertig ist, ungeändert laßen und unverrückt conserviren wollen'. Haake, 'Die Wahl', 55n.

15. Radziejowski to Augustus, 24 May 1697 (French), in J. Ziekursch, 'August der Starke und die Katholische Kirche in den Jahren 1697–1720', *Zeitschrift für Kirchengeschichte*, XXIV (1903), 86–135, 232–80; 97n.

16. Baron Johann von Loen (1694–1776), in Ziekursch, 'August der Starke', 93.

17. 'Ne soiges pas bigos ni hybocriet, mes (d')une vres devossion, le peubles en veusst estres pries'. Haake, 'Die Wahl', 39n.

18. The Latin text of Raab's 'attestation' of 2 June 1697 is printed in P. Hiltebrandt, 'Die polnische Königswahl von 1697 und die Konversion Augusts des Starken', *Quellen und Forschungen aus Italienischen Archiven und Bibliotheken*, X (1907) 1, 152–215; 203.

19. 'Comme Votre Eminence a voulu etre assuré par moi meme touchant la religion catholique, je luy dis, que, si l'affaire se pourroit achever de la manière que je pouvois etre élevé sur le trone de Pologne, je ne fairois point de difficulté alors de professer publiquement la religion catholique, ce que je ne scavrois faire avant pour les grandes raisons, qui ne peuvent pas etre inconnu a V.E., et à cause des quelles je la prie de vouloir menager l'affaire le mieux qui se peut. Voilà ce que je crois suffira pour l'assurance de la religion, dont elle peut encore prendre plus exacte information par celui qui vous rendra celle-ci [Flemming], en qui je me remete pour vous dire plus que je ne fais a present'. Augustus to Radziejowski, 4 June 1697, in Hiltebrandt, 'Die polnische Königswahl', 179.

20. Haake, 'Die Wahl', 36.
21. The Latin text of da Via's *testimonium credulitatis* of 27 June 1697 is printed in Hiltebrandt, 'Die polnische Königswahl', 203–04.
22. 'Wählt den Kurfürsten von Sachsen, wählt den Teufel selbst, nur nicht Conti'; in K. Piwarski, 'Das Interregnum 1696/97 in Polen und die politische Lage in Europa', in J. Kalisch and J. Gierowski (eds), *Um die polnische Krone: Sachsen und Polen während des Nordischen Krieges 1700–21*, Berlin 1962, 9–44; 42.
23. '[E]t aggiuntosi loro l'ambasciatore Cesareo, vennero a protestarmi di tutto il male, che sarebbe derivato al regno, s'io non davo un attestato d'haver veduto l'accenato documento, giacche anche quelli del principe di Conty si sarebbero accostati al Sassone, purchè fossero sicuri nel punto della religione'. Da Via to Spada, 28 June 1697, in Hiltebrandt, 'Die polnische Königswahl', 207.
24. On Augustus's relationships with his States, see: G. Wagner, *Die Beziehungen Augusts des Starken zu seinem Ständen während der ersten Jahre seiner Regierung (1694–1700)*, Leipzig 1903; F. L. Carsten, *Princes and Parliaments in Germany from the Fifteenth to the Eighteenth Century*, Oxford 1959.
25. Stepney to Blathwayt, 2/12 April 1695; Stepney to Cresset, 2/12 April 1695; Stepney to Blathwayt, 14/24 May 1695, all in SP105/55.
26. Stepney wrote later that Frederick was 'extremely pleased with the purchase he made lately of Quedlinburg for RT 340,000, and thinks he may have more such pennyworths' as long as Augustus 'lies under want of ready-money'. Stepney to Vernon, Warsaw, 7/17 May 1698, SP105/51.
    Stepney's quoted sum is much higher than the figure in the text of this book, which comes from a detailed list in K. Czok, *August der Starke und Kursachsen*, Leipzig 1987, 50–51. Czok's figures for Borna and Mansfeld tally with those given by Augustus (see n27 below), but for Lauenburg he gives the meticulous price of RT 733,333 and 6 pfennigs. Other 'prices' for Lauenburg are 1.1 million guilders and RT 800,000 in Haake, 'Die Wahl', 63, 77n.
27. Some 15 years later, the then English envoy with Augustus was camped with him at Güstrow in Pomerania. From there he sent a letter from Augustus to Queen Anne on the 'veritable etat de mes affaires', plus a 'list writ by the King's own hand' of the outlays involved in gaining the Polish crown. It is not the most legible of records, but it is the only authentic example known to me of a document from the pen of Augustus himself, to be found in the British archives. Fortunately, some kind contemporary has transcribed his French. Scott to Secretary of State, 19 December 1712, SP88/20.
    In this list Augustus details that he obtained 800,000 guilders for jewellery and other precious works in Holland and Hamburg, and a further 500,000 in capital from Dutch sources. He raised 1.2 million from the sale of Lauenburg to Hanover, 0.5 million for Borna and 0.6 million for Mansfeld. Against the sale of Quedlinburg to Prussia there is a blank. Can't he remember? Does he no longer wish to recall such matters, from a time when his life was so much easier? Has something – a serving-wench, a refill of his goblet, a joke – distracted him?
28. 'La mattina de 25 giugno 1697 cominciarono ad accostarsi al campo elettorale i palatinati della Polonia numerosi di circa 100,000 cavalli'. Da Via to Spada 28 June 1697, in Hiltebrandt, 'Die polnische Königswahl', 204.

29. Plantamour to Ellis, Frankfurt, 13/23 June 1697 and 20/30 June 1697, enclosing a copy of a letter from Dresden dated 15/25 June 1697 (French), all in AM 28899.
30. Sutton, *Lexington Papers*, 273.
31. 'Omnia contraria atque haereses, quascunque ab Ecclesia damnatas et rejectas et anathematizatas, Ego pariter damno, rejicio et anathematizo'. Haake, 'Die Wahl', 59n.
32. Lexington to Blathwayt, Vienna, 25 September 1697, in Sutton, *Lexington Papers*, 307.
33. Liselotte to Sophie, 14 November 1697, in Scott-Stevenson, *Letters of Madame*, 156.
34. Lexington to Blathwayt, Vienna, 3 July 1697; Blathwayt to Lexington, Cocklenberg, 19 July 1697, in Sutton, *Lexington Papers*, 273, 282–83.

CHAPTER 14

OCS 14: The main sources for this chapter are SP105/51, 52 and 53, which are Stepney's letter-books detailing his missions to Berlin and Warsaw in 1698–99. Two minor items come from his despatches in SP90/1.

1. Reporting upon the battle, Plantamour wrote that 'le nombre des Blessez, des Tuez et des Prisoniers est considerable aussy bien que la perte du Bagage'. He noted that the German troops had not been involved in this action, but added that 'le Duc de Wirtemberg voyant qu'il n'y a pas grand chose a gagner dans ce Pays s'en retournera bientot'. Plantamour to Ellis, Berlin, 21 September/1 October 1698, AM 28902. At this time Stepney was away from Berlin meeting William III.
2. George's account of his stay in Saxony is in Stepney to Ellis, Leipzig, 7/17 October 1699; Stepney to Blathwayt, Berlin, 17 October 1699(OS), both in AM 28904.
3. The collective presence in Dresden of Sophie Charlotte and the Princess of Anhalt, as well as a 'covey' of mistresses apparently 'well-disposed' towards each other, at least provides the requisite personnel for certain events described by K. L. von Pöllnitz, *The Amorous Adventures of Augustus of Saxony*, London 1929 [1734], 184–91. The happenings he relates, which required the joint participation of four major (former or current?) mistresses – Aurora von Königsmarck, Countess Esterle, Eleonore von Klengel and Countess Lubomirska – may well have taken place in Dresden in autumn 1699. However, if I remain sceptical about this account, it is not because of any logistical problems. It is simply because no comparable version appears to have been bruited by Sophie Charlotte, her mother Sophie of Hanover, or Liselotte; a sinister silence.

CHAPTER 15

1. Stepney to Hedges, Vienna, 27 December 1702, SP105/66; Robinson to Hedges, Warsaw, 15 September 1703, SP88/15.
2. R. Przeździecki, *Diplomatic Ventures and Adventures: Some Experiences of British Envoys at the Court of Poland*, London 1953, 23.

3. 'Mit Patkul ist keine Mittelstraße zu gehen, sondern man muß ihm entweder einen kurzen Prozeß machen und den Kopf abschlagen lassen oder ihn zum Obristen machen und ihm ein Regiment geben'; in Y. Erdmann, *Der Livländische Staatsmann Johann Reinhold Patkul*, Berlin 1970, 33.

4. I. Grey, *Peter the Great*, London 1962, 105.

5. Grey, *Peter the Great*, 133.

6. The reference to future use of his sword is in a letter of Werner, the Brandenburg envoy to Warsaw, of 29 August 1698, in P. Haake, *König August der Starke: eine Charakterstudie*, Munich–Berlin 1902, 5. Stepney's papers refer to the stag beheaded by Augustus with one blow in East Prussia on 6 June.

   According to the Austrian envoy, Augustus and Peter exchanged clothes as well as swords at Rawa. The two rulers were 'in solche Bruderliche vertraulichkeith kommen, daß beede einen Kleidertausch getroffen, auch der Czar mit des König in Pohlen rokch, hueth und slechten Degen in Moscau ankommen'. R. Wittram, *Peter I, Czar und Kaiser*, 2 vols, Göttingen 1964, i, 166.

7. L. R. Lewitter, 'Peter the Great and the Polish Election of 1697', *Cambridge Historical Journal*, xii (1956), 126–43; 143. Peter always wore the sword that Augustus had given him. There is a report (which may be apocryphal) that, 'upon the news of his army's flight [at Narva, p 180]', Peter 'split the heads of the first two messengers with that very scimitar which was presented to him by the King of Poland, and which he values so much that he always wears it'. Aldersey to Ellis, Hamburg, 28 December 1700, AM 28906.

   Augustus lost Peter's sword, presumably at the battle of Kliszów in July 1702 (p 184). Peter retrieved it from the Swedish baggage after his victory at Poltava in July 1709. He returned it to a mortified Augustus when they met at Thorn the following October: R. K. Massie, *Peter the Great: His Life and World*, London 1989, 520.

CHAPTER 16

1. 'Sie ahneln Affen, denen man ein Taschenuhr gibt'. Y. Erdmann, *Der Livländische Staatsmann Johann Reinhold Patkul*, Berlin 1970, 108.

2. '[D]aß Er nicht den Braten, den Wir ans Spies gestecket, uns vor dem Maule weg freße, das ist, daß er uns nicht Lieffland selbst mit der Zeit weg fische'. R. Wittram, 'Patkul und der Ausbruch des Nordischen Krieges', *Nachrichten der Akademie der Wissenschaften in Göttingen*, 9 (1952), 201–33; 221.

3. '[U]nd was sonst noch mehr zu unseres Vaterlandes Besten'. Erdmann, *Johann Reinhold Patkul*, 72.

4. In December 1698, the Swedish envoy in Warsaw reported how Peter often discoursed in the following terms: 'Wann er freye hände von anderen kriegen [with Turkey] bekäme, gedencken wolte, wie Er Narva und anderes wieder unter seine botmässickeit bringen möchte'. Wachslager to Charles XII, 16/26 December 1698. About the same time the Tsar spoke to Carlowitz about 'tous ses ports de mer dans la Baltique'. In October 1699, Poul Heins remarked of Peter, 'combien il a la Livonie en

teste'. R. Wittram, *Peter I, Czar und Kaiser*, 2 vols, Göttingen 1964, i, 205, 207, 215.

If Peter was considering the capture of the Livonian ports even before his entry into the war, then his comment to the Swedish resident in April 1700 can be made to read rather differently. Seeking to allay rumours of an imminent Russian attack upon the Swedish Empire, the Tsar declared: 'You cannot think that I would begin an unjust war against the King of Sweden, and break an eternal peace, which I have just promised to preserve'. As for Augustus, if he captured Riga from Sweden, 'I will tear it from his hands': I. Grey, *Peter the Great*, London 1962, 168–69. The reinterpretation might therefore run as follows: a war to retrieve Narva, 'stolen' from Russia by the Swedes, could not be 'unjust'; the promise to preserve the Treaty of Kardis was not sealed with a kiss of the cross; and Riga was never intended to belong permanently to Augustus.

5. These auxiliaries were seen merely as cannon-fodder. Patkul had advised Augustus that 'Russian infantry would be most serviceable for working in the trenches and for receiving the enemy's shots, while the troops of the King could be preserved and used for covering the approaches': E. Schuyler, *Peter the Great: Emperor of Russia*, 2 vols, London 1884, i, 447.

6. Heins' letter of 28 November 1699, in Wittram, 'Patkul', 231.

7. The news of this fiasco had reached Berlin by early February. 'Le Bruit a couru icy et ailleurs que quelques Regiments Saxons de ceux qui sont en Quartier d'hyver en Lithuanie avoient en dessein de surprendre la ville de Riga en Lithuanie [*sic*] et que cette entreprise devait etre conduite par le General Peichol [Paykul], mais que le Gouverneur en ayant été averti assez, a temps l'avoit fait échouer par les bons ordres qu'il avoit donnez'. Plantamour to Ellis, Berlin, 30 January/9 February 1700, AM 28904.

8. The story of Flemming marrying and honeymooning in early 1700 comes from Russian sources and would appear to be untrue. Plantamour reported to Ellis on 5 October 1700 that Flemming had just arrived in Berlin. He had been in Warsaw for several days with his *future* bride Princess Sapieha. AM 28906.

When Flemming had negotiated the treaty with Brandenburg, his rather lame attempt at disguising the reason for his presence had failed: 'Ce Lt-General [Flemming] dit étre venu icy pour voir ses parens, mais c'est là son pretexte ordinaire et il n'est pas croyable que toutes ses allées et venues ne soient pour autre chose que pour cela, c'est pourquoy l'on tient qu'il se negocie quelque affaire entre le Roy de Pologne et Mr L'Electeur'. Flemming did better at masking his motives for going to Lithuania: 'Il prit hier congé de la cour et il doit étre parti aujourd'huy [2 February] pour aller en Lithuanie tacher d'appaiser les troubles qui y regnent a l'occasion des Troupes Saxonnes qui y sont en Quartier d'hyver'. Plantamour to Ellis, Berlin, 20/30 January 1700 and 23 January/2 February 1700, AM 28904.

9. Frederick to Sophie, 30 May 1700, in L. and M. Frey, *Frederick I: The Man and his Times*, New York 1984, 242.

10. 'Es seind nicht mer als zwey wege die antreprisse vorzunehmen a quelque pries que cla soit oder suchen es gar ligen zu lassen, welches leztre nicht zu rahtten, dieweillen außwertig peussansen [personnes

sont] engagiret und wier zu sehr inpengiret, alsoh man das werck for-tsehzen mus'. P. Haake, *August der Starke*, Berlin–Leipzig 1927, 86.

11. 'Die Evenements dependiren von Gott und nicht von Menschen, alsoh hat er sich aller Gnade zu versehen. Ich habe Eure Difficultaeten wohl erwaget, allein ich hoffe doch, daß die sache wohl gehen soll. Ihr mueßt nur ein gutes Herz haben. Gelder will ich Euch schon schaffen. Das Land ist degarniret von Volk, und ehe die Huelfe aus Schweden kommt, bin ich mit meiner uebrigen Armee auch in Livland'. Haake, *August*, 86–87.

12. According to Heins, the Russians thought that Augustus was remaining in Saxony 'pour se divertir avec les Dames et pour vacquer aux plaisirs de ces pays là'. Wittram, *Peter I*, i, 221.

    'Le Roy de Pologne n'est pas encore parti de Saxe. Il ne paroit meme pas resolu d'en partir si tot qu'on avoit cru, puisque les Divertissements vont recommençer a Dresden comme si l'on alloit entrer dans le Carna-val. Les Troupes Saxonnes sont toujours prétes à marcher mais Dieu sçait quand elles marcheront'. Plantamour to Ellis, Berlin, 17/27 February 1700, AM 28904.

13. Wittram, 'Patkul', 232.

14. A copy of Héron's letter of 2 September is in AM 28905: 'Il arrive tous les jours de l'Artillerie au camp et il semble qu'on se prepare à un bom-bardement'. The letter notes that Augustus had called for sheepskins to be supplied to his troops, and the Frenchman concluded that 'ces pre-cautions donnent lieu de croire qu'il ne veut pas separer si tot son Armée'.

    Letters 'du Camp devant Riga' of 19 September and 24 September 1700 are enclosed with Plantamour to Ellis, Berlin, 28 September 1700 and 2 October 1700(NS), AM 28906: 'Tout étoit prest pour bombarder la ville [Riga], mais le Roy par des raisons particulieres a changé de resolution. L'on a demonté les batteries et renvoyé les Canons et Mor-tiers a Augustusbourg ['Augustenburg']. S.M. [His Majesty, i.e. Augustus] decampera icy au premier jour pour aller prendre Kockenhausen'. He had still not broken camp on 24 September, but it was his intention 'de se saisir de Kockenhausen pour l'en servir comme d'une téte de pont afin d'avoir la communication libre avec la Courlande et la Lithuanie'. For the fate of the Saxon artillery sent to 'Augustenburg' see p 183.

15. Grey, *Peter the Great*, 308.

16. MacKenzie to Queensberry, Marienburg, 8 August 1710, SP88/18.

CHAPTER 17

OCS17: Letters written to Ellis by Stepney, Plantamour and William Aldersey can be found in AM 28907–28912, the six volumes of the Ellis papers for 1701–02.

1. R. Nisbet Bain, *Charles XII and the Collapse of the Swedish Empire*, New York 1895, 16–17.

2. F. M. A. de Voltaire, *History of Charles XII: King of Sweden*, London 1912, 13.

3. Charles told his tutor that 'when I meet the King of France I will address him in French. But if he sends me a minister, then it will be

more fitting for the minister to learn Swedish on my account than for me to learn French on his. For I esteem my language as highly as he does his own'. F. G. Bengsston, *The Life of Charles XII: King of Sweden 1697–1718*, London 1960, 9. He read French literature constantly from an early age and out of necessity spoke the language during his years in Turkey, 1709–14. Charles also acquired a varying knowledge of Finnish, Polish, Italian and Turkish.

4. Despatch of 19 August 1699, in K. Waliszewski, *Peter the Great*, London 1898, 301. His predecessor d'Avaux had remarked similarly that Charles was 'very good-looking and very tall for his age': despatch of 15 July 1697, in E. Godley, *Charles XII of Sweden: a Study in Kingship*, London 1928, 8. From studies of his exhumed skeleton, it has been variously estimated that Charles was between five feet nine inches and six feet in height. He was considerably taller than Augustus, who was himself about five feet nine inches, so the latter assessment seems nearer the mark.

5. There are two stunning snapshots of Charles, written when he was in Saxony in 1706–07. One, by the Swedish student Alstrin, is in Bengsston, *Life*, 230–31; the other is in O. Browning, *Charles XII of Sweden*, London 1899, 160–63. Browning attributes its authorship to Stepney, who he wrongly says 'was at this time British envoy in Poland' and saw Charles and Augustus in Saxony. This is incorrect: Stepney was in Vienna, the Hague and Brussels while Charles occupied the Electorate, and was often too ill to travel anywhere. Since Browning provides neither references nor bibliography, it proved impossible to track down his original source.

6. R. M. Hatton, *Charles XII of Sweden*, London 1968, 15; Bengsston, *Life*, 12; Bain, *Charles XII*, 285.

7. Robinson to Stepney, Stockholm, 15 May 1701(OS), AM 7075.

8. Bengsston, *Life*, 388.

9. Voltaire, *History*, 37.

10. These words of Arvid Horn (p 205), dating from the time when he had broken with his King, are in Bain, *Charles XII*, 71.

11. Bengsston, *Life*, 209.

12. Godley, *Charles XII*, 138.

13. Voltaire, *History*, 75.

14. G. Scott-Stevenson, *The Letters of Madame*, Vol. 1, London 1924, 200. 'What they say about King William is quite true', Liselotte asserted in December 1701, 'but all our heroes have been the same'. Some four years later she pronounced that 'nothing, however, is more ordinary in England than this unnatural vice'. She cited Lord Raby, England's then ambassador in Berlin (p 219), as being so inclined (despite his very public affair with the wife of the Grand Chamberlain of Brandenburg). 'Bible reading makes no difference to it', she confirmed. Generously she conceded that there were 'many in Germany, too, who practise this vice'. That Liselotte scattered her allegations widely seems obvious, and is perhaps understandable, given the charade of her marriage to 'Monsieur'. Following his death, she confessed to Sophie that 'I found in his coffers all the letters that his young men had written to him, and I burnt them all without reading them, in case they fell into other hands'. Scott-Stevenson, *The Letters of Madame*, 212, 218, 256–57.

15. Bengsston, *Life*, 11.

16. Godley, *Charles XII*, 167.

17. Hatton, *Charles XII*, 118, 128.

18. Bengsston, *Life*, 60.
19. I. Grey, *Peter the Great*, London 1962, 171; E. Schuyler, *Peter the Great: Emperor of Russia*, 2 vols, London 1884, i, 460. At the end of August 1700, Langen, the Saxon ambassador in Moscow, informed Patkul and Augustus that he and Poul Heins had done all they could to 'distract' Peter from his intention to attack Narva. However, he found the Tsar so adamant that he 'feared to touch any more on such a delicate subject, and must be satisfied with the Tsar's break with Sweden, in the hope that in time Narva will not leave our hands'. Grey, *Peter the Great*, 175.
20. Bengsston, *Life*, 73.
21. Bain, *Charles XII*, 67.
22. Bengsston, *Life*, 82.
23. Robinson to Ellis, Stockholm, 19 December 1700(OS), AM 28906.
24. Bengsston, *Life*, 92. 'It is particularly observed', wrote William Aldersey, 'that His Majesty was so hotly engaged that he lost a boot in the throng and had his stocken [*sic*] torn down to the heel'. The Briton also mentioned 'the bullet found in the folds of the King's neckcloth' after the battle. Aldersey to Ellis, Hamburg, 7 and 11 January 1701.

    Aldersey appears to have sought to be a protégé of 'my very worthy friend Mr Stepney', but there is no indication that George took him under his wing, as he did Whitworth (C20 n18) and his cousin Erasmus Lewis. This cannot have been because he lacked ability. A fluent German speaker, Aldersey's letters from Hamburg are packed with information, particularly upon the sparring between Augustus and Charles prior to the battles of the Düna crossing and Kliszów. That said, I have used only a small selection of material from his correspondence.
25. Hedges to Robinson, 14 January 1701(OS), SP104/153.
26. Bain, *Charles XII*, 79–80.
27. Grey, *Peter the Great*, 185.
28. Waliszewski, *Peter the Great*, 305.
29. Bain, *Charles XII*, 85.
30. Stepney to Blathwayt, Vienna, 10 September 1701, SP105/63. G. M. Adlerfeld, *The Military History of Charles XII*, 3 vols, London 1740, i, 102–03, details the booty in artillery (73 cannon and mortars, including 32 24-pounders), nearly 50,000 cannon-balls, some 10,000 grenades and bombs, plus cartridges, powder, muskets and corn. He also observes that 'the fort was delivered to the Swedes in a condition infinitely better than when it was taken'.

    In a letter to Ellis of 31 December 1701, Plantamour described the surrender of 'Augustenburg'. 'Il n'y avoit dans toute la Garnison que 40 hommes capable de porter les armes, tout le reste étant mort ou malade. La Capitulation permet aux Saxons de sortir avec Armes et Bagage le 23 [December] mais toute l'Artillerie, Munitions etc. doivent demeurer aux Suedois qui y ont mis 400 hommes ...'
31. Hatton, *Charles XII*, 565n.
32. Voltaire, *History*, 80; Stepney to Sutton, Vienna, 27 May 1702, SP105/65.
33. There is a contemporary engraving of the Battle of Kliszów, together with a relation written by a participating officer in German, in Stepney's miscellany on Sweden and Poland in SP105/61.
34. Bain, *Charles XII*, 111; Bengsston, *Life*, 148; Godley, *Charles XII*, 83.
35. Hatton, *Charles XII*, 187.
36. Hatton, *Charles XII*, 174, 178.

CHAPTER 18

OCS18–22: Stepney's papers relating to his mission in Vienna (1701–06) are in SP105/62–77. His years there are also covered by the State Papers relating to events in the Empire, SP80/18–28. I have only researched these latter volumes to plug gaps in the SP105 collection.
OCS18: The three volumes SP105/62–64 cover the period March–December 1701. There are no papers for January–February 1702 in the Stepney collection; to fill this hiatus I consulted SP80/18, which holds no important material upon Augustus. SP105/65 runs March–August 1702. Papers for August–December 1702 are in SP105/66.

1. Vernon to Stepney, 28 April 1702(OS), in G. P. R. James, *Letters Illustrative of the Reign of William III*, 3 vols, London 1841, iii, 218–19. On 19 July 1702 George thanked Vernon for 'the many (almost fatherly) kindnesses you were pleased to show me during the course of your ministry'.
2. Hedges to Stepney, 26 June 1702(OS), SP104/200. Around this time the allies feared that Sweden would make 'an irruption into Saxony': Hedges to Robinson, 2 June 1702(OS), SP104/53.
3. SP105/65 contains an extract from a letter sent from Cracow on 17 June 1702, discussing the Swedish negotiations with Radziejowski. It is written in French and contends that Charles, because he did not understand enough Latin or French to explain matters, handed over to Piper. We have already noted that Charles had a fluent understanding of both languages (p 176), while even from the above account it is evident that both Charles and Piper knew more than just Swedish and German. It is possible that Charles feigned ignorance here, either to avoid commitments or because he had no time for Radziejowski's latest evasions of his clear-cut demand for dethronement.

CHAPTER 19

OCS19–21: Stepney's papers for 1703 are organized quarterly (January–March etc.) in SP105/67–70, and likewise for 1704 in SP105/71–74. For 1705 there are two volumes: SP105/75 covers January to June and SP105/76 July to December. Most of Robinson's letters to Stepney are in the above tomes, but some can be found in AM 7075. Whitworth's despatches from Vienna, while he deputized for Stepney during the latter's absence from November 1703 until March 1704, are in SP105/70 and 71.
Robinson's despatches from Poland in 1703 are divided rather arbitrarily between SP95/15 (Sweden) and SP88/15 (Poland) and may still be incomplete. In 1704 and 1705 his letters are reunified in two (complete?) volumes, respectively SP88/16 and 17.
Raby's letters from Berlin in 1703–05 are in SP90/2 (April 1703–July 1704) and SP90/3 (July 1704–December 1705).
Whitworth's despatches from Russia in 1704–05 are in both SP91/4 and AM 37354. The latter volume also contains letters to Stepney and others.

1. On Robinson and his mission, see his DNB entry, and J. Milne, 'The Diplomacy of Dr John Robinson at the Court of Charles XII of Sweden, 1697–1709', TRHS (1948), 75–93.
2. Robinson's instructions of 11 December 1702(OS) are in SP104/53. This volume also contains identical instructions of the same date made out to Stepney, as envoy extraordinary and plenipotentiary. It is possible that the final decision regarding whom to send was only taken on 11 December. On that day Hedges informed another candidate that Whitehall had 'pitched upon the expedient of sending Mr Robinson to the King of Sweden': Hedges to Cresset, 11 December 1702(OS), SP104/204.
3. 'On dit icy que Le Roy de Pologne n'a été en Saxe que pour voir un jeune homme qui est dans la Forteresse de Königstein et qui a la reputation de sçavoir faire de l'Or depuis une experience qu'il fit dans cette Ville-cy [Berlin]; il y a environ un an en presence de personnes dignes de foy qui l'ont attestée; ce qui fut cause aussy qu'on fit icy tout ce qu'on put pour avoir ce jeune homme lorsqu'on sçeut qu'il s'étoit retiré en Saxe'. Plantamour to Hedges, Berlin, 28 November 1702, SP90/1.

    The prisoner in Königstein was the alchemist Johann Friedrich Böttger (1682–1719), who was later to play a crucial role in the discovery and production of porcelain, which would stimulate the development of that profitable industry in Saxony. J. Gleeson, *The Arcanum: the extraordinary true story of the invention of European porcelain*, London 1998, offers considerable detail upon the relationship between Augustus and Böttger. P. Haake, *Christiane Eberhardine und August der Starke: eine Ehetragödie*, Dresden 1930, 97, dates this meeting as late 1701. This is an error; Augustus could not afford to leave Poland in that year. This is confirmed by Ms Gleeson's work.
4. F. M. A. de Voltaire, *History of Charles XII: King of Sweden*, London 1912, 84.
5. F. G. Bengsston, *The Life of Charles XII: King of Sweden 1697–1718*, London 1960, 161.
6. Augustus's main assistance to the allies was at last to send a Saxon contingent of 8000, agreed by treaty in January 1702, into the Emperor's service. The Saxons saw action against the pro-French Bavarians in 1703.
7. After fighting a duel in late 1701, Patkul was dismissed from his Saxon offices. In 1702 he was taken onto the Tsar's payroll, although he had returned to Poland by the time of Kliszów in July of that year. He was back in Moscow in March 1703. That August, Peter made Patkul a Russian privy counsellor and his envoy extraordinary to Augustus.

CHAPTER 20

1. E. Godley, *Charles XII of Sweden: A Study in Kingship*, London 1928, 95.
2. R. Nisbet Bain, *Charles XII and the Collapse of the Swedish Empire*, New York 1895, 121.
3. Godley, *Charles XII*, 97. Other dates in February, and even January 1704, are offered by various authorities for Augustus's dethronement. I have used that given by both Stepney and Raby.
4. Originally, like Sweden and several other states, Augustus refused to recognize Archduke Charles as Carlos III, a second King of Spain, in

opposition to Louis's grandson Philippe. He was possibly fearful of setting a precedent for Poland; but it was also a means of pressurizing Vienna.

5. F. G. Bengsston, *The Life of Charles XII: King of Sweden 1697–1718*, London 1960, 167.
6. Godley, *Charles XII*, 103.
7. Godley, *Charles XII*, 101.
8. Godley, *Charles XII*, 104.
9. Godley, *Charles XII*, 99–100. Stanisław was hardly penniless, since his wife was one of the wealthiest women in Poland.
10. In reality the Cardinal was opposed to Leszczyński and not to a 'native' king as such. He was supporting the pretensions to the throne of Crown General Hieronymous Lubomirski, who had defected to the Swedes in March 1704. Stepney attributed this support to Lubomirski giving 'his daughter in marriage to the Cardinal's favourite, Towianski'. Towianski's first wife had been the Primate's 'long-time mistress, whom the Swedes sardonically referred to as 'Madame la Cardinale'. Presumably she and her husband had now divorced, doubtless with primatial blessing.
11. F. M. A. de Voltaire, *History of Charles XII: King of Sweden*, London 1912, 98; Bain, *Charles XII*, 124.
12. R. M. Hatton, *Charles XII of Sweden*, London 1968, 199.
13. Bengsston, *Life*, 172.
14. Voltaire, *History*, 102–03.
15. I. Grey, *Peter the Great*, London 1962, 233.
16. Godley, *Charles XII*, 107–08.
17. Peter had made Patkul both a Russian privy counsellor and a lieutenant-general and had appointed the Livonian to be the commander of the Russian auxiliary forces which had recently arrived in Jaworów. It was Patkul who insisted upon keeping 10,000 infantry as an independent force under his orders; Augustus had wanted to form them, together with some of his own troops, into a larger army. Patkul had also opposed Augustus's capture of Warsaw.

    The Livonian had anticipated that the siege of Poznań would be another walkover. 'Je suis sur le point d'aller dans la Grand Pologne pour la reduction de Posen', he blithely informed the Danish ambassador to Warsaw: in K. Jarochowski, 'Patkuls Ausgang', NASG III (1882), 201–28, 257–289; 215. The stout resistance of 700 Swedes ensured his failure. With the westward advance of Charles, Augustus ordered him to break off the siege. After bloody skirmishes on the Silesian border, Patkul brought only 4000 Russians into Saxony.
18. Charles Whitworth (1675–1725), later Baron Whitworth, was born in Staffordshire and educated, like his mentor, at Westminster School and Trinity College, Cambridge. He was in other respects too a clone of Stepney, who now played the role of patron. Whitworth (as well as Lewis and Plantamour) was part of Stepney's entourage (at least for some of the time), when he was envoy extraordinary at Berlin in 1698–99 (C14). Stepney took Whitworth with him to Vienna as his secretary in 1701, and it was largely at the older man's instigation that William III appointed Whitworth as his representative to the Imperial Council in Ratisbon in early 1702. Whitworth remained there until being recalled to Vienna to hold the fort, while Stepney journeyed to England, in the winter of 1703–04. In September 1704 Whitworth was appointed envoy

extraordinary to the Tsar and in October, barely 29 years old, he left
for Russia, where he served until May 1710.

CHAPTER 21

1. For Countess Cosel, see G. Hoffmann, *Constantia von Cosel und August der
   Starke,* Bergisch Gladbach 1984; K. von Weber, 'Anna Constance Gräfin
   von Cossell', ASG 9 (1871), 1–78.
2. According to another source, Esterle had quit Poland in fear of her life:
   'La Comtesse d'Isterle qui est partie d'icy a la Sourdine a écrit qu'Elle
   ne s'est retirée que parce qu'elle avoit été informée de bonne part
   qu'on vouloit l'assassiner. Il n'y a pas d'apparence qu'on ait voulu
   pousser la cruauté si loin contre elle, mais il se peut bien que la Jalousie
   ait trouvé moyen de luy inspirer cette terreur panique pour l'eloigner de
   la Cour'. Plantamour to Ellis, Berlin, 26 November 1701, enclosing letter
   from Warsaw of the same date, AM 28910.
     It seems that Esterle left Poland in 1701, perhaps in early autumn.
3. C. Gurlitt, *August der Starke: ein Fürstenleben aus der Zeit des deutschen
   Barock,* 2 vols, Dresden 1924, 160, writes that Lubomirska lived from
   1680 until 1744. However, unless otherwise noted, I have relied upon
   the details in K. Czok, *Am Hofe Augusts des Starken,* Stuttgart 1990, 160,
   for the life-spans of Augustus's mistresses and his eight legitimized bastards.
4. 'Dieser König müßte kassirt werden', Ilgen in Y. Erdmann, *Der Livländische Staatsmann Johann Reinhold Patkul,* Berlin 1970, 179; 'Ei, so lasset
   ihn ins Teufels Namen fallen, so wissen wir alle einmal woran wir sind',
   Kaunitz in K. Jarochowski, 'Patkuls Ausgang', NASG III (1882), 201–28,
   257–89; 259.
5. For Fürstenberg, see H. Pönicke, 'Politisch einflußreiche Männer um
   August den Starken', *Archiv für Sippenforschung,* 40 (1974) 56, 599–610.
   On the arcane subject of governmental reform and absolutism in
   Saxony, see J. Durichen, 'Geheimes Cabinett und Geheimer Rat unter
   der Regierung Augusts des Starken in den Jahren 1704 bis 1720', NASG
   51 (1930), 68–134; P. Haake, 'Joh. Friedr. v. Wolfframsdorff und die
   "Portraits de la Cour de Pologne"', NASG 22 (1901), 69–101, 344–78; P.
   Haake, 'Ein politisches Testament Königs August des Starken', *Historische
   Zeitschrift* LXXXVII (1901), 1–21.
6. On 12 April 1704 Raby reported that the King of Prussia was 'assured'
   that Emperor Leopold was making a treaty with Augustus. Under its
   terms, Leopold promised to marry his grand-daughter (Maria Josepha,
   the elder daughter of Joseph, the King of the Romans) to Augustus's
   son Friedrich August and 'to settle upon her all the hereditary countries
   in case the King of the Romans and the King of Spain [Archduke
   Charles] should not have sons' (C12 n4). If the Habsburgs failed to
   produce any male issue, then the plan was to have the Saxon Kurprinz
   elected Emperor. In return for all this, Augustus 'by a secret article promises to breed up his son a Roman Catholic, and to use his endeavours
   to introduce that religion as far as he can in his Electorate'.
     A copy of this letter to Hedges went to Stepney, who commented
   rather superciliously that 'the prospect for both [Habsburg] princesses is

at a good distance, our eldest lady not being yet five years old'. However, the prospect became reality when the nuptials of Friedrich August and Maria Josepha were celebrated in Vienna in August 1719, after the Kurprinz had converted to Catholicism.

The idea of replacing the Habsburgs on the Imperial throne with the Wettins was an ambition that Augustus pursued to the end of his life and with a very real chance of success, until the Emperor Charles VI produced offspring of his own. Whether there was a treaty in the offing as early as 1704 seems unlikely, as does any idea of reintroducing Catholicism into Saxony, particularly while fighting against the Protestant champion Charles XII.

7. '[S']appercevoyant que l'argent destiné pour Mars se tourne vers Venus'. E. Hassinger, *Brandenburg-Preussen, Schweden und Russland 1700–13*, Munich 1953, 169.

 Raby had heard that Augustus and his court 'have been treated magnificently at Carlsbad by commissioners appointed by order of the Emperor [Joseph]': Raby to Stepney, Berlin, 13 June 1705, AM 7061.

8. In a letter to her father in July 1705, Eberhardine described herself as 'the most miserable wretch on earth', beset by so much pain and sorrow that she 'longed for death every hour of the day': text in Czok, *Hofe*, 65. Her 'deliverance' only came in September 1727.

9. F. G. Bengsston, *The Life of Charles XII: King of Sweden 1697–1718*, London 1960, 195. One account attributes Charles's severity to a letter written to Augustus, in which Paykul bragged that 'I hope within a fortnight ... to deliver into your Majesty's hands the wild and mad young King of Sweden, dead or alive': O. Browning, *Charles XII of Sweden*, London 1899, 124.

10. Robinson did not think that Radziejowski's death would 'be of much consequence one way or other', since he had 'outlived all credit and interest with any of the parties'. Yet his demise was hardly nugatory at the institutional level, as the envoy unthinkingly made clear. There would now be two successors to the Primacy, and all the other major Polish offices would be duplicated, with candidates nominated by both Augustus and Stanisław. This Polish pork-barrelling would 'introduce a new scene of ruin and destruction, and engage a fierce war for places, among those that would fight for nothing else'.

11. This suggests that Augustus had no intention of using this army in 1705, although several letters to Stepney in July–August from a rather gullible Raby posit the contrary. For instance, he reported on 18 August that the Saxon 'is getting his troops together with a resolution to force his passage into Poland'. See AM 7062.

12. This was certainly Augustus's view, expressed in his most exotic French to his ambassador at the Hague: 'En premier lieus jes for ... quon saches que ces dietes trouppes me sont stipules par une allianse, par laquelle il les diet, qui me resteron si longtems que la guerres dureras contres la Suedes, et que jen dispose quommes des miens prospres'; Augustus to Gersdorf, Grodno, 8 January 1706, in J. H. Kemble, *State Papers and Correspondence 1618–1714*, London 1857, 435–36. The agreement in question was the 1703 Treaty of Warsaw (p 202–03).

13. Raby reported that on 18 December a courier had arrived in Dresden 'with despatches from the King of Poland to the [Regency] Council, which assembled the next day, and at night sent an officer' to arrest

Patkul. Raby added that a day or two before his arrest Patkul had become engaged to Frau von Einsiedel, a widow 'said to be worth 300,000 crowns'. Moreover, the Livonian had 'lately talked of retiring from the service, and purchasing an estate in some other country with the money he has got in the Czar and King Augustus's service'. Raby to Stepney, Berlin, 26 December 1705, AM 7062.

CHAPTER 22

OCS22–23: Stepney's reports from Vienna in 1706 are in SP105/77 (January–June) and SP80/28 (January–September). His letters from the Hague and Brussels (October 1706–July 1707) are in SP84/230, part I.

Robinson's letters for 1706–07 are in SP88/17. Whitworth's despatches for 1706 are in SP91/4 and for 1707 in SP91/5. Raby's reports from Berlin in 1706–07 can be found in SP90/4. The source of his letters to Stepney is AM 7062.

1. R. Nisbet Bain, *Charles XII and the Collapse of the Swedish Empire*, New York 1895, 136.
2. Schulenburg's own account to his sister of 17 February 1706 is printed in J. H. Kemble, *State Papers and Correspondence 1618–1714*, London 1857, 437–38. He was not imprisoned, nor did he even lose his command.
3. Plantamour expressed less optimism in the letter he sent to Stepney that same day. 'Les affaires étoient entierement deséspérées pour le Roy de Pologne'. Augustus 'pretend de maintenir a Cracovie et il en fait fortifier le chateau'. Plantamour to Stepney, Berlin, 24 April 1706, AM 37155.
4. 'Unss mit Deroselben völlig reconcilijret und die vormahlige gute intelligence zwischen Ihro und Unss retabliret zu sehen': A. Günther, 'Die Entstehung des Friedens von Altranstädt', NASG 27 (1906), 311–29; 314n.
5. Possibly Pfingsten was the person referred to by Robinson in his letter of 1 September 1706. 'A minister of King Augustus is lately passed through this place [Danzig] going to Saxony, with orders relating to the present state and danger of that country'. He contended that Augustus was 'resoluted to remain in Poland whatsoever happens in the Electorate', and 'they pretend not to defend the Oder but the Elbe'.

   How desperate Augustus was to retain the Polish throne is a matter of conjecture. Whitworth reckoned that he only clung on to the Polish crown 'out of a point of honour and reputation'. Otherwise, as he told the envoy in early 1706, 'he would rather live [as] a private citizen in Leipzig than reign over such a people'. Robinson received a letter from a Swedish official on 17 September, which assumed that the envoy was aware 'that King Augustus is not averse from freeing himself at once from all his trouble and vexation'.
6. As the Swedish protocol of the conference worded it: 'Daß König August zuerst und vor allen Dingen sich der polnischen Krone begebe, allen Ansprüchen darauf entsage und König Stanislaus anerkenne. Das sei die Grundlage des Friedensschlusses und dieser könne auf keine andere Weise zustande kommen'. Günther, 'Die Entstehung', 323n.

7. A full German text of the treaty can be found in H. Kretzschmar, 'Der Friedensschluß von Altranstädt 1706–07', in J. Kalisch and J. Gierowski (eds), *Um die polnische Krone: Sachsen und Polen während des Nordischen Krieges 1700–21*, Berlin 1962, 161–83. A Latin version is in SP88/17, a French summary in SP84/230, and an abbreviated translation into English in SP90/4. The main provisions of the 22 articles were as follows:

Under Article 3, Augustus abdicated as King of Poland and recognized Stanisław as the lawful king. Augustus was allowed to keep the titles and honours of a king during his lifetime, 'but without either the arms or title of King of Poland'.

Article 5 required Augustus to renounce his alliances against Charles. He also undertook to give no further assistance to the Tsar. If Peter should now attack Augustus, then Article 20 obliged Charles and Stanisław to come to his aid and ensure, on making peace with Peter, that the Saxon received 'satisfaction of his just pretensions'.

Augustus was to restore to Poland its regalia and archives, to free the Sobieskis and other Polish prisoners and to work on the Pope to liberate the Bishop of Posen (Articles 7–9).

Under Article 11 Augustus promised to hand over all Swedish traitors and keep Patkul a 'close prisoner till delivered up'. Article 12 required the surrender of Muscovite troops in Saxony as prisoners of war.

Articles 15–17 covered the evacuation of Saxon garrisons in Poland, the provision of winter quarters for the Swedish army; and Swedish occupation of the Electorate until the treaty's provisions were implemented. Article 18 specified that hostilities should cease immediately in Saxony and within three weeks in Poland.

Augustus and Charles were to work to preserve the religious provisions of the 1648 Treaty of Westphalia (Article 19).

Article 21 obligated Augustus to seek English, Dutch and Imperial guarantees of the treaty. Ratifications of the treaty were to be exchanged six weeks after signature (Article 22).

8. For a detailed study of the background to Kalisz, as well as the battle itself, see J. Wimmer, 'Die Schlacht bei Kalisz am 29 Oktober 1706', in Kalisch and Gierowski, *Um die polnische Krone*, 184–207.

9. Stepney left Vienna on 25 September 1706. In the first days of November he took up his new post, as envoy extraordinary and plenipotentiary to both the Dutch States-General and the Council of the Spanish Netherlands in Brussels.

10. R. M. Hatton, *Charles XII of Sweden*, London 1968, 215. The Secretary of State told Whitworth that if the Russians mentioned the subject of the peace, the envoy could assure them 'that they cannot be more surprised at it, than we were here'. Harley to Whitworth, Whitehall, 19/30 November 1706, AM 37355.

11. Stepney to Davenant, 23 November 1706; Stepney to Raby, 2 December 1706; Stepney to Robinson, 3 December 1706, all from the Hague, AM 7075.

12. Liselotte to Raugräfin Luise, 2 December 1706, in G. Scott-Stevenson, *The Letters of Madame*, Vol. 1, London 1924, 266. The German original can be found in P. Haake, *August der Starke im Urteil seiner Zeit und der Nachwelt*, Dresden 1922, 8.

13. D'Alais to Stepney, Hanover, 5 October 1706, AM 7075.

14. Augustus had scrounged 10,000 ducats from Menshikov on the march to

Kalisz. Peter wrote in disgust to his general, 'You know very well that one always hears from the King, "Give, give! Money, money!"' E. Schuyler, *Peter the Great: Emperor of Russia*, 2 vols, London 1884, ii, 50.
15. F. G. Bengsston, *The Life of Charles XII: King of Sweden 1697–1718*, London 1960, 231.
16. E. Godley, *Charles XII of Sweden: A Study in Kingship*, London 1928, 122–23.
17. Bengsston, *Life*, 232.

CHAPTER 23

1. For the tense Austro–Swedish relations, see C. Ingrao, *In Quest and Crisis: Emperor Joseph I and the Habsburg Monarchy*, W. Lafayette 1979, 56–69.
2. H. Snyder, *The Marlborough–Godolphin Correspondence*, 3 vols, Oxford 1975 (hereafter '*MGC*'), ii, 747, 767 (Spelling modernized).
3. Stepney to Davenant, the Hague, 23 November 1706, AM 7075.
4. W. S. Churchill, *Marlborough: his Life and Times*, vol. 2, London 1936, 250. Marlborough's meeting with Charles is described in the biographies of these two men. See also A. E. Stamp, 'The meeting of the Duke of Marlborough and Charles XII at Altranstädt, April 1707', TRHS, New Series, Vol. XII (1896), 103–16.
5. Snyder, *MGC*, ii, 753, 760–62.
6. I would imagine that Charles's absence from the hunt upon this occasion is the same as that referred to by O. Browning, *Charles XII of Sweden*, London 1899, 155. This has it that Augustus had invited Charles to a massive boar-hunt at Liebenwerda, with the intention of having his cousin murdered sometime during the tumult attendant upon such events. Charles accepted the invitation, but reportedly lost his way, either by accident or design. Finding himself near to the residence of his aunt, Anna Sophie, he paid her a visit and allowed the time set for the hunt to trickle by, before returning directly to his headquarters at Altranstädt. While nothing can be excluded with Augustus, I confess that I find it unlikely that he would have risked the probability of the Swedes torching Saxony, if they had judged their King to have been murdered.
7. 'Ich Endesgenannter bescheinige, daß mir der Herr Generaladjutant Arnstedt den Arrestanten Johann Reinhold Patkul am 6. April Glocke 12 Uhr in der Nacht wohl abgeliefert, welches hiermit attestiere. Die Festung Königstein 6. April anno 1707. E. v. Vietinghoff; Otto Reinhold Stakelberg'. Cited in Y. Erdmann, *Der Livländische Staatsmann Johann Reinhold Patkul*, Berlin 1970, 271.
8. F. M. A. de Voltaire, *History of Charles XII: King of Sweden*, London 1912, 125–26.
9. F. G. Bengsston, *The Life of Charles XII: King of Sweden 1697–1718*, London 1960, 242.
10. R. M. Hatton, *Charles XII of Sweden*, London 1968, 247. Other dates in September are given for this encounter, but the letter of 6 September from Flemming's secretary, which is cited by Raby, is unambiguous: 'Le Roy de Suede vint hier [5 September] dans cette ville pour donner visite au Roy mon Maitre'.
11. Voltaire, *History*, 144.

12. Whitworth to Powys, Grodno, 27 October/7 November 1705, AM 37354.
13. Voltaire, *History*, 129. He dates this meeting as occurring in 1713.
14. The contemporary references to Stepney suffering from 'bloody flux' and to his burial are in E. K. Halbeisen, 'George Stepney: A Calendar', *Notes and Queries* (August 1930), 93–96, 114–17; 117. H. Snyder, 'The British Diplomatic Service during the Godolphin Ministry', in R. Hatton and M. Anderson (eds), *Studies in Diplomatic History*, London, 1970, 47–68; 59, states (without a source) that Stepney was stricken with consumption.
15. Snyder, *MGC*, ii, 935.
16. H. Schreiber, *August der Starke: Leben und Lieben im deutschen Barock*, Munich 1981, 259, estimates the number of bastards fathered by Augustus as 100 sons and 150 daughters, while the total of his paramours was more than 300 and might well have numbered 700. He informs us that this expert conclusion results from a detailed study of all the sources. I must confess that if I could produce such a precise result, I would have published it as a historical and demographic document; if only to demonstrate that a significant chunk of Europe's current population must be descended from Augustus.
17. G. Hoffmann, *Constantia von Cosel und August der Starke*, Bergisch Gladbach 1984, 19.

Index

Ingram Content Group UK Ltd.
Milton Keynes UK
UKHW020832250423
420735UK00006B/113